Creating Mexican Consumer Culture
in the Age of Porfirio Díaz

Creating Mexican Consumer Culture
in the Age of Porfirio Díaz

STEVEN B. BUNKER

University of New Mexico Press | Albuquerque

© 2012 by the University of New Mexico Press
All rights reserved. Published 2012
Printed in the United States of America

First paperbound printing, 2014
Paperbound ISBN: 978-0-8263-4455-7
19 18 17 16 15 14   1 2 3 4 5 6

LIBRARY OF CONGRESS CATALOGING-IN-PUBLICATION DATA
Bunker, Steven B., 1970–
  Creating Mexican consumer culture in the age of Porfirio Díaz / Steven B. Bunker.
    p. cm.
  Includes bibliographical references and index.
    ISBN 978-0-8263-4454-0 (cloth : alk. paper) — ISBN 978-0-8263-4456-4 (electronic)
1. Consumers—Mexico—History—20th century.
2. Consumption (Economics)—Mexico—History—20th century.
3. Mexico—Commerce—History—20th century.
4. Mexico—Social conditions—20th century. 5. Mexico—History—1867–1910.
6. Díaz, Porfirio, 1830–1915. I. Title.
  HC140.C6B86 2012
  306.30972—dc23

                    2012028934

Book design and type composition: Lila Sanchez
Body type: Dante MT Std 11/13.5
Display type: Myriad Pro

CONTENTS

ILLUSTRATIONS

PREFACE

IN THE BEGINNING OF HIS NOVEL *ONE HUNDRED YEARS OF SOLITUDE*, Gabriel García Márquez expresses the intertwined fascination with goods, technology, and modernity of many Latin Americans early in the twentieth century.[1] In the first forty pages he recounts the powerful ideas and goods brought by a ragged family of gypsies who set up camp every year outside the small, isolated community of Macondo. He constructs the triangular relationship of the indefatigably curious José Arcadio Buendía, his wife, Úrsula, and the old gypsy Melquíades. The showman Melquíades spins tales of international travel and a magnificent material culture as he introduces inventions such as magnets, telescopes, and other articles from a much larger world that fired the imagination of Buendía. Through the carnivalesque filter of Melquíades and subsequent gypsy peddlers, Buendía and his village are introduced to the scientific wonders of progress sweeping the nineteenth-century world. For years, Buendía acquires these goods at considerable cost in the hopes of adapting them to aims such as finding gold (the magnets) and military purposes (the telescope, for solar warfare), all with the aim of somehow finding this seemingly fantastic world beyond his *patria chica*. Buendía does not find an escape route to the modern world despite all of his efforts. Interestingly, García Marquéz leaves this feat not to the man but to the woman, Úrsula, who instead *brings* this world to the village after disappearing for five months. She returns "exalted, rejuvenated, with new clothes in a style that was unknown in the village."[2] She introduces Buendía to the crowd she has brought with her, "men and women like them. . . . They had mules loaded down with things to eat, oxcarts with furniture and domestic utensils, pure and simple earthly accessories put on sale without any fuss by peddlers of everyday reality." Although they had never made contact before, they lived only two days away, in towns that received mail every month of the year and "where they were familiar with the implements of good living."

Earlier, Buendía had declared to his wife that "incredible things are happening in this world."[3] Perhaps in a significant caveat for this book and for understanding deep changes in human daily lives, García Marquéz points out that Buendía did not find these "incredible things" in his search for great inventions. Rather, the source of potentially revolutionary change was Úrsula (the consumer?), who brought modernity to her village and her village into the nation and modern world through an abundance of cheap and useful goods—the "implements of good living."

At its heart, this book seeks to introduce the ways in which goods and consumption helped to materialize notions of modernity in the time of Porfirio Díaz, how they provided proof, both big and small, for the beliefs of many Mexicans that "incredible things are happening in this world."

ACKNOWLEDGMENTS

AS AN UNDERGRADUATE AT THE UNIVERSITY OF BRITISH COLUMBIA I could not have foreseen that research for my honours thesis would eventually lead to my first book, a career that I love, and a network of friends and colleagues to whom I owe a great debt for their support over these many years. I am grateful to three mentors whose intellectual, professional, and moral support for me as a (once) young scholar cannot be overestimated. First, my undergraduate and master's advisor Bill French, who sparked my interest in Mexican history and supported my idea to research the relationship between a developing consumer culture and the rapid modernization experienced during the presidency of Porfirio Díaz. Second, at Texas Christian University (TCU) my dissertation director, Bill Beezley, set a high standard of creativity, generosity, and intellectual rigor that I try to emulate as a scholar and teacher. After so many years of discussing this project with him he still never fails to listen to an idea of mine and then convince me to make it better. Finally, Susan Ramírez at TCU provided timely support and counsel, two gifts that I continued to take advantage of as I worked on the book manuscript.

At TCU, the University of Alabama (UA), and elsewhere, many have earned my gratitude for their editing skills, insights, response to questions, knack for *le mot juste*, sundry forms of aid, and sometimes just memorable companionship and conversation over a drink. Heartfelt thanks go to Susan Gauss, William Schell, Marie Francois, and Helen Delpar for reading and commenting on drafts of this manuscript. My compadre and writing collaborator Víctor Macías proofread numerous conference papers and served as an invaluable sounding board for issues of consumption in Mexico. Others include Jürgen Buchenau, Paul

Garner, Daniel Newcomer, James Garza, Susie Porter, Shannon Baker-Tuller, William B. Taylor, Arturo Flores, Don Coerver, Sarah Sohmer, Margaret Peacock, Holly Grout, Harold Selesky, Larry Clayton, Jenny Shaw, Stephen Schwab, Teresa Cribelli, Dave Michelson, Rich Megraw, John Beeler, Chuck Clark, Dan Riches, Diana Jeaneth Montano, Michael Matthews, and Monica Rankin. The staff at the interlibrary loan departments of both TCU and UA earned my respect and appreciation for their diligence and speed, while Brett Spencer of the UA Libraries worked wonders in acquiring microfilm and special-order books crucial for my research. Working with the University of New Mexico Press has been a delight and I thank all involved for their talent and professionalism, especially the anonymous reader of my manuscript and my copy editor, Joy Margheim. Special praise goes to Clark Whitehorn, the editor in chief at New Mexico, for his patient shepherding of me through the publication process for the first time. I couldn't have asked for a better experience.

Assistance in Mexico came from many individuals. Special thanks go to Kitzia Nin-Castillo Poniatowska de Romero de Terreros for allowing me access to the archives of the Palacio de Hierro and to Víctor Macías for arranging our introduction. Verónica Zárate Toscano at the Instituto Mora shaved off hours of bureaucratic hassles for me at her institution and several others. The friendly and efficient staff at the Centro de Estudios de Historia de México Carso, the Archivo General de la Nación, the Biblioteca Miguel Lerdo de Tejada, the Instituto Mora, and the Hemeroteca at the Universidad Nacional Autónoma de México allowed me to dedicate as much of my precious time as possible to productive research. At the AGN, special thanks go to Alma Vázquez in the Centro de Información Gráfica for bringing me countless images to consider for the book and to the director, Aurora Gómez Galvarriato, for her timely assistance in acquiring the permissions to publish them. As the director of the Biblioteca Miguel Lerdo de Tejada, Juan Manuel Herrera graciously extended every courtesy to me on my trips over the years. His staff, particularly Alfredo de Jesús Pantoja Oláco, even delayed closing times to help me take the last images for my book. Finally, I owe a particular debt to Javier Pérez Siller at the Universidad Autónoma de Puebla and his México-Francia research team. From the moment he introduced himself after spying me reading French newspapers at the UNAM Hemeroteca, Javier has deepened my understanding of the French presence in Mexico and kept me in stitches with his remarkable sense of humor and remarkably poor taste in pulque.

Funding for this project came from a number of sources. A two-year research grant from the Social Sciences and Humanities Research Council of Canada, the Green Fellowship from Texas Christian University, and additional funding from the Graduate Studies Committee at TCU and the Paul Boller Travel Fund supported my early research. At the University of Alabama, generous support from the Research Grants Committee, the History Department, and the Williams Travel Fund permitted me to expand my research and refine my conclusions.

As always, I reserve the highest praise for my immediate families, the Bunkers and the Chatametikools, for their good humor, assistance, and suspension of disbelief over these many years. To my mother-in-law, Susanna, whose support covered the field, not the least with her understated Mainer patience. To Dad, whose belief in my success never wavered. To my immensely supportive mom, who finally got to see this moment, and to Pong, who I dearly wish had. To my children, Ian, Kitzia, and Alex: you arrived during a break in my career and gave me three more reasons to finish. I love you all. And finally Barb, whose patience I have taxed the greatest and whose solid support never cracked. Conversant in Mexican historiography, supportive of research trips and conferences, and levelheaded during highs and lows, you know what you mean to me. I promise you Enchiladas Suizas for life.

INTRODUCTION

If the great credit establishments, the important railroads, and the various factories . . . reveal the wealth of Mexico's soil and the industriousness of its inhabitants, the luxuries and good taste of its retail stores reveal the culture and civilization of its people.

—J. FIGUEROA DOMENECH

J. FIGUEROA DOMENECH CAPTURED THE MODERNIZING ESSENCE OF THE regime of Porfirio Díaz (1876–1911) in his eight-hundred-page compendium of Mexican economic development, the *Guía general descriptiva de la República Mexicana.*[1] His paean to material progress belongs to an extensive body of contemporary literature that credited the government for living up to its motto, Order and Progress.[2] By progress, Domenech and other allies of the Porfirian state meant a strong central state that had aligned the nation with the economic and cultural imperatives of global capitalism. This alignment involved imposing social order, fostering rapid economic growth, and engineering in its people a cultural transformation consonant with that achieved by nations such as France, the United States, and Britain. Like Domenech, generations of scholars have evaluated almost every aspect of the regime's claims to have brought about the modernization of Mexico. Unlike Domenech, they have produced a nuanced and generally more critical view of the extent and the limitations of the regime's success in achieving order and progress through their examination of the political, economic, and cultural dimensions of its policies.[3] Despite these more critical interpretations, the

1

state as subject and central agent remained the touchstone in analyses of the rapid social, economic, and cultural changes of the era. Furthermore, that Díaz's regime ended not with adulation but rather revolution lasting a decade and leaving nearly two million dead (the Mexican Revolution, 1910–1920) ensured that lines of scholarly inquiry would concentrate on causation of the Revolution, specifically identifying the weaknesses of state-sponsored modernization and the resistance it engendered. As a consequence of this focus, most scholarship has followed Domenech in conceptualizing Porfirian-era modernization as a state-generated process imposed upon a resistant and disenfranchised population.

The field of Porfirian studies has reached a point of maturity where the tethers binding histories of Porfirian-era modernization to those of the state have begun to loosen. Modernization now appears not simply as a top-down creation but as a richly complex process influenced by polyphonic forces. For example, Emilio Kourí does not excise the state from his analysis of the privatization of rural communal lands in Papantla, Mexico.[4] He instead subsumes it within the broader complex interplay of diverse global, national, and especially community forces involved in the wrenching changes that transformed this community. In lieu of the conventional victims of modernization (the aforementioned resistant and disenfranchised population), Kourí locates in his local subjects as much impetus for as resistance to social and economic transformation. This book assumes a similar perspective, viewing modernization as a phenomenon that arose from the bottom as much as it descended from above. This more complex interpretation may lack the bright lines and clean edges of a state-driven modernization model but it provides a deeper and more complex understanding of Porfirian Mexico and the evolution of Mexican modernization.

The purpose of this study is to examine consumption as a measure of the popular and participatory nature of the Mexican modernizing process. "Becoming a consuming people," as Porfirian writer and newspaper editor Alfonso Luis Velasco described the goal of national progress, was a cultural, social, political, and economic process forged by national and international players representing all classes, genders, and races.[5] In urban areas, and especially Mexico City, being a consumer increasingly defined what it meant to be Mexican. A history of consumption is, therefore, a history of everyday life.[6] In an effort to reconstruct a history of everyday life in modernizing Porfirian Mexico, this book surveys the institutions, spectacles, and discourses of consumption but also explores how individuals and groups used the goods, practices, and spaces of urban consumer culture to construct meaning and identities in the rapidly evolving social and physical landscape of the capital city and beyond.

The choice and utility of consumption as an analytical category to explore modernization is a logical one. Defined most simply as the processes by which consumer goods are created, bought, and used, the breadth of consumption as a category of analysis allows it to colonize other fields of study such as material culture, industrialization, visual culture, spectatorship, urbanization, and mass culture, among others. In doing so, it offers greater explanatory power for phenomena as complex as modernization. With a nod to Eric Van Young's call for a cultural approach to history that subsumes other genres of historical inquiry, including economic, social, and political, this history of consumption is a cultural history of modernization at its most imperial.[7]

Nevertheless, this book is the first analytical survey of Porfirian consumption. It adds to a young but slowly developing historiography on consumption in Latin America generally and Mexico specifically.[8] As recently as 2006, historian Alan Knight cited consumerism as a "neglected theme" in Mexican historiography.[9] A handful of studies published in English identify consumption as a category of analysis and link it to the modernization process in Porfirian Mexico, but none in as direct or encompassing a manner as this book.[10] A few more volumes explore consumption over a broader time period or study aspects of consumption during the twentieth century.[11] Although somewhat more prolific, Mexican scholars publishing works in Spanish favor a more narrow and descriptive focus. Some do engage theoretical models of consumption, though often at the expense of the uniquely Mexican characteristics and experience of consumption and modernization.[12] A notable highpoint is the six-volume series *Historia de la vida cotidiana en México*, a project directed by Pilar Gonzalbo Aizpuru that attempts to reconstruct the experience of daily life in Mexico from the Aztecs to the present day.[13]

Scholars of North American and Western European societies established the field of consumption and have produced a vibrant array of studies. Often cited as the first major study is *The Birth of a Consumer Society: The Commercialization of Eighteenth-Century England*, by Neil McKendrick, John Brewer, and J. H. Plumb, published in 1982.[14] A year earlier, however, Michael Miller revolutionized histories of retail institutions with his study of the Bon Marché, situating the history of the department store within the larger context of French social, economic, and cultural change.[15] Since then, historians, anthropologists, literary critics, and scholars from a variety of disciplines have contributed histories of consumption with subjects as varied as department stores, discursive constructions of femininity and masculinity, advertising, specific commodities, and national identity, with a particular emphasis on the intersection of consumerism and modernity.[16]

Consumption is at once a study of the local and the global; thus the paucity of studies on regions beyond Western Europe and North America has raised considerable concern among scholars reviewing the state of the field.[17] This is the first monograph contribution for Mexico and joins the work of Arnold J. Bauer in representing Latin America in this field.[18] It adds to works by Christine Ruane, Timothy Burke, and Jeremy Prestholdt on Russia, Zimbabwe, and East Africa, along with outstanding studies of Asian consumer cultures, to explore the local experiences of this global phenomenon in peripheral societies.[19]

While historians have been slow to recognize the centrality of consumption in the production of meaning in Porfirian society, Porfirians themselves made abundantly clear in their writings that nothing indicated individual and national progress better than changes in consumption and material culture. Commentators from across the social spectrum used a language of consumption as a means to engage in much larger sociopolitical debates over the direction of Mexican society.[20] The photographic and written record illustrates the ubiquitous practice of employing consumer institutions, goods, practices, and spectacles as indicators of national and personal progress. Commemorative albums, national guides, newspaper photos and articles, travelers' accounts and guides, contemporary literature, and official government inaugurations all reveal this.[21] Social commentators such as economist Andrés Molina Enríquez and criminologists Julio Guerrero and Miguel Macedo employed categories of consumption patterns as a major determinant in their social classifications of modern Mexican society and as an indicator of the behavior and moral character of each group.[22] Porfirians, like their contemporaries around the globe, most certainly celebrated the achievements of production in the economy, such as new railroads, factories, ports, smelters, and other indicators of progress. Yet following Adam Smith's famous dictum that "consumption is the sole end and purpose of all production," these achievements served as a means to an end: the proof of progress came not in GDP reports but in the abundance of goods, entertainments, and retailing institutions that reassuringly confirmed the correctness of current political, economic, and social policies.[23] J. Figueroa Domenech expresses this in the epigraph at the head of this introduction, concluding that "the luxuries and good taste of [Mexico's] retail stores reveal the culture and civilization of its people."[24] Discussing the increased wants of Mexico and opportunities for American business, the magazine *Modern Mexico* wrote in 1897, "A dozen years ago there was not a plate glass window in San Francisco street; now it is lined with them; and behind them are displayed goods from every part of the world."[25] The newspaper *La Semana Mercantil* proudly observed in 1895 that the rows of store windows along the streets of the capital were "radiant with light, where products and articles often worth a fortune were displayed, the most noticeable manifestation of the productive force of our epoch and a lovely and grandiose display of our work and progress."[26] Foreign and domestic observers referred to the stores, the plate-glass windows, and the advertising as shorthand for the modern cosmopolitanism of Mexico City and the nation's progress.[27] Many applauded or groused at the increased wants, needs, and expenditures of modern Mexicans.[28] They used this voracious consumer appetite to explain increased prices, personal and family financial sacrifices to maintain increased consumption, and of course, the inevitable and apparent march of national progress.

Many Porfirians recognized the central role of consumption in their society and economy insofar as they spoke the language of consumption and of its importance to modern societies. They spoke of consumption, consumers, and the consuming public and even referred to Mexico in the near future becoming a "consuming people" (*pueblo consumidor*).[29] They proclaimed that the great interest of nations is to assure consumers for their production, talked of establishing direct relations between the producer and the consumer, and observed the rewards of tending to the tastes, needs, and demands of consumers.[30] Internationalist debates over the nature and importance of consumption reached local presses. Discussions included the role of consumption in national development, the latest manifestation of a longstanding argument seeking to distinguish "productive" from "unproductive" consumption.[31] When textile industrialists mentioned the possibility of reducing production in Puebla, they were met by protests not just from workers but from leading businessmen, who declared that such a move would be disastrous for commerce as workers would have less to spend at their establishments.[32] Mainstream newspaper editorials from 1877 proposed that raising wages would benefit agriculture, commerce, and industry by providing workers with the means by which to purchase more of their products.[33] Many evidently understood that a modern economy was based on both production and consumption. These calls for higher wages to promote popular consumption anticipate Fordism by decades and indicate a progressive streak in Porfirian economic debates that has received minimal attention in the historiography. While this consumerist language may not have carried the day in determining macroeconomic government policy, it appears to have found purchase in the language of both the business community and the public at large.

Dramatic social and economic changes in Mexico set the stage for this consumer culture. After independence from Spain in 1821, the new nation experienced a half century of civil wars, foreign invasions, and occupations (Spain in 1829, France in 1838, the United States from 1846 to 1848, and France again from 1861 to 1867) and the loss of half its territory to the United States. Chronic instability, rampant banditry, deplorable roads, and a weak and capricious rule of law failed to attract foreign or domestic investment and left the nation fractured and vulnerable. Things began to change during the Restored Republic after Benito Juárez and the liberals defeated Emperor Maximillian and his conservative allies in 1867. The ascension of Porfirio Díaz to the presidency in 1876 confirmed and accelerated this turn. Fearing further predations at the hands of the United States and the European powers, the Porfirian leadership sought to strengthen and consolidate their nation by modernizing it. Emulating the economic and cultural models of those same powers became the blueprint for this change. Expanding and strengthening the central state, the Díaz administration (and the interregnum of president Manuel González, 1880–1884) pushed through a series of laws and institutional reforms that established a welcome environment for foreign investment and the integration of the nation into the global capitalist economy.

The growth of urban centers and urban culture was a signal consequence. The land hunger of large foreign and domestic agribusinesses was abetted by laws such as the "Baldíos Law" of 1883, which led to widespread land dispossession and the migration of tens of thousands to the cities. By 1910 Mexico City had more than doubled its population of two hundred thousand in 1895, and more than half of its inhabitants were born in other states.[34] Mexico's seventeen largest cities grew by 30 percent between 1895 and 1910, while the nation's population increased 20 percent.[35] Once in the cities, these rural migrants became integrated into larger national and global processes, including the consumer economy and market relations. They were exposed to a world of consumer goods and experiences heretofore unknown or encountered only obliquely through peddlers, traveling salesmen, or trips to regional markets. In the urban milieu they adopted new attitudes of desires and expectations that they were able to fulfill to varying degrees. To be sure, life was not easy and often grim. Migrants usually experienced poverty, lived in cramped, dilapidated, and unhygienic housing, and suffered abuses from state agents such as the police and judicial system.[36] At the same time, a vibrant working-class and popular urban culture flourished during the Porfiriato, a culture constructed on particular patterns of consumption, as this book will show.

Industrialization, improvements in distribution, and increasing literacy also contributed and gave character to Porfirian consumer culture. Goods of mass consumption became cheaper and more abundant as domestic industrial production grew rapidly after 1890, particularly in the consumer goods sector. Industrialization drove down prices for a number of popular goods, notably cigarettes, beer, and textiles and reduced the demand for imported goods and artisanal production. Consumer goods dropped from 75 percent of total imports in 1876 to only 43 percent in 1911.[37] Many industries were located in urban areas, further driving urbanization and the expansion of the money economy by attracting rural migrants in search of a livelihood. Workers were also consumers, and it should be noted that while women made up 17 percent of the industrial labor force nationally, they composed almost half in Mexico City.[38] The construction of a modern transportation and communication infrastructure further facilitated the growth of a domestic market. Ports in Veracruz, Mérida, Tampico, and elsewhere were deepened and modernized to facilitate trade, and an extensive telegraph network developed along with an extensive railway system, whose mileage grew from six hundred kilometers at the beginning of the Porfiriato to over nineteen thousand by 1910.[39] Literacy, crucial for reading the mass-circulation press that rose during the Porfiriato, grew nationally from a rate of 17 percent in 1895 to 29 percent in 1910, while that in the Federal District rose from 45 percent to 65 percent during the same period.[40]

To clarify, this book does not claim that the history of Mexican consumption began with the Tuxtepec Rebellion that elevated Porfirio Díaz to the presidency. From before the arrival of the Spanish until today, "both the production (supply) and the consumption (demand) side of

material culture created meaning for the gendered, classed, or racial-
ized structures of social life in the public and private spaces" of Mexico.[41]
The importance of imported goods, consumption patterns, and customs
has also remained a constant in Mexican history since contact. With the
Conquest, the transference of Mediterranean material culture to the
New World was an essential part of Spanish evangelization and accul-
turation of the indigenous populations. A hybrid society resulted from
the mixing of indigenous, European, African, and Asian material cultures. Another wave of foreign material culture washed over the new
nation's shores after independence in 1821 when Mexico's elites embraced
all things British and then French. British and French merchants vied for
control of Latin American markets opened by the defeat of the Spanish
and their mercantilist policies.[42] Although hyperbolic, José María Luis
Mora expressed this well in his 1836 memoir: "In the first years after
Independence, England set the tone of Mexican society: the clothing,
the fashions, the furniture, the food, the social gatherings, everything,
everything was then English, even our customs began to be modeled
after those of the British even though they were so different. But then
the French began to introduce themselves, and as their habits and fashions were more in conformity with those of Mexico, of course they were
preferred to the ones we had just adopted. From that point on, French
fashions and habits have set the tone of Mexican society."[43] Mexico's
material culture incorporated these changes to varying degrees depending on the subject's social and physical proximity to this new influence.
The influx of foreign goods and influences would only accelerate with
the French Intervention (1862–1867) and then during the Porfiriato as
Mexico became thoroughly integrated into the global economic system
and developed its domestic market.

This allure of the foreign reached an unprecedented level during the
Porfiriato.[44] Food, fashion, arts, architecture, leisure entertainments,
and all manner of technologies from Western Europe and the United
States pervaded Mexican society, particularly urban society. Their influence reached further down the social ladder than ever before. Yet the
portrayal of Porfirian slavish imitation of foreign models is inaccurate.
While cultural nationalists accused and still accuse those who embrace
this influence of aping foreign models, they fail to recognize that, from
the arrival of the Spanish, Mexicans have continuously fashioned and re-
fashioned their hybrid identities and patterns of consumption by incorporating selective elements from each new foreign material culture.

In other words, Mexicans possessed postmodern identities long before the idea of postmodernity existed. Engagement with foreign material culture and consumption patterns (or buying foreign-looking goods produced domestically—but more on that later) did not mean wanting to become French, or British, or German, or American. It meant buying into the ideal that those nations represented; it meant grappling with what it meant to be modern. Mexicans shaped an imaginative future for their nation and themselves through their perceptions of France's or Britain's or America's present.[45] Consumption, identity, and the idea of becoming modern—always related from the birth of the nation—became tightly woven as the modernization process transformed Mexico.

The chapters of this book consist of six snapshots of Porfirian consumer culture, all of which share the unifying themes of consumption, identity formation, and modernization. Although set mostly in Mexico City, they offer glimpses of what was occurring elsewhere in the republic. They illustrate the Mexican experience of a global phenomenon. Although influenced heavily by foreign goods, businesses, and citizens, Mexico's experience was directed by domestic rather than imperial imperatives. Those foreign influences were numerous, but this book argues that the French and Western Europeans generally were the leading foreign influence in forging a modern consumer culture, not the Americans, as recent historiography has contended.[46] American economic investment in Mexico certainly did exceed that of the French by 1900, but French cultural cachet and high investment in the retailing and domestic consumer goods sectors stamped a distinctive Gallic imprint on Mexican consumption patterns and tastes. After World War I, the United States would assume its modern place as the preeminent foreign economic and cultural presence in Mexico, but it has never fully erased the distinctively European encoding of many Mexican consumer proclivities. Each of the following chapters emphasizes this French contribution to a distinctly Mexican history.

Chapter 1 focuses on the manufacture and marketing of a single commodity: machine-rolled cigarettes. This chapter traces the mechanization and consolidation of the tobacco industry into three leading firms dominated by the El Buen Tono company. Publicity spectacles and marketing strategies reveal not only the links among consumption, spectacle, and modernity but also how even at this point the search for a mass market required the application of niche marketing strategies. Emphasis throughout remains on the changing meaning that society ascribed to the cigarette and how changes in technology, business organization, and cultural perceptions turned the once-lowly cigarette into a symbol of national progress.

Chapter 2 shifts to advertising and the popular characteristics of its production and audience. Emphasizing the range of advertisers, advertising forms, and intended markets, this chapter considers the history of advertising in Mexico as longer, more decentralized, and more popular than existing studies of the subject have indicated. Advertising concession petitions to the Mexico City Ayuntamiento (city council) and patent applications to the Development Ministry (Fomento) reveal a diverse class of entrepreneurs united by a belief that in their promotion of the new science of advertising in the public spaces of urban Mexico they were promoting a modern agenda synonymous with national progress. Working-class consumers, a group overlooked in existing studies, were an important market and attracted the attention of advertisers. The second half of this chapter analyzes advertising in the penny press, revealing a world of working-class consumption and a vision of a modern Mexico distinct from that of the more affluent classes but indicative of a widespread embrace of material progress, if not the terms on which it was offered.

Chapters 3 and 4 highlight the greatest institutional symbol of modern consumer culture: the department store. An expanding historiography on this subject elsewhere in North America and Europe allows for illuminating transnational comparisons. In analyzing department stores and a broader evolution of retailing in Mexico City the chapters provide a wealth of data on a much commented on but little studied phenomenon of Porfirian urban life. Additionally, they identify and correct a number of misconceptions about these stores, including the source of their goods and their customer base. They do so as they outline the origins, ownership, organization, financial success, and clientele of the stores. Department store owners—from Aristide Boucicault of the Bon Marché in Paris to the Tron family of the Palacio de Hierro in Mexico—had always trumpeted the "democratization of luxury" that their institutions brought to the mass of consumers. How Mexican stores interpreted this democratization and took on a larger cultural role as promoters of constant innovation and progress receives consideration. Finally, these chapters look at how the stores and their magnificent buildings were part of a steady visual transformation of central Mexico City into a secular commercial zone, a transformation in which private capital took on a leadership role.

Chapters 5 and 6 move away from more traditional manners of viewing consumption. Here, store crime and the public discourse on crime provide another angle from which to consider the impact of department stores, consumption, and the meaning of goods on Porfirian society. Together, the chapters help probe how the Porfirian motto of Order and Progress, with its emphasis on the security of both person and property, conveys a necessary precondition for any modern consumer society. Both chapters illustrate how property theft and thieves increasingly dominated discussions of crime and how a growing perception of their visibility found expression in a discourse of crime characterized by a transatlantic belief in a shift from violent to property crime in modernizing societies. Chapter 5 considers department store crime generally, beginning with observations on the nature of department store shoplifting before moving on to other forms of property crime committed in these establishments. It concludes with an account of the preexisting Mexican model of criminality and its modification as Porfirians viewed the modernization of crime occurring in lockstep with that of the larger society. From this platform, chapter 6 offers the La Profesa jewelry store robbery-homicide as an early case study of this phenomenon and provides a more intimate account of the changes that modernization, consumption, and crime brought about in the daily life of residents in the capital.

Chapter 1

PERSONALIZED PROGRESS

The Production and Marketing of the Machine-Rolled Cigarette

ON CHRISTMAS EVE 1907 MADAME CALVÉ CAME TO TOWN. NEVER one to miss out on free publicity, the famous French opera singer visited one of the republic's largest stages: the El Buen Tono cigarette factory in Mexico City. At the invitation of the general director, Ernesto Pugibet, Madame Calvé toured the state-of-the-art industrial facility that symbolized all that Mexico's leaders wanted their nation to be. Stepping out of her automobile she met the warm applause and proffered flowers of top government officials, factory directors, and two thousand neatly dressed workers. Above the assembly towered the Longines clock, imported from Switzerland not merely to decorate but to instill in industrial workers the time discipline of a modern labor force. Entering the factory, Madame Calvé toured the main shop floor, where young women dressed in white smocks and sashes in the national colors attended to the two hundred high-speed French machines that rolled and cut over 3.5 billion cigarettes each year (figure 1). Continuing on, she proceeded through "Porfirio Díaz" corridor—the long, marble-floored spine of the factory—to inspect the connecting work areas, modern lithographic presses, opulent administrative offices, vast tobacco warehouses, and other departments. The delegation finished its tour with a champagne lunch in the magnificent boardroom, where Pugibet announced that factory lithographers would print all of the posters, programs, and handbills promoting Madame Calvé's Mexican tour, grandly concluding by presenting the renowned diva with a new brand of cigarettes named for her to commemorate her visit.[1]

The performance proved a public relations success for El Buen Tono, Madame Calvé, and the Díaz regime. Upon making her farewell, Madame Calvé promised to return the next day in her costume as Carmen for portraits with both workers and high officials. As an experienced performer in the world of spectacle and appearances, Madame Calvé recognized the stage set—and the leading role played—by El Buen Tono in the Porfirian drama of modernizing Mexico.

Cheap and ubiquitous, machine-rolled cigarettes symbolized Mexico's economic and cultural progress more than any other mass-produced consumer commodity during the Porfiriato. To smoke the cigarettes of El Buen Tono and its two major industrial competitors was to demonstrate

Figure 1. French opera star Emma Calvé poses with cigarette rollers at the El Buen Tono cigarette factory. Note the cigarette-rolling machines on the left. Source: *El Mundo Ilustrado*, January 5, 1908, 22.

oneself as modern. This chapter explores the production and marketing changes involved in making this happen, examining the mechanization and consolidation of the tobacco industry, the industry's collaboration with the Porfirian state, and the industry's leading role in introducing new advertising techniques and consumer technologies to promote its brands to Mexican consumers.

A study of the industry's marketing, particularly that of El Buen Tono and its general director Ernesto Pugibet, provides a colorful and entertaining exploration of Porfirian urban culture as it demonstrates how the city served as "consumer culture's classroom."[2] In pursuit of a mass market for mass production, tobacco marketers contributed to the making of a Mexican mass culture. Yet as in any classroom setting, the supposed pupils were far from passive. Rather than simple manipulation and imposition of change from above, the iconic status and commercial success of the machine-rolled cigarette was far more complex and derived in part from consumer demand and changing tastes and attitudes. Companies worked hard to win over urbanites through visual display and exhibition, pouring immense resources and creative energy into reaching as wide an urban and national market as possible. In Mexico City tobacco advertisers marketed in every possible neighborhood and venue in the growing city, from the *pulquerías* in the Tepito barrio to affluent gatherings at the Tivoli de Eliseo.

Tobacco advertising in the press and on the street combined with industry-sponsored spectacles enacted not only to sell branded and machine-rolled products but also to advance simultaneously individual and group identities as consumers and citizens. By offering to fulfill individual aspirations with consumer choice these promotional efforts tapped into and encouraged individualization—the emergence of the individual, distinct in identity from a larger group entity—that defined Porfirian (and, indeed, Western) cultural trends.[3] At the same time, spectacles and print advertising constituted and promoted a larger community identity at an urban and even national level. A new and unifying identity for Mexicans, that of consumer, thus became entwined with a Mexican national identity as tobacco marketers promoted cigarette smoking as universal and modern.

Continuity and Change

Tobacco production and consumption has a long history in Mexico. Pre-Columbian societies harvested, dried, and traded tobacco leaf. During the colonial period Mexicans smoked tobacco in cigars, cigarettes, and pipes and snorted it as snuff while Indian laborers chewed it with lime juice (*pisiete*) in much the same way as Andean peoples chewed coca leaves for endurance. Cigarette manufacturing in Mexico reputedly began in the early eighteenth century with Antonio Charro, who rolled and sold cigarettes to theatergoers outside of the Teatro de Comedias in Mexico City. By the late colonial period cigars and cigarettes dominated consumption, composing over 90 percent of tobacco monopoly sales.[4] From 1768 until 1810 tobacco production, manufacture, and retail became a monopoly under the Bourbon reforms. Sale of tobacco products became the second-largest revenue source for the colonial government, exceeded only by the silver tithe.[5] The turmoil of the War of Independence that began in 1810 led to a decline in crop yields, the destruction of the monopoly, and the decentralization of the industry. The tobacco sector slowly recovered, and by 1862 the value of tobacco products manufactured in the capital trailed only that of the textile and clothing sector.[6]

Contemporary travel accounts indicate the Mexican love of tobacco never diminished throughout the half century of economic instability and conflict that followed independence. Foreign observers confirmed a senior colonial bureaucrat's assertion that "a Mexican would forsake a tortilla for a cigarette." In 1822 U.S. minister to Mexico Joel Poinsett expressed surprise when he observed "several young ladies, pretty and well-dressed, smoking cigars . . . the Mexican gentlemen do not seem to dislike it and the tale of love is whispered and vows of fidelity are interchanged amidst volumes of smoke."[7] Two decades later Fanny Calderón de la Barca peppered her memoir with accounts of both sexes smoking cigarettes after breakfast and cigars with hot punch after an evening of diversions.[8]

Representations of tobacco filled the literature and iconography of the new nation. In 1849 Ignacio Cumplido included in his two-volume *El álbum mexicano* a comprehensive essay on the history of tobacco in Mexico, accompanied by a full-page color lithograph showing the various implements used to smoke. Shortly after, the famous descriptions and images of Mexican types in *Los mexicanos: Pintados por si mismos* included numerous popular representations of tobacco in daily life, including the classic pose of a smoking China Poblana as well as less-well-remembered images such as "La cajista," the tobacco street vendor. Writing in 1865, Luis G. Inclán romanticized the incessant conflict between larger, state-sanctioned growers and manufacturers and small-scale farmers and rollers in his novel *Astucia: El jefe de los hermanos de la hoja; ó, Los charros contrabandistas de la rama.* When Porfirio Díaz assumed the presidency in 1876, tobacco was firmly established as a staple consumer commodity, tightly interwoven into Mexican social customs and the material culture of everyday life.[9]

Changes associated with Porfirian modernization altered both the quantity of tobacco consumed and the way in which it was consumed. New technologies and other developments drastically increased the cultivation, manufacture, and distribution of tobacco products after 1890. Tobacco cultivation burgeoned and quality improved to the point where the price obtained for tobacco grown in the Valle Nacional exceeded that of the coveted Cuban harvest. The opening of new growing areas like the Valle Nacional in Oaxaca and an infusion of new capital and horticultural techniques led crop yields to rise from 7,116 tons in 1892 to nearly 11,000 tons three years later. They continued to increase rapidly before peaking in 1905.[10] Transformations in tobacco production began in the mid-1880s and accelerated in the early 1890s in large part due to the actions of French-born entrepreneur Ernesto Pugibet. Pugibet took advantage of new Mexican incorporation laws, foreign technology, and investment capital to modernize, mechanize, and concentrate the cigarette industry. The development of a national rail network combined with the abolition of the *alcabalas* (internal tariffs) created potential for mass markets. Mechanization favored the rolling of cigarettes over cigars and the price of a pack fell to less than five centavos. Furthermore, quality improved as new adhesive-free rolling machinery removed glue and other impurities from the production process. Consumption of cigarettes swelled from 328 million cigarette packets in 1898 to 493 million in 1910.[11]

Pinning the cause for increased consumption solely on availability and lower price achieved by industrialization places the proverbial cart before the horse by ignoring changing consumer tastes and demand. First, as Mexican society steadily urbanized, city dwellers found that cigarettes better fit the faster pace and social etiquette of the urban social world than the messier, leisurely smoked cigars and pipes. Second, and most significant, machine-rolled cigarettes—created by the latest technology in large, modern, heavily capitalized factories—captured the Porfirian spirit of progress in a way that hand-rolled cigarettes or cigars did not. For good reason did the major tobacco companies use images of their factories and machinery in their advertising. Whether consumed conspicuously in public or inconspicuously alone, machine-rolled cigarettes allowed individuals to express affordably their participation in, and contribution to, national progress. A wide variety of brand choices allowed smokers to stake out or even try out different individualized or group identities. Much as factory-produced beer and its association with modern societies and supposedly more efficient working classes (the United States, Germany, England) grabbed market share from producers of traditional pulque (a mildly alcoholic fermented beverage made from the sap of the maguey cactus), so too did the cigarette overtake the cigar, pipe, and chewing tobacco. Changes in supply as well as demand, spurred by well-financed marketing campaigns that captured and attempted to direct this cultural zeitgeist, resulted in the quintupling of domestic cigarette consumption within the first twenty years of the Porfiriato. Cigarette consumption further increased by 50 percent between 1898 and 1910 as cigar consumption tumbled from 110 million to 76 million cigars per year during the same period.[12]

By the Revolution, cigarette consumption and etiquette permeated nearly every aspect of public and private life. British travel writer William English Carson described shopping in the capital's fancy department stores, where a salesman would "measure off a yard of cloth or fit you with new collars between puffs of his cigarette."[13] Mexican elites concluded dinner with coffee and cigarettes—not cigars—while newspaper columnists advised young women to buy their *novios* elegant cigarette holders.[14] Percy Martin expressed his annoyance that smoking had so thoroughly penetrated social etiquette; he observed how cigarette paraphernalia had become a stylish gift, and when two acquaintances met one would invariably offer his cigarette case "and it is considered impolitic to refuse, even if one be a non-smoker." Martin then went on to echo travelers who had noted that Mexicans rarely bothered to buy unrolled tobacco, since "cigarettes are so cheap that few take the trouble to make their own [and] . . . one sees but very few pipes in use, though occasionally perhaps among some old Indian man or woman. The cigarette is universal."[15]

Foundations of Success:
Ernesto Pugibet and the Porfirian Tobacco Industry

The mechanization of the tobacco industry during the 1880s presaged larger trends and marked a significant development in the Porfirian economy. As Edward Beatty demonstrated, large-scale factory production steadily eroded foreign imports, artisan workshops, and home production as the main source of consumer goods for Mexicans by 1900.[16] The transition to mechanized production increased demands on workers within modernizing factories and for those in smaller firms struggling to compete. In 1884 the Mexico City tobacco firm El Modelo installed the first cigarette-rolling machines, a mere three years after Joseph Bonsack patented the first model and the same year James Duke introduced the technology into his factories in Durham, North Carolina. Three different imported makes transformed the Modelo factory: Bonsack, Winston, and Comas. One year later Ernesto Pugibet and Luis Josselin patented a French rolling machine on behalf of El Buen Tono.[17]

With the advent of this machinery, public controversy intensified over child labor and the maltreatment of the predominantly female workforce under constant pressure by factory owners to increase its productivity.[18] Factory owners professed their sensitivity to these issues both in their public relations battles in the press and in the language used in their patent applications. For example, Josselin and Pugibet claimed that their newly invented rolling machine was better than those of competitors, primarily because it "did not disturb the operator in her work, a significant advance over those machines presently employed." Productivity soared with the new machinery, a fact that helps to explain why factory owners disregarded a government dictate in the early 1880s that dropped the daily workload from 2,600 to 2,185 cigarettes per worker and instead increased the number to 3,200 in certain cases.[19] Increased mechanization signaled to traditional artisan workshops that their days were numbered, yet the quantity of factory jobs created in the consolidating industry exceeded the number of positions lost in traditional shops. Mexico City's "Big Three" tobacco companies routinely recruited female employees throughout the country in advertisements placed in local newspapers.[20]

The El Buen Tono cigarette company, founded and directed by Ernest Pugibet, quickly positioned itself at the forefront of this change. Better known as Ernesto in his adopted homeland, Pugibet would eventually out-invest, outspend, and outmaneuver his competitors as El Buen Tono became a de facto monopoly. Cosmopolitan, urbane, and refined, he traveled frequently to New York, Paris, and Geneva. He returned to Mexico from these centers of the modern world with fresh capital, new business techniques, and cutting-edge advertising innovations. He was one of the founding members of the Moctezuma Brewery (now part of the Grupo Modelo), the Compañia Nacional Mexicana de Dinamita y

Explosivos, the French-Swiss investment group Société Financière pour l'Industrie au Mexique, and the thoroughly modernized and expanded San Ildefonso wool textile mill and electric power facility. His administrative duties and stock holdings also involved establishments such as the Banco Nacional. In 1907 the French government awarded him the Legion of Honor, and he played an active role in the French community in Mexico as administrator and patron in social organizations such as the Cercle Français, the French Commercial School, and the July 14 Independence Day Committee. His well-known philanthropic largesse extended to the Mexican community at large through his construction or donation of fountains, buildings, and churches, such as the Iglesia de Nuestra Señora de Guadalupe de El Buen Tono.[21] Throughout the last two decades of the Porfirian regime, Pugibet successfully established himself as one of the leading architects of Mexican modernization, with the El Buen Tono cigarette company at the top of his portfolio.

Pugibet committed few mistakes on his path to industrial monopolist. Raised in the Haute-Garonne department in the French Pyrenees, Pugibet immigrated to Cuba in 1868 at the age of fifteen, where he found work in the tobacco industry. With the growing disruptions caused by the Ten Years' War (1868–1878), Pugibet fled to Mexico and in 1875 arrived in the capital. He hired four employees and established a small cigarette factory that would become the embryo of La Cigarrera Manufacturera El Buen Tono in 1889. In the mid-1880s Pugibet assured his business success by marrying Guadalupe de la Portilla y Garaycoechea, a daughter of the Mexican aristocracy with noble family origins in eighteenth-century Spain. In addition to bearing him two sons and a daughter, Portilla brought him investment capital, useful contacts in the tobacco-growing region of Veracruz, and invaluable connections within the Porfirian government. One of the most useful was her uncle, Juan Bárcena y Zugalde, governor of Veracruz. Control of the capital and patents of El Buen Tono was in the name of Guadalupe de la Portilla when Pugibet transformed El Buen Tono into a corporation in 1894, illuminating the influence she held and would continue to hold in her partnership with Pugibet.[22]

In addition to the political patronage afforded by his marriage to Portilla, Pugibet curried and obtained the support of the Mexican political elite. He offered them lucrative stock-purchase options and packed the administrative council of El Buen Tono with powerful notables such as the son of Porfirio Díaz, Secretary of War General Manuel González-Cosío, Deputy Finance Minister Roberto Nuñez, and Julio Limantour, the finance minister's younger brother and a well-known real estate developer.[23] Pugibet unconditionally supported the government via his company's publicity campaigns. Identifying brands as "Dedicados al Presidente de la República y á su Ministerio" or awarding every member of the newly inaugurated Congress a silver medal with the El Buen Tono factory on one side and the president astride his horse on the other were merely the beginning. Pugibet and his administrators placed El Buen Tono in the forefront of businesses cheerleading at the biennial *fiestas presidenciales* by introducing new brands dedicated to Díaz and constructing elaborate, enormous floats that involved up to two hundred parading workers.[24] In the last years of the regime, when aerial advertising came into vogue, the pilot of the company zeppelin would switch from publicizing cigarettes to supporting Díaz-controlled politicians. The dirigible would also occasionally escort the presidential train beyond the city limits en route to points throughout the republic.[25]

Through connections with the Porfirian political and social leadership, Pugibet intertwined the interests of business and state with a goal of advancing the progress of the Mexican nation. His particularly close business, political, and social ties with Finance Minister José Yves Limantour demonstrate the fusion of business and politics among the Porfirian elite. Limantour, considered the mastermind of Porfirian economic progress, held the top post in the Secretaría de Fomento from 1893 until 1911. His personal papers reveal a lively correspondence with Pugibet beginning in the late 1890s. Both men had extensive stock holdings in the same firms. For example, Limantour purchased El Buen Tono stocks for himself and for family members such as his daughter María Teresa Iturbe. Pugibet enabled Limantour to buy shares in his other business interests, such as the San Ildefonso wool textile mill, and Limantour reciprocated by guaranteeing Pugibet five thousand shares of the San Rafael paper factory, the newsprint source for the republic's largest dailies.[26] Limantour received regular updates on the San Ildefonso factory as well as samples of the newest products.[27] Pugibet also accommodated Limantour's need to dispense patronage within his own *camarilla*, or network of political and family allies, the Científicos. Upon request from Limantour he provided jobs as varied as traveling salesman, shop foreman, and lottery manager. In one case Limantour asked Pugibet to hire a young man, Agusto Agacino, who "committed the stupid act of marrying and now asks you for a job, any job, and will do so on a trial basis at whatever wage you will pay him."[28] Pugibet also provided Limantour's wife with pure nicotine to destroy mites in her home.[29] The relationship between the two men grew comfortable enough for Pugibet to offer Limantour the use of his Paris home and also the run of his New York apartment-suite when Limantour returned from his transatlantic voyages.[30] When Pugibet decided to enter the Mexico City real estate market in 1906 he consulted with Limantour's brother, Julio, who advised him to purchase the downtown Hotel Guardiola and then handled the transaction.[31] In 1892, Limantour replaced Matías Romero as the head of Fomento, signaling a power shift in the administration toward the Científico camarilla.

With political patronage and protection secured through the camarillas of Pugibet's wife's family and of Finance Minister Limantour, the fortunes of both Pugibet and El Buen Tono began their stellar ascent in 1889. That year El Buen Tono won the prestigious first prize at the Paris Universal Exposition, the first of many international honors. The next year Pugibet moved the company to its new factory facing the Plaza de San Juan, just five blocks south of the Alameda. Over the next two decades the factory complex would engulf neighboring properties as the company added housing for employees, expanded tobacco warehouses, and constructed new production departments.[32] Pugibet, like his main competitor, Antonio Basagoiti of La Tabacalera Mexicana, recognized the value of new production technology and confidently believed that increased output would not only crush competitors but also find ready absorption in an increasingly accessible national market. His greatest coup was the 1891 acquisition of the patent rights for the French Decouflé high-speed and glueless cigarette-rolling machines for a period of twenty years. The replacement of manually applied glue with mechanized crimping by this new innovation was so significant that the company named its first glueless brand Pedid los Cigarros sin Pegamento de Ernesto Pugibet (Ask for the glueless cigarettes of Ernesto Pugibet). The new machines also garnered praise in the press.[33] The company aggressively protected the competitive advantage afforded by the Decouflé machines and spent much of the next twenty years in litigation to fend off competing technology and extend the length of its patent privilege. With sixty Decouflé machines and initial capital of 1 million pesos, Pugibet reorganized the company as a corporation (*sociedad anónima*) in 1894 and became the new general director of the firm.[34] Over the next two decades the factory, production, and revenue would grow, with

annual sales increasing from just over 1 million pesos in 1894 to plateau
at nearly 7 million pesos in 1907 until the Revolution, based on capital
of 10 million pesos and the production of over two hundred machines.[35]

New technologies of image production and reproduction were as
important as those of cigarette production for the success of El Buen
Tono. Mass production required mass consumption, and the company's
state-of-the art lithographic department produced not only the artwork
for cigarette packaging but also all newspaper advertising as well as posters, handbills, trading cards, and other printed ephemera. In other words,
the lithographic department was instrumental in producing the images
and visual associations of the cigarette with modernity that helped define
the machine-rolled cigarette as an icon of progress. What distinguished
modern consumer culture (and modern life) from earlier periods was
the "democratization of the image," an achievement stemming from the
invention and confluence of lithography, chromolithography, and photography along with advances in mechanical reproduction such as the
rotary press.[36] El Buen Tono was one of only a handful of companies in
Mexico with an in-house publicity department. El Buen Tono promoted
the department as yet another facet of a progressive image. Few publications reviewing Mexican economic and cultural progress failed to laud
the department: one described it as "amazingly well-equipped" with
"the most modern and expensive machines"; another, by French economic analyst Raul Bigot, remarked on the quality of the color posters
and the advertisements and illustrations destined for the newspapers.[37]
Domingo Gómez was the first and a long-term manager of the department and oversaw more than a dozen employees working three lithographic presses.[38] Equipment changes and expansion characterized the
department as propaganda needs and technology improvements intertwined. By 1907 the company had purchased new rotary lithographic
presses from France that replaced printing stones with aluminum sheets
and offered better quality and a greater range of colors and printing sizes.
About the same time two more French imports arrived to take advantage of these advances. By replacing the Mexican Gómez with the highly
acclaimed artistic talents of Alexandre Prudhomme and Auguste Ussel,
the company signaled a decisive embrace of and emphasis on the creative
and artistic over the technical. In the wake of this latest innovation to
woo consumers, one observer praised the genius of Ussel, who "covered
the walls of Mexico with advertising posters full of originality and possessed of a Parisian flavour and exotic *parfum* that matched the classiest

of European masters in the field."[39] Prudhomme and Ussel ensured that representations of tobacco consumption contributed to what Mexican historian Julieta Ortiz Gaitán has called the "omnipresence of the image in the urban world."[40]

The success of El Buen Tono convinced smaller firms to merge in 1899 to form the second and third largest cigarette manufacturing companies in Mexico—La Tabacalera Mexicana and La Compañia Cigarrera Mexicana. Pugibet's innovation forced consolidation that transformed the industry from a hodgepodge of hundreds of parochial, labor-intensive firms into one dominated by three firms of national scope, employing modern forms of business organization and heavily invested in new manufacturing, marketing, and distribution technologies. Consolidation led to competition that spurred a tobacco publicity war with heavy press advertising, sponsored lotteries, popular entertainment, and other public spectacles whose expense appeared to defy fiscal responsibility. Fortunately, the leadership of the firms possessed deep pockets. Competition and efficiency shrank the number of tobacco factories in Mexico from 766 in 1899 to 341 by the Revolution. In Mexico City the number dwindled from 43 to 14 by 1905. As the number of producers plummeted, cigarette consumption rose from 4.9 million to 8.4 million kilograms per year. By the turn of the century the product of Mexican manufacturers was so inexpensive that the importation of foreign tobacco products, particularly Cuban and Virginian, virtually halted.[41]

Pugibet's main rivals in the cigarette market were La Tabacalera Mexicana, headed by the Spanish-born Antonio Basagoiti, and La Cigarrera Mexicana. Basagoiti, like Pugibet, pursued a wide range of business opportunities, with interests in the sugar, banking, textile, and steel sectors.[42] In response to El Buen Tono's growth, Basagoiti combined his small tobacco companies with the wholesale operation of Veracruz tobacco brokers Zaldo y Compañia to form La Tabacalera Mexicana.[43] La Cigarrera Mexicana was a consolidation of four factories, including the Negrito factory of Antero Muñúzuri, El Modelo of Ampudia y Sucesores, Iñigo Noriega's La Mexicana, and Pesquera Sucesores. Unlike La Tabacalera, which remained privately owned, La Cigarrera incorporated as a publicly traded company and a significant number of its shares entered the portfolios of high-ranking Porfirians such as Enrique Creel and Ignacio de la Torre y Mier.[44] Both companies moved into expanded facilities located in Mexico City and both possessed government connections who officially blessed their enterprises. At the inauguration of

La Cigarrera Mexicana, Porfirio Díaz offered the toast before touring the plant to praise the "manufacture of cigarettes and cigars on a large scale . . . using all the mechanical advances and perfections that this industry had achieved."[45] These "mechanical advances and perfections" primarily referred to the use of increasingly efficient rolling machinery from American companies such as Bonsack and Winston. El Buen Tono stood by its French Decouflé technology.

Freed of the onerous internal tariff barriers (the alcabalas, abolished in 1896) and blessed by a rapidly expanding rail system, the companies marshaled a network of traveling salesmen, rural agencies, and peddlers to bring their products and advertising to an emerging national market. El Buen Tono led the industry in the use of advertising to capture and expand market share. While its bull's-eye remained Mexico City, the greatest market in the nation, it worked to develop provincial and rural markets as well. From Chihuahua and Monterrey to Guadalajara and Mérida, its advertising became a regular topic of conversation among the citizenry and was integrated into popular culture nationwide. El Buen Tono staged a constant parade of spectacles that sought to transform a rather pedestrian consumer product into an icon of modernity through a visual and text-based advertising program that linked its vision of progress to progress within Mexican society. Smoking the machine-rolled cigarettes of El Buen Tono and its major competitors became, for many Mexicans, affordable conspicuous and inconspicuous consumption that demonstrated modernity, that demonstrated that they were keeping pace with the rapid changes occurring in their society and were on the cutting edge of history.

Unsuspected Consumers and Niche Marketing

In their affordability and widespread consumption machine-rolled cigarettes served a market whose size and composition challenges the conventional wisdom on the Porfirian consumer market. This wisdom, slowly changing but tenaciously resilient in scholarly works, holds that only a small elite and a slightly larger but insecure middle class had the capacity to consume. A lack of interest or a lack of purchasing power inhibited or prohibited working-class and popular participation in the market, an odd argument since urban life and reliance on a money economy by definition makes one dependent on the market for the material bases of life.[46] The legacy of dependency-theory analysis, which minimizes analysis of domestic industrialization and overemphasizes the importance of luxury imported goods, combined with Marxist interpretations and a healthy dose of overemphasis on vilifying the Old Regime by post-Revolutionary historical narratives, has propped up this viewpoint.

The numbers and evidence on cigarette production and consumption argue for a strong correction. By 1910 the three major firms produced 5.2 billion cigarettes per year, with El Buen Tono churning out 3.5 billion alone, and they controlled anywhere from 62 to 90 percent of the national cigarette market.[47] To absorb this massive production, economic historian Stephen Haber estimates that Mexico possessed a consumer market of five million people (out of a national population of nearly thirteen million) sufficiently incorporated within the money economy to be capable of purchasing manufactured goods. Every man, woman, and child in this market could have (but in all probability did not) smoked 1,040 cigarettes a year (or a pack a week), if we divide this market into cigarette production figures for 1907.[48]

Marketing strategies of tobacco companies suggest they viewed their consumer market as deep and wide and dispel the myth of a shallow and narrow base of potential. Tobacco companies adopted a multitiered branding structure laden with class- and gender-specific meaning by modifying price, packing, and advertising language and imagery. Niche marketing was an integral part of their strategy to construct a mass market for their products. Moreover, archival records corroborate the calculation above: itemized family budgets of semiskilled urban workers listed cigarette purchases of approximately thirty packs a month; those of unskilled workers ranged from six to ten.[49] While most Mexicans lived financially precarious lives during the Porfiriato (and before, and after), this did not preclude their participation in a consumer culture (particularly in one stocked by lower-priced goods produced by a growing domestic industrial base) that was becoming synonymous with urban culture.[50]

Cigarette manufacturers recognized that capturing a mass market demanded that they target their products in varied ways to accommodate the social, economic, and cultural diversity of Mexican society. At the same time, offering different tiers of cigarette brands offered the illusion or at least the dream of social mobility for only a few centavos through the purchase of a premium brand. Companies employed graduated pricing as the most basic distinguishing factors between their brands. All three big companies did this. El Buen Tono pricing in 1906 ranged from a few centavos to over fifteen centavos per pack.[51] With premium brands consumers received better tobacco, often finer paper (usually rice paper), more elaborate and elegant packaging (including foil lining), and of course the social cachet of being seen smoking cigarettes such as Parisienses, Cycle, Jockey Club, High Life, Elegantes, or Reina Victoria. The names of these luxury brands reflect the modern, cosmopolitan, and cutting-edge self-image or aspirations of those who smoked them. Brands aimed at a more plebeian clientele include the wildly popular Canela Pura of El Buen Tono and Flor de Canela from La Tabacalera Mexicana as well as Canarios, Chorritos, Granaderos, Mexicanos, Sabrosos, Sirenas, La Popular, and Torpederos. This sample is merely a small fraction of the enduring brand names offered by the Big Three, not to mention those of their competitors.[52] The companies regularly launched new brands and frequently named them to commemorate special events. El Buen Tono created Cigarros El Centenario for the 1910 celebrations, Alfonso XIII when the company was named the official provider of the Spanish Royal House, and Judic, Mazzantini, and Calvé to pay tribute to the Mexican tours made by these French and Italian actresses and chanteuses.[53] The different pricing, packaging, images, and language served as markers of meaning well understood by consumers, and the implication of brands positioned at the upper tiers "was that smoking these cigarettes would bring the sensation of luxury."[54] Whether viewed as duping or fulfilling the fantasies of individuals, the multitude of brand names indicates not only the fluid cultural literacy of Mexican consumers but also the never-ending demand on advertisers to pair and promote a title and an image that had meaning for and would entertain and entice potential buyers.

Where companies spent their advertising dollars reflected the target markets of the companies and their products. El Buen Tono covered the broadest spectrum of the market while La Cigarrera and La Tabacalera concentrated on the middling to lower segments. La Tabacalera coveted and challenged the range of El Buen Tono but lacked the packaging technology and luxury cachet to make serious inroads into the premium market. In the commercial press, El Buen Tono dominated in papers such as *Actualidades* and *Frivolidades*, aimed at the affluent and hedonistic segment of the capital's population, and the company's ads outnumbered those of La Tabacalera and La Cigarrera in journals such as *El Mundo Ilustrado* and *El Tiempo Ilustrado*, aimed at a respectable readership. The ratio reversed slightly in the penny press, which offered a potential market of wage-earning laborers.

Working-class individuals are the most unsuspected of consumers in histories of the period, yet tobacco companies advertised heavily and continuously not only in their neighborhoods but also in the penny press that catered to them. Cigarette ads joined those for furniture, aluminum beds, watches, phonographs, and photography and suggested that many producers believed a lucrative mass market existed in the capital.[55] These ads did not just appear in papers advocating a more moderate, mutualist approach to labor relations; in fact, the greatest number and frequency of ads occur in *El Diablito Bromista*, one of the most radical papers, which advocated labor strikes. It covered and commended cigarette companies for providing spectacles for workers at venues such as the Orrin Circus or for hosting bullfights at which they handed out quantities of free packets exceeding ten thousand.[56] Equally important and illustrative of the sophisticated niche marketing practiced by the companies is the way in which they adapted specifically to the technical limitations of the penny press and catered to the tastes of its readership. Most of these papers ran on a shoestring and did not have sophisticated presses; as a result the tobacco companies reigned in their increasingly splashy visual ads used in better-equipped papers. Still, they occasionally mixed text and image, as with El Buen Tono's placement of their famous cartoon strips or La Tabacalera's inclusion of mixed text and pictogram riddles possibly designed by the likes of José Guadalupe Posada.[57] The use of humor and wordplay demonstrates the recognition by cigarette advertisers of the popular practice of *albures*, or language games, among the Mexican lower class.[58] Other advertisers in the popular press used this popular custom, as did newspaper editors on page one, but no one matched the cleverness or length (often two-thirds or a whole page of a four-page paper) of the stories told by La Tabacalera. These involved popular themes set in quickly identifiable or working-class places with easily recognizable characters. Take the story titled "La Mansión de Luzbel," in which two agents of the company travel to hell to gain an audience with the devil. Lucifer, his minions, and his captive clientele made up of cheating moneylenders, flirtatious women, drunks, thieves, and scoundrels try the products after enduring a hard-sell pitch of the merits possessed by the brands Sirenas, Supremos, and Flor de Canela. Instantly the mansion of hell "becomes a palace of light, of opulence, of music, and of aromatic flowers" as the residents dance "cuadrillas . . . cake-walks, and polkas," compelling Lucifer to permit the smoking of La Tabacalera brands one hour per day.[59]

Children are another category of unsuspected consumers. Considerable evidence points to the marketing of cigarettes to—and ready acceptance by—Mexican children and youths. Numerous ads featured children smoking, and one for the La Tabacalera brand Flor de Canela humorously depicts a cigarette as the only cure for a crying baby.[60] While these ads did not directly cultivate children as current or future smokers, the sale of chocolate cigarettes by El Buen Tono certainly did.[61] Another indication of child smokers comes from the middle-class narrative against the habit. The newspaper La Clase Media (The middle class) occasionally pointed out the health costs of smoking, especially by children, as it fought a losing battle against the contrary arguments of the tobacco companies and many doctors.[62] Ten years later, in 1919, the moral debate over juvenile smoking as part of a larger package of youthful vices reached the chambers of the Municipal Council in Mexico. Arguments in council never translated into action, as many dismissed the dangers. One councillor drolly suggested that children caught smoking should be taken to the home of one antismoking council member and forced to play piano for a quarter of an hour.[63]

Porfirian women are the last category of unsuspected consumers. Evidence is contradictory, as the practice and meaning of female smoking was undoubtedly controversial and multivalent. On the one hand, smoking appears to have become gendered masculine. In upscale private homes smoking rooms reserved for men appeared, undoubtedly borrowing from architectural fashion in the United States and Western Europe. Among respectable society, women, as the "gentler sex," were to find smoke disagreeable and merited certain considerations for their delicate nature. A gendered battle over smoking in enclosed public spaces erupted in the last two decades of the Porfiriato as women protested the practice, or certain men protested on their behalf. Not surprisingly, the conflict came as women increasingly and more autonomously moved into public spaces, and it reflected growing social anxiety over the female's lack of enclosure and perceived threats to patriarchal privilege.[64] Theaters became gendered battle zones as men complained about the plumage and elevated grandeur of women's hats in response to the objection of women to the stench emitted and noxious clouds formed by men's cigars and cigarettes. The Mexico City Ayuntamiento periodically debated whether to ban smoking in theaters and elicited strong passions on both sides. After enacting a ban in 1893 that met great opposition and was eventually lifted, the council tried again in 1902.[65] As one male petitioner against a ban frothily ranted, women's hats were "extremely disagreeable, rather bothersome, and even anti-hygienic to the public" before adding almost as an afterthought that they also blocked his view.[66] In a letter published in *El Imparcial* one woman suggested that women would stop wearing hats in theaters if men stopped smoking in the city tramcars.[67] The trams joined the theaters as another contested smoking zone, with newspapers taking sides and printing letters, all of which reinforced the notion of women as offended nonsmokers.[68] Finally, in March 1909, Governor Guillermo de Landa y Escandón decreed a ban on smoking in trams. This led to another escalation in the print gender wars. In desperation, nicotine-deprived smokers such as the German civil engineer F. Mathis wrote open letters to Ernesto Pugibet pleading with him to do something, perhaps provide smoking cars, since he was the dominant cigarette producer in the country.[69] Meanwhile, the newspaper *Actualidades* best captured the friction between the sexes. Three days after the ban started, the paper printed a cartoon image of a tram in which a single primly dressed lady and the conductor ride inside while fifteen men cling to the outside as they smoke. In an accompanying article an indignant patron, writing under the pseudonym "Cyrano," recounts how after a conductor caught him smoking he angrily declared, "I'll smoke whenever I want." In response the conductor threatened to call a nearby policeman and warned, "Sir, . . . the fair sex requires certain considerations."[70]

On the other hand, strong evidence indicates that Porfirian women smoked cigarettes. In 1877 the cigarette manufacturer El Borrego advertised "small cigarettes for ladies," while another promoted the brand Damitas (Little ladies) as "cigarettes well-known by the fair sex in Oaxaca" and promised, "In these little cigarettes we do not omit or sacrifice anything to please the delicate tastes of our kind female consumers [*nuestras consumidoras*]."[71] In January 1897 *Modern Mexico* noted that "nobody chews tobacco, but nearly everybody smokes cigarettes, including most of the women of the lower classes."[72] Numerous foreign traveler accounts indicate smoking among women was not a habit limited the lower strata of Mexican society. In 1888 William Curtis wrote, "Everybody smokes, women as well as men."[73] Nine years later Percy Martin spent considerable time describing the smoking habits of Mexicans and concluded, "Practically every man and many women smoke."[74] Shortly after, W. E. Carson observed the habits of Mexican elite women and remarked, "Smoking is very general among them, and this is very often done in quite an open manner and in company with the male member of the family."[75] Both El Buen Tono and La Tabacalera marketed brands targeted toward women. They bore names like Gardenias and were further coded feminine by their size, slimness, delicacy of rolling paper, and package color.[76] Furthermore, as in France and elsewhere, smoking was also associated with the New Woman and actresses by the late nineteenth century, which made it both sexy and subversive, an association reinforced by El Buen Tono advertising depicting photos or paintings of famous actresses smoking its brands.[77] Although the historiography does not exist to elucidate the extent, complexity, and significance of the female smoker in Porfirian society, women did smoke and cigarette companies did cater to and target a female audience as part of a larger strategy to plumb the depths of a mass consumer market crossing class, gender, and even age lines.

Spectacles of Progress

To win over consumers, create new ones, and inculcate the relatively recent idea of brand recognition, El Buen Tono coordinated its marketing campaigns to create a commodified, carnivalesque street culture that was embraced by residents of all social classes in Mexico City. The newspaper El Imparcial summed up this vision of boulevard-centered spectacular progress promoted by El Buen Tono:

> El Buen Tono has always believed that in order to stimulate consumption it must use the most effective means to please the public and not spare any expense or effort to do so. It recently installed a free public cinema that provides innocent and enjoyable distraction to both middle and lower classes. Tomorrow it launches its dirigible balloon and will soon enter into the Flower Festival parade nothing less than its luxurious automobile that now serves to deliver its magnificent brands to stores across the Metropolis. This doesn't even include its free lottery that showers its consumers with thousands of pesos, nor the other irrefutable proofs of its generosity to the public that grow day by day and earn thousands of rounds of applause.[78]

Effusive in its praise and probably paid copy, this snippet from the Porfirian press reveals not only the entertaining innovations sponsored by El Buen Tono but also the language used to convey a sense of power to—and participation by—the consumer.[79] This appeal to consumers and desire to constitute and please the urban crowd—"the public" mentioned so often in the excerpt above—characterized the strategy of marketing tobacco in Porfirian Mexico. Tobacco companies, therefore, were leaders in the spectacularization of city life and the development of an urban mass culture. In the consumer-oriented city, the crowd experience increasingly became less a threat of potential violence than an act of collective consumption.[80]

The El Buen Tono dirigible, initially launched in late 1906 and early 1907, was the most famous and enduring of the company's spectacles (figure 2). Until its inauguration, no organization, not even the military, had ever flown a self-propelled and controllable airship anywhere in the republic. Although hot air balloon ascensions first occurred in 1785 and continued through the Porfiriato (El Buen Tono had maintained its own since 1900), the dirigible offered spectators the first opportunity to view a pilot no longer at the mercy of prevailing winds.[81] Emblazoned

Figure 2. An El Buen Tono dirigible at a horse race sponsored by the German community. Source: *El Mundo Ilustrado*, February 2, 1908, 9.

on all sides with the company's name, measuring also one hundred feet in length, powered by a ten-horsepower engine, and steered by pedal rudders, the dirigible promised mankind's conquest of the air for the first time in Mexico.

After a month of heavy promotion in the press and company advertisements, the dirigible embarked on its maiden voyage. Its flight path provided telling insight into its commercial and cultural purpose. Piloted by the American citizen Charles Hamilton, the dirigible aimed straight for the heart of the city rather than for a safer location such as the Valbuena Flats, which had none of the obstacles and dangers of an urban skyline. Entering the Zócalo as he skimmed only meters above the National Palace, where President Díaz watched the flight from his balcony, Hamilton proceeded to climb above the towers of the National Cathedral. Turning to the west, then south, he overflew the Portal de Mercaderes commercial zone and the Municipal Palace before completing another circuit around the plaza. "Handling the machine like a fine horseman handles his steed," the pilot then returned to the airfield after first buzzing the fashionable shopping thoroughfares of Plateros and San Francisco, then crossing Alameda Park and, at the statue of Carlos V, turning southwest down the Paseo de la Reforma to Chapultepec Castle. Thousands of bystanders applauded and whistled from the crowded streets, sidewalks, balconies, and plazas beneath the flight path. Finally, after symbolically marking the most significant political, religious, and commercial sites of the capital and of the nation, he veered north to end his journey at the Tivoli de Eliseo.[82]

Commentators commended the company for educating the population in the ways of the modern world. Various journalists waxed on about how El Buen Tono had "popularized flight in Mexico" and pointed out "the incessant fight between old and modern means of transport," as its dirigible "characterized the conquest of the air, the pride of the twentieth century." Not forgetting the commercial aspect of the flight, another added that "El Buen Tono, thanks to this audacious advertisement —which represents a considerable financial sacrifice . . . —has achieved the popularization of science. Although others will undoubtedly imitate its achievement, only El Buen Tono will accrue the glory of having introduced to the Mexican public one of the noblest inventions of the century."[83]

Over the next three years this dirigible and its successors became a regular sight over the capital and beyond. In addition to repeating its first itinerary, it circled over special events as diverse as those at the Peralvillo race track frequented by Mexico's bon ton, the French business school while high-level government ministers were visiting, and of course, the bullfights attended by a cross-section of *capitalino* (residents of the capital city) society.[84] Díaz, attending the races at Peralvillo, "commented on the visit very favorably" and remarked that "the attractions of the balloon have eclipsed those of the race course."[85] As part of its national marketing strategy, the company sent the aircraft for a tour of the republic, entertaining residents of Guadalajara, Puebla, and other cities. In Puebla the airship "flew over the highest buildings and the towers of the Cathedral." One observer noted that "the popular classes loudly expressed their admiration for the nimble flying of the dirigible." In Guadalajara the bullring El Progreso received a flyover for at least ten minutes as the crowd "warmly applauded" the diversion.[86]

The dirigible remained popular through the centennial celebrations of 1910, but by then a French-made Bleriot monoplane captivated residents in search of the latest spectacular novelty. Thomas Braniff may have earned the honor of flying the first heavier-than-air craft in Mexico when he successfully took off from the dusty Valbuena Flats in 1909, but it was Ernesto Pugibet who earned widespread praise for allowing free public attendance to his sponsored plane's flights in 1910. Pugibet's pilot, Maurice Raoul-Duval, navigated a number of short flights beginning on February 22, garnering much publicity and attracting large crowds. Raoul-Duval also took the opportunity to engage in healthy self-promotion: as the general agent in Mexico for Perrier mineral water and Pommery & Greno champagne, he used his aeronautic achievements to boost his own businesses' advertising campaigns in the newspapers.[87]

Pugibet's emphasis on the public displays of the newest technological wonders underscores the clarity of his understanding of how consumption, spectacle, and modernity reinforced each other. As one newspaper remarked, "El Buen Tono has always been distinguished by the originality with which it attracts the attention of consumers to its unsurpassable products."[88] Whether those "unsurpassable products" were their cigarettes or spectacles did not really matter: urbanites delighted in consuming both. Each epitomized the modern condition: as mass-marketed commodities, their entertaining qualities of novelty, ephemerality, and cutting-edge technology required constant refreshment to retain their allure to the public. On a visceral level the cigarette advertisers understood this and provided a steady stream of spectacular promotions calculated for their broad appeal that acted as selective infomercials on the latest wonders devised by science.

Take, for example, Electric Man. El Hombre Luminoso walked through the main shopping area of Mexico City, elegantly dressed, "awakening the curiosity of all." Wearing a frock coat and pants of "an irreproachable cut," a hat of silk, expensive rings on his fingers, and a gold-tipped walking stick, he garnered the praise of one newspaper writer as "the epitome of elegance . . . a 'dandy' in every sense of the word (figure 3)."[89] Every detail of the attire of Electric Man conformed to social prescriptions of good taste. As one of the many popular social etiquette books of the era advised the nouveau riche, a gold-tipped walking stick like Electric Man's was fine for evening perambulations, but morning and afternoon constitutionals required no more than unadorned wood to remain "truly *chic*."[90] What distinguished him from other, similarly dressed men of progress was his electrical wiring. Wandering the downtown streets at night, he could light three lines of incandescent lightbulbs woven into the back of his coat that illuminated the words "Eureka, Cigarettes 'Calvé,' El Buen Tono, S.A," referring to the brand of cigarettes named in honor of French soprano Emma Calvé, whose visit opened this chapter. Power flowed from six dry-cell batteries strapped around his waist that activated with the press of a button hidden in his pocket. Nightly he "blended with the most elegant gentlemen who strolled along Plateros, San Francisco [and other central streets] . . . until he paused to linger in front of a group of people standing before the doors of a club, business, or a family engaged in window shopping. Unexpectedly the bulbs would light up with a miraculous effect . . . today Electric Man is the topic of all conversations on the boulevard."[91] Electric Man represented an idealized modern consumer with his attention to appearance, ease with new technology, and familiarity with the urban environment; in short, Electric Man epitomized the cosmopolitan citizen. A walking billboard, he offered a didactic model of emulation for the population of the capital as much as an advertisement for cigarettes.

Roaming further across the urban landscape than Electric Man and emulating a Parisian innovation, ten-foot-long advertising coaches pulled by two or four horses attracted crowds with multicolored lightbulbs, electric bells, and phonographs synchronized with the displayed ads for El Buen Tono cigarettes.[92] The advertisements on the sides and rear of the coach either rotated on canvas cloth (a *banda sin fin*) or were projected from inside onto translucent sidewalls by a slide machine.

Figure 3. Electric Man posing before an evening perambulation downtown. The brand advertised on his back, Cigarettes Calvé, commemorates the visit of French opera diva and transatlantic celebrity Emma Calvé to the El Buen Tono factory several months before. Source: *El Mundo Ilustrado*, April 19, 1908, 24.

One even provided a cinema show advertising multiple businesses, with the screen mounted on the rear and powered by an electric motor.[93] These schemes were not without their flaws. The cinema coach required a large tank of water in case the heat from the lens set fire to the highly flammable acetate film, a common occurrence.[94] A longstanding tradition of El Buen Tono and its competitors was the elaborate decoration of their horse-drawn delivery carriages in processions commemorating civic holidays and other special occasions, such as the fiestas presidenciales in 1900. On that occasion La Cigarrera Mexicana paraded all of its "advertising carriages" and its employees while El Buen Tono sent out two carriages covered in bougainvillea preceded and followed by 350 of its workers. By 1897 El Buen Tono deployed five carriages for urban deliveries and two more traveling exclusively to the rail stations with the aim of supplying retail agencies across the republic.[95]

Figure 4. An El Buen Tono delivery truck decorated for the
Fiesta Floral parade. Source: *El Mundo Ilustrado,* May 3, 1908, 21.

By late 1907 Pugibet again distinguished himself from the competition when he imported from Paris the first of a fleet of internal combustion engine delivery trucks to supplement, and then replace, the
company's horse-drawn delivery carriages (figure 4).[96] Shortly thereafter
he added a far more elegant French-made Daracq sedan to his publicity
fleet. Night and day, the company ran the car strung with colored lights
through the city streets and in parades, distributing thousands of packets
of "its magnificent brands" to the crowds.[97] With an eye to not only entertaining but also educating the crowd this was a master stroke. Up to that
point, vehicles powered by the internal combustion engine had remained
the playthings of the elite. Finance Minister José Yves Limantour had
imported the first vehicle in 1896, and by 1903 over 150 roamed the urban
streets of Mexico, mostly in the capital, where both fortunes and paved
streets were most abundant.[98] Much like bicycles and electric trains first
had, the new technology engendered both the curiosity and animosity
of the masses.[99] Now Pugibet helped to popularize them by putting them
to work advertising and distributing products. He also offered three as
additional grand prizes in his nationwide lotteries in which tens of thousands of Mexicans throughout the republic participated.[100] By removing

the technology from a charged social context of haves versus have-nots and focusing on its marvel, utility, and accessibility (via the lottery), Pugibet provided more than spectacle; with his savvy, street-level marketing of the automobile he injected into the urban popular discourse a favorable view of national progress in its latest manifestation.

Free national lotteries sponsored by El Buen Tono and La Tabacalera captivated Mexicans from the first announcement in late 1905 until the beginning of the Revolution. Lotteries were not new to consumers, having raised funds for charitable institutions since the colonial period. After independence they served as means by which state and national governments raised capital for infrastructure projects such as railroads.[101] By the early 1890s tobacco companies offered giveaways of small prizes, including popular games like *lotería de figuras*, a board game similar to bingo.[102] What was new to residents in 1905 were free lotteries offering extravagant prizes and promoted on a scale heretofore unseen. La Tabacalera initiated this new marketing approach by announcing its gratitude to its customers and its wish to thank them with a lottery drawing on January 1, 1906. Shortly thereafter, El Buen Tono thanked its customers for helping monthly sales reach a new high of 400,000 pesos and reciprocated with four lottery drawings, on April 2, June 2, September 15, and December 23.[103] Thus began a lottery mania that captivated the capital and spawned a host of imitators—even the electric tram company held its own free lottery by using the numbers on its ticket stubs.[104] El Buen Tono yet again sought to ingratiate itself with Díaz and identified consumption of its products with Mexican nationalism: its September draw coincided with the national holiday celebrating Porfirio Díaz's birthday; the April draw commemorated the president's victory over Emperor Maximilian's forces in the final battle of Puebla in 1867.[105]

Consumers did not have to buy lottery tickets but rather acquired them by purchasing cigarette packets. Each company distributed tickets differently: El Buen Tono required one hundred empty cigarette packets returned to the company's factory or kiosk in the Alameda in order to receive a single lottery ticket; La Tabacalera offered one ticket inside each packet. La Tabacalera argued for the democratic nature of its rules; El Buen Tono did so for the higher chance of winning prizes with a more stringent policy. In both cases, public participation was intense. In the first lottery (April 2, 1906), consumers of El Buen Tono cigarettes exchanged as many as 3.6 million empty packets for thirty-six thousand tickets.

Exactly one year later the number of lottery tickets distributed rose to seventy thousand, indicating consumers exchanged as many as 7 million packets over the course of four months.[106] La Tabacalera did not release ticket information as readily but claimed that over fourteen thousand customers received prizes totaling 24,000 pesos in one of its earlier draws.[107]

Both El Buen Tono and La Tabacalera Mexicana embarked on a media blitz in the streets and crowded the daily papers with full-page advertisements, regular updates, and cartoons advertising the draws. They offered impressive sums of cash for each draw, ranging from 10,000 to over 30,000 pesos, depending on the date.[108] La Tabacalera also included pictures of various animals on each ticket and offered instant free cigarette packets if the animal matched the one announced in the daily papers, yet another example of the close relationship between the commercial press and business in promoting a new culture of consumption.[109] On a grander scale, El Buen Tono offered three French sedans in 1907 that it displayed in the show windows of the Trutz carriage store (not coincidentally, located across the street from El Buen Tono's main retail kiosk). Not to be outdone, La Tabacalera offered a two-story house on Zarco Street. The company cleverly combined the concerns of the middle class (and those aspiring to the middle class) over high real estate prices and the economic contraction of 1907, reasoning that the middle class suffered most from financial recessions because downturns endangered their chances to buy a home of their own. Thus they offered a new house "full of amenities and good taste" and recommended the lottery to "persons who desire a tranquil future as they put behind them the monthly nightmare of rental payments."[110]

The spectacle and suspense built to a crescendo for the drawing of the winning numbers and the delivery of the major prizes to the lucky recipients. Both companies staged their heavily publicized draws at their factories. To ensure that the event seemed legitimate, they combined the aura of scientific impartiality conveyed by a newly patented lottery machinery with the presence of government representatives and large crowds as witnesses. Photos of the El Buen Tono factory draws attest to the social range of the crowds, as the number of attendees wearing traditional sombreros approximated those sporting western-style hats.[111] Because of the El Buen Tono procedure for dispensing tickets, company officials had the name and address of every ticketholder and could announce winners immediately after the draw. Sometimes the lucky ones were in the crowd, other times they lived beyond the capital and the winnings were sent to them. For example, Miguel Ramos of San Blas, Tepic, and David Samuel Maceda of Puebla both won 5,000 pesos from El Buen Tono, and Antonio Vicente of Mérida received 1,000 pesos from La Tabacalera (figure 5).[112] These lotteries appear to have been legitimate. Companies reported lottery costs in annual reports and newspapers devoted considerable paid and unpaid copy to winners (including photographs and reproduced letters of thanks with signatures). In addition, El Buen Tono donated all unclaimed or undeliverable prize money to the public charity Benificencia Pública.[113]

LOTERIA DE "EL BUEN TONO," S. A.

Tenemos el gusto de presentar á Udes. al simpático joven David Samuel A. Maceda, hijo del Sr. Agustín A. Maceda, empleado de la Secretaría del Gobierno de Puebla, que ganó el premio mayor de $ 5,000.00 de la Lotería de "EL BUEN TONO," S. A., que se celebró el 30 de Junio pasado, y que, muy agradecido, está dispuesto á seguir coleccionando los Registros núm. 12 de las cajetillas vacías de nuestras mascas que le obsequian su papá y sus amigos.

"EL BUEN TONO," S. A.

Figure 5. Young Puebla resident and El Buen Tono lottery winner David Samuel A. Maceda. Source: *El Mundo Ilustrado*, July 15, 1906, 22.

Newspapers and cigarette companies promoted the rags-to-riches angle of the top prizewinners. With uncanny similarity to countless Greek dramas, El Buen Tono performed quarterly acts as deus ex machina as it randomly plucked members of the honest but downtrodden classes from a life of desperation and provided them with unexpected and previously unimaginable wealth. Their agent in these performances was Paul Pugibet, the nephew of Ernesto Pugibet. He would travel to the tenement homes of impoverished winners in the city to announce their good fortune and deliver the money. Publicizing these performances, the newspapers granted extensive coverage to children, women, and men of humble origins, who often provided testimonials of their hard life and the responsible ends to which they intended to put these windfalls. Félix Gómez, winner of 1,000 pesos in a 1906 La Tabacalera lottery, was an archetype of the fortunate male. He wrote that he had worked in various printing presses for thirty years, but with growing expenses and the hardships of life he had never been able to save a nest egg. He had lost hope, but thanks to his being an "assiduous consumer of the excellent 'Flor de Canela' cigarettes" he could now securely live the rest of his life "as a humble worker, in union with [his] family."[114] In addition to men like Gómez, a surprising number of women and children won the lotteries. In fact, approximately 12 percent of prizewinners were women and children.[115] This fact belied the Porfirian ideal that only men smoked. Newspaper and company accounts usually explained this away by portraying women and children as collectors of tickets and cigarette packets from older, male members of the family. Thus the stories attributed the success of young boys David Samuel Macedo in Puebla (5,000 pesos) and Alfonso Aceves of the capital (4,000 pesos) to the generosity of fathers and friends.[116]

Accounts treated women as thrifty "guardian angels" of the home, calling them "thoughtful and wise for taking care to ask their husbands for their lottery tickets."[117] In one instance an eighteen-month-old girl named Elena Montañez won 6,000 pesos when, in her name, her mother mailed one hundred packets smoked by her husband in return for a single lottery ticket. This was to be Elena's Christmas present because her father, in his job as a magazine vendor, "earned barely enough to nourish the family and his only pleasure was to smoke his daily packet of Canela Pura." Another winner, of 2,000 pesos, was the wife of a poor policeman. Just like Elena's mother she lived in a "small room in a tenement [*casa de vecindad*]" and carefully collected the empty packets of Chorritos left by her husband. She worried about the danger of her husband's job and his growing frustration, "caused by the sumptuous residences he protects with nothing to show for it." Then suddenly, one day, Paul Pugibet showed up and the lucky couple planned to return to Oaxaca and start a business where they grew up and their families still lived. Notably she— along with other major prizewinners—planned to spend their earnings in traditional, practical, and commendable ways befitting their socio-economic station.

These accounts appeared in publications read not only by the middle classes or members of the expatriate communities (*El Imparcial, Le Courrier du Mexique,* etc.) but also by members of the working class (usually skilled or semiskilled) who asserted a place for themselves within respectable society by adopting its manners, morals, and when possible, patterns of consumption. They serve as valuable texts by which to understand the ongoing intertwined processes of class and gender formation during the Porfiriato.[118] Representations of these working-class winners invariably emphasized an ethos of thrift, hard work, and self-improvement located within a strong family unit anchored by a wife and mother whose careful management of home economy acquired the winning ticket. These qualities made up the core moral or "cultural" criteria by which the Mexican middle classes, self-proclaimed as the *gente decente,* or respectable society, used to define themselves against the popular classes, whom they viewed as undisciplined and vice-ridden degenerates.[119] For middle-class readers, these stories of social mobility achieved by "worthy" members of the working class warmed their hearts and confirmed their vision of national social evolution. For working-class readers, they not only served to further internalize gente decente values but also raised hopes and dreams that a happy end to the modernization trail existed. For all readers, participation in patterns of modern consumption, in this case smoking machine-rolled cigarettes, opened the door to personal, familial, and by implication, national progress.

Combined with the mass-circulation press, the lotteries were an integral component in constructing a common set of consumer-oriented experiences for residents of Mexico City and those of the entire republic. Through company advertising of ticket sales, Mexicans knew that thousands of fellow citizens joined them in this endeavor. Moreover, the publication of lists of winners with their addresses meant that individuals could insert themselves into an urban narrative and experience a sense of belonging and order amid the chaos of the city as they read the names of friends, relatives, neighbors, drinking buddies, and perhaps even themselves. For many, the calendar of the late Porfiriato included anticipation not only for the change in seasons or the latest festival but also for the advent of the next tobacco lottery and the chance to *sacar el gordo* (hit the jackpot). In this developing urban and national narrative of notable events and daily rhythms the lotteries and the considerable publicity surrounding them positioned the cigarette companies as translators between the rich and poor, between modern and traditional. Through these spectacles they disseminated the message that the prosperity, technology, and modernization of the Porfiriato benefited all Mexicans.[120]

El Buen Tono also incorporated into its marketing perhaps the most powerful new consumer technology of the era: cinematography. Although cinematography debuted in Mexico only one year after the Lumière brothers' invention premiered in Paris in 1895, the rise of the cinema as a form of mass entertainment in Mexico did not proceed smoothly. Initially it was hailed as a marvel of science and progress, yet according to film historian Aurelio de los Reyes, by 1899 its popularity nose-dived among respectable society. Cinema entrepreneurs and filmmakers had to rely on consumer support in the provinces after encountering growing criticism of the moral quality of the films and the makeshift viewing tents for lower-class audiences. Yet in part due to the efforts of El Buen Tono and other commercial interests the cinema rose to new heights of popularity, and by 1904 residents of the capital converged en masse to view the free, open-air shows sponsored by El Buen Tono.[121]

Pugibet hired French filmmaker and spectacle impresario Enrique (Henri) Moulinié, a true pioneer of early Mexican cinema, to coordinate a two-pronged promotional campaign.[122] First, in all the major state capitals Moulinié organized free screenings or charged an admittance of empty packets of El Buen Tono cigarettes. Within a year these shows included the first film advertisements in Mexico, consisting of a still slide positioned between short films.[123] Second, Moulinié and Pugibet opened the first public and free cinema in Mexico City, differentiating the company from the nighttime spectacles of advertisements projected onto city walls and rooftop screens that had become common over the previous decade.[124]

Hundreds of spectators—men and women from a wide range of social classes—packed the streets to watch these performances of Mexican, French, and sometimes U.S. film productions.[125] The diverse crowd experienced together in these "frames of living photography . . . comic and grotesque scenes, theatrical and dramatic episodes, romantic stores of love, adventures of miraculous journeys, and subtle and innocent children's stories."[126] They did so in several locations throughout the city, including El Buen Tono's famous retail kiosk located on the fashionable Puente de San Francisco next to Alameda Park and on the prepared site of the new National Theater. Kiosks, serving as retailing outlets and regulated advertising space, had first appeared in Paris in 1857 and at least by 1875 Mexican entrepreneurs had successfully petitioned the ayuntamiento to establish them in the capital by appealing to their vogue in Europe and the United States.[127] Yet in El Buen Tono's case, the term *kiosk* seems inadequate for their structure. Set in the middle of a central city block with the company's name carved ornately into the arched stone façade, rising three stories high, and spanning eight meters in width, the kiosk sold cigarettes, provided a working display of the factory's famous high-speed machinery, and included a cinema screen on the third floor. On either side of the kiosk a two-story-high wall wrapped around the block. The top half of the wall sported advertisements for the Palacio de Hierro department store, the bottom half displayed three-meter-high advertisements for each of El Buen Tono's brands, and on each corner gigantic posters publicized the Moctezuma Brewery.[128] Within two years, in 1906, the company had replaced the original screen with an octagonal tower that held not only a newer screen but also a public clock and advertising space for all of its brands.[129] In its heyday the kiosk exhibited films nearly every night, the spectacle amplified by the profligate use of expensive and relatively new electrical lighting before and after the show. Here onlookers watched snippets of Mexico City and beyond come to life, frequently seeing in local productions places they had visited, events they had seen, people they knew, or sometimes even themselves. The chaos of urban life received a narrative through the technological spectacle of cigarette-sponsored cinematography.

Pugibet fought hard to receive permission to show these films. Like all entrepreneurs wishing to entertain the public, he had to gain the approval and licensing of the city council. The kiosk was the first of the public screens, and Pugibet personally wrote the application in June 1903. He asked not just for a license to run the free shows but also for permission to turn off a streetlight located in the median of the street directly in front of the screen. This last request required that the petition pass through the hands of the Comisión de Alumbrado (Lighting Commission). The commission's chair, Nicolas Mariscal, would then give its recommendation to the council. Pugibet persuasively argued that his activities would benefit the public by "providing this colorful distraction free of charge to passersby" and would cause negligible disorder. He offered to pay for an automatic switch that would turn off the light only during the film presentation in the early hours of the evening, which happened to be the prime time for the residents of the capital to stroll along the fashionable boulevard. He noted that other light from the "great number of electric bulbs" decorating the kiosk, the two streetlamps on either corner of the block, and stores located across the street would be sufficient to "dispel the fear of a lack of light." He concluded with an appeal, or perhaps a taunt, to the council to keep up with the modern world by adding that "it's unnecessary to invoke examples of [free street cinema presentations] in other great capitals [of the world]." Mariscal and the Lighting Commission recommended against the proposal for fear of the danger of combining diminished lighting with heavy pedestrian, coach, and electric tram traffic. Moreover, Mariscal added that the disruption of service would break the contract with the electric company, which required continuous service through those hours. Despite the opposition of the Lighting Commission, the city council approved the petition.[130] Surely Pugibet's political connections helped his application, but more importantly, the council seemed to have recognized that the diversionary benefits of this public spectacle far outweighed the considerable fears of disorder caused by urban crowds.[131]

Moulinié and El Buen Tono also produced a number of films, tapping into the growing celebrity culture that was developing in France and elsewhere.[132] In his first memorable cinematic coup, Moulinié hired cameraman Salvador Toscano and popular actor Gavilanes (of Teatro Principal fame) and produced *Gavilanes aplastado por una aplanadora* (Gavilanes flattened by a steamroller). This trick film, unusual among Mexican productions, appeared to come straight from the Paris "special-effects" studios of Georges Méliès. Gavilanes begins the film walking along the central streets of the city but is run over by a steamroller and reduced to a two-dimensional figure. A passerby saves him by peeling his face off the ground and sticking an El Buen Tono Canela (a recently launched and heavily advertised brand) into his mouth. Gavilanes inhales and regains his three-dimensional shape before dancing happily to the laughter of the audience as the film ends. Toscano achieved the effect by stopping the filming and replacing Gavilanes with a cut-out replica. An assistant (presumably a small one) knelt behind the turned-up head and smoked the cigarette offered by the pedestrian. El Buen Tono publicized the film in a variety of ways, including in its famous twelve-panel cartoon strips, which condensed the narrative.[133] El Buen Tono advertising regularly featured endorsements of famous celebrities, including the bullfighter Bombita and a constant parade of singers and actresses in vogue on the capital city's stages. The company also had a close relationship with the most famous clown of the Porfiriato, Ricardo Bell, who not only appeared in advertising but also smoked El Buen Tono cigarettes during his performance (and drank Moctezuma Brewery beer).[134]

The location of the El Buen Tono screens reveals the wide advertising net cast by the company and demonstrates that, contrary to much scholarship on the period, urban working and popular classes were participants in the Porfirian culture of consumption.[135] In addition to its famous kiosk in the heart of the city's retail and leisure zone, the company erected permanent screens atop the public markets of Carmen and Loreto. Both these locations were in clearly lower-class, peripheral areas of the city: Loreto five blocks east of the National Palace, Carmen about six blocks north and slightly east. Poverty may have limited but did not preclude participation in a consumer society. Far from marginal consumers disinterested in the offerings of modernization, residents of these barrios attended these company-sponsored free cinemas and bought machine-rolled cigarettes advertised in these productions and in many other mediums encountered in their daily lives. El Buen Tono's shows were merely one facet of the citywide dissemination of images and texts to urban crowds, linking consumerism, spectacle, and notions of modernity. The difference between the screens in the working-class neighborhoods of Carmen and Loreto and the one at the kiosk in the Alameda is that the former two reached an audience in areas of the city often neglected by state officials and services. Understanding the historical significance of consumption requires moving past the dated definition of consumption as merely the act of purchase.

The cigarette companies added to this abundance of free shows by sponsoring private performances for which patrons received admission in exchange for empty cigarette packets. In the capital all three big tobacco companies booked local theaters and entertainment venues for cinema, light opera (*zarzuelas*), comedies, dramas, circuses, and variety shows. To commemorate Independence Day in 1905, La Tabacalera Mexicana rented out the Circo Orrin for a variety show. The company packed the house with patrons, who admired the lights and decorations specially purchased to adorn the exterior, the vestibule, and the main hall. Nearly two thousand people watched films by Pathé on the Russo-Japanese war, applauded the sleight-of-hand skills of the "Brujo de los Salones," and delighted in the singing debut of the lovely Jovita. Throughout the film, female employees of the company handed out free packages of cigarettes to the crowd. This kind of publicity extended beyond Mexico City to the major cities of the republic. After El Buen Tono offered free shows in Veracruz La Tabacalera countered with its own offerings at Christmas that starred the popular dancing midget Emilio Romano (aka Lagardere), who led the crowd in "vivas" to the generous company and danced his two-foot-four-inch frame "until he could dance no more." La Tabacalera probably holds the record for the most impressive mass rental of these theaters. To commemorate Independence Day in 1906 the company rented out the Principal, Renacimiento, Circo Orrin, Hidalgo, Lelo de Larrea, Guillermo Prieto, Popular, and Apolo theaters to perform a wide variety of shows. Considering that the first four venues alone could hold between them at least seven thousand people, quite a number of capitalinos celebrated the *dieciseis* as the guests of the La Tabacalera Mexicana cigarette company.[136]

Undergirding these larger spectacles was the daily saturation of cigarette advertising and marketing efforts in the press, on the streets, and in more intimate venues of sociability such as theaters, drinking establishments, and corner stores. As photos, literature, and archival records attest, the three tobacco companies advertised everywhere: in newspapers to reach a literate audience and in the streets not only with text but also with bright graphics, images, and logos to attract the illiterate. Capitalinos could not avoid the cigarette vendors nor the colorful tobacco-advertising posters like those on the El Buen Tono kiosk, which covered walls in many parts of the city. Men passed out handbills advertising brands in the train stations and ads were posted inside streetcars, not unlike those in mass-transit vehicles today.[137] Smokers could trade accumulated packets to receive a 25 percent discount at one of a number of famous downtown retailers, including the Palacio de Hierro department store or the Esmeralda jewelry emporium.[138] Urban residents may have encountered one of the many other new advertising forms for cigarettes, including rotating billboards, leaflet dispensers, and even a Pavlovian-inspired cigarette sample dispenser. In this last item an electrically backlit mini-billboard housed a motor to rotate a cloth band of advertisements (the approved patent application used El Buen Tono's Chorritos brand) while buttons on the side allowed passersby to press them for free samples of whatever product was featured at that moment.[139] Waiting for a theater performance to begin left spectators exposed to advertisements dangling before, printed on, or projected onto the stage curtain.[140] If one desired a pre- or postshow drink and did not have the time to drop by a local cigarette *expendio* on the way to a pulquería, *figone*, or cantina, he could pick up a pack from the cigarette vendor parked by the door.[141] Inside drinking establishments as well as grocery stores (*tiendas de abarrotes*) shopkeepers plastered walls with thick paperboard ads for bottled beer and cigarettes that typically measured eleven by fourteen inches (figure 6).[142] Even vendors at public markets and popular festivals set up covered stalls to sell machine-rolled cigarettes, their posters conspicuous amid rows of unadorned tables that sold fruit, sweets, and other unbranded items to a lower-end clientele.[143]

While some Mexicans were undoubtedly repulsed on aesthetic or moral grounds by the ever-present and at times intrusive advertising and marketing efforts, many more developed a more complicated and negotiated relationship dependent on individual aspirations and ways of understanding the rapidly changing world in which they lived. Machine-rolled cigarette consumers even incorporated advertising and marketing tools into their home life and daily rituals in a variety of ways. At Christmas customers could visit the El Buen Tono kiosk or factory and pick up beautifully lithographed calendars for home display, pocket agendas and almanacs whose use as reference and organizational tools further integrated consumerism and urban life, and even pencil cases shaped like cigarette packets.[144] Throughout the year smokers collected, traded, and even framed cards included in cigarette packets featuring photos of celebrities, personages, beautiful women, and sometimes women shedding articles of clothing.[145]

All of these spectacles by tobacco companies, both big and small, sought to win over the hearts and minds of consumers and develop brand loyalty. In print and street advertising tobacco marketers sought to create and entertain a unified entity, what scholars would call "the crowd" and what contemporaries referred to as "the public." In doing so, in promoting mass consumption of their mass-produced products not only in the cities but throughout the republic, tobacco advertisers also promoted

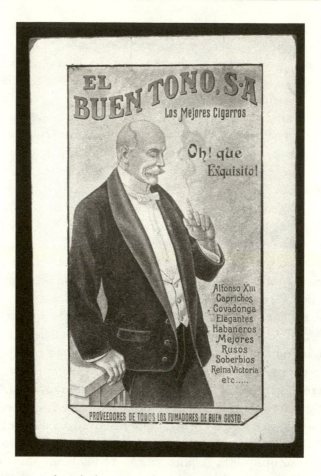

Figure 6. Paperboard advertising placard for El Buen Tono, makers of
"the best cigarettes" and "provisioners for all smokers of good taste."
Such ads were typically found in bars, restaurants, and other commercial
establishments. The brands listed along the right side were among the
premium offerings of El Buen Tono. Source: Author's collection.

the formation of an urban and even national identity crucial to Mexican modernization based on a common consumer good (machine-rolled
cigarettes), a common brand and increasingly common popular culture
reference (El Buen Tono, for example), common experiences (nationwide
spectacles such as the lotteries, the dirigible, the cinema), and a new, universal, and primary self-identification—that of consumer.[146]

Purchasing as Politics: The Unión Mercantil Affair

The final episode of urban spectacle generated by the tobacco companies is the 1906 Unión Mercantil boycott of El Buen Tono products. The boycott reveals the extent to which advertising and marketing promoted not only individual fulfillment but also a particularly acute sense of personal and collective empowerment through participation in the market. In this manufactured crisis-spectacle, Porfirian political and consumer culture merged as both sides of the boycott urged consumers to envision their individual and collective purchasing decisions as a form of voting. The narrative of the boycott pushed citizens to view themselves as citizen-consumers by equating market action with political and civic action, a fitting metaphor for the Porfirian brand of liberalism in which political rights, including effective suffrage and fair elections, had been sacrificed for thirty years in the name of securing social order and material progress.

A history of El Buen Tono and La Tabacalera Mexicana appealing to Mexican consumers in the court of public opinion set the stage for the Unión Mercantil affair. In the Bonsack controversy of 1900 El Buen Tono was the plaintiff, claiming patent infringement of their Decouflé rolling machines and their glue-free technology by the Bonsack rolling machines employed by La Tabacalera and several small companies. The dispute lasted five years and involved three major court decisions before the Supreme Court found in favor of the plaintiff. During this time both sides received considerable coverage in the press and also paid to publish page-long articles in the major papers in an effort to win over public opinion.[147] Shortly after the decision El Buen Tono began savaging La Tabacalera in the press for trademark infringement. Not even bothering with the judicial system, El Buen Tono took its case before the court of public opinion. It argued that La Tabacalera stole and slightly modified El Buen Tono names for its own products. El Buen Tono certainly had a legitimate claim, citing such examples as Canela Pura turned to Flor de Canela, La Yucateca transformed to Yucatecos, and Chorritos to Chorrito-Sirenas.[148] La Tabacalera retaliated with ads depicting working-class Mexicans that disputed the charges. It also published articles asking consumers to view its ads in tramcars and other public places that visually compared each pair of brands and demonstrated the packaging dissimilarities between the two.[149] To gain further public support and sympathy throughout these private-turned-public controversies each side accused the other of mistreating their mostly female workers and crowed about their own labor practices. They frequently resorted to the popular technique of personal testimonials from their own employees to make their case.[150]

The Unión Mercantil affair began in the midst of this highly publicized spat. The Unión began as a commercial association made up mostly of *abarroteros*, or owners of small food, tobacco, and beverage retail establishments; in essence, they were corner store owners. Mostly Spanish, the association elected Antero Muñúzuri as its first president in 1894 with the stated aim of reducing adulteration of its wares and eliminating the circulation of false money in its stores (a national problem).[151] In February 1906 the association decided to raise its commission considerably, to 25 percent on each pack of cigarettes sold. Every tobacco company accepted except for El Buen Tono. As a result, on February 15 the Unión boycotted El Buen Tono as a way of bringing the company to its knees.[152] El Buen Tono fought back.

The company initiated a two-pronged attack consisting of the creation of an alternate retailing network and a media blitz portraying itself as a defender of the consumer on whom the company relied for its existence. El Buen Tono launched an army of sandwich-board men and basket-carrying cigarette girls (*cantineras*) to sell their products. Publishing photos of these two groups in the press, the company described its plan and expressed the logic in an advertorial with two full pages of text and photos, titled "The mobile army of 'El Buen Tono,' S.A." It noted, "This important cigarette factory that enjoys so much public favor is constantly devising new ways to make it easier for consumers to purchase its accredited brands so well known throughout the Republic." One of these new ideas was the service of male vendors, on whose sandwich boards was written, "YES, I SELL EL BUEN TONO CIGARETTES BECAUSE THEY ARE PREFERRED BY THE PUBLIC" (figure 7). Assisting this mobile army was a group of cantineras to improve the success of their "bellicose operations." The girls, who were "beautiful and truly elegant uniformed youths wearing hats of the best taste" carried their wares for sale in the Alameda, San Francisco and Plateros Streets, the Zócalo, and Chapultepec Park; "that is to say, the most central and aristocratic sites where the most enthusiastic consumers of El Buen Tono cigarettes pass their time." The article claimed that this new effort provided "proof that El Buen Tono would not spare any expense to benefit and comfort the consumer." After listing all the brands available for purchase, the

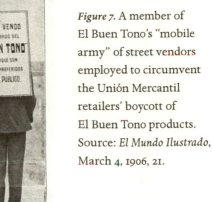

Figure 7. A member of El Buen Tono's "mobile army" of street vendors employed to circumvent the Unión Mercantil retailers' boycott of El Buen Tono products. Source: *El Mundo Ilustrado,* March 4, 1906, 21.

argument concluded with a laundry list of why the company earned the support of the public, including its awards from expositions, the construction of its magnificent factory, with the "most modern machines, like those which absorb the dust from the tobacco leaving it completely clean and hygienic," and its effort of "procuring all the means possible to please the consumer" for which it merited "the applause of all smokers of good taste."[153]

El Buen Tono also practiced a strategy of dividing the opposition. It listed its supporters, including forty-three cigarette retailers and forty-five members of the Unión who did not participate in the boycott.[154] To further undermine its opposition's morale, El Buen Tono published monthly lists of its sales, painting a picture of increasing revenues and a failing boycott effort.[155]

Within a month La Tabacalera entered the fray. It probably did so for two reasons: first, the La Tabacalera ownership was Spanish; and

second, one of its founding members was Antero Muñúzuri, the first
president of the Unión and owner of the now-defunct El Negrito cigarette factory. It declared the army of "Sandwiches" a failure, publishing
cartoons in which they were run out of town.[156] El Buen Tono shot back
with rising sales figures. La Tabacalera created rhyming ads accompanied by sketches playing on social attitudes toward women on the street
to question the morality of the cantineras. In one advertisement, titled
"One Who Is Sorry," a gentleman in top hat and tails takes a demoralized
cantinera by the arm. He points at a nearby poster advertising the phe-
nomenal 20,000-peso La Tabacalera lottery prize and advises her that it
is "best not to expose yourself to the mirth of the people! You will see, if
you are true, that there is no small difference between a lady of the house
and a street salesgirl."[157] El Buen Tono countered with a letter signed by
twenty-five of the girls, angered at being compared with "women without honor," in other words, prostitutes. They finished by writing that they
were responding in their own way, "as many others are," to "the ignoble
campaign that some businesses are waging against El Buen Tono."[158]

As these examples have suggested, El Buen Tono used the real or
imagined voices of individuals to convey a sense of consumer participation and empowerment. It is this construction of a public discourse, a
consumer discourse, that is most striking in this debate. El Buen Tono
frequently cited "our numerous consumers" for supporting them, even
creating the powerful image of the company "surrounded and favored
by its consumers so that they must necessarily win however many battles are forced upon it."[159] Both sides constantly appealed to consumers
to vote with their pesos. One maverick shopkeeper who supported El
Buen Tono wrote a letter to both *El Imparcial* and *Le Courrier du Mexique*
in which he reiterated the power of consumers five times. He concluded
with the advice that when a shopkeeper tells a customer that he does not
sell El Buen Tono brands, the buyer should simply inform the owner that
he will choose to go next door and buy not only his cigarettes but all his
other groceries.[160]

The counterattack succeeded. El Buen Tono's sales increased and the
Unión dropped the boycott after several months. El Buen Tono's brilliant strategy of winning over consumers and excoriating its opponents
in its cartoons, ads, and press columns combined with its deep pockets to carry the day. Pugibet's side convincingly portrayed their Goliath
as David. The instructive aspect of this battle lies not in who won but

rather in the crash course in consumer choice sponsored by the company. El Buen Tono's rhetoric and actions empowered Mexican citizen-consumers, giving them the opportunity to feel in control of their life through purchases, to feel modern.

The irony of this discourse is that just as its rhetoric of consumer democracy and choice reached its peak the industry was monopolizing and ossifying just like the Porfirian political system. In fact, El Buen Tono's actions serve as an apt allegory for the Porfiriato. Within eight months of the end of the boycott El Buen Tono had purchased La Cigarrera and moved it next door.[161] Two years later the company bought out La Tabacalera.[162] Much as Porfirio Díaz maintained the illusion of democracy and political options, the cigarette conglomerates kept up the appearance of free markets and competition by maintaining separate companies and keeping spectacles and advertising at a high level. All the while the El Buen Tono conglomerate denied the reality of monopoly. Again Porfirian politics and business met over the importance of illusion and appearances for the maintenance of the status quo.[163] Yet at the same time, what did the message of consumer/political agency of the boycott and of the culture of consumption more generally mean to consumers? Did citizens even connect the boycott and consequences of market participation with political action? Did voting in the market serve as a safety valve for the lack of a meaningful participatory political system? Or did individuals recognize the boycott as a metaphor or even a parody of the lack of political influence of the social groups that, ironically, were most expanded by the material progress of the era and made up the majority of the cigarette market—the urban middle and working classes? Unfortunately, the limited research so far on consumption in Porfirian society makes a definitive answer beyond the scope of this study. The question, however, serves as a reminder that consumption is not just an economic act nor defined merely by the act of purchasing. Rather, consumption has social, cultural, and political consequences, the investigation of which holds open the potential for fresh perspectives and better understanding of historical processes and the questions they raise.

The machine-rolled cigarette industry that developed in the latter half of the Porfiriato became a potent cultural and political as well as economic force at the vanguard of the modernization process in Mexico. The interaction between its marketing strategies and consumer responses provides vivid insight into how Mexican modernity and development were stated and affirmed through the medium of consumer goods during this era. The three largest companies, El Buen Tono, La Tabacalera Mexicana, and La Cigarrera Mexicana, positioned themselves at the forefront of broad economic, social, and cultural changes in Mexican society and the economy. In their efforts to capture a mass market for their mass-produced products their advertising helped to shape an interrelated and distinctly Mexican consumer culture and urban mass culture that became increasingly national in scope in the last decade of the era.

A confluence of developments made cigarettes the most widely consumed branded commodity in Mexico by 1910. First, with its tradition as a widely consumed commodity (a popularity no doubt aided by its addictive qualities), tobacco was a foreseeable and logical choice for a new industry based on modern organizational principles.[164] What changed during the Porfiriato was the format in which Mexicans consumed it (through mechanization El Buen Tono and others made the cigarette dominant) and the meaning smokers attached to its consumption. Second, the potential market for manufactured goods such as cigarettes expanded as urbanization spurred and was spurred on by industrialization and heavy internal migration to the cities, leading to the concentration and incorporation of an ever-increasing number of Mexicans in the money economy. In addition, the development of an extensive rail and communication system facilitated the development of a national distribution system and advertising program. And third, new technologies in cigarette production and image production (chromolithography, etc.) combined with new consumer technologies (such as electricity and cinematography) to allow for the manufacture and marketing of tobacco products at a level unimaginable before the last decade of the nineteenth century.

New production technologies brought tangible and salutary benefits that supported the transformation of the cigarette into an icon of Mexican progress by marketers and consumers. No longer based on hand-rolling and gluing, cigarette manufacture became mechanized and hygienic (glueless and hands free), conducted in enormous factories requiring great amounts of investment capital and under the most modern methods of organization. Little wonder advertisers used images of the factories, machines, and other connections to production to sell their product.[165] Consumers could see, feel, and taste the difference that these changes made. Uniformly crisp and neatly crimped rolling paper visibly improved on hand-rolled and glued cigarettes of old. Even better, machine-rolled cigarettes were less expensive than their predecessors. Moreover, modern packaging exceeded older versions in both quality and aesthetics, as shiny aluminum foil combined with colorful lithographic images to add an element of sensory pleasure and sharply distinguish between brands. For many, discussion of national progress could be distilled into the dramatic material improvements made to the cigarette.

Publicity campaigns reinforced this popular association of the cigarette with progress. Linking the latest technologies and images of abundance to cigarettes helped to popularly disseminate the vision of linear progress and promise of earthly utopia so forcefully and ubiquitously promoted by Western societies in the decades prior to World War I. In Mexico this society-wide loose sense of progress, aptly termed the "Porfirian persuasion" by William Beezley, received concrete reinforcement not just by actions of the government but also by business, as demonstrated by El Buen Tono and others sponsoring free public displays of the dirigible, the airplane, the automobile, the cinema, and other spectacles of technology.[166]

These public spectacles sponsored by tobacco companies functioned in concert with other marketing forms to shape a new urban mass culture forming in Mexico. Cigarette marketing facilitated the formation of collective identities in its efforts to constitute and entertain a crowd, whether through the unifying experience of street spectacles, national lotteries, or print advertising. These collective experiences of consumption created yet another set of common values and images and a common vocabulary that fostered a sense of urban and increasingly national community forming during the Porfiriato. In this respect, the Mexican experience with modernity was a global one replicated in Paris, London, New York, Tokyo, and other rapidly changing urban areas around the globe. At the same time, cigarette marketers did not ignore class and other social distinctions, engaging in niche marketing as an essential component of a mass-marketing strategy. Moreover, advertising facilitated the powerful trend in modern society toward individuation. It spoke to the psychological needs of individual consumers, promising through consumption the fulfillment of personal hopes and desires and offering a means to negotiate and a find a sense of belonging in the rapidly changing world of urban Mexico. Viewed on these multiple levels, the mass-marketing campaigns (like the consumer market) of the Porfiriato were more complex than previously imagined. This approach suggests that the consequence of mass marketing both shaping an urban mass culture and facilitating individuation was not a contradiction but rather a necessity of modern marketing and a characteristic of modern consumer societies.

Machine-rolled cigarettes came to represent personalized progress through the confluence of the industry's mechanization, savvy mass-marketing campaigns, the historical place of national tobacco consumption, and the appeal of the cigarette in the contemporary social and cultural context. The possession and consumption of machine-rolled cigarettes, as objects of both inconspicuous and conspicuous consumption and indicators of urban taste and modern living, indicated as much to the consumer as to others a forward-leaning individual demonstrating and contributing to national pride and progress. In other words, the machine-rolled cigarette exemplifies how commodities served as important repositories of meaning. In the urban mass culture developing during the Porfiriato, individuals, groups, manufacturers, retailers, advertisers, and many other actors and interests sought to construct and define identities and meaning through goods and the language of goods (especially advertising). Chaotic, colorful, and entertaining, the marketing spectacles surrounding the cigarette illuminate the street-level negotiation of what it meant to be modern and Mexican in the Porfirian capital and beyond.

The marketing campaigns of El Buen Tono and its major competitors were the most elaborate, original, and coherent of the Porfiriato. They were, however, only the most salient expression of a highly diverse and decentralized advertising and commercial culture established long before El Buen Tono and Pugibet became a major presence.

Chapter 2

Selling in the City

The Growth of Popular Advertising

LATE IN AUGUST 1874 MEXICAN ENTREPRENEUR ILDEFONSO ESTRADA Y Zenea petitioned the ayuntamiento of Mexico City to establish permanent advertising kiosks in the Zócalo and other principal plazas in the capital city in preparation for the Independence Day celebrations of September 16. He began his application by noting "the custom in the principal capitals of Europe and many in America to establish kiosks in the major plazas and major thoroughfares on which to affix advertising" and how, among its other benefits, such advertising space reduced one of the great eyesores of the modern city: advertising posters and handbills attached to building walls, often without the permission of property owners. Estrada lamented how in Mexico City these advertisements piled up on the walls, one on top of the other. Considering "the enlightenment and importance that this beautiful capital claims and to which it aspires," his column-shaped kiosks made of glass would "contribute to the tastefulness" of the city and demonstrate to its many foreign visitors "the enlightenment and progress that our patria is achieving." On September 4 the combined Comisiones de Policía y Obras Públicas supported the application before the council. It confirmed that such kiosks existed in the major cities of Europe and the United States and would beautify the capital's streets as well as support commerce and industry.

The council voted unanimously to approve the application.[1] As in Paris and other cosmopolitan capitals, advertising kiosks would become a feature in Mexico City throughout the Porfiriato.[2] The very presence of advertising mediums signified modernity and material progress as much as the commodities and lifestyles sold on their surfaces.

This episode reveals how city leaders, entrepreneurs, and commercial interests grappled with public advertising and an urban landscape increasingly characterized by publicity images, iconography, and spectacles. It also suggests that the history of advertising offers another means by which to track the transformation of Mexico City into a secular and commercial city, an effort begun by the Liberals in the 1850s. Existing scholarship has produced excellent studies of Porfirian commercial art and artists and drawn attention to the significance of consumption, yet its exclusive focus on the commercial press and only a handful of publications (skewed toward an affluent readership) has obscured our understanding in two ways.[3] First, in overlooking the vibrant world of public advertising represented by entrepreneurs such as Estrada, the literature has conflated the timeline of the history of advertising with that of advertising in the commercial press. Although these studies have understandably emphasized the time period after the mid-1890s (or even the early twentieth century), when rapid improvements in image production and reproduction technologies transformed the commercial press and its publicity, their choice of periodization truncates a longer and broader history of advertising.[4] Second and more importantly, by favoring a narrow range of publications targeted at a more affluent audience, scholars have also repeated the inaccurate conclusion that members of the working class were either negligible or not members of the consumer class.[5]

By expanding the traditional source base on advertising and consumption this chapter seeks to correct these misconceptions. In part one, advertising patent applications to the Ministry of Development (Fomento) and petitions like Estrada's to the ayuntamiento reveal the ubiquity and salient position of public advertising in daily urban life and the language of progress used by its promoters. Part two analyzes the rise of the newspaper as a mass-marketing medium and then revisits the perception that the working class had a negligible presence in the Porfirian consumer market. By expanding the range of newspapers consulted to include the working-class penny press and analyzing it for the first time from the perspective of consumption, this section reiterates the larger argument of this study—not only that a working-class consumer culture existed in Mexico but that its constituents embraced consumerism and broad notions of personal and national progress, if not on the terms presented by their social superiors.

Pre-Porfirian Advertising

Advertising—defined at its most basic level as drawing attention to products, services, or events for the purpose of promoting a sale—long predates the Porfiriato, although no scholarly study exists on such early advertising. Three distinct major forms operated by Independence in 1821: newspaper advertising, street hawking, and shop signs. The latecomer to the trio and frankly the most limited in audience and likely effectiveness was newspaper advertising. Credit for Mexico's first newspaper advertisement belongs to the Bourbon-era *Gaceta de México*, which in 1784 announced its new service for those who might want "to sell slaves, horses or haciendas, lost or found jewelry and other things of this sort."[6] These tiny, black-and-white texts fit the bare minimum criteria of advertising: to make something known, publicly and generally. Over the next ninety years advertising in the press managed to migrate from the last page to the first and from text only to the addition of small images. In 1857 *El Eco Nacional* devoted half of its first page to advertising. These ads, which often included basic graphics, were for clients such as clothing stores, bookstores, tobacco manufacturers, patent medicine producers, and candle merchants.[7] Despite these quantitative changes in advertising content the fundamental nature of the newspaper had changed little. Moreover, advertising and general consumer issues remained distinct from—and subordinate to—the rest of the copy. Newspapers would slowly increase their advertising space in the following decades but only acquired their modern connotation as a mass marketing medium once they themselves became an object of mass consumption in the 1890s.

The second form of advertising, street hawking or performative advertising, most closely fit the modern criteria of advertising by not only announcing items or services for sale but also seeking to engage and persuade customers to buy. In a primarily oral culture, vendors hawking their wares drew on popular cultural forms and values such as proverbs, satire, allusion, and mnemonic devices (alliteration and rhyme) and adapted them to commercial ends.[8] The effectiveness of this strategy continues today in the best slogans and jingles produced by advertisers.[9] Colonial vendors often favored *décimas*, appropriating these ten-line stanzas used by the Church in its sermons and plays for the purpose of

moral exhortation for the purpose of humorous and pranksterish advertising.[10] Colonial street advertising was an extremely aural experience,
as music and noisemakers competed with the voices of vendors. Records
attest to efforts by officials to silence what they considered the most
egregious excesses of this vibrant soundscape. For example, during the
Early Republic officials frequently sought to ban the use of whistles and
drums, and President Antonio López de Santa Anna himself sought to
crack down on this urban cacophony (possibly due to political content
mixed with the sales pitch) when in 1834 he supported a ban on "youths
advertising by way of [songs and verse] the sale of anything" and threatened incarceration for transgressors.[11]

Shop signs were the third form of early advertising. Combining art
and commerce in a visual and textual medium, shop signs arguably fore-
shadowed modern advertising in their creativity and in the controversy
they could generate.[12] Studies of shop signs in Paris and Moscow identify
the eighteenth century as the beginning of the use of increasingly elaborate and controversial shop signs that attracted considerable condemnation or praise but always marked the rising tide of modern commerce.[13]
In Mexico City shop signs had existed since at least 1571, when the ayuntamiento passed an ordinance requiring taverns to post color-coded signs
on their door alerting customers to the provenance of the wine served
within: white if from Castile, black if from the Indies.[14] This was perhaps
the first example of government regulation of advertising but certainly
not the last. On March 21, 1833, shortly before banning musical advertising, the Mexico City Ayuntamiento cited the abundance of "ridiculous
figures" and the poor taste and spelling on shop signs throughout the
city as it passed a law forbidding the painting of animals or images of
any sort on the façades of businesses and requiring inspection of all signs
for decency and correct orthography.[15] All signs had to pass inspection
by the local alderman, and noncompliance resulted in a fine of twelve
reales. This law appears to have remained on the books throughout
much if not all of the Porfiriato, although at some point before 1871 the
council unloaded inspection and enforcement duties onto a sign inspector (*inspector de letreros*). The occasional lamentation in ayuntamiento
records of the widespread flaunting of and contempt for the law suggests inspection and enforcement remained sporadic and halfhearted.[16]
Most of the controversy throughout the nineteenth century came from
establishments catering to a popular-class clientele and reflected competing visions of urban space, a legacy continued through the Porfiriato,

most famously in the disgust of respectable onlookers at the ornate and piquant shop signs of pulquerías but also in the reports of sign inspectors scandalized by business names containing sexual innuendos, such as The Valley of the Señora.[17]

The origins of modern advertising in Mexico are found in the Liberal project to transform Mexican society and the economy, in particular the sustained effort to secularize and commercialize the capital city begun with the Ley Lerdo of 1856. One of the famous Reform Laws that became enshrined in the Constitution of 1857, the Ley Lerdo was the first major land redistribution policy to apply to corporate landholding and required the Church to sell much of its property, including its extensive urban holdings, to either its tenants or bidders in real estate auctions. This law transformed urban centers. Demolished churches, convents, hospitals, and monasteries made room for new boulevards, cafés, and retail shops (and eventually department stores). Over the following decades Mexican governments, whether the French-imposed Second Empire of Maximilian I, the Restored Republic of Benito Juárez, or the authoritarian Liberalism of Porfirio Díaz, cultivated a secular and commercial urban landscape patterned after Haussmann's Paris.[18]

Advertising expanded as major public works, transportation improvements, and commercial modernity transformed the capital. Under the Second Empire, Maximilian began construction of the great boulevard Paseo de la Emperatriz (today Paseo de la Reforma), while dependency on France and the sumptuary demands of Maximilian's court society accelerated developments in retailing, established regular transatlantic service between France and Mexico, and "entrenched French goods' cachet as the benchmark of modernity and good taste among the upper and middle classes."[19] These trends help us to understand why the first advertising agency in Mexico opened in 1865. The Agencia General de Avisos, owned by the Frenchman Eugene Maillefert and managed by Fermin Marchand, claimed representatives in Paris and demonstrates again the active channel of cultural and commercial innovations that flowed across the Atlantic, especially from France.[20] With the restoration of the republic in 1867, the victorious Liberals looked to foreign investors and models of development to expedite the redesign of the capital and their efforts to ensure that economic, social, and political liberalism would find purchase in Mexican soil. Completion of a railroad between the port city of Veracruz and the capital in 1872 spurred commerce in Mexico City and was the first important segment of what would become a national rail system over the course of the Porfiriato. In the history of advertising, perhaps the signal event of the era was the establishment of La Escuela de Artes y Oficios (School of Arts and Trades) as part of the Ley de Instrucción Pública of 1867. Until then, no formal training program had existed in the commercial and industrial arts. Students in the school received technical and creative training in lithography and subsequent graphic production technologies that would pave the way for the explosion of commercial poster and press art that would come to define the last two decades of the Porfirian visual landscape.[21] In addition, new public advertising forms already common in Paris, New York, and other cities where consumption and representations of consumption were becoming ingrained in modern urban culture began to appear around Mexico City's central plaza, the Zócalo. The trickle of concession applications by the likes of Estrada or Simón López—who in 1875 requested permission to post cigarette advertising in the four corners of the plaza—would open to a torrent with the Porfirian era's peace and prosperity and the remarkable pace of new technologies advancing production, transportation, and consumption.[22]

Brokering Urban Space:
Advertising Systems, Entrepreneurs, and Government Regulators

By the 1860s text-based advertising had broken free of the shop sign and begun to colonize the public and private space of the commercial city.[23] A new group of people in the capital began to earn a livelihood by selling advertising space whereby manufacturers, retailers, and other commercial enterprises could promote their products and establishments. These were the first advertising agents, small-time entrepreneurs who collectively inscribed an ever-widening number of urban surfaces such as walls, public transportation, theater curtains, and billboards with commercial messages and representations of consumption. Throughout the Porfiriato the principal activity of advertisers and advertising agencies like Ildefonso Estrada y Zenea, Simón López, and the Agencia de Avisos was the selling and manufacturing of space, both in newspapers and in the urban landscape. These space brokers were middlemen but they were also innovators as they introduced the Mexican public to new advertising systems, such as illuminated or mobile advertising designed to increase the amount of available space and capture the attention of spectators and consumers. Sometimes these agents invented these advertising systems, but as patent applications reveal, many inventors earned their living in other jobs. Both space brokers and inventors of advertising systems shared the language of progress and faith in advertising as agents of economic and national development. Those creative tasks we associate with advertising today, such as planning, designing, and producing ads, were typically performed by independent printing shops, imported from the United States and Europe (a task taken over by local talent during the last decade of the Porfiriato as Mexican commercial art became increasingly sophisticated), or in house in the case of larger companies such as El Buen Tono or the Palacio de Hierro department store. The modern iteration of the advertising agency began in the United States in the late nineteenth century with N. W. Ayer & Son but did not appear in Mexico until near or after the Revolution began in 1910.[24]

The advertising business in Porfirian Mexico was remarkably decentralized and nonprofessionalized and its practitioners and innovators numerous and notably diverse. One major business guide listed nine advertising companies in 1899 but did not include individual agents or the established firms of José D. Gayosso and David Camacho.[25] In addition to these space brokers, public advertising businesses specializing in publicity signs, customer gifts, and other advertising paraphernalia also developed.[26] For the next decade new firms continued to open, including John H. Greaves & Co., the Publicity Company, the Compañia de Anuncios Mexicanas, S.A., and the Empresa Explotadora del Anuncio de Movimiento sobre Vehiculos.[27] The three hundred advertising patent applications that make up part of this section's sources are particularly helpful in understanding the demographics of this population.[28] These were the successful applicants, having either received provisional (patent pending) or definitive patents.[29] Many applying for these ten-year patents were Mexican citizens and most lived in the capital, though a few resided in other cities.[30] A large percentage—perhaps even a majority—were foreign nationals, mostly of North American or European citizenship, although a smattering of Guatemalans and Venezuelans also registered. Those living in Mexico usually applied on their own, while the few who lived abroad used the services of an agent to shepherd their application through the process—frequently Julio Grandjean or Ignacio Sepúlveda or, in one case, a Mexican army general.[31] Applicants listed their occupations as advertising agents, commission agents, store owners, store clerks, industrialists, pharmacists, and even an employee for the War and Navy Secretary.[32] Companies began to apply for patents in their own name only well after the turn of the century and then infrequently.[33]

While this section focuses on space brokerage and advertising systems in the urban landscape, space brokering in newspaper advertising, which was widespread during the Porfiriato, is the usual subject of attention when considering nineteenth-century advertising.[34] Not that advertising agencies would have drawn a sharp distinction between the fields. Many agencies shared the Publicity Company's ecumenicism in its claims to expertise in "newspapers and magazines, railroad stations and street cars, bill and sign posting, distributing and mailing."[35] Space brokers either bought up space from newspapers and resold it or served as agents for the newspaper and received 15 percent of the revenue. An example of the latter was the exclusive relationship between the G. y B. Goetschel agency and *El Imparcial*, the most widely distributed newspaper in the nation, although the famous *El Imparcial* columnist José Juan Tablada writes in his memoirs that journalists themselves had to drum up clients and include favorable commentary in their regular articles.[36] A contract brokered in 1892 between the Hermann advertising agency and the Palacio de Hierro department store provides an example of the former. The agency typed on its form the promise to procure insertions in the following Mexico City papers: *El Tiempo, El Monitor Republicano, El Universal, La Nacional, Two Republics, El Correo Español,* and *El Voz de México.* In addition, an insertion in the newspapers would be included in each of the following cities: Chihuahua, Guadalajara, San Luis Potosi, Monterrey, Puebla, and Veracruz. Julio Tron—the director of the store—wrote in the size (twenty-four by thirty-six, presumably centimeters), the location (third and fourth page), and the day of publication (preferably Sunday). The agency did not create the ads. An establishment as large and advertising-conscious as the Palacio managed that task itself. The contract began in January 1893, lasted for a year, and for a fee of 4,200 pesos undertook 248 insertions in the capital and 310 in the interior. Tron also reserved the right of the Palacio de Hierro to change the text of the ads once per week in the capital and once a month in the other cities.[37] In addition to providing the details of what exactly Mexican newspaper space brokers did, this extensive contract demonstrates yet again how large Mexican firms such as the Palacio or El Buen Tono envisioned a national profile for their brand and market for their goods—and how advertising agencies like Hermann were themselves large enough to help them achieve it.

What united these advertisers (the term I will use for both space brokers and patent applicants unless otherwise specified) was their common belief in the efficacy of "the science of advertising" and their ability to modernize trade practices and promote national economic development. As Xochimilco resident Pedro F. Martínez stated, "Advertising is the powerful lever that elevates and moves the arts, agriculture, industry and commerce."[38] The object of patented marketing innovations was "to facilitate for industrialists of this country a new medium to advertise their goods," added fellow capitalinos Pedro Miliner and César Morán.[39]

Advertisers both promoted and were challenged by the transformation of nearly all public space into potential spaces of consumption and commerce over the course of the Porfiriato. Their main goal was to attract as many sets of eyes as possible to the visual marketing texts of their clients. The ideas of repetition and saturation marketing possessed considerable currency and led to a race to secure advertising space and plaster every conceivable and available public location (even electricity transformer boxes) with posters, handbills, and signs.[40] A careful look at Porfirian- and Revolution-era photographs reveals a city whose brick and stone structures are blanketed with paper and painted advertising (figure 8).[41] Property owners placed notices on walls demanding (more likely pleading) "Se Prohibe Anunciar"—advertising prohibited (figure 9).

Inventors of advertising systems sought solutions to cut through this advertising clutter, already noted by Estrada in 1874, while simultaneously colonizing new space for commercial purposes. Novelty best achieved this aim, in the form of advertising mediums that adopted new technologies to attract, amaze, and eventually win over the consumer. Inventors banked on newness and the consumer's receptivity toward progress and spectacle as the modern way of advertising. The applicant for "Improvements in Advertising Apparatuses" summed up this approach: "Considering the multitude of advertisements, notice boards for posters and handbills, signs in windows that change and disappear automatically, apparatuses constantly or intermittently illuminated, all used now in or above display windows, on the walls of stores, in vacant lots, in effect—to be brief—in whatever location where they are in a position to be observed by the public, the effectiveness of such publicity methods depends on some original and noteworthy novelty in its construction. Something must be unique and fantastic in its design that attracts—even if for no more than a moment—the attention of passersby."[42] Juan Begovich of Popotla received a patent for such a device. His Anunciador Standard consisted of a clock resting atop a long, horizontal glass case. The case would be illuminated at night, backlighting a roll of

Figure 8. Advertising on the corner of Avenida Cinco de Mayo
and the Zócalo. Source: Archivo General de la Nación, Fondo
Instrucción Pública y Bellas Artes, Colección C. B. Waite, exp. 8.

advertisements that would pass across the front of the glass, pulled by an
electrical motor. As each ad entered the full field of vision it would stop
for a set period of time before the device moved on to the next. During
the pause a poster of the company in the ad would pop up next to the
clock and products from that company ("attractive and desirable gifts,
souvenirs, price lists, etc.") would dispense from one of the thirty-four
slots below the case, one slot for each advertiser. "The combination of
operations produces an effect similar to the public cinema exhibitions
sponsored by large businesses," Begovich explained, referring to the publicity campaigns of El Buen Tono and the Cuauhtémoc brewery, among
others. Expressing the popular psychology involved in the science of
advertising, Begovich concluded that "the passerby is halted by a screen
showing at that moment; he stops, interested in seeing what will happen
next, and involuntarily fixes in his memory the name of the business
producing the spectacle."[43]

Figure 9. In an attempt to ward off the appropriation of public space for unregulated advertising, both private and government property owners resorted to painting notices like this one on their walls, prohibiting advertisements. Source: *La Semana Ilustrada,* April 29, 1910, 5.

To circumvent restrictions on posting advertisements, advertising agents teamed up with advertising innovators to devise mobile advertising systems that used the streets as their venues. The most basic involved a large, hollow figure of the business's product (medicine bottles, alcohol bottles, tins, books, cigarette boxes, etc.). Mounted on a wheeled platform, the advertisement could be pushed along the central thoroughfares of the city by an employee hidden inside or pulled by a horse or even an automobile.[44] Adding an aural and far more technological dimension to his successful patent, Domingo Arámburu invented a mechanical dog designed to walk the city, play music from a phonograph inside, and dispense ads from his mouth (figure 10).[45] Following this line of creativity, Napoleón Valero Martin, a Spaniard, received a patent in 1905 for an advertising system consisting of a human dummy containing a phono-graph. With the push of a button or pull of a ring the dummy would provide information about the client's business, product, or service. Like so many others, Valero Martin pitched his invention as a method to cut through the visual clutter of advertising that overwhelmed the urban landscape. He declared his system worked "with the object of sparing the public the bother of fixing its attention on the signs, cards, sheets and posters that are used today." He added that his system would have a sizeable public relations benefit for the advertiser since customers would actively seek it out: "The advantages of my advertising system are incontestable, since for curiosity and distraction the public will hear without being bothered the most complete details of the goodness and value of the advertised products."[46] By the 1890s the most common and successful category of mobile advertising was horse-drawn carriages and then automobiles.[47] One such company belonged to Mexican citizens Vicente Villada Cardoso and Luis Rivas Irúz, who in 1908 patented and formed the Empresa Explotadora del Anuncio de Movimiento sobre Vehiculos. The newspaper La Clase Media supported their effort and explained how moving ads were better than fixed, how they drew more attention, covered more area, and ensured clients, "No longer will you be stopped by 'Se Prohibe Anunciar.'"[48]

Sites of commercialized leisure—privately owned spaces of public sociability—became prime locations for marketers and advertising innovations. Holding thousands of spectators, bullrings not only offered advertising space around the walls but made ideal venues for promotions sponsored by large businesses such as El Buen Tono.[49] Matadors became important icons in Porfirian consumer culture, celebrity figures whose popular cultural cachet made them sought-after endorsers of consumer products.[50] For this reason inventors like Felipe Buenrostro viewed bullfights as a place to use advertising systems with prizes. In Buenrostro's system customers purchased event tickets imprinted with numbers. Products sponsors at the event would use the numbers for prize draws. Buenrostro also adapted this for use by cigarette and railroad companies, claiming it would increase sales by interesting the "consuming public" (público consumidor) with a cash prize.[51] Fellow Mexican E. Ureta joined a trend of combining clocks with advertising, using the clock to regulate the viewing duration of each illuminated ad appearing in a frame beneath it. He envisioned its use at bullrings, theaters, event halls (salones de espectáculos), street corners, and anywhere the public

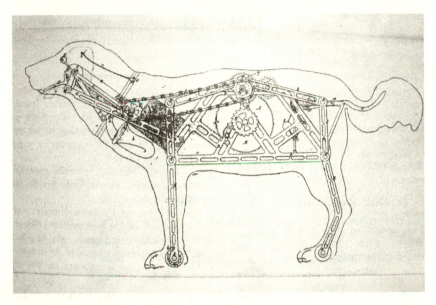

Figure 10. Domingo Arámburu's patent application drawing for his talking and walking advertising dog. Source: Archivo General de la Nación, Fondo Secretaría de Comercio y Fomento Industrial, Patentes y Marcas, Legajo 207, exp. 1.

gathered.[52] Player pianos, a new phenomenon, became advertising tools as they entertained in cantinas and other locations. An attachment to the piano's mechanism advanced a hundred-foot-long roll of advertisements across the top of the piano between two posts, the whole cycle taking over an hour to complete.[53] Billiard halls became potential advertising spaces, not just on their walls but also on the tables themselves. The Mexican Franco brothers applied to patent their billiard game titled "Títulos de Marcas de Efectos Nacionales y Extranjeros," in which each ball would be painted with a brand or business name and image.[54] Theater curtains, already hung with fixed ads, now improved with the help of technology.[55] Juan Maqueda Aguilar, a Spaniard residing in the capital, was one of two successful applicants in 1907 for a patent on a moving advertising curtain for theaters. He called his version "Telón anunciador sin fin," which, like the player piano and the Anunciador Standard described above, moved ads across the curtain in an endless cycle. He extolled the superiority of moving ads, which, he asserted, "more easily caught the attention of the public."[56] Even the barbershop deserved attention. Domingo Arámburu invented personal ad viewing for each customer in the *barbería*. A roll of paper ads skewered by a rod would hang from the ceiling above each chair. A second rod near the chair would collect the roll as the seated viewer turned a crank "at his leisure," which turned the roll. Arámburu portrayed it as a pleasant diversion, noting in his conclusion "the useful-ness that this great distraction provides [the customer]."[57]

Tramcars—first horse drawn and then electrified after the turn of the century—represented both the promise and dangers of the modern city, but advertisers considered their interior and exterior walls premium real estate.[58] Traveling throughout the city, tramcars offered excellent visibility among the urban crowds for advertising on their exterior sur-faces. Only when parked at the Zócalo might the trams lose the eye of the urban observer, whose gaze transferred to the central terminal kiosk with its large public clock and color posters for cigarette brands, brewer-ies, department stores, and other companies.[59] The most publicized and enduring ad campaign on trams belongs to the distributor for Jules Robin cognac. It coordinated a two-tier advertising campaign, placing ads on the exterior of all city trams and then making them the central image for its humorous newspaper ads (figure 11). Advertisers also prized the inte-rior space of trams for its promise of captive audiences looking for visual stimulation. Foreign visitors to the capital remarked with surprise at the amount of advertising within the trams.[60] Mexican citizen and Saltillo resident Eduardo Hay sold his advertising system, Anunciador Viajante, by claiming it ideal for trams and trains, hotels, theaters, and other pub-lic locations. Focusing on trams and trains, he describes his reliance on a captive audience: "An advertisement placed in my system will have the advantage of being continually viewed by the traveler who will be seated together with it, and since travelers generally look for some distraction, no matter what it might be, they will be strongly drawn to pay attention to the advertisement, reading it perhaps more than once, and by so doing satisfying the goal of the business advertising."[61] Applicants even found a way to install the ubiquitous "tela sin fin"—the moving rolls of advertise-ments—inside the tram.[62]

The combined technologies of electricity and the incandescent light-bulb transformed not only urban life but also public advertising. They allowed for the invention of *anuncios luminosos,* a catchall term for any illuminated advertisement, from lamppost installations and shop signs to still-image projections and cinematography. The significance of these technologies clearly extended far beyond advertising and, as elsewhere, transformed life in Mexico City.[63] Electrification of the capital's street

Figure 11. Tramcars in the Zócalo advertising Cognac Robin. The liquor distributor coordinated this street advertising with a newspaper publicity campaign featuring the trams. One long-running newspaper ad shows a stationary streetcar filled with passengers waiting on a man with one step on the stairs. The conductor asks him, "What's it going to be, friend? On or off?" The man replies, "Don't hassle me! I'm reading the advertisement for Cognac Robin and I've got a right to do so. I guess that's the reason why they put it there!" Source: Archivo General de la Nación, Fondo Instrucción Pública y Bellas Artes, Colección C. B. Waite, exp. 10.

lighting began in 1888 and rapidly replaced older and dimmer sources such as turpentine.[64] Electric lighting assisted in maintaining public order and, combined with the newly formed gendarmerie, provided better security for the growing number of stores with high-value inventories. It also extended the hours and breadth of public life on the streets as well as that of private commercialized leisure such as theaters, circuses, roller-skating rinks, and restaurants. Electricity further aided a culture of consumption by providing stores much better display opportunities and longer hours with clearer, brighter light and cleaner air than kerosene and hydrogen lamps provided.

Not surprisingly, advertisers quickly jumped on this marvel as a way to attract public attention. Juan Begovich's Anunciador Standard and an earlier patent for a similar device were both powered and illuminated by electricity.[65] Electrically lit store signs were popular, and the Mexican Light and Power Company held contests for the best.[66] In 1889 and 1892 Eduardo Barreira and Michael Ximénez were among the earliest advertising agents to successfully petition the ayuntamiento for concessions to establish illuminated signs on city street corners, mounting tin and glass rectangles or parallelograms approximately five feet high by two or more feet wide on top of ornate steel poles to publicize businesses and products.[67] Patent applicants also used dry cell batteries to make electricity portable, with the result that advertisers could send men lit up with advertising messages out on the street at night. At least three inventors filed patents for an Electric Man, or El Hombre Luminoso, in 1907 and 1908. Two received definite status and at least one, filed by Y. D. Arroyo but owned by El Buen Tono, appeared in the streets in a much-publicized advertising campaign (see chapter 1).[68] Illuminated billboards also appeared, but few compared with the installation of twelve hundred incandescent lights on the wall of the former convent of Saint Isabel to advertise the cigarette company El Buen Tono and department store Palacio de Hierro in the months leading up to the Pan-American Congress meeting in Mexico City in 1902.[69]

Advertisers pounced on evolving image-projection technologies such as cinematography and the magic lantern not only for their popular appeal but also because they dramatically expanded the time and space available for advertising images in the city. Building walls, rooftops, and other urban surfaces either unavailable for publicity during the day or limited to a single, fixed advertisement became canvases for a brilliant and colorful procession of images, in the case of the magic lantern, or blended advertising and entertainment short films, in the case of the cinema. Moreover, as advertising mediums they made a popular consumer technology and commercial entertainment free to a highly receptive public and by doing so promoted another set of common commercial experiences around which an urban mass culture formed during the Porfiriato. In this sense both magic lanterns and the cinema were similar to the newspaper: at first primarily a commodity but subsequently transformed into powerful marketing tools with which to promote mass consumption more generally. A magic lantern could either act as a slide projector, casting a large still image onto a screen, or it could backlight an image onto a smaller, transparent or translucent surface such as a store window or the screen walls of a mobile projection carriage. Mirroring its vogue in France and other nations, the magic lantern became a nighttime entertainment standard for the last quarter of the nineteenth century at public events ranging from sophisticated expatriate celebrations to more plebeian gatherings.[70] Cinematography came to the republic much later. In 1896 President Porfirio Díaz attended the first motion-picture viewing, a date notable for being only a year after the Lumière brothers introduced the new technology in France and an indication of how important the French viewed Mexico to be as a new market. Although scholars of the cinema in Mexico and abroad have discussed many facets of the socially and culturally transformative role of projection technologies during this era they have given short shrift to their use as advertising mediums.

The first application to transform the magic lantern from a commercial entertainment device into an advertising medium came in 1882, when Juan H. Purdy y Compañia requested a license for his new advertising system, creatively named "The Magic Lantern."[71] A trickle of patent applications and license requests turned into a flood as advertisers, commercial entrepreneurs, and businesses competed for the most dramatic nighttime publicity stunts that invariably drew urban crowds. Mexican citizen Enrique Ángulo received a patent in 1889 to project three-inch-diameter photographic images onto a twenty-five-foot-wide screen (whether a wall or cloth) and noted, "As these ads will be shown at night they will without any doubt call the attention of passersby and will be more effective than any other system."[72] The same year Ignacio Alarcón received a license for a horse-drawn advertising projector carriage that would cruise the streets of the city between 6:00 and 10:00 p.m. and stop every fifteen minutes to project advertisements and diverting scenes onto city walls.[73] License petitioners frequently noted that advertising images would be interspersed with images of "landscapes, portraits of notable men, buildings, and fantastic views."[74] Entrepreneurs heightened the sensation of the experience with additional visual and aural stimuli. Most commonly on mobile platforms, advertisers combined a phonograph for sound, a projector for cinematic or slide images, and sometimes strands of colored lightbulbs and electric bells to attract attention. A generator powered by petroleum or more volatile oxygen or hydrogen gas powered the devices.[75] Applicants for mobile projectors envisioned their territory and clientele broadly. Agustín Vélez, from Puebla, intended his modestly named Vélefono vehicle to be "installed at train stations or run through the principal streets, public plazas, avenues," and other public locations with the goal of "showing, to the passersby, one ad after the other."[76] The more numerous and typically successful fixed-location requests were concentrated in the center of the city. Advertisers and commercial establishments received approval to permit projectors to illuminate building façades, balconies, and screens on rooftops—commercial and private—as long as the applicant received permission from the property owner and operated within a prescribed and variable range of hours between 6:00 p.m. and 1:00 a.m.[77] Seemingly no location could be too large, too public, or too sacrosanct to serve as a screen on which to project images of consumption, not even the walls of the Alameda Park or the roof of the Teatro Nacional.[78]

Requests for licenses to advertise with cinematography began to appear in 1900 and resembled those for magic lanterns in their language, locations, and variety of commercial and "educational" images. Alberto Jauregui asked for and received permission to project color cinematography from one rooftop to another on the centrally located Puente de San Francisco, across from the Alameda.[79] Others followed in central locations. Mario Vázquez received permission to establish a "diorama-anuncio" for cinematography and other forms of "electric projections" from the roof of the Portal de Mercaderes overlooking the main plaza, the Zócalo.[80] In doing so, Vázquez capitalized on the "o-rama" craze that swept France during the late 1890s, when mechanical panorama commercial entertainments began to incorporate cinematography into their mechanical tableaux.[81] One can only imagine how he adapted the panorama to advertising purposes. Although most of these licenses were for the commercial heart of the city, in an echo of El Buen Tono's placement of public screens in working-class neighborhoods at least one applicant, Emilio Bellan, established his screen on the periphery of the fashionable thoroughfares just north of the cathedral on Santo Domingo and Escalerillas Streets.[82]

Space brokers required the permission of the city council to carry out their plans. Their applications and the council's deliberations and decisions allow us to glimpse how their language expressed a shared cultural ethos of progress so widely prevalent in Porfirian society. Petitioners aligned their interests with the aspirations and concerns of council members for the city's material progress, order, public safety, and finances. Both parties shared a common cosmopolitanism that they envisioned extending from Paris, London, and New York to Mexico City.

The majority of applicants self-consciously made their activities analogous with those in other cosmopolitan centers, referencing advertising innovations in other cities as a way to legitimize both their plans and their position in Mexican society. So harmonious did the urban vision of advertisers and council members appear at times that "modern" and "commercial" seemed synonymous. Yet while a common vocabulary and generalized vision of progress served to bond these two groups whose social circles and economic status likely differed considerably, that bond had its limits, as demonstrated by council members who periodically—and sometimes spectacularly—diverged.

All parties generally agreed that modern cities required modern advertising. Publicity and its spectacles, novelties, use of new technologies, and representations of consumption served as a nexus of culture and commerce in late nineteenth-century global cosmopolitan centers. For many proponents, advertising facilitated material and therefore human progress. As Alberto Díaz began his application for advertising towers in 1892, "Advertising is considered in all the enlightened nations of the world as one of the principal factors encouraging commercial development and for this powerful reason we are constantly devising ingenious and costly means to call the public's attention to mercantile establishments that, because of their importance, are able to provide exceptional advantages TO THE CONSUMER."[83] Most petitioners to the council (and most patent applicants to the Fomento) took the same tack as Ildefonso Estrada y Zenea, described at the start of this chapter, claiming European (and occasionally U.S.) precedent for whatever advertising system they were offering. Two months before Alberto Díaz's submission, Vicente Moyano concluded his application by stating, "Our system is not new. It has been adopted with success in the principal cities of Europe, and for that reason we are endeavoring to implement it in this city."[84] Federico Bodet asked to establish an advertising agency "in a modern European style," Alberto Jauregui described his advertising with color cinematography as "European style," and José Gastaldi claimed his ornate billboards were "already in use in various European nations," as did Alfonso Hermann, who added, "and in the United States" for his system of advertising on the interior and exterior of coaches.[85] To support its recommendation of Mario Vázquez's Diorama-Anuncio to the council, the Comisión de Policía asserted, "That advertising system is in vogue in all the civilized nations."[86]

A desire for order, regulation, and urban aesthetics also united both

parties. The chaos and exuberance of public bill posting decried by
Estrada long predated and superseded his kiosks. As representatives of
respectable society, the council had long sought to bring bureaucratic
rationalization to bill posting and other forms of public advertising.
Throughout the Restored Republic and the Porfiriato, the Comisión de
Policía lamented the popular production of store signs and advertisements that failed to comply with an 1833 law prohibiting the painting of
"ridiculous images" on storefronts and demanding proper orthography.[87]
In 1875 the ayuntamiento even passed the commission's recommendation to rescind the business licenses as a penalty for noncompliance,
but complaints by members of council for the next thirty years suggest
enforcement was futile.[88] By the Porfiriato, the sheer volume of advertising had become an issue. Bill posters plastered "posters of all sizes and
colors, [on] the front of public and private buildings, corners, posts, portals, and other high traffic sites" using various substances that stained
and deteriorated the walls and left a dirty and unappealing appearance
(figure 12).[89] These bill posters fell outside of the purview of government
regulation discussed in this chapter and indicate a large pool of second-
or third-tier advertisers worthy of future research.

Applicants offered a solution to the council, promising revenue, public safety, and urban beautification. In return for a concession for a monopoly over a certain area of the city, space brokers offered generous fees
(or free public services like street cleaning) to erect billboards on rooftops and street corners, to build kiosks and twenty-foot-tall "Advertising
Towers," to attach advertising placards to street lights, and to create
other new spaces on which all public advertisements would have to be
placed after receiving permission.[90] José Gayosso, who received approval
in 1894 to establish an advertising agency to promote rationalization of
publicity, exemplifies this appealing offer. He promised to place ads only
in locations where he had the express permission of property owners
and council. He would ensure the cleanliness of the area, that the ads
possessed tax stamps and stayed up for their contractual period, and
that "they would be affixed in frames and kept in good appearance." All
notices by the city, district, and federal governments would be free.[91]
Federico Bodet merely offered free government notices and 500 pesos per
year for the concession that he received in 1895.[92] A number of applicants
received concessions to expand public lighting, like Francisco Gutiérrez
Solorzano, who, in 1882 (before the city installed electric lighting),
offered free of charge to the city to set up over one hundred streetlights

Figure 12. The exterior walls of the Hospital de Jesús demonstrate the consequences of bill posting for the appearance of buildings in the capital. Concession and license applicants to the ayuntamiento frequently referenced unsightly façades such as this to promote the merits of their orderly and rationalized advertising systems. Source: Archivo General de la Nación, Fondo Instrucción Pública y Bellas Artes, Colección C. B. Waite, exp. 80.

on streets, in plazas, and at railroad stations. The lights would contain transparent advertising over the glass, and Gutiérrez left open the possibility of placing advertising on the poles.[93] Several applicants, including El Buen Tono, even sought concessions to paint color ads on city sidewalks (especially around the Alameda Park) and offered the argument that they were saving the city money by applying a "protective cap of paint" and thus preserving the surface from heavy pedestrian traffic.[94] In every case, however, the council denied the request.

Council members did have their limits. While they granted concessions and licenses to the majority of applicants, on numerous occasions they turned down petitions, such as José Gastaldi's plan to attach billboards ornamented with latticework atop public walls, including those of the Alameda, where residents took their evening and weekend strolls.

They declared the location of the ads "unattractive" and "inharmonious" with the foliage and special ornamentation of the paseos.[95] In 1889 the Comisión de Policía revealed its guiding philosophy after granting a concession for illuminated advertising to Eduardo Barreira, writing that it and the council reserved the right to grant concessions and licenses only when they contributed to both the "adornment of the City and an income for the city."[96]

Council members possessed a vision of modernity that shared elements but not the whole of the vision held by those in the advertising business. Applicants to the ayuntamiento and the Fomento embraced a bustling, colorful, noisy, and chaotic capital city whose transforming visual landscape reflected the secular commercial city on which modern Mexican urban mass culture was based. Theirs was one of crowds engaged no longer in collective violence but in collective consumption of spectacles ever-refreshed by new technologies and marketing ideas that, as this study shows, often combined entertainment and advertising.[97] Those on the council also believed in material progress and identified consumption as a tangible indicator, yet their model of a modern Mexico City differed in significant ways. Theirs was a more sensible, rational, hierarchical, and ordered city imbued with an aesthetic sensibility that often clashed with that of advertising and other commercial entrepreneurs. Most importantly, theirs was a city that possessed a strong sense of history and decorum, and they reacted strongly when those lines of decorum were crossed.

In 1896 José Mariano Crespo crossed at least one of those lines when he petitioned to place a projector and screen atop the Municipal Palace in the Zócalo and show ads during the evening rush hour, between 6:00 and 8:00 p.m. He must have thought he sweetened the deal by touting his additional exhibition of "instructive and curious views, free to the public for whom the images will provide solace and distraction." For the members of the Comisión de Policía this request was the last straw. In a letter signed by "Camacho" to the president of the ayuntamiento, the commission lashed out at the crassness of advertising and the impudence of its practitioners. It began by explaining Crespo's request before initiating its criticism by observing that he wanted the benefit of the building and its honest reputation exclusively for himself, "to the prejudice of the decorum and good appearance of a public building that is the residence of the Offices and principal authorities of this Capital who must be cloaked in the respect and consideration inherent in the object of their institution, and for that very reason the building must not be degraded by assuming the ridiculous role of a common street corner assigned to advertise to passersby." Camacho continued that any private residence would not welcome advertisements affixed to it "promoting miraculous pills or unguents . . . to cure all the ills that afflict humanity and using slick talk to attract those who suffer. In a building that bears the name of Municipal Palace, occupied by the Government of the District, by the City Council, by the Civil Registry and other important offices of the Capital, it would be unpardonable to transform it into an advertising poster in order to please an individual who cannot argue on any grounds for his pretension."[98] Crespo had gone too far and, not surprisingly, council members rejected his application. Camacho's stand became ingrained in the institutional memory of the ayuntamiento. Three years later, in 1899, the chairman of the Comisión de Policía, Juan de Pérez Gálvez, quoted passages of Camacho's diatribe verbatim when he turned down a request by Daniel R. de la Vega to advertise on the exterior walls of Belén prison.[99]

Although the city council had either colluded with or acceded to space brokers in the colonization of public space for advertising, Camacho's visceral attack demonstrated that the council's members possessed a vision of modern Mexico that overlapped but did not fully overlay with that of the petitioners. An analysis of newspapers and their rise as a mass-marketing advertising medium, in particular the penny press, reveals yet another vision of modern Mexico and the perspective of a working-class consumer culture.

The Rise of the Commercial Press as a Mass-Marketing Medium

When historians talk about advertising and consumerism in the Porfiriato they almost invariably cite newspapers as their source.[100] Though driven by their ready availability, this focus on newspapers likely also reflects a degree of presentism, assuming the greatest mass entertainment and marketing medium of the twentieth century occupied the same cultural niche in the nineteenth.

Benedict Anderson grants newspapers a similar long-term and venerable social function and cultural significance by imprudently jumping from their role in late-colonial nation building among colonial elites to the "mass ceremony" of newspaper consumption in the late-nineteenth century, with little discussion of the intervening 150 years.[101] He centers the birth of nationalism in the Americas in the narrative of the early gazettes that the colonial creoles read to learn of the latest in "commercial news . . . colonial political appointments, marriages of the wealthy, and so forth." This narrative "created an imagined community among a specific assemblage of fellow-readers, to whom *these* ships, brides, bishops, and prices belonged."[102] He describes the widespread shared experience of newspaper readership without considering how and why the newspaper transformed into a commodity of mass consumption and why it would appeal to a broad spectrum of the public.

This assumption tends to overprivilege the newspaper and its message(s). In her study of Porfirian advertising Nora Pérez-Rayón Elizundia selected a single year, 1900, and a single newspaper group, Rafael Reyes Spíndola's *El Imparcial* and *El Mundo Ilustrado*, to make sweeping claims about newspapers' impact on society.[103] Phyllis Smith used a much broader range of periodicals in her fine study but overreached with her conclusion that "their [newspaper advertisements] growth in size and importance attests to the power of the medium itself and its almost single-handed creation of a consumer culture."[104] In fact, early Porfirian newspapers utterly failed as a mass-market advertising medium.

Newspaper editors did not see their mission and responsibility to their readers in terms of advertising, particularly given the small readership characteristic of nineteenth-century newspapers. News of ship arrivals and the goings-on of the elite still dominated their pages, along with world news and long political essays. The scarcity and high price of newsprint resulted in a single copy costing ten centavos or more, far out of reach for laborers whose daily wage was but thirty or forty centavos. Moreover, newspapers were predominately the upper classes talking to each other, with the emphasis on politics and "serious" matters unlikely to interest potential readers in the popular classes. Journals, seeking to maintain an aura of social respectability, Enlightenment rationality, and gravitas, disdained entertainment, spectacle, and other traditional marketing techniques. Politics were extremely important, yet in the newspapers they were discussed in a way that had little relevance to the great majority of Mexicans.

The newspaper's emergence as a mass-market advertising medium was not a historical inevitability. Newspapers are themselves commodities, bought and sold. Although they served a circumscribed market, there was no inherent need to sell space to advertise goods and services. The newspaper's historical destiny was applied ex post facto. Newspapers changed as the societies in which they functioned changed. As the market economy consumer revolution washed over Mexico, its newspapers adapted to explain and provide meaning to the social changes in progress, of which they were a part.

As in any evolution of a cultural form, the change was neither sudden nor smooth. Evidence of this adaptive process exceeds the simple tracking of increased advertising quantity and quality throughout the nineteenth century. Numerous dead ends ensued. The newspaper *El Anunciador Mexicano* represents one of these attempts at finding the right formula in this new age.

El Anunciador Mexicano: Organo del Comercio e Industria published its first edition on November 22, 1877.[105] It attempted to overhaul both the economic model and the cultural function of the newspaper, discarding the notion of the newspaper as a commodity itself and embracing the idea of newspapers as a mass-marketing advertising medium by giving away its copies for free. Its prospectus stated that one should advertise because "it is the axiom of the century that, *he that doesn't advertise, doesn't sell*." *El Anunciador* charged five centavos per line, per edition and promised to publish twice a week with eleven thousand copies in each run, for a total of eighty-eight thousand copies freely distributed to willing consumers every month. The paper did not last long and some of its distribution claims seemed farfetched. Still, its publishers had recognized a national market, pinpointed the capital's key centers of consumer activity, and identified a public need to know "the manufactures of the whole country, the prices of the articles in each locality, the places where they can buy the cheapest, and the good production houses of the Republic." Although a prototype of the modern newspaper, *El Anunciador* lacked the technology and capital to succeed in the newspaper market economy. In addition, while providing plenty of advertisements, its content remained traditional and lacked the elements of entertainment and the spectacularization of daily life, those compelling qualities that could confer mass appeal. Newspapers continued to edge toward this realization, but not until 1896 did a newspaper hit the magic formula of content, capital, and technology to transform the newspaper in Mexico into a true object of mass consumption and vehicle of mass-marketing.

In 1896 Rafael Reyes Spíndola and Carlos Díaz Dufóo launched *El Imparcial*, which transformed the role of the newspaper in Mexican society.[106] Reyes Spíndola revolutionized the newspaper business model in Mexico and made the mass-circulation daily a permanent reality. From a purely economic perspective he removed the cost barrier to a mass market by driving down the per-copy price to a single centavo. To attain this low price he relied on government subsidies, revenues derived from reserving roughly 50 percent of the paper's space for advertising, and adoption of the modern retail model of "sell cheap and sell often" ascendant in Mexico among department stores and the big tobacco companies. By undercutting its competition in search of a mass market *El Imparcial* ground down and then eradicated such stalwarts of the traditional press as *El Siglo XIX* and the *Monitor Republicano*. Reyes Spíndola offered a product seemingly apolitical yet thoroughly supportive of the regime's policies. This pro-development stance was most overwhelmingly conveyed in the consumer orientation of the publication, not just in its innovative and conspicuous advertisements but also in its general coverage of businesses, products, fashion, and consumer behavior. Because of all these characteristics—ties to the government, emphasis on consumption, and "commercialization" of the press—the paper became the bête noire of contemporary and future opponents of the Díaz regime, who cited it with a mixture of loathing and awe.

A low price helped to achieve unheard-of circulation figures. Daily runs of 70,000 by 1902 occasionally peaked at 125,000 during 1907 before settling at a consistent 100,000 by 1910.[107] Reyes Spíndola further plumbed the downscale market with *El Popular*, which attained daily runs of up to 50,000 and reached the more affluent with the relaunch of the weekly news and photo magazine *El Mundo Ilustrado* in 1900. Editors trumpeted these circulation numbers on the front page for a city and federal district whose combined populations in 1910 totaled 720,000.[108]

A low price made a mass-market commodity possible; a change in conditions and content made it happen. Historians might consider that, culturally, *El Imparcial* was the right paper at the right time in Mexican history. A confluence of printing technologies, increased consumption capacity, a deluge of goods needing a far-reaching advertising medium, and a rapid growth in the size and population of a city in search of an identity all created a historical moment in which *El Imparcial* could be launched and thrive.

To understand the success of *El Imparcial* is to address the questions Anderson left unasked. The city, like the nation-state, is an imagined community. In the metamorphosis of the city under the strains of what Karl Polanyi has called the "Great Transformation," the technological, production, and cultural revolutions accompanying the entrenching market economy led to the simultaneous rise of a consumer economy and an urban mass culture.[109] Focused across the Atlantic on fin-de-siècle Paris, Vanessa Schwartz implicitly begins from this point as she considers the omissions of Anderson through the lens of the relationship between the press and the visual entertainments that constituted a developing urban mass culture. Schwartz agrees with Anderson that the newspaper created a mass community but seeks to understand and explain why the newspaper enjoyed such widespread and sustained appeal among individuals. She argues that "the newspaper served as one of the most powerful forms of modern mass cultural urban entertainments in the sense that it constituted a collective and then aimed to please it through a newspaper reading."[110] It is the spectacularization of city life and the narrative provided for it by the pairing of images and stories in the press that made the newspaper a mass commodity and the city an imagined community. Schwartz therefore associates modernity with the fusion of visual and written texts, in direct contradiction of Anderson, who asserts that it is the rise of written and the decline of visual texts that characterizes modernity.[111] For Schwartz, "a culture that became 'more literate' also became more visual."[112] In Mexico, *El Imparcial* led the Porfirian press in adopting this new formula.

Reyes Spíndola did not just change the content of newspapers, he also changed their presentation. He contributed to the "spectacularization of city life" by sensationalizing the everyday in Mexico City and in so doing attracted a mass readership. Transforming the written text, he favored journalists with an exuberant style and a proclivity for factual embellishment while devoting considerable space to crimes, disasters, and other events deemed likely to horrify, titillate, but most importantly, attract a readership. As he candidly explained early in his career, "A journalist, in my opinion, must exaggerate to touch the imagination of the masses."[113] *El Imparcial* provided the vehicle by which to put his ideas into practice, delivering to readers four pages of news and advertisements from around the country and the globe as well as a chronicle of their urban world that ranged from the sober to the salacious. He placed a high premium on the power of images and pioneered the widespread insertion of illustrations and then photographs to verify and spectacularize the written text. He quickly upgraded his presses when halftone photoengraving enabled photographs to be reproduced on cheap paper such as newsprint. In 1903 he imported new rotary presses from the United States and specifically noted that he could "illustrate the new paper with finer engravings which I will now have the occasion to do with the new machinery."[114] Photos served to convey accuracy, authenticity, and "reality" to his stories, even more than illustrations.

Reyes Spíndola bore similarities to William Randolph Hearst in his transformation of his nation's press, but he was in truth uniquely Mexican. *El Imparcial* tapped into existing popular tastes for the sensational, the carnivalesque, and the spectacular. The flavor of the broadsheets produced by Antonio Vanegas Arroyo and José Guadalupe Posada captured this tradition and antedated *El Imparcial* by nearly a decade. Reyes Spíndola merely repackaged, commercialized, and modernized traditional forms of entertainment. Advertisements mirrored this development, taking advantage of new printing technologies to better incorporate entertaining elements of the spectacle, the huckster, and the half-truth into their testimonial texts and creative images.

To attract a mass audience, *El Imparcial* went beyond the contents of the broadsheets. It focused on a selective account of urban events and made the often-mundane entertaining. While critics then and now attack *El Imparcial*'s infatuation with the trappings of consumption—its heavy emphasis on articles on fashion, urban entertainment, store openings, or other similar and arguably pedestrian topics—they overlook that in these accounts the readership identified their lived reality, or a version of it. The paper featured a host of writers, including Juvenal, Figaro, Manuel Gutiérrez Najera, and José Juan Tablada, who contributed social commentaries on life in the capital. They chronicled the pleasures, travails, and serendipity of modern urban living while creating such famous characters as El Duque Job along the way.[115] They created a narrative of urban life that made order from disorder and gave meaning and form to the transformation and dislocation that characterized Porfirian Mexico City. They helped readers anchor themselves in a city strained by rapid physical growth, strong inflows of rural Mexicans in search of a livelihood, and the awe and thrills that science, technology, and business brought to the residents in the way of architecture, urban design, consumer goods, and entertainments. Together the commentaries, articles, advertisements, and graphic images gave readers a way to see or interpret the city, while the simple participation in the daily ritual of newspaper reading promoted the notion that the reader formed part of a larger community whose members shared a common reality.

The Reyes Spíndola papers helped generate the spectacles that they covered and inserted themselves into the urban narratives that they reported. Reyes Spíndola's journals sponsored or cosponsored bullfights, charity banquets, and advertising contests. Each year the entire city awaited *El Imparcial*'s publication of its illustrated almanac. For a mere ten centavos the buyer received four hundred pages filled with a calendar, city and national maps, government and business directories, lists of religious and secular events, a compilation of cooking and pharmaceutical recipes, sections on topics such as hygiene and advice, and plenty of advertising throughout the text. A booklet of coupons good for theater and store discounts accompanied the almanac. *El Imparcial*, its sister publications such as *El Mundo* and *El Mundo Ilustrado*, and even the French *Le Courrier du Mexique* ballyhooed the almanac's release and published cover stories and photographs of the mixed sombrero and homburg crowd that attended the event.[116]

The depiction in the photo published by *Le Courrier du Mexique* on February 20, 1901, staged or not, of an intermingled readership dressed in traditional and Western attire cuts to the core difference between *El Imparcial* and its predecessors. Setting aside his pro-regime editorials, Reyes Spíndola actively sought an ecumenical readership by placing the themes Vanegas Arroyo used in his popular broadsheets in the same four pages as the wry social commentaries of Juvenal. *El Imparcial* actually tried to speak to a cross-class readership; previous papers mostly involved members of the same small class talking to each other. With a price of a single centavo *El Imparcial* put itself within reach of a mass audience, and by discarding the notion of the press as simply a respectable forum for ideas it also provided content and an urban narrative that its readership found compelling. Price, audience, and content distinguished *El Imparcial* from earlier formats. Social and economic currents combined with technological innovations in print made its existence possible and its success assured. In this sense the market for *El Imparcial* was less created than tapped into.

El Imparcial may have played a leading role in the mass-circulation press, but it was not alone. Mexicans of the Porfirian age were voracious readers, judging by the number of dailies and weeklies published. National adult literacy rates in the republic rose from 17 percent in 1895 to 29 percent in 1910, while those in the Federal District rose from 45 percent to 65 percent in the same time period.[117] The number of people who actually derived information from the press was likely even higher, given the way newspaper reading occurred at the time. One common tradition was for several people to come together and hear the paper read aloud.

This practice had both social and utilitarian aspects, as it required only one literate member to relay information, it energized the contents as it converted written texts into lively oral accounts, and finally it allowed participants to transform the individualist act of bourgeois culture into a communal experience. Historian don Luis González confirms the deep historical roots of this tradition in the prologue to his *San José de Gracia: Mexican Village in Transition*.[118] This practice and the act of passing along newspapers probably laid the foundation of Reyes Spíndola's assertion that each paper in Mexico changed hands four times during its short lifetime.[119]

The Mexican press adapted to the Reyes Spíndola juggernaut and seemed to fill every conceivable niche market. Business, politics for or against don Porfirio, bullfights, cinema, family life, fashion, women's issues, crime, humor, and numerous other topics were frameworks of cultural life on which publishers were willing to hang a newspaper. Newspapers not only spoke to the public's interests but also spoke their language. Every expatriate could find a local publication in his or her language. Some of the more prominent were the English-language *Two Republics* and *Mexican Herald* and the French-language *L'Echo du Mexique* and *Le Courrier du Mexique* as well as the monthly *Mexique Moderne*. Prices among this diverse field ranged from a centavo, to match *El Imparcial*, up to twenty-five centavos. This does not include the untold number of free newspapers that followed the business model of the 1877 *El Anunciador Mexicano*. The mainstream press did not take kindly to this threat and wrote warnings to advertisers to distrust the claims of the free papers.[120] Such diversity and conspicuousness of leisure and fashion provides more evidence of a modern consumer lifestyle defining the capital city for many of its residents.

In this sense the broader press mirrored *El Imparcial*. An acceptance of and reliance on advertising and a consumer discourse characterized nearly every publication. Prominent front-page solicitations for advertising preceded more elaborate house ads scattered throughout many of the papers. A review of nearly one hundred publications confirms an upward trend in advertising space during the Porfiriato that paralleled trends in American newspapers. Advertising spread throughout the paper, from a ratio of ads to unpaid copy at seventy to thirty in the 1880s with the bulk of the ads on the last page (usually page 4) to nearly fifty-fifty by the Revolution. Those periodicals falling short of high advertising levels did not fail for a lack of effort. An 1895 front-page house ad from one of the first copies of *La Semana en el Hogar* conveys this desire for clients: "ADVERTISERS LOOK AT THIS!!! This newspaper, because of the sections that it contains, is destined to be read by ALL MEMBERS OF THE FAMILY, in such a way that a notice placed in it has a very high probability of success for the advertiser."[121] Moreover, as the Porfiriato progressed, the vast majority of publications increasingly covered the same kind of consumerist-oriented news that *El Imparcial* had made its signature. For example, Catholics could count on *El Pais* and *El Tiempo* to deliver the news with a pro-Catholic slant while finding ads for the latest medicine, devotional items, and fashions within their pages. With the launch of the weekly *El Tiempo Ilustrado* in 1901 to match Reyes Spíndola's splashy, photograph-filled *El Mundo Ilustrado*, devout Catholics could read and see with a clear conscience the latest fashions, behavior, and consumer trends of the Porfirian bon ton at the Peralvillo track or at the Tivoli Eliseo.

Newspapers became not only a medium for advertising but also educators and advocates of its efficacy. Economic self-interest as well as a genuine belief in the power of advertising drove newspapers to make claims for advertising that rang true to many readers. "Publicity is the lever that moves and fuels the machine called COMMERCE," declared *El Anunciador Mexicano* back in 1877.[122] "Publicity in our time is a necessity for the retailer and the industrialist," claimed *Le Courrier du Mexique*, while *El Imparcial* observed, "Our age, full of curiosities, is seduced by information and by the ADVERTISEMENT; there exists a new art—advertising." It added that the best artists were foreign and that "European journals are full of perfect examples of this careful work."[123] The working-class paper *Don Cucufate* counseled the retailers among its readership, "He that advertises more sells more, and he that sells more make much more money. This is as obvious as the midday sun."[124] The *Mexican Herald*, in one of a series of house ads, outlined the logic and necessity of advertising: "You should advertise to create a demand. People need things but usually remain unconscious of the need until some farseeing advertiser points out such need. People believe they could not get along today without thousands of things their forefathers never dreamed of. Why? Because advertising has created demands and suggested easy means to satisfy them."[125] In the self-promotion efforts of the Porfirian press the modern, mass-circulation press alone possessed the skill and expertise not only to bring together producer and consumer in an increasingly mass market but to persuade consumers to satisfy previously unrecognized desires.

The cutting edge of modern advertising appeared to have left the quaint world of the *Gaceta de México* in the distant past.

The Working-Class Penny Press

The publications mentioned so far targeted primarily the white-collar and relatively economically privileged portion of Mexican society. Certain papers, such as *El Imparcial* and *El Tiempo*, enjoyed a broader readership, but their language and vision of progress fit them within the usual historical imagination of the profile of Porfirian consumers and consumerism. That profile involves middle- and upper-class Mexicans consuming imported goods. Consider Nora Pérez-Rayón Elizundia's definition of Mexico's consuming class. She declares the "middling classes, above all urban" are those in which "publicity found its receivers [*receptores*] and commercial production, its consumers."[126] Historians overlook the engagement of the lower classes in this consumer culture, considering them neither culturally inclined nor economically capable of consumption beyond the "essentials" of life (beans, corn, chile, pulque, and coarse cotton cloth).

Such self-imposed categorical restrictions seem baffling. Certainly the wealthier strata of Porfirian society had more disposable income, and they certainly spent more—per capita—than the lower classes. Yet why cut out the 85 percent or so of the population that did not fit into these categories and define them as nonconsumers? What did they do to eat, drink, court, clothe themselves, entertain themselves, or fulfill religious and social obligations? In other words, without knowing what they consumed and the material culture that they constructed, how does one know how they lived? Clearly, consumption patterns between classes are different. The poor have always spent less on durables (furniture, home decoration, and private transportation) and more on entertainment, food, and drink in pulquerías, figones, and other public sites of diversion, often for cultural as well as practical reasons (e.g., if you cannot afford a house, let alone a big one, you are not going to furnish it).[127] Yet there is an overlap of consumption patterns for numerous items, such as mass-produced goods or certain entertainments, such as cigarettes or circus performances. Within these categories there is a considerable price differentiation through which social distinctions can be made. As Carole Shammas points out, "Being poor and being a consumer . . . were not mutually exclusive conditions."[128]

The working-class vision of a modernizing Mexico expressed itself in abundant forms within in the Porfirian press. Discussions of the popular press in Mexico typically start and frequently end with the broadsheets produced by the team of Antonio Vanegas Arroyo and José Guadalupe Posada. These broadsheets deserve such attention, but studies often posit them as guardians of an unchanging, traditional Mexico, in contrast to the modernizing press symbolized by *El Imparcial*. Overlooked is the fact that Vanegas Arroyo imported the broadsheet idea and format from France, although he and Posada undeniably transformed the medium into a vessel for popular values and concerns over the pace and strategy of modernization implemented by the Díaz regime.[129] The point here is that the lower classes often adopted the material culture of modernity (such as Posada's use of lithography), adapting goods and technologies—often imported—to reflect and express their lived experience. Popular or privileged, social groups in Mexico often adopted new goods and made them their own.

The penny press reveals a working-class consumer culture. Like their more affluent counterparts, these papers constructed an urban narrative particular to their readership. Unlike the broadsheets of Vanegas Arroyo, they followed the format and business model of *El Imparcial* by relying on advertising (Vanegas Arroyo did not) and providing local and national stories that more directly dealt with the economic, political, and social issues facing labor. Historian María Elena Díaz has analyzed these papers from their political positions and concluded that even the most radical (such as those advocating the strike) still sought to work within the market economy system.[130] Surprisingly, Díaz makes no mention of the consumer goods and services advertised in these papers and what this implies about the purchasing power, material culture, gender construction, and politics of their readership. Research into working-class consumption in the United States provides ways of thinking about these conclusions and understanding how those Mexicans tied into the cash-based market economy, particularly in urban areas, and how they viewed the possibilities and not just the perils of modernization. Most useful is Lizbeth Cohen's notion of "moral capitalism," the belief that capitalism was not corrupt in itself so long as it operated according to standards of morality and fairness.[131] Also instructive is William R. Leach's study of U.S. department stores in the Progressive Era. In it he cautions readers to avoid the dangers of presentism and to study consumer capitalism in its historical context, noting "the opportunities and . . . imaginative culture that arose from early consumer capitalism."[132] To deny this element of popular enthusiasm for the possibilities of human progress—even though that capitalism may have failed miserably in living up to its promises—is to miss an important social and cultural crossroads in Mexican and world history.

Penny press papers published mostly once a week, typically on Sunday or Thursday, and charged, as their name announced, one centavo. All of these papers published in Mexico City, but the penny press also existed in other urban areas.[133] To distribute their papers they employed the same techniques as the rest of the press, contracting with *vocedores* (street agents) to whom they sold one hundred copies for 72 centavos, guaranteeing successful sellers 28 centavos profit for each unit.[134] Publication numbers are harder to quantify, although one paper, the progressive *Don Cucufate*, claimed runs of 12,500.[135] Whatever their actual readership, the papers were popular and powerful enough to raise the ire of Rafael Reyes Spíndola, who in 1902 confided to José Yves Limantour that the penny press "is tormenting us [*El Imparcial*, etc.] with their foolishness."[136] Advertisements reinforced these editorial assaults, with an ad for the patent medicine Pildoritas Antibiliosas del Dr. Enrique Hernández Ortíz including the barb "that the newspaper *El Imparcial* tells the truth" in its ad titled "Cosas Imposibles."[137]

In the penny press the laboring classes found a representation of city life that reflected their lived reality. Front pages paired satirical images with equally biting explanatory *corridos* (popular ballads) or décimas castigating politicians, factory owners, government regulations, high food prices, competitors in the press, or a number of other subjects. Popular nationalism commonly entered through such avenues as corridos for the deceased beloved president and liberal hero Benito Juárez. Interestingly, the attacks on capital characteristically took the form of "bread and butter" issues reminiscent of the AFL trade union in the United States rather than the radicalism of the IWW. These included attacking factories for paying workers with false money or local governments for allowing possible monopolies in meat butchering under the guise of public health.[138] Never does the actual economic system come under attack. Moreover, *Don Cucufate, El Diablito Rojo, El Diablita Bromista*, and other papers María Elena Díaz characterizes as reformist, progressive, and even radical carried the most advertising. Political opposition to the regime did not necessarily translate into a dislike of the consumer goods resulting from Mexico's modernization.

The penny press, like their more upscale cousins, advertised a wide range of products. Economic realities did circumscribe the types of products and services as well as the printing technologies used to advertise them. These boundaries nevertheless allowed for the offering of a wide range of goods. Nor did these limitations discourage the papers from soliciting advertisers and touting their power to increase sales by reaching consumers. Even the ad agency Compañia Anunciadora Mexicana used the radical *El Diablito Bromista* to offer its services to the public.[139] The press advertised products and services that catered to working-class sociability and entertainments in addition to medicines, medical services, clothing, and home furnishings. In each instance they were conscious of price, message, and utility for the target audience.

Given the squalid state of housing for the poor of Mexico City one understands why working-class consumers sought so much companionship and entertainment in establishments of commercialized leisure. Commonly advertised venues included cafés, *neverias*, and restaurants, including those "served by young ladies."[140] More frequent were penny press ads for pulquerías, cantinas, figones, and other drinking establishments, which were sites of working-class sociability and bonding.[141] One could, of course, buy both imported and domestic alcohol from a variety of stores.[142]

Newspapers injected themselves into this aspect of their readership's life and spectacularized it. They did this through such means as *La Guacamaya's* contest for the best pulquería, in which enthusiasts sent in coupons voting for their favorite establishment. Started at the end of June 1904, by September 1 the leader El Ancla had received 1,417 votes while runner up El Sueño de Amor had garnered 1,000. By mid-December El Ancla reached 6,660 votes while El Atrevido assumed second place with 6,603 votes.[143]

These establishments were also hubs of working-class consumption, spaces in which not only pulque and increasingly beer and falsified liquors were consumed, but also where vendors peddled knickknacks and novelty items as well as the ubiquitous machine-rolled cigarettes of El Buen Tono, La Tabacalera Mexicana, and La Cigarrera Mexicana. These cigarette companies, as discussed in chapter 1, targeted a number of their brands at the lower classes. La Cigarrera claimed that its products were "preferred by the working classes," while La Tabacalera took a page from Dr. Hernández Ortíz as it wrote ads such as the one in which it claimed, "Police commit as many legal infractions as smokers choose 'Flor de Canela' [brand cigarettes]."[144] La Tabacalera Mexicana advertised the most in the penny press, often inserting lengthy, humorous articles under the guise of actual stories.[145]

Commercialized leisure for the readership extended far beyond the drinking holes. Bullrings, cinema salons, and theaters all placed advertisements in the press.[146] At least eight circuses advertised, although interestingly the popular Orrin circus did not, even though its star, Ricardo Bell, Mexico's most famous clown, did when he struck out on his own.[147] Popular nationalism stands out in these ads, as each circus vied to claim the status of being the most Mexican. The Circos Treviño, Guerrero, Victoria, and others made this claim to distinguish themselves from American circuses entering the capital.[148] Other than ownership, this meant shunning the three-ring circus in favor of the traditional single ring, and the Gran Circo Victoria's claim to have a Mexican clown (U. Noceda, aka "Tonche") likely sought to draw attention to Bell's foreign origin.[149] As with the pulquerías, newspapers such as *El Diablito Bromista* placed themselves into the lives of their readership, in this case by offering discount coupons to the circus that reduced the price from twenty to fifteen centavos.[150]

The technology of photography also grabbed the imagination of Mexico's working classes. The heaviest advertiser was the Gran Fotografia Daguerre, located in the heart of the city shopping district, Number 16, Puente de San Francisco.[151] They invited readers to come and visit their photo exhibitions, offered gold-leaf framing, and charged fifty centavos for a dozen miniatures, ten centavos for larger sizes, and twenty-five centavos for portraits, all well within the reach of semi-skilled and skilled workers. Of course, the store also offered a number of higher-priced options.

Advertisements in the penny press also reveal a working class that devoured cheap novels. The Biblioteca Brillante offered two novels for one centavo, including *Una victima del gran mundo* and *La esposa del muerto*.[152] Samuel Sánchez sold racy "Novelas Prohibidas" for two centavos, describing them as "Dramas íntimos del Amor. Misterios del Amor en la Mujer. Todo por el Amor!" Reflecting how quickly and how far new printing technologies trickled down, Sánchez noted that the novels were made of high-quality paper (a dubious claim), with color photoengravings.[153] The "immense selection of [chromolithographic] calendars for the New Year" advertised by a printing company reinforces this technology diffusion.[154] Other novels and offerings were more expensive, up to twenty-five centavos. The single most popular novel advertised was *Los 41*.[155] Rather than being completely fictitious, *Los 41* narrated and sensationalized the scandal rocking the Porfirian elite after forty-one sons of prominent families were caught at a transvestite ball. The fascination of the lower classes with this event offers intriguing possibilities for studies of sexuality and gender as well as the mass-cultural means by which *los de arriba* and *los de abajo* constructed their understanding of each other. Both *La Cagarruta* and *Don Cucufate* offered readers coupons to purchase the account for only fifteen centavos at their offices.[156] The latter described it as "a sensational Mexican novel. A true and graphic relation of the scandalous queer dance [*baile de maricones*] in La Paz Street." It added that readers should rush their requests for the few copies remaining, noting that they constituted the last of the first edition of the novel, "which has been so well-accepted across the Republic." This last point about a national audience is important, as the vendors of this novel and others all offered to mail book orders anywhere in the republic for ten centavos more per copy. As with so many other products, booksellers relied on the agency system to distribute their product, with Samuel Sánchez soliciting "agents in all of the Republic" and another seller offering its agents discounts of 25 percent on orders larger than a dozen copies.[157] What becomes obvious from these sales as well as the penny press itself is that by the mid-Porfiriato literacy had become relatively common among the lower classes and literature an essential transmitter of popular culture.

Purveyors of medicines and medical services also sought to reach a market through the penny press. Notably, the number and variety of ads were less than in more mainstream publications. All of the purveyors except one advertised Mexican rather than imported products.[158] One possible reason for the limited print advertisement is that Mexican products tended to rely on other forms of advertising, such as "snake-oil salesmen," who were known to draw crowds on urban streets. The most prolific advertiser was Dr. Enrique Hernández Ortíz, who placed ads for his "Pildoritas Antibiliosas" in five penny press journals.[159] Particularly humorous, his ads reflected the concerns and anger of his potential clientele toward the injustices and abuses of Porfirian modernization. One ad, titled "Cosas Imposibles," listed dozens of impossibilities in modern

Mexico, including *El Imparcial* telling the truth, electric trams no longer killing people, a policeman who did not beat his victims, a federal deputy who spoke against the government, effective suffrage, labor recruiters (*coyotes*) who possessed noble instincts, and finally, the ineffectiveness of Dr. Enrique Hernández Ortíz's Antibilious Pills.[160] Another example of how poorer Mexicans accessed modern forms of medicine comes from the ads for Dr. Gual. With the coupon attached to his advertisement and twenty-five centavos he offered the presenter both a consultation and free medicine. Without the coupon he offered private consultations between nine in the morning and noon for a peso or general consultations between three and six o'clock for fifty centavos.[161] This description of his practice places Dr. Gual at the lowest tier of the westernized medical system in place during the Porfiriato.[162] The real surprise in this field comes from the presence of ads for Dr. S. S. Hall's Instituto Eléctrico Medico, located on Coliseo Viejo.[163] Dr. Hall advertised heavily in the mainstream press about the healthful benefits of his electric belts and electricity in general.[164] Advertising from at least 1900 until the Revolution, the longevity of his business suggests his success in the capital. In light of this, his attempts at penetrating such a seemingly unpromising market raise questions about how contemporaries viewed the consumption capacity of their society.

Advertisers in the press offered products ranging from the predictable to the startling, given our assumptions about the Porfirian popular classes. Candle factories offering products for religious obligations as well as domestic use understandably found a market for their solicitations.[165] Life insurance offered by La Mexicana Life Insurance Company to workers piques interest, while the funeral service ads of La Compañia Nacional de Inhumaciones display a likely unintentional black humor, as they offer free caskets to the indigent and a discount for workers (or, more likely, their families) who present a copy of the advertisement.[166] Ads for sewing machine repairs bolster the importance of the sewing machine as an integral business technology among the working classes.[167] Equally intriguing are the ads for the Compañia Tortillera Mexicana, "seeking 200,000 individuals of both sexes to consume [our] clean and delicious tortillas."[168]

Ads for clothing and accessories figured prominently in the pages of the newspapers. Mexican hatmakers (*sombrererías*) advertised regularly, not a surprising fact given the importance of the sombrero to the identity and honor of the Mexican male.[169] The presence of ads for *platerías*, or silver shops, elicits no sense of wonder, as silver decorated hats, boots, and jackets.[170] Haberdashery shops (*mercerías*) popped up occasionally, supplying outfits for a male clientele, from gloves and neckties to shirts and hats.[171] Ads for *ropa hecha*, or ready-made clothing stores suggest the degree to which the working class had begun to patronize fixed-location stores rather than open markets for their essentials.[172]

Although popular consumption patterns differed from those of the more affluent, particularly in the realm of home furnishings, a surprisingly high number of retailers for these items marketed quite heavily in the penny press. Wallpaper, wood furniture, and crystal ware sought a clientele.[173] Blas Pahisa y Compañía offered an inventory, including wardrobes, trousseaux, dressers, nightstands, beds, and mattresses.[174] The bed factory El Vulcano offered "an immense selection" of tin and iron beds as well as mattresses in "all sizes and prices."[175] El Vulcano was probably the largest bed frame maker in the republic and advertised heavily in the mainstream press, both alone or, often, cross-advertising with the El Buen Tono cigarette company in its famous cartoons, which frequently ended up with the hero smoking a Canela Pura brand cigarette and drinking a Moctezuma brand beer while relaxing on a Vulcano brand bed. Given the competition between the cigarette companies around this time period it should come as no surprise that just as El Vulcano teamed up with El Buen Tono, the competitor La Tabacalera Mexicana should do the same with the bed maker La Industrial. In one such ad on the front page of *El Diablito Bromista* a *charro* smokes a Flor de Canela while lying on a bed from La Industrial.[176]

When historians speak of Porfirian modernization on a social and cultural level they often point to the consumption of imported goods by the middle and upper classes. This assumption has a considerable element of truth. Imported goods (and establishments selling them) were the most commonly advertised goods in the big dailies and weeklies. As new products and not "necessaries," they needed to find a market. They had the budgetary resources to do it, and newspapers did hit their target demographics. Beyond advertising visibility, the actual quantity and variety of foreign goods entering Mexico during the Porfiriato was impressive. Their element of "foreignness" marked them as items of social display and conspicuous consumption. For this reason historical accounts list off displays of foreign finery in the form of clothing, carriages, automobiles, phonographs, and of course, those famous banquet menus.[177]

Yet these accounts overlook the banal and quotidian. They focus on the extravagant and on only the largest papers thought both to carry advertisements for these goods and to reach the respectable classes who consumed them. Less glamorous yet monumental domestic production and consumption transformations go unnoticed or at least unrelated. Domestic light manufacturing of consumer goods and foreign investment in their production expanded considerably during the Porfiriato, making local production more responsive and more capable of filling domestic consumer demand in areas including food, textiles, cigarettes, pulque, beer, and furniture, among others—exactly those items advertised in the penny press and, to a lesser degree, in the pages of their competitors.[178] We should keep in mind that most Mexicans could not afford on a daily basis the imported clothing, food, and other goods that were heavily advertised in the newspapers.

Instead, historians and other commentators of the period trot out a list of stock luxury items when discussing Porfirian-era commodities because their seeming incongruity within the host country offers a delicious shock value. It also provides a convenient device by which to express disgust as well as to parody the Porfirian elite. Focusing on "luxury" and "foreignness" makes the attack easy. It makes consumerism, and by extension capitalism, appear imported and not something with which good Mexicans associated. This ahistorical approach should be reconsidered, given that Mexicans have been importing many of their consumer goods from Europe since the Conquest. By using the familiar trope of associating luxury with decadence and femininity, writers portray the consumers of these goods as demonstrating their unsuitability as leaders. Of course, these consumers—always elite—are typically portrayed as engaged in a wholesale adoption of foreign goods and meaning, never an adaptation.

In most cases, for authors of these portrayals the meaning and consumer of these goods are fixed. The label "import" becomes conflated with "elite" and "luxury." Rarely if ever do they consider that meaning is fungible, that consumption is less about the purchase than the possession of a good—what the consumer does with it.

Consider the phonograph. By all accounts it was an imported good targeted at the elite and especially the gente decente as yet another indicator of the bourgeois obsession with domesticity and the increasing role of the house interior as a public display of social status.[179] President Díaz himself received a phonograph finished with gold leaf and a personal inscription from Edison himself, a clear indication of both the target market for the good and Edison's grasp of the social phenomenon of trickle-down emulation.[180]

Yet the phonograph quickly became a staple of popular urban culture. Too expensive for working-class individuals to own, phonographs achieved widespread diffusion among the popular classes through the entrepreneurs who set up the music boxes on the streets and attached headphones or charged crowds for the thrill of hearing recorded voices.[181] As mentioned earlier with the patent applications, advertising also picked up the phonograph as a medium and incorporated it as a street attraction. One editorial complaint about these phonograph *ambulantes* conveys this transformation: "We earnestly call the attention of the authorities to the itinerant phonographs which are a veritable danger to public health and morality. Outside of the skin maladies which they claim to cure, the phonographs produce popular songs [*chansons ordinaires*] that perhaps delight street urchins but are an attack on public morality. We ask the police to control the repertoire and to conduct surveillance close to the street empresarios."[182] Advertising in the penny press supports this diffusion and cooption of this imported luxury. Edison's agent, Jorge Alcalde, advertised phonographs and cinema projectors—which other imported bourgeois entertainment transformed into a popular form.[183] More assertive proof of the Mexicanization and popularization of the phonograph comes from the advertising of Joaquin Espinosa, located on Calle Tacuba. He offered "a complete selection of talking machines, all classes and prices." More importantly, he reveals a domestic recording industry as he highlights "popular recordings [*fonogramas populares*], pressed by Sres. Rosales y Murillo."[184] Phonographs are but one example of how certain imported goods, even supposed luxury goods, found a much deeper market than is traditionally assumed.

By this constant reworking of consumer goods and the texts used to sell them—advertising—Porfirian social groups generated the cultural meaning that provided an identity for both the self and the world around them. We can observe this process by discarding traditional notions of cultural production, diffusion, and adoption as well as by embracing a more ecumenical definition of sources. The rewards include unequivocal evidence of a broad-based culture of consumption. Deeply fractured, this consumer market included a working-class consumer culture. The acceptance of the market economy as well as modernizing consumer goods did not imply an acceptance of Porfirian policies. Instead, through

the emission and consumption of cultural meaning attached to the
advertising and consumer goods that increasingly defined the visual
reality of the city, competing social groups developed multiple images of
possible urban modernity. Consumerism transformed public and private
physical space in the capital; advertising and the urban press provided a
portion of the major narrative and the perceptual filters for capitalinos to
evaluate the transformation. Envisioning the city as a cultural creation
constructed through efforts to realize social and political objectives, one
better understands how the daily actions and choices of a multitude of
businesses, ad agents, marketing innovators, lithographers, printers,
journalists, and consumers—not just "the State"—made the city in some
degree their own. Rather than simple dichotomies of consumers versus
nonconsumers, mindless modernizers versus unflinching traditional-
ists, I argue that the competing visions of Mexico City were all modernizing, merely debating over the pace, strategy, and social structure of
the change. This was a competition over how—not whether—to shape
the future of the city. And in the case of such a highly centralized polity
as the Mexican Republic—in which the capital overwhelmingly concen-
trates political, religious, economic and cultural influence—the significance of portraying the most accepted image takes on added resonance.
As goes the capital, so, too, goes the nation when it comes to envisioning
oneself as part of an imagined community.

Chapter 3

CAPITAL INVESTMENTS

Porfirian Department Stores and the Evolution of Mexico City Retailing

NOTHING MADE MODERNITY MORE TANGIBLE FOR URBAN MEXICANS than the department store. Born in 1891, midway through the Porfiriato, the Mexican department store signaled a maturing and deepening consumer market capable of supporting no less than nine such stores by the Revolution. Respectable society and their political leadership invested themselves deeply in these institutions. Stocked with the goods of a modern national and global economy, serving as an institution of the gente decente, and securing an urban transformation program jointly undertaken by the state and private capital, the department store symbolized the apparent triumph of the Porfirian modernization project and the ascendance of its dominant class. The department store functioned as an essential cultural primer, educating its customers on how to look, behave, think, and therefore *be* modern. Department stores marked the latest refinement in a transnational process whereby members of modern nation-states learned that citizenship meant engaging in proper consumption activities as well as production.

Still, the history of what most consider the "classic" department store in Porfirian Mexico is in its infancy.[1] While Porfirians chattered incessantly about the significance of department stores, the academic historiography addresses this issue only tangentially. John Lear and others touch on the stores' labor relations but most scholars dismiss them as elite institutions.[2] Only Jürgen Buchenau, in his research on Casa Boker, the famous German hardware store in Mexico, has given the department store its due as a modernizing institution in Porfirian Mexico.[3]

Casa Boker, praised by President Díaz as "one of the best ornaments of the capital and a demonstration of its culture," was undoubtedly a department store.[4] It had distinct merchandising sections, although the Bokers emphasized hardware and only grudgingly moved into other product lines. Moreover, they did not pursue modern advertising and display techniques until much later in the Porfiriato. What this study considers is the stores along the lines of the Bon Marché in Paris or Wanamakers in Philadelphia. Such stores maintained an inventory weighed heavily toward a mix of garments, fashion accessories, and home furnishings, among other items, as well as employing modern advertising and display techniques designed to cultivate desire. Often mentioned but never carefully examined, the Porfirian department store and, more generally, the evolution of retailing in nineteenth-century Mexico remain poorly understood. Part of this absence in the historiography stems from the difficulty of writing business histories in Mexico. Mexican family companies and corporations alike are far more guarded with their archives than other North American firms, assuming records even exist.[5] Fires, neglect, and the troubles of the Revolution further diminished sources.[6] These difficulties with sources, combined with the ideological imperatives of the Porfirian Black Legend produced by the Revolution, continue to shape the popular image of Porfirian department stores as vendors of imported goods and preserves of the elite who could afford them. This stereotype, like any other, possesses an element of truth, but this chapter will demonstrate that department stores were far more complicated institutions than the standard characterization allows.

A variety of sources help to answer questions of store ownership, staffing, customers, retailing practices, provenance of goods sold, and cultural role in Porfirian society. Despite the lack of studies in Mexico, since the early 1980s historians of Europe and the United States have enriched an existing historiography of department stores in these centers of modern consumerism by incorporating social and cultural dimensions into their work.[7] These establish a baseline of comparison with stores established in "peripheral" nations such as Mexico. Newspapers, including those of the American and French colony, join travelers' accounts, commercial directories, and the archives of Finance Minister José Yves Limantour in piecing together the characteristics of general retailing as well as department stores. Rare access to the surviving *copiadores* of the Palacio de Hierro department store provides insight into the internal workings of arguably the most important of these stores and verifies secondary accounts. Finally, a surge of interest in regional history in France supports this endeavor. Over the past three decades historians of the Barcelonnette region in southeastern France have marshaled findings in local and Parisian archives to account for the nearly incredible role of the Barcelonnette immigrants in the economic development of Mexico prior to the Revolution in 1910.[8]

This cultural history strives for inclusivity, taking into account not only how department stores participated in the production of meaning but also the social, economic, business, technological, and political dimensions of these institutions.[9] An introductory case study of the Centro Mercantil inauguration serves to demonstrate the cultural and symbolic meaning these institutions possessed for the gente decente and the Porfirian regime. What follows is an overview analysis of the department stores of Mexico City (and, to some degree, those throughout the republic). Consideration of ownership, organization, product sourcing, financing, employees, clientele, and a range of marketing techniques precedes a concluding observation on the place of these institutions within a broader commercialization of the city and Mexican society.

Inaugurations

Department store inauguration ceremonies reflected both the kind of society Porfirians desired and their perception of the cultural utility of these institutions. They acted as "dramatic statements of the dominant culture" in much the same manner as colonial viceregal processions or contemporary elite-sponsored public spectacles such as charity kermesses or increasingly secularized and commercialized holiday festivities.[10] In these celebrations Porfirians staged a drama projecting their cultural principles and categories as they acted out a world organized the way they saw it. Specifically, through the use of goods they expressed gender roles, class hierarchies, and—ever an issue in Mexican modernization plans—racial solutions. This enactment served both to reaffirm their beliefs and to educate onlookers—whether they be in attendance or reading about it the following day in the newspapers. Unlike other time-specific "rituals of rule" (including the World's Fair exhibitions analyzed by Mauricio Tenorio-Trillo), the stages of these cultural dramas remained.[11] Department stores became permanent fixtures in the urban geography, their cultural impact continuous.

The inauguration of the Centro Mercantil offers an exemplary introduction to the grafting of commerce onto public rituals of domination.[12] The Centro hosted its party on the cusp of the new century, September 2, 1899, and—more importantly—only two weeks before the purse strings loosened for celebrations surrounding President Díaz's birthday and national independence. Surging crowds at the downtown intersection of Tlalpaleros and Monterilla made transit a near impossibility. Granted, at five in the afternoon on *any* day, even on a Saturday, the traffic flow at this southwest corner of the Zócalo could never be described as uncongested. The inauguration merely made a bad situation worse. Even the vigilant presence of a mounted gendarmerie unit could barely contain the unpredictability of the "enormous crowd of the curious."

The building itself generated a sense of civic pride, and its sheer size compounded the sense of spectacle surrounding the ceremony. Its architecture unabashedly stamped Porfirian taste on the physical space of the

Figure 13. The Centro Mercantil department store viewed from the Zócalo. Source: Archivo General de la Nación, Fondo Instrucción Pública y Bellas Artes, Colección F. Miret, exp. 14.

city. Although not the first department store in the city, it could now boast, however briefly, to be the largest. The first of its three storefronts occupied one-third of the Portal de Mercaderes, then wrapped its four stories of glass and columns around the first full block of Tlalpaleros Street before concluding its presence on the equally trendy Palma Street (figure 13). Twelve-foot-high glass display windows housed the latest in imported and domestic finery as well as Mexican flags and bunting in the national colors. This elegance and progressive spirit defined the internal as well as the external qualities of the new edifice. Upon entering the foyer the eyes of visitors would be drawn to the grand staircase before them. Italian white marble steps and burnished mahogany railings divided to deliver shoppers to departments on the left or the right side of the second and third floors. Before ascending they could peruse the flawless glass display cases of each department, all artfully arranged and beautifully lit with odor- and soot-free electric incandescent light, supplemented by arc lighting for the inaugural event. High above the entrance way an enormous stained-glass window complete with the monogram of the store provided more light and color for the interior. An electric elevator transported shoppers and goods to the upper floors.[13] Among other conveniences, the Centro Mercantil, reportedly emulating the Louvre department store in Paris, installed a dining room offering a free buffet and refreshments.

Through the hoi polloi strode the leadership of the city and nation. The political importance of the event could not have been clearer. A veritable "Who's Who" of Mexican society appeared for the champagne lunch and tour, upstaged only by the star power of the attending President Díaz and most of his ministers, District Governor Guillermo W. de Landa y Escandón, and an assortment of other high functionaries and members of the foreign diplomatic corps. Each guest received a ribbon of national colors attached to a commemorative medal: on one side, the Virgin of Guadalupe; on the reverse, images of Centro Mercantil president José de Teresa y Miranda and two other top officials.

The ritual representation of a hierarchical society unified through noblesse oblige began with plate glass separating the symbolic head of Mexican society within the store and the body without. Days earlier, members of the assembled elite had received from Teresa y Miranda coupons valid for free clothing redeemable at the inauguration. The city's elite were to distribute the coupons among the urban poor. The recipients, numbering between five hundred and three thousand, depending on the account, now filed one by one into the store to receive their gifts. Officially this act of charity served to bring prosperity to the new establishment, but beneath this lay a pattern of action typical of Porfirian elites at their public ceremonies. Selfless acts by the individual or, in this case, private enterprise, theoretically negated the need for organized state assistance and reaffirmed the historical, indeed Biblical, social covenant by which the poor traded obedience and deference in return for the protection of the powerful. Moreover, the choice of clothing as a gift highlights the perceived pedagogical role of consumption in the Porfirian modernizing vision and underscores the unity of vision shared by the political and commercial leadership of the period. True national progress required not only economic but also cultural modernization. The need to shift the behavioral and consumption patterns of the lower classes to achieve visually the idealized efficiency and well-ordered society of more advanced North Atlantic nations antedated the Porfiriato, but it is during this period that the Mexican elite had the wherewithal and cultural momentum to make a concerted effort to educate their social inferiors with a variety of carrot-and-stick approaches.

As to be expected, President Díaz personified the national paterfamilias or *patrón* of the nation at this event. Less expected was his part as the nation's shopkeeper, for not only did he distribute ten of the clothing coupons prior to the event, he also stood behind a shop counter to receive the first recipient. Handing out cuts of high-quality percale fabric, he performed his role of benevolent provider in this high social theater. Perhaps suffering flashbacks from his earlier days as a shop assistant in Oaxaca, he repeated the act only a few times before turning over the chore to "high-ranking [male] employees," who added shoes and other components necessary in the assemblage of a respectable outfit.[14]

A respectable but not fancy outfit. Percale was the fabric of the Porfirian working class: durable and aesthetically civilizing, distinct from traditional and coarser Indian cottons.[15] In 1892 Emile Chabrand specifically noted this hierarchy of clothing in the *cajones de ropa* of the capital.[16] He described the stocking of the *tarima*, the massive wooden shelving system located behind the shop counter (the *mostrador*) that separated customer from attending clerk. On the lowest level employees stocked "Indians and percales," with each ascending level supporting a better class of material.[17] The inauguration ritual thereby reinforced traditional social hierarchies with the idea of proper consumption wherein each citizen consumed appropriate to his or her social station.

The tarima serves as a metaphor not only of class but also of racial attitudes. Mexican society has always interwoven categories of race and class as tightly as the fibers used to make those percale and "Indian" fabrics (in fact, probably tighter). Historically, darker skin signaled a lower social and economic class that those advancing up the social ladder sought to lighten through the use of better clothing, skin-whitening chemicals, and—in the case of the colonial period—the outright purchase of official documentation declaring the bearer as criollo, or of Spanish and not Indian blood.[18] In Porfirian Mexico, the drive for economic progress required a labor pool imbued with the productive habits (attitudes toward hygiene, time, thrift, and sobriety) and consumption patterns (diet, clothes, leisure activities, home utensils, and adornments) associated with the apparent success of Western European and North American workers. For both foreign and domestic observers Indians represented the antithesis of this model and a drag on the development of internal production and consumption markets.

"Indian" cloth in Mexico exemplifies nineteenth-century globalization while illustrating the shifting meaning of words. *Indian* refers not to Mexico's indigenous population but rather to the South Asian origin of the printed calico imported into England and France. Industrialized mills in Manchester, Alsace, and Rouen destroyed the textile economy in India but retained the name for this type of cloth.[19] Mexico imported this material for much of the nineteenth century, but by the last decade its modernized and expanded textile industry satisfied most of the domestic demand. Coarser than percale, this calico or Indian fabric was popular with the indigenous population in Mexico, and I suspect that this situation transferred the meaning of "Indienne" cloth from the Asian subcontinent to the native population of Mexico. Percale is usually a much finer fabric than calico, hence the prestige attached to percale bedsheets. However, Porfirian Mexican textile mills produced differing qualities and a cheaper and more durable version of percale became the common material for both the uniforms that clothed the thousands of female workers employed in the modern manufacturing sector as well the daily clothes that marked the humble respectability of members of the lower economic rungs of respectable society.

While switching from Indian to percale fabric did not necessarily change one's situation economically, it did so culturally, constituting a horizontal move on the social ladder. Such a move—voluntary or not—suggested the renouncement of economically and culturally backward indigenous attitudes and behaviors and identified the wearer as a participant in the Porfirian modernization program and thus a pretender to membership within the gente decente.

This emphasis on outward appearances, so important to the Porfirian image construction of a modern society, provides a clue as to why contemporary society placed such a premium on consumption generally, and department stores specifically, as civilizing agents. Department stores, with their attraction of a clientele spanning most of the social spectrum and professed direction toward the "democratization of luxury," seemed the ideal institutions through which to achieve this. Perhaps one of the starkest examples of this common attitude comes from Auguste Génin in his *Notes sur le Mexique*, written at the end of the Porfiriato. Génin, a prominent member of the French community, had lived in Mexico most of his life and had carved out a career as both a businessman and an indefatigable booster of the Porfirian regime. In *Notes sur le Mexique* he expresses Porfirian positivist and social Darwinian attitudes as he portrays the overwhelming success of Díaz's modernization program.[20] At the same time, he positions the French community as integral to this achievement, particularly in the modernizing of the populace, as he discloses characteristically French attitudes toward their global civilizing mission and fascination with exotic cultures. He masterfully combines mutually reinforcing visual and written texts, most notably the juxtaposition of department stores with images of nearly naked Indians or "traditional Mexican types" such as the China Poblana. His visual implication becomes statement in his narrative that these charming but backward Mexican categories will soon become little more than museum displays under the civilizing force of modern consumption. "Under the equalizing process that occurs to all those who have experienced the displays of the Palacio de Hierro, the Ciudad de Londres, or the windows of the Fábricas Universales . . . or the Importador—which are the Bon Marchés, the Louvres, and the Printemps of the Mexican capital—the *Jarrochos* of Veracruz, the *Apaches* of Sonoras, the gracious *Poblanas* . . . and the *Indias* of Amatlán, all are white under their veils, having disappeared forever."[21] Génin simply expressed the prevalent hope that department stores and the modern consumption and fashion that they promoted could homogenize, whiten, and modernize the citizenry of the republic so that it could take its proper place among the fraternal order of civilized nations.

The lucky recipients of presidential service at Centro Mercantil's inauguration were all of low social class and probably of Indian or mestizo racial background. Moreover, all were female. This exclusivity of gender begs for an explanation. One could glibly claim that confining the gift to a single sex made the distribution task easier. Another reason could be that Díaz simply liked young ladies. A final explanation could be the visual symbolism of father Díaz providing for the daughters of the nation. In any case, the exclusion of males in this public performance neatly represented the intersection of a growing consumer culture with gender roles idealized by gente decente society.

Nineteenth-century bourgeois culture, Porfirian, Victorian, or Gilded Age, separated gender by defining spheres or realms as masculine and feminine, public and private, production and consumption.[22] In his analysis of conspicuous consumption, Thorstein Veblen suggests that one of the most important expressions of a family's social position and respectability stems from the appearance of female members, particularly the wife.[23] In the most simplistic form of this vision men produced in the public sphere so that women could consume for the family and develop the private, or domestic, sphere.[24] The fact that women increasingly frequented the quite public downtown shopping areas to acquire the goods for their families readily belies the shaky practicality of this ideal. Nevertheless, the image of masculine Díaz providing for his extended family of female consumers seems to make this ideal explicit. Another fact supports this analysis: the strict gender segregation and male-to-female direction of this charitable aid stands in sharp contrast with most noncommercial charity events, where elite women catered to the poor, usually of both sexes.[25]

Press accounts of the event reflect this gendering of consumption. Although husbands undoubtedly accompanied wives and fathers daughters, when it came to reporting the effects of the tour the guests consisted of "a great number of ladies and misses" freely roaming through the departments, assisted by "a veritable army of personnel" of both sexes. "Elegant ladies" received much attention as they naturally became "seduced by the value and elegance of the . . . articles" illuminated and displayed so professionally in their glass cases.[26] The only male references described how Díaz, accompanied by the president of the corporation, José de Teresa y Miranda, "appeared enchanted on his stroll through the store."[27]

The celebrants continued until eight o'clock after dispensing with the charity cases. They interwove their necessary first purchases with a champagne lunch and a tour of the store. In commercialized rituals of rule, an act of consumption necessarily accompanied the symbolic representations of a modern, hierarchical society.

This inauguration, expressing the degree to which department stores stocked Porfirian ideals and dreams of national progress, was far from an isolated event. Similar celebrations marked the renovations and expansions of existing establishments as well as the entrance of new stores into the commercial fray. In May 1907 no less than six department stores in Mexico City had recently inaugurated or were soon to inaugurate new or extensively expanded and redesigned buildings. By this time the city of barely four hundred thousand possessed nine true, purpose-built department stores and at least fourteen other major dry-goods stores organized on the department store principle in which distinct sections sold clothing, accessories, home furnishings, and other goods.[28] This business development extended throughout the major cities of the republic, including Guanajuato, San Luís de Potosí, Puebla, Monterrey, Chihuahua, and Guadalajara, where the October 1899 inauguration of the newly renovated Fábricas de Francia prompted one commentator to sniff, "It is unnecessary to state that the interior is appointed luxuriously and in the style of the great stores of Paris."[29] In the capital, Díaz's wife—Carmen Romero Rubio de Díaz—seemed to grace any important inauguration missed by her husband. In May 1903 El Paje, the new *almacén de novedades* on the corner of Plateros and Empedradillo on the Zócalo proudly announced that Carmelita was their first customer. Not long before she had enjoyed guest-of-honor status at the inauguration of the high-end jewelry store La Perla, for whose ceremony the owners (the Diener brothers) sent out nearly two thousand invitations.[30] The mixture of high society and high politics appeared unfailingly to characterize these historical events. New buildings, new business technologies, and new shopping venues provided Díaz with both the opportunity and forum to announce the realization of his regime's development programs.

Modernizing Attributes

In the flourishing consumer culture of late nineteenth- and early twentieth-century Mexico City the department store stood out as a modernizing institution par excellence. Their association with the metropolitan centers of Europe and North America enhanced their appeal to the modernizing mindset of Mexican society. Nearly every aspect of these stores, from their origins to their ownership and their advertising, reinforced this impression.

Department stores were not a Mexican creation, but Mexico was in the global vanguard of their development. Although both New York and Paris have claims to the first purpose-built department store, Aristide Boucicault's Bon Marché, constructed in 1869, served as the template for the iconic institution of the twentieth century.[31] Over the next two decades now-famous stores such as the Louvre or Le Printemps in France or Macy's, Wanamakers, Lord & Taylor, and Marshall Field's in the United States were established. Department stores became transnational phenomena, appearing first in leading centers of cultural modernity—though not necessarily industrial centers—before establishing outposts around the globe.[32] Comparatively speaking, Mexicans, with their first department store in 1891 and five before 1900, were indeed "civilized consumers" on the cutting edge of Western cultural progress. Although Timothy Eaton established Canada's first store in 1883, Germany waited until the 1890s and England until 1909.[33] South American centers of modernity also lagged behind. Brazil did not receive its first store until after 1900, and both Santiago, Chile, and Buenos Aires, Argentina, waited until 1910 for the inauguration of Gath y Chaves, despite their large markets and excruciating attention to European fashions and consumption patterns.[34] The vast interior space of these buildings, their attention to visual appeal, and policies that made transactions more time-efficient and less stressful transformed shopping into a refined leisure activity and carved out a new, private social space for the ascendant class of the age: the bourgeoisie.[35]

Department stores celebrated and memorialized the transnational ascendancy of bourgeois culture that in Mexico equated with the gente decente social class. This class was as much a cultural as an economic category that represented a particular way of looking at the world. In Mexico, this worldview manifested itself in the ongoing development or modernization program that embodied the gente decente values of "thrift, sobriety, hygiene, and punctuality."[36] These values served to develop the "peaceful and working people" required for a capitalist economy and society to function.

Gente decente values were mobilized for consumption as well as production, glorifying the material abundance produced by factories, hard work, and technological prowess that made it possible for the middle class to consume. Consumption complemented production while levels of access to goods served to define an individual socially and culturally. Thus the increased production delivered by the capitalist economy and culture of the bourgeoisie fulfilled a demand for goods resulting from a centuries-long trend in Western culture in which goods and the act of consumption became increasingly important repositories of cultural meaning.[37] Importantly, one central goal of bourgeois society was improvement, often measured by manners and morals but equally by the material culture with which one surrounded oneself. Consumption not only aided economic progress but also expressed tangible evidence of improvement for the individual, the family, the nation, and humankind in general.

Department stores, therefore, were the ideal institution to further this logic. They appeared to mark the apex not only of modern retailing but also modern living as they brought together new building technologies, recent display innovations, evolving retail models, and a transformation of shopping into a leisure activity. Michael Miller best described the link between institution and social class in his study of the Bon Marché in Paris: "In its architecture it brought together the culture's commitment to functionalize its environment and the culture's irrepressible need to secure solidity and respectability for its works. In its values it flaunted the culture's identification with appearances and material possessions, reaffirmed the culture's dedication to productivity, personified the culture's pretensions to an egalitarian society. The department store was the bourgeoisie's world."[38] Furthering the development and success of the department store and a broader urban culture of consumption were demographic trends toward urbanization, state policies of urban renewal favoring commercial development, an economic pattern that steadily raised urban wages as well as increased the number of those reliant upon wage labor, and social and cultural investments in goods and the pursuit of those goods.

Ownership and Organization

Mexico's advanced status in global retailing owes a great deal to owners with French names such as Tron, Ebrard, Proal, Ollivier, Reynaud, Signoret, Donnadieu, and Robert, who came from a single region in France—the Barcelonnette. During the Porfiriato this community controlled the national garment and fashion trade.[39] Barcelonnettes established eight of the nine Porfirian department stores and owned all of them after Sebastian Robert (founder of La Valenciana) bought out the shareholders of the Centro Mercantil in 1901.[40] Barcelonnette stores brought the cultural cachet of France to Mexico. Keep in mind that at the end of the nineteenth century Paris was the uncontested consumer capital of the world in terms of dictates of good taste generally and feminine fashion specifically.[41] Store names reveal the French—or at least Latinate—influence in their fanciful or descriptive qualities: the Iron Palace, the Importer, the Port of Veracruz, the Surprise, and the New World. A parallel may be drawn with the whimsical appellations of Mexico's popular drinking holes, the pulquerías, which so fascinated contemporary travel writers as well as several of today's historians.[42] This contrasts with the Anglo-American influence in South American stores exhibited by their adoption of names of company proprietors, such as Gath y Chavez and Harrod's.

Business organization of the department stores weighted heavily toward the partnership model. This was partly a function of Mexican commercial law and partly a preference among the Barcelonnette community for spreading both the risks and benefits of their ventures. Still, two firms eventually adopted the new organizational form of the joint stock company (the Sociedad Anónima, or S.A.): in 1898 the Palacio de Hierro became the first retailer in the republic to do so, followed by the Puerto de Liverpool in 1907. Both companies were listed not only on the Mexican stock market—the *bolsa*—but also on the prestigious Paris bourse.

The Barcelonnette Emigration and Early Settlement

Barcelonnettes forged an extremely close-knit social and business community in Mexico. In many respects their financial and cultural support networks resembled those of other commercial emigrant communities in Mexico. They did not come to Mexico with the intent of assimilating into the host society but rather to work hard, make a fortune, and return home to marry and retire in financially secure bourgeois respectability. Marriage—particularly to a Mexican woman—was frowned upon.[43] Barcelonnette immigrants carried with them not only their social class's perceptions—most were from the middling classes—but also racial prejudices. Achieving personal enrichment and furthering the European *mission civilisatrice* merged in the Barcelonnette community. They were, as Jürgen Buchenau aptly labeled participants in this process, "trade conquistadors."[44]

The Barcelonnettes came from an isolated valley in southeastern France with a population of less than eighteen thousand. Nestled—or imprisoned—in the Basse-Alpes bordering Italy, the Barcelonnette region refers to the Ubaye valley, in which over half the population lives in the town of Barcelonnette. The town provides the name for the larger administrative arrondissement and the people from the region. The valley possessed a long tradition of economic migration that facilitated this emigration to Mexico. Historically, men would leave the valley before the winter snows came in order to peddle the products of their domestic woolens industry throughout southern France. As French industry and transportation systems expanded they increased their range and expanded their product line to include textiles of other regions, particularly those of the nearby textile center of Lyon.[45] Migration to Mexico therefore marked a simple extension of the *colporteur* tradition for residents of this economically disadvantaged valley.

Barcelonnette involvement in the Mexican retail trade long preceded the department stores. Not surprisingly, given the fashion reputation of the French and their regional economic traditions, the Barcelonnette immigrants gravitated toward investment in the textile and garment sector. The first Barcelonnette store in Mexico opened in 1821, when the Arnaud brothers, Jacques, Dominique, and Marc-Antoine, established the Cajón de Ropa de las Siete Puertas on Portacoeli Street in the capital city. Even after Jacques was brutally murdered, disemboweled, and robbed of 35,000 pesos en route to Veracruz in 1828 the remaining brothers hung on, prospered, and eventually sent home for help.[46] Three employees who answered that call would later set up their own store, El Gran Oriental, in 1838 under the Portal de las Flores on the Zócalo. The pace of immigration quickened after flooding at home in 1843 pushed young men to seek their fortunes in Mexico, a career option that became more attractive after two of the Gran Oriental owners returned home two years later with 200,000 francs each. Young Barcelonnette men and a few women swelled the community in Mexico, with almost seventy arriving in 1849 and 1850. Barcelonnettes owned forty-four businesses in Mexico by 1848, including nine clothing stores in Mexico City, Puebla, Zacatecas, Guadalajara, and Toluca. Still, between 1845 and 1852 they made up only 7.5 percent of French emigrants to Mexico.[47]

The following decades saw the number of Barcelonnettes expand to the point that Mexicans came to use the name *Barcelonnette* to label all

French. For at least the last two decades of the Porfiriato they made up 80 percent of the French community, counting for forty-eight hundred of six thousand French living in Mexico in 1910. By 1867 they ran twenty-seven clothing stores in the capital, and at the time of the Revolution they possessed a network of 214 firms trading in thirty-one cities and twenty-three states of the republic before the Revolution. While they ventured into a number of business fields they specialized in retailing and producing textiles and articles of fashion. As the new century began, 80 percent of Barcelonnette immigrants worked in garment stores.[48] So associated were the Barcelonnettes with the textile retail trade that a stock Mexican stereotype of the Frenchman was, "Vende mucha manta y hace buena cocina" (He sells a lot of cloth and cooks well).[49] The Mexican nickname for the French was "calicot," for the low-priced, printed cotton cloth that the Barcelonnette-owned garment stores sold so much of.[50]

The Barcelonnettes adapted to the Mexican market at the same time that they introduced new ideas about retailing brought with them from France. The retention of transatlantic financial and family ties ensured that subsequent successful strategies in Paris often found their way to Mexico. The early Barcelonnette retail model of low price and high turnover allowed merchants to prosper and the community to expand slowly through the 1850s. These first stores, called the traditional cajones de ropa, would gradually give way to the larger and fancier *almacenes de novedades* and eventually the *grandes almacenes* (department stores). While competitors charged that they sold commensurately low-quality goods, the Barcelonnettes were implementing the beginnings of a business model of high-volume sales on lower profit margins with origins in Western Europe that would revolutionize retailing and result in the department store.

Despite these early inroads into the Mexican market the economic position of the Barcelonnette community remained far from secure. Mexican and Spanish retailers controlled much of the retail garment trade through midcentury and offered stiff competition. Furthermore, Barcelonnette and other French merchants remained captive to German and, to a lesser extent, British wholesalers whose compatriots controlled commercial credit and transatlantic transportation.[51]

From the 1860s onward, domestic and international developments and the Barcelonnette community's deft capitalization on these events paved the way for French domination of the dry-goods trade in Mexico. The stranglehold of German and British wholesalers began to weaken in 1863 when French retailers in Mexico took advantage of Napoleon's Intervention and succeeded in establishing a French-owned steamship route directly from Saint-Nazaire to Veracruz. Seven years later the eruption of the Franco-Prussian War would prove disastrous for the French nation but allowed the French merchant community in Mexico to finally declare its independence from German middlemen. With the onset of war, French merchants boycotted the German wholesalers and a number of Barcelonnettes returned home and used their wealth to open export houses in France that extended generous credit in order to fill the vacuum. As a consequence, eighty German import houses went bankrupt and the last German textile import house in Mexico liquidated in 1892.[52] Further assisting this consolidation of French preeminence was the 1880 diplomatic reconciliation between France and Mexico.[53] In addition, the rise a decade later of the Científico faction in the Porfirian government signaled a shift toward a European counterbalance to growing concerns of American influence in Mexico. José Yves Limantour, the finance minister and most prominent member of the Científicos, enjoyed a close relationship with the Barcelonnettes. A dramatic example of this came in 1903 when Émile Meyran, a Barcelonnette director of the Centro Mercantil, returned from his native valley and presented Limantour with a live eagle from his hometown of St. Ours.[54]

Product Sourcing

One of the greatest misconceptions about Porfirian department stores is that imported goods lined their shelves and filled their displays. These stores, often perceived as institutions of the elite, were believed to retard national development by promoting the consumption of imports and limiting the growth of a domestic market for national industry. This perception fit within the economic model of Mexico as a colonial, export-oriented economy controlled by foreigners and elites who had no interest in developing internal industries or markets.[55] Recent works by Mexican economic historians such as Aurora Gómez Galvarriato Freer and Sandra Kuntz Ficker have provided convincing evidence that a domestic market and national industry did expand steadily during much of the Porfiriato.[56] American economic historian Edward Beatty has also demonstrated federal support for the growth of national industries and markets in his analysis of Porfirian economic policies such as import tariffs.[57] My own research from a retail approach supports these revisions, at least in textile manufacturing and selling.

In fact, the progressive reputation of the Barcelonnettes rested on the modernization not only of Mexican retailing but also manufacturing. Barcelonnette textile factories produced many of the clothing items sold in their stores. The movement of the Barcelonnette community into textile production strengthened their retail position. Indeed, it would eventually spur its expansion. This vertical integration of textile production and retailing marked a distinct innovation over French retailers such as the Bon Marché, whose direct involvement in production went no further than certain items in high demand being manufactured in house or in its neighboring annex building.[58] In Mexico Barcelonnette investors had staked a presence in this sector by the mid-nineteenth century, the first Barcelonnette textile mill opening in Puebla in 1831.[59] The American Civil War proved a windfall for the community, allowing its members to make hefty profits by filling the demand for troop uniforms and wisely modernizing their factories. In doing so they transformed an industry whose longstanding importance in the Mexican economy was matched by its horrendous inefficiencies. The Pax Porfiriana set the stage for the next round of Barcelonnette expansion, and in the 1880s they established new textile factories and purchased existing ones. Most notable was the formation of CIDOSA (La Compañia Industrial de Orizaba, S.A.), which incorporated a number of textile factories. It included Río Blanco, the largest and most modern facility in the country, constructed in 1892 and the scene of arguably the largest, bloodiest, and most iconic labor conflict of the Porfiriato. CIVSA (La Compañia Industrial Veracruzana, S.A.) formed in 1896 and began operations at its flagship Santa Rosa factory in 1898.[60] The Barcelonnettes also branched into hydroelectric power plants to feed the energy needs of the factories and, often, neighboring population centers. Two notable examples of this energy generation are the Rincón Grande plant paired with CIDOSA and San Ildefonso with the woolens factory of the same name.

These and other textile factories deployed modern machinery and production techniques that required a mass consumer market to absorb their goods. Not surprisingly, the owners of four of the five department stores built before 1900 happened to be founding members of CIDOSA.[61] Another group of influential Barcelonnette retailers shut out of this investment put up the money behind the subsequent CIVSA.[62] In fact, many department stores advertised on their exterior façade the names of domestic factories that supplied them. Sebastian Robert's La Valenciana, located under the Portal de las Flores, announced in large letters above its second floor, "Productos de las Fábricas de Santa Rosa y La Hormiga."[63] The Centro Mercantil likewise ran banners on its façade advertising its imports as well as "wools and cottons from the principal factories of the country."[64] Francia Maritima acted as an outlet for the woolens produced by Santa Teresa and the cottons of La Magdalena.[65] The Cajón de Sol of Denis Ollivier paired with the Rio Hondo mill to such an extent that the bankruptcy of the store in 1901 led to the sale of the factory.[66]

Palacio de Hierro archives illuminate this domestic sourcing of goods that spanned a wide variety of materials (cashmere, cotton, wool) and classes. The company contracted with a variety of mills, including La Magdalena, Miraflores, San Lorenzo, La Minerva, Rio Hondo, La Carolina, and San Ildefonso, among others. The common Barcelonnette strategy of joint mill ownership bears out in the familiar practice of those factories supplying the stores owned by investors, sometimes exclusively. La Magdalena, for example, produced primarily for the eight Barcelonnette business partnerships that owned it.[67] While Barcelonnettes did not own all the textile factories in Mexico, they did use their retailing clout to forge exclusive contracts with producers, prohibiting sales to retail competitors. One such contract was that made by eight leading retailers with the Watson Phillips Company, owner of La Minerva, for seven thousand pieces of *manta*—coarse cotton cloth—in three different classes, ranging from 3.37 to 7.75 pesos per piece. The contract concluded, "You are obligated not to sell Miraflores manta to any other buyers who may present themselves."[68] Barcelonnettes also used their economic position and social clout to push for favorable tariff policies, such as dropping the tax on raw cotton, that reflected their textile investments.[69] Palacio archives detail the extent to which store directors owned shares in various textile factories, such as CIDOSA, as well as other Porfirian businesses.[70] The achievements of domestic textile manufacturers to expand the domestic market at the expense of imports received regular adulation in the business and general press.[71] In 1900 Limantour wrote to Swiss-French financier Eduard Noetzlin on this subject: "The brilliant success achieved by the cotton textile factories established or developed in the years between 1895 and 1898 is undoubtedly owed to the skill of the owners of the retail clothing stores [*tiendas de ropa al menudeo*] who understood very well the advantages that could come from the union, under the same hands, of the manufacturing sites with the establishments that have achieved a *de facto* monopoly on retail sales [*ventas al pormenor*]."[72]

This information contradicts any assumption of department stores and other dry-goods retailers in the central commercial zone as exclusive purveyors of imported goods. Instead, the evidence demonstrates that these retail establishments were outlets for the increased capacity and diversity achieved by the domestic textile industry of the late nineteenth and early twentieth centuries. Department store shelves stocked a mix of goods produced domestically and imported from a variety of nations.

The enduring success of French Barcelonnette department stores appears counterintuitive for those familiar with Porfirian macro-economics and import statistics, which state that French imports to Mexico slid precipitously during the last two decades of the Porfiriato. The nation fell from second place among importers to a distant fourth, behind the United States, Great Britain, and Germany.[73] French commercial commentators criticized their compatriot manufacturers in France for their complacency in Mexico and around the globe. They blamed producers for relying solely on the cultural cachet of French goods to sell their products instead of advertising heavily and supporting a network of commercial agents and traveling salesmen to promote their goods as the Americans, British, and Germans had. Furthermore, the French did not—and haughtily would not—adapt to the tastes and economics of their overseas markets, a strategy that the Germans had used to great success to capture market share.[74] In the late nineteenth-century context of economic and territorial colonialism national pride conspicuously infused this struggle over foreign markets.[75] Battle imagery colored the language of global trade, metaphors that eventually translated into reality in 1914.

What explains this contradictory development of a shrinking French import presence and an ascendant French merchant class in Mexico? Pat assumptions of national identity, loyalty, and actions need reexamination. The obvious answer to this dilemma is that the Barcelonnette cart was not attached to the French manufacturing horse. French merchant communities did not live or die on the sale of French goods alone. As described above, the linkage between Barcelonnette-owned manufacturing facilities and retail outlets in Mexico illustrates a primary reason for the success of the community in the face of shrinking markets for products from the mother country. A second crucial reason is that Barcelonnette retailers sold not only domestically produced goods but also those imported from other Great Powers. A brisk transatlantic trade continued with English, German, Belgian, Swiss, and other suppliers, while American goods entered through the seaports of Veracruz and Tampico as well as via the rail lines of the Mexican Central and the Mexican National.[76] For the Barcelonnettes, business reality outweighed national loyalty. Moreover, unlike French manufacturers, Barcelonnette merchants transplanted traditional economic patterns into Mexico and established a network of Barcelonnette traveling salesmen—four times larger than that in France—to fill in the gaps of the brick-and-mortar latticework they were carefully constructing throughout the republic.[77]

In some respects the Barcelonnettes were not French at all. They distanced themselves from the rest of the French community and reserved jobs for residents of the valley to the exclusion of those from other regions of France.[78] A French national identity was far from complete in the nineteenth century, and among the Barcelonnettes its development was recent and imperfect. This resilience of their local identity explains the insularity of the Barcelonnette community in Mexico. While they pragmatically took advantage of the benefits and protections offered by French citizenship, they considered themselves Barcelonnette first and French second.

Store Finances and Banking Function

The remarkable stability and financial success of Barcelonnette department stores and fashion stores (the almacenes de novedades) furthered their image as agents of progress. The expansion projects and sheer numbers of Mexico City department stores suggest that the prosperity of the Palacio was not an isolated case. This conflicts with blanket statements on the unprofitability and overcapacity of Porfirian businesses and the scarce purchasing power of consumers made by many current American economic historians of Mexico, headed by Stephen Haber.[79]

Palacio de Hierro account books state that in 1896, two years before incorporation, twelve shareholders in the company (all French) shared 330,000 of the 520,000 pesos in net profits earned that year.[80] The rest of the earnings were plowed back into company reserves. Earnings on the sale of merchandise rose to 672,000 pesos in 1899, 751,000 in 1901, 833,000 in 1902, 1 million in 1905, and 1.2 million in 1907—the first year of a brutal depression and the last year in which information is available in surviving company books.[81] More impressive is that the market could support the expansion to full department store status not only of the Palacio but also the Puerto de Veracruz in 1894, the Puerto de Liverpool in 1898, the Centro Mercantil in 1899, and the Correo Frances by the turn of the century.[82] Investors, regardless of political philosophy, do not continue to sink money into losing propositions. Nor do companies expand repeatedly in such an environment. The balance sheets of the Palacio de Hierro reveal the lucrative potential of Porfirian merchandise retailing, much as the net profits and dividends shared by the El Buen Tono cigarette factory owners show the profitability in the tobacco-manufacturing sector.

Bankruptcies among Barcelonnette establishments were unusual. A spokesman for the North American Manufacturer's Association informed *Modern Mexico* magazine in 1897 that "Mexican laws regulating bankruptcies are very strict, and business failures are very rare indeed."[83] He claimed that no failure of any consequence had occurred in the past ten years and that business was conducted on a "very conservative basis." The operating practices of the Barcelonnette community only strengthened this general characteristic. The Barcelonnettes constructed a social and business network that provided mutual support as it spread risks and benefits. Begun in the days of the almacenes de novedades and cajones de ropa, the same principles continued through the Porfiriato. A careful selection process preceded the establishment of a new Barcelonnette store. First, only senior and capable employees established new stores. An employee's patron could loan him enough money, credit, and product to either become a traveling salesman and then set up an establishment in the interior or to directly set up a business. Or, if the patron amassed more than 100,000 francs, he was expected to retire and return to France. He would leave two-thirds of his assets to the new member of the partnership and would continue to receive a share of profits until bought out of the business. New businesses usually located in virgin or expanding markets. This resulted in a web of Barcelonnette retailers throughout the republic, branching out from the capital, where the largest firms acted as wholesalers and creditors for their protégés.[84] Most creditors did not worry even when a bankruptcy occurred. They knew that they would receive full payment from partners and family members associated with the debtor. When the Cajón de Sol, owned by Denis Ollivier, collapsed financially, J. Ollivier—owner of La Ciudad de Londres and presumably a family relation—assumed the responsibility of repaying creditors. A report of the situation noted that the liquidation was amiable and "all creditors are to be paid in full."[85]

The peculiar Mexican approach to credit, both commercial and consumer, also stabilized businesses but required deep capital reserves

on the part of owners. Successful retailing in Mexico necessitated the
lengthy extension of credit to wholesale and retail purchasers and therefore cut out smaller entrants into the field. American observers were
baffled by the widespread use of credit and lengthy terms that characterized Mexican retail trade, but most concluded that "in the end they
cover their accounts."[86] Often stores issued account statements to their
regular clients on an annual or semiannual basis. This contradicted the
retailing model in leading French stores such as the Bon Marché, which
operated on a strict cash-only basis.[87] One journal in Mexico noted that
the practice of lending credit required "immense capitalization" and
reported that a leading jewelry house had outstanding accounts totaling 100,000 pesos. On the other hand, they wrote off less than 2 percent of accounts as a result of bad debt prior to 1900.[88] The Palacio de
Hierro wrote off a paltry 9,000 pesos for 1903.[89] As a consequence of
the peso devaluation and inflation caused by Finance Minister José Yves
Limantour's transfer of the peso to the gold standard, losses climbed to
28,000 pesos in 1905 before spiking to nearly 53,000 pesos for 1906 and
finally 70,000 pesos in 1907, the last year of available data.[90] The same
terms applied between businesses.

The Palacio de Hierro also illustrates two ways by which stores may
have increased their liquid capital. In the absence of a stable Mexican
banking system the Palacio acted as a savings institution and investment vehicle for employees, Barcelonnettes, and affluent Mexicans.
For employees it offered savings accounts and loans. Such a benefit had
a moral dimension in promoting thrift as well as continuing a long
Barcelonnette tradition in which the store owner held back a portion of an employee's salary with the understanding that the accrued
sum would provide the initial investment when the employee eventually opened his own establishment. This savings and loan function for
employees was likely a common practice among department stores,
given the paternalistic organization of these institutions.[91] The letters
of department store clerk Anselme Charpenel home to his family in
the valley described how he sent home ten of the sixty pesos he earned
each month and placed another ten pesos in the store bank of the Centro
Mercantil at 6 percent interest.[92] Unfortunately the Palacio books offer
only one year of these accounts, but they suggest that the arrangement benefited employees more than the company: in 1901 employee
deposits (cuentas de empleados acreedoras) totaled 25,387 pesos, in contrast with loans to employees (cuentas de empleados deudoras) equaling

128,178 pesos.[93] Whether this imbalance was commonplace or an exception remains unknown at this point.

The banking function of the Palacio for the Barcelonnette community and beyond proved a far more lucrative proposition. In 1901 deposits totaled over 1.1 million pesos.[94] This bestowed on the Palacio a considerable degree of financial flexibility, given that its capitalization was 4 million pesos and gross earnings less than 1 million pesos at this time. Depositors tended to be French. They included famous perfumer and former Intervention soldier Paul St. Marc, lesser-knowns such as Luis Bouler and Luis Vizcarra, the influential Alfonso Ebrard of the Puerto de Liverpool store, and Louis Ollivier, depositing for the department store group Signoret Honnorat y Compañia.[95] The last two deposits suggested that other Barcelonnette dry-goods stores placed investments with the Palacio.[96] Barcelonnette firms in other business lines, such as the El Buen Tono cigarette factory, also used the banking services of the Palacio.[97] Depositors resided throughout the republic and beyond, including Barcelonnettes or their surviving spouses who had retired and returned to Paris or the valley.[98] Victor Audiffred from Guanajuato (probably a store owner given his famous last name) as well as the Lions Brothers of Puebla (who owned an almacén de novedades in that city from 1880, which they transformed into a department store in 1910) joined a long list of investors from the states.[99] The Palacio was presumably considered a secure investment and attracted deposits from women and widows of well-known families, including (among many others) the Señoras Josefa Gallardo, Victorina Garcin (deposited by Eduardo Garcin), Delfina G. de Caire, Estella Peker, Julia Maupuy, the powerful widow Génin, and the Viuda de Teresa and her daughters.[100] The famous Fortoul, Chapuy y Compañia of Guadalajara, owners of Las Fábricas de Francia department store in that city, deposited over 20,000 pesos in the name of Fortoul's wife in 1900.[101] In 1909 a Palacio director wrote the widow Chapuy that the business successors of her recently deceased husband had deposited his two hundred shares of the San Rafael paper factory and that of the Electricity and Irrigation Company with the store in the capital.[102] Earlier, in 1899, the Guadalajara firm had deposited over 24,000 pesos on behalf of two other widows.[103] The size of the deposits varied, from as low as 3,000 pesos to upwards of 50,000 pesos, with interest rates ranging from 6 to 8 percent.[104] Because the company books noted only deposits, the total balances of individual accounts remain elusive. One exception is the account of Antonio Proal in Paris, which reached over 100,000 pesos by 1906.[105] That depositors had to provide at least one month's warn-ing—and often two—before withdrawing their investments reinforces the likelihood that the Palacio invested these funds into various projects.

Employees

Department store hiring practices retained characteristics of those in the earlier cajones de ropa and almacenes de novedades while chang-ing to accommodate the increased demands of the big stores as well as Porfirian ideas of paternalism toward workers. Department stores strove to maintain a positive public impression of their institutions as establish-ments of respectability and progress through their well-publicized treat-ment of employees. This treatment involved benefits to employees such as housing, profit-sharing, and savings programs as well as the imposi-tion of moral codes of conducts. Store owners realized that their employ-ees were an important part of their strategy of "selling the store" as an institution of respectable society.[106]

Barcelonnette owners relied heavily on Barcelonnette labor. This practice hearkened back to the earliest days of the community, when emigrants from the valley exclusively staffed the stores.[107] Fellow valley emigrants, often linked by ties of family, were considered more reliable and trustworthy and were indebted both socially and financially to the owner.[108] The result was a family atmosphere (with all its personality conflicts) among store personnel. Hiring exceptions were made in the case of Basques and French from the Pyrenees region, who often allied with the Barcelonnettes in Mexico.[109]

The labor demands of the department stores broke this tradition of exclusivity. In the past, when the personnel of a store could range from a handful to thirty or forty, emigration from the valley sufficed. By the twentieth century the Barcelonnette population of eighteen thou-sand could not possibly staff all the stores. The Palacio de Hierro alone hired sixteen hundred employees, a number that included one thousand employees at the downtown store, many of them clerks, and six hun-dred seamstresses in its main workshop on the outskirts of the city.[110] Barcelonnettes were by far the largest employers in the retail field; by comparison, the famous German hardware department store Casa Boker employed 170.[111] Visitor Wallace Thompson noted the presence of French and Mexican clerks in the French dry-goods stores.[112] The 1903 *Massey-Gilbert Blue Book of Mexico* supports this in its list of English-speaking businesses and employees. Included were department store clerks with surnames such as Anda, Manuel, and del Mazo.[113] This listing also underscores stores' need for polyglot employees to deal with a cosmopolitan clientele, particularly the lucrative expatriate market. Porfirian stores often advertised their ability to converse with customers in their preferred language, a marketing strategy with a long history in Mexico.[114] Despite this increasing diversity in hiring practices I suspect that the vast majority of clerks—the public face of the store—remained Barcelonnette. The presence of a French clerk assisting in fashion purchases undoubtedly carried a higher degree of prestige with a Mexican clientele. For Mexican employees the department store proper (not counting its off-site workshops) offered positions in the local delivery, shipping and receiving, administration, and mail order departments, among others.

Following not only Mexican custom but also the realities of the Barcelonnette emigration pattern, the majority of department store employees, especially clerks, were men. Across the Atlantic, department stores in France and Britain also overwhelmingly hired male clerks, although after 1870 the feminization of the British clerks exceeded that of the French.[115] This contrasted starkly with the early French retail tradition of the female modiste and the infamous *grisettes*—her young and reputedly sexually exploitable female assistants.[116] The boutique and seamstress trade in Mexico also continued this tradition, but the area behind the counters of the almacenes de novedades and most department stores remained a masculine preserve.[117]

Women did find limited employment opportunities within the department stores. The new Centro Mercantil described its staff as "composed of misses in the *modas confecciones* sections and young men in the other parts of the establishment."[118] A 1902 photo of the Puerto de Veracruz department store floor staff pictured two women and over sixty men.[119] At the Palacio in 1903, one of the Tron family members wrote a letter of reference for a Miss Jeanne Colón, noting that she had worked in the departamento de confección de sombreros (hat-making department) since January 1900.[120] In a 1906 advertisement in the *Mexican Herald* the Palacio announced that its staff included "Many English speaking Clerks—both Ladies and Gentlemen."[121] Henri Tron of the Palacio wrote to Oaxacan governor Emilio Pimentel in 1906 in response to a visit from a widow, Señora Guadalupe Santaella Viuda de Cortés, who carried a letter of introduction from Pimentel. After the usual pleasantries he promised that "the first vacancy at the counter will be offered to one of the daughters (*señoritas hijas*) of the lady under discussion."[122] This is a surprising letter given that the petitioning woman was of a respectable social station—of the gente decente—belonging as she did to the patronage circle (camarilla) of Pimentel. She may have fallen on hard times with the death of her husband, but we do not know if this was a recent event or what her financial situation was. For her to seek employment for her daughters not only in a department store but also one in a different state (Oaxaca City did not yet have a purpose-built department store) implies that she was either extremely desperate or else such a position in the department stores (or at least in the Palacio) was acceptable—even desirable—for daughters of decent families. Not enough data exists to draw conclusions, but this letter undermines the possible assumption that female clerks in Mexico mirrored the lower-middle-class social status that characterized their Parisian counterparts at the Bon Marché.[123]

Far and away the most visible and prestigious public placement for women in the big stores was as a modiste imported from France. In 1905 the Puerto de Veracruz department store announced the recently arrived modista Parisiense Madame Damaris. After her voyage on the French steamer *La Navarre* she took over management of the department for women's fashions, hats, and lingerie.[124] In 1909 Madame Rosa Warin, contracted as a modiste for the fashion and hat department (modes et chapeaux) of the Ciudad de Londres, wrote Finance Minister Limantour asking his assistance in releasing her goods from Veracruz customs. She noted that she was not wealthy and had brought six crates of furnishings and other belongings to avoid the cost of renting a furnished hotel room in Mexico.[125] Other department stores also publicized their in-house French modistes, who could conjure up the most fantastic and luxurious creations for a ball at the Casino Español or the races at Peralvillo, but only out of materials purchased on the premises.[126]

In spite of this increasing female presence in the retail sector the male clerk remained ubiquitous in the popular imagination. Written and cartoon dramatizations of encounters between clerks and customers always involved men behind the counter and women in front. The only depiction of female clerks appeared in carnivalesque accounts of the world such as the one imagining society if feminists had their way.[127] In 1909 W. E. Carson observed that "the custom of employing female clerks is only beginning to be adopted in Mexico's capital."[128]

Paternalist capitalism shaped the relationship between department store owners and employers. Leading employers during the Porfiriato often touted benefits to workers such as employee housing, medical care, education, and other services.[129] The Porfirian regime often pointed to these policies to show how Porfirian progress benefited workers as well as employers. As in the United States and other industrializing nations, most of these policies were undertaken in company towns dedicated to extractive industries or at factories of major manufacturers such as the Cervecería Cuauhtémoc in Monterrey or the El Buen Tono cigarette company in Mexico City. But these were mostly blue-collar employees (and, depending on the industry and location, often of rural origin) engaged in the manufacturing and "production" side of the economy. Much less work has considered these policies as they related to employees in the service or "consumption" side of the economy, who were usually white collar and urban and considered themselves current or future members of the same cultural class of not only their employers but also the customers whom they served. In this light, department store employee relations need to be viewed in terms of how owners balanced traditional labor relations techniques with the class aspirations of employees and the perceptions of customers who viewed these clerks as members of an urban respectable society with greater "needs" than peons working on a hacienda.

At the same time, Barcelonnette retailing traditions and transatlantic influences were as significant as the need to maintain a positive public image of worker relations for business and political reasons in determining certain policies. The longstanding Barcelonnette custom and Parisian department store practice of live-in staff stands out as a salient example. The Palacio de Hierro reserved its fourth and fifth floors for employee quarters. The store also fed employees in a grand dining hall located on one of the floors.[130] Whether both men and women employees resided in house remains unclear. Even today, walking along Avenida Carranza, one can look up at the old Fábricas Universales building and the 1920s Palacio de Hierro store and see that the top floor and its windows are much smaller. Employees continue to eat upstairs, where an employee kitchen remains, at least in the Palacio de Hierro. During the Porfiriato most, if not all, of the department stores offered this benefit. In the *Blue Book* directory a considerable number of the listed English-speaking employees gave their employer and listed their residence as "same." Multiple entries for "clerks" and "employees" (*empleados*) appear for the Palacio de Hierro, Ciudad de Londres, Puerto de Veracruz, and Centro Mercantil.[131] Although several of the names are those of important Barcelonnette families, suggesting that perhaps family members received special treatment, a majority are either not French or not identified with the ownership elite. While many employees resided in the store, the directory also lists a number of clerks and employees who lived in rooms or apartments separate from the store. In-store residence combined equal parts of tradition, supervision of employees, and paternalism that allowed owners to demonstrate their public commitment to the advancement of their workers.

Pay, while not exactly generous, exceeded averages in the capital. Furthermore, considering that many employees received heavily subsidized room and board, salaried clerks did fairly well for themselves and could afford to place a considerable portion of their pay into the store bank or send money home to their families. Salaries for clerks began at approximately twenty to thirty pesos per month and increased with experience and responsibility. Anselme Charpenel started at twenty pesos per month at the Centro Mercantil in 1910, received his first raise, to forty pesos, the next year, and enjoyed another a year later, bringing his salary to sixty pesos.[132] Léon Martin began work for Las Fábricas Universales in 1902 at twenty pesos per month and complained that the annual salary review was unfair and that the owners kept telling him he was too young for a raise. Nevertheless, by June 1904 he was earning thirty pesos monthly, forty-five by September, and by the time of his death of appendicitis in March 1905 he received a monthly salary of seventy-five pesos.[133] Overall, clerks with any experience enjoyed salaries exceeding those of most workers in the capital, which ranged from thirty pesos for unskilled labor and upwards of sixty pesos for skilled and semiskilled.[134] Profit-sharing also figured into at least the Palacio de Hierro pay structure. It based its 1898 incorporation on that of the Bon Marché, which made employees shareholders in the company.[135] Whether other stores followed this lead (especially the Puerto de Liverpool, which incorporated next, in 1907) remains unknown.

Employees followed house rules on morality and conduct befitting members of the gente decente in return for the benefits and status associated with working for a department store. Undoubtedly department store employees faced conduct rules traditionally imposed on workers in Barcelonnette stores as well as in practice at the large Parisian stores.[136] Restrictions applied to what little free time employees (especially those living on premises) possessed. Store management usually steered their charges toward educational and "healthy" diversions, such as concerts, sports, social events, or classes sponsored by the Employee Mutualist

Society, French social clubs such as the Cercle Français, or the YMCA.[137] Drinking was prohibited. Curfews were enforced. Sexual misconduct brought serious punishment. Employers likely fined or fired employees for such infractions. Gente decente values and management anxiety over store image made the protection of the virtue of female employees a priority for store employers. Concerns over the morality of unescorted young ladies outside the house and engaged in wage labor troubled middle-class minds. Since hiring married women was out of the question (they were to tend to the home and the family), only young, single— and therefore vulnerable—girls were eligible for hire. As for the Parisian modistes hired in Mexico, the available documentation suggests they were unmarried, and given that the stores touted their experience we can assume that a woman with some degree of maturity made the crossing. The Limantour-Tron letter suggests that their assistants and female clerks were young and single. In Western Europe and the United States mixed salacious and fearful imaginings about girls such as these mingling with smooth male clerks and sweet-talking male customers drove a whole international literary genre, fueled a social commentary niche, and compelled owners such as the Bon Marché's Boucicault to publicly demand and enforce the strictest moral codes for girls so as to reaffirm bourgeois values and the proper image of the department store.[138] Future studies on this subject in Mexico will likely reveal similar sentiments, given the ready adoption of foreign literature and cultural trends among respectable society.[139]

Although granted gente decente status, employees nevertheless had to earn their wage. They also united among themselves and often in solidarity with employees of other stores to achieve certain improvements, such as shortened hours and holidays. Store owners varied in their approach to these requests. Some placed themselves at the vanguard of these concessions while others strenuously opposed change.

Department store employees organized under the rubric of the Sociedad Mutualista de Empleados de Comercio in 1892.[140] The idea for a permanent association of commerce employees was finally accepted among the different sectors during the fight for Sunday as a day of rest.[141] The society grew quickly and built its own center at which members could enjoy various recreations.[142] In 1905 the society voted to admit non-store employees but only at a ratio of four employee members for each nonemployee.[143] As a mutualist society, the organization also assisted with payments for funerals, medical treatment, and pensions for widows.

Department stores typically opened at seven or eight o'clock in the morning, closed between one and three o'clock for lunch, then reopened until eight at night.[144] Employees officially worked thirteen-hour days, and by 1902 a number of stores reduced their hours by closing earlier, at seven o'clock. When two of the stores, El Centro Mercantil and La Francia Maritima, opted out of the agreement over three thousand workers protested and forced compliance.[145] Junior employees did not enjoy the long meal break, often wolfing down their food during a paltry rest of thirty minutes to one hour while senior employees enjoyed the full period. Beyond official hours, employees spent more time cleaning, stocking shelves, unpacking crates, and preparing samples for traveling salesmen.[146]

These hours continued a long Mexican tradition and mark a distinct difference from American and European department stores. In the name of progress the business paper *La Semana Mercantil* urged stores to adopt American business hours of ten to five for the betterment of employees and consumers. It noted in 1896 that the Mexican custom was injurious to all, prejudicial to the many workers in other economic sectors who had only their lunchtime to shop, and detrimental to store employees, whose late hours deprived them of the ability to "leisurely enjoy the pleasures of family."[147] This argument overlooked that most clerks were young, single males unable to afford a family.

Employees also fought for a day of rest on Sundays. Historically, most owners of the Barcelonnette clothing stores (cajones de ropa and almacenes de novedades) had given Sunday afternoons off after a morning of unpacking and restocking of goods. Employees at smaller garment stores owned by other nationalities, especially the Spanish, did not fare so well. Several agreements among owners fell apart as stores broke the rules and owners feared that employees "abused" their free time.[148] In May 1904 the Palacio de Hierro spontaneously granted Sunday as a day of rest, and employees marked the first anniversary with celebrations.[149] Employees still worked most holidays; León Martin at Las Fábricas Universales complained that he worked until midnight most days and two in the morning on New Year's Day.[150] In 1909 the Puerto de Veracruz granted All Saints' Day and Day of the Dead (November 1 and 2) as employee holidays. When other stores did not comply, French, Spanish, and Mexican employees protested, showing their solidarity as they marched in the streets singing in French the famous socialist song the *Internationale*.[151]

Importantly, new Barcelonnette emigrants employed in their compatriots' stores found their social status diminished, no longer being treated as part of an ethnic family but rather considered as little more than a reliable, exploitable pool of labor. The notion of apprenticeship, of arriving as an employee with a chance of rapid advancement and eventual ownership, faded as the Porfiriato advanced. "Trade conquistadors" became "proles" singing the *Internationale* in the streets of Mexico City. The fluid, merit-based system that had characterized the early decades of Barcelonnette emigration ossified and became more prone to nepotism and exploitation during the department store decades of the 1890s and 1900s. The hierarchy of the community became much more rigid. Family members of this elite still worked in the store but often received better treatment and faster promotion over other Barcelonnettes. In 1904 Léon Martin bitterly wrote home to his brother describing his disillusionment. "In this dump only the nephews of the owners advance and they shit on the rest [*qui emmerdent les autres*]." He declared his patrons "avaricious," continuing, "they are not like bosses in France" and "Spanish and Mexican owners seem better than our compatriots." Bosses who were so nice when they recruited back home in the valley "changed completely once you arrived." In Mexico employees did not speak to the patrons, said Martin, and he concluded, "One must be rich to be accepted by these people and in Mexico I only rarely visit our cousin Pellotier [a member of one of the successful families]." Martin expressed a likely widespread sentiment among those at the bottom of the community that the system was rigged against them. He expressed indignation that "the bosses are travelling to France, and on the account of the employees! Our first patron is going to France this year, the Derbez brothers will certainly go next year. They are all rich and they would be able to retire comfortably [and follow the tradition of passing down the business to new blood], but of course it is the employees and the rest of the unfortunates who must continue to labor."[152] Department store organization in Mexico was becoming more bureaucratized, hierarchical, and specialized, reflecting not only the maturing of the Barcelonnette community but also trends occurring throughout Mexican and Western societies more generally.[153]

Clientele

Who were the clientele of these department stores? Popular misconception stubbornly holds that the stereotypical shopper at department stores and other respectable commercial establishments was a light-skinned, middle-to-upper-class female. Most foreign travelers viewing Mexico through the cultural lens of gendered consumption dominant in their own societies continued this popular image. Besides, for Mexicans the opportunities for double entendres and other manifestations of popular humor provided by male clerks serving female customers made the ubiquitous female consumer a received wisdom. For historians favoring a dependency-theory approach, this class-race-gender image travels hand in glove with the belief that these stores sold only luxury imported goods.

A particular oddity of travelers' accounts is the frequent rehashing of the dying custom of women customers purchasing their goods from their carriage while parked at the curbside in front of the store. In 1888 William Curtis repeated this, claiming, "It is a common thing to see a row of carriages before a fashionable store with a clerk at the door of each one exhibiting silks or gloves or ribbons." He did admit that "in some of the stores are parlors in which a señora can sit if she likes and have goods brought to her" but added that "none but foreigners and the common people stand at the counter and buy."[154] As late as 1907, Nevin O. Winter feverishly fantasized, "Another example of the Oriental exclusiveness is seen in the life of the ladies of the wealthier classes who always drive in closed carriages . . . and, when shopping, do not deign to leave the carriage."[155] While possibly true for an infinitesimally small number of consumers patronizing exclusive shops such as the tailor Louis Sarre, by 1907 *no one* shopped by carriage at department stores or the fashionable almacenes de novedades.

These stereotypes make no sense from either from a business or historical perspective. The department store business model of leaner profit margins on a high-volume turnover—one that the Barcelonnettes had practiced for a half century—by necessity cannot work without a broad base of consumers. The praise department stores received for their "democratization of luxury" was not mere hyperbole but rather caught the essence of this cultural and economic phenomenon.[156] In a shallow market like Mexico, a mass retailer had little choice but to promote a democratic admission policy. Early on, most Barcelonnette retailers adopted a pragmatic approach to reach deep into the Mexican market while at the same time retaining an image of respectability.

Thus even prior to the creation of department stores the clientele of Barcelonnette cajones de ropa and later almacenes de novedades included both sexes and a broad spectrum of society. Clients were both male and female. An 1867 commercial directory includes illustrated ads for leading almacenes de novedades such as Las Fábricas de Francia, El Puerto de Liverpool, and La Francia Maritima featuring both male and female customers window shopping and purchasing at the counter.[157] Emile Chabrand's 1892 portrait of a Barcelonnette store includes customers of both sexes.[158] Importantly, both these examples located customers inside and at the counter—not out on the curb. Jürgen Buchenau places respectable women's shift from curbside patronage to shopping (often unattended) in store interiors in the 1880s, but I suspect the shift may have begun much earlier, possibly during the Intervention.[159] In addition to loosening cultural restrictions on respectable women in public, the move out of the carriage and into the store accelerated with the arrival of the tram system, first mule-drawn and later electric. Chabrand's account records a clientele spanning a wide range of economic classes—from those purchasing silks down to the consumers of printed calico—as well as a range of racial and national backgrounds. Chabrand describes a Spaniard and an English woman whom he postulates was likely the wife of an Anglican minister. He confirms that store personnel collectively spoke a number of languages in order to service the expatriate colonies, usually offering German, Italian, Portuguese, and English in addition to the standard French and Spanish. He also includes a vignette on an Indian from a hacienda among the crowd at the counter, whose shirt and pants probably cost less than a peso but whose hat probably cost a hundred times that.[160] Continuing, he tells of a group of Indians entering the store and how one who could speak Spanish bargained for the rest, beginning with an offer barely a quarter of the clerk's asking price before finally working upward. At least a portion of Mexico City's indigenous population felt comfortable enough and sufficiently understood the retailing rules to enter Barcelonnette stores in pursuit of at least some of their material needs. They also had enough money to do so.

French commercial commentators such as F. Bianconi in 1889 explained this market and its possibilities and limitations. Bianconi informed manufacturers about the wide gulf separating the rich and poor in Mexico and explained that in order to succeed they must follow the rule that while the elite are prodigious consumers, "the mass of consumers above all demands articles at a good price."[161] Importantly, he included the indigenous population as a market for French goods such as jewelry and candles.[162] He pleaded with producers to adapt to the Mexican market, not only its ability to absorb goods but also its tastes. Given the slide of French imports his compatriots apparently did not heed him, but the Barcelonnettes did. So too did Finance Minister Limantour, who kept a copy of the book in his library.[163]

To be sure, Porfirian department stores were unabashedly institutions of the gente decente. They reflected a gente decente social vision of order, progress, and abundance consonant with that of a larger transnational class of the bourgeoisie. But the gente decente was more a cultural than an economic category comprising a membership ranging from semiskilled laborers to business leaders and united more by a compatible worldview and value system than a comparable financial situation.[164] To accommodate both this shared vision and the wide range of disposable incomes required a varied price structure. Expensive and often imported goods provided the more affluent with their material piece of modernity and social prestige while domestic factories and cheap imports served the same purpose for the middling and humbler classes. Moreover, one should not overlook that while the values of the stores may have been those of the gente decente, their attractions in terms of abundance, novelty, color, and display appealed to all economic strata and racial categories, not to mention gender and sexual orientation.

I add this last point to remind readers that while Porfirian society may have gendered production and consumption as masculine and feminine, respectively, Porfirian males did not leave all the shopping to women. Male fashions consumed considerable space in both stores and catalogs.[165] In addition, large almacenes de novedades such as New England and High Life catered exclusively to men.[166] Certain newspapers, such as *Frivolidades* and *La Risa*, catered to an affluent (or at least free-spending) male clientele. The papers of José Yves Limantour reveal that he was quite the shopper in Paris and often made purchases for others, among them President Díaz and his wife.[167] Finally, Víctor Macías-González continues to compile a body of work on the construction of the Porfirian male (and gay male) consumer.[168]

This democratization of luxury illuminates the way in which material abundance not only formed the cornerstone of modern Mexican retailing but also served as the most visible and widespread benefit to mankind during the age of progress. Both for cultural purposes and out of economic pragmatism stores commonly advertised the sale of "Luxury and Common Goods" or, as the banner outside the Centro Mercantil stated, of "Fine, Half-Luxury, Common Goods" to tap this market.[169] A typical description of the Palacio de Hierro in 1900 expressed its wish to serve all of respectable society, asserting, "So it is in that store that one can find articles ranging from the most modest and indispensable to our working class to the most exquisite and the most tasteful goods that can appeal to the middle and aristocratic classes of this refined capital."[170] Even as far back as 1867 the commerce directory of Mexico City featured ads such as that of the Ciudad de Londres offering an "elegant selection of luxurious and common goods," while an illustration for the Fábricas de Francia ad included a range of window shoppers that spanned rebozo- and sombrero-wearers to those sporting top hats and tails.[171] Department stores continued in the tradition of the earlier stores described by Chabrand in 1892. Wallace Thompson remarked, "The French dry-goods stores, with their French and Mexican clerks . . . seem the ablest of all foreigners to give the Mexican women, from the most exclusive ladies to the humblest peon, the peculiar attention which custom has made them desire. . . . Always there is a subtle understanding of class, a subtle patronage of the woman in a *reboso* and a subtle deference to the lady with a hat."[172] What becomes clear from these observations is that Barcelonnette department stores, like the almacenes de novedades and cajones de ropa that preceded them, offered a wide variety of goods to an equally broad spectrum of society. A composite portrait of their products, clientele, and business practices suggest that this appeal may not have reached the poorest of the poor or the richest of the rich, but it certainly attracted a far wider swath of the population than previously imagined. Perhaps the *Mexican Herald* newspaper expressed this best in 1895 when describing the department stores: "Here the rich lady, who has her liveried coach without, stands side by side with the poor, weather-beaten Indian from the mountains. And there is that with which to satisfy them both."[173]

As this chapter has shown, a considerable source of the modernizing aura possessed by the department store in Mexico derived from its origins, ownership, organization, financial success, broad clientele, and democratization of luxury. But what was it about the institution itself that proved so attractive to late nineteenth-century societies around the globe? The following chapter pursues this question, considering the historical-anthropological as well as social significance of the goods and novel retailing techniques adopted by Mexico City department stores. Placing department stores and other retail architecture within the context of the Porfirian effort to radically transform the visual landscape of the city into an expression of national progress reinforces the modernizing significance of the goods, practices, and organization of the stores in Mexican national culture.

Chapter 4

MODERNIZING CAPITAL

*Constant Innovation and the
Expression of Progress*

FROM THEIR BEGINNING, DEPARTMENT STORES THRIVED ON INNOVA-
tion and novelty. Their readiness to adopt new retailing practices, new
products, and new displays placed them as the representative institution of a progressive age. Yet while these stores reflected the values of
a modernizing culture, they also shaped and constructed that culture.
Department stores may have admitted a broad swath of Mexican society,
but the image they created and sold with their architecture, displays,
organization, and consumer rituals solidly represented the aspirations
and material culture of the gente decente. Department stores anchored a
host of fixed-location retail stores (*casas de comercio*) such as jewelry and
home decoration stores that moved the market off the street and into a
controlled private-public marketplace. In these locations retailers spent
considerable effort, imagination, and capital displaying goods on the
store floor, in street windows, and in sales literature such as print advertisements and catalogs in a way that tapped into the broader culture's
association of goods and modernity and then invested goods with significance that encouraged a particular way of viewing the world. In short,
department stores sold the material culture of modernizing Mexico, or
more specifically of a gente decente vision of a modern Mexico.

So powerful were they in their role as producers of cultural meaning that department stores did not even need goods to sell this image of modernity. Department stores led the business community in transforming the visual reality of the capital through their breathtaking architectural styles and highly conspicuous position within public rituals such as holiday parades. Efforts to rationalize, beautify, and remake the city as an expression of Mexican economic and cultural progress reach back into the colonial period. The 1856 Ley Lerdo accelerated this project by prying urban land from Church control and opening the door to the greater commercialization and secularization of the capital. Not until the government of Porfirio Díaz, however, did the national leadership have the resources and internal unity to undertake fully this task. Historians have concentrated on the myriad efforts of the Porfirian government to transform the city into a showcase of Mexican economic and cultural modernity. As photographs of Porfirian Mexico City clearly reveal, however, department stores and other modern retailers played a monumental role in expressing Porfirian progress to Mexicans and foreign visitors alike.

The brilliance of department stores is that they capitalized on a long-developing trend in Western societies whereby people invested in—and derived meaning from—the man-made cultural artifacts that constructed their environment to an ever-growing degree. The work of material culture anthropologists helps us consider this phenomenon.[1] Goods are invested with connotations of class status, race, age, gender, and other categories by which cultures bring order and sense to the world around them. The meaning of goods, however, is not necessarily cross-cultural. The significance of colors, materials, and styles are equally culturally specific. Moreover, the goods used by one society may be unknown in another.

Numerous scholars have observed the increasingly important role of goods in Western society over the past half millennium, spurring and spurred on by increasing trade and commercial capitalism. The abundance of goods appears equally in artistic depictions from the Italian Renaissance, seventeenth-century Holland, and colonial Mexico, where paintings pointedly feature the inaugural procession of the new viceroy passing through the abundance of goods offered in the Parián market in Mexico City. Conspicuous consumption and the meaning of goods did not originate in the late nineteenth century.

But a cascade of technological progress and corresponding advances in production, transportation, and communication accelerated the significance of goods in nineteenth-century societies. Not only did the economic engines of modern society achieve the mass production of traditional goods, but they created a plethora of new ones. These goods often suited the specific cultural requirements of the leading class of this economic transformation: the bourgeoisie. Examples of this include new leisure goods such as parlor games and beach paraphernalia or the explosion of home appliances and furnishings catering to the middle-class obsession with the home as a site of consumption.

Department stores and other leading retailers of the Porfirian Age served not only to bring these goods to Mexico and popularize them but also to educate Mexicans as to their use and social significance as defined by the bourgeois culture of France or perhaps England, Germany, or the United States. Through displays, advertising, and employee-client relationships department stores helped to define and place goods within a cultural web of meaning. This served to visibly mark social and other hierarchies in an increasingly anonymous city environment dominated by the "urban crowd."

For Mexican consumers, a sign of membership in modern and respectable society was the ability to purchase goods—to consume—in quantity and quality appropriate to one's social station. Such a task was not an easy one. With an ever-increasing abundance of goods, the creation of new goods, a quickening fashion cycle, and the pronouncements of a commercial press and pressure of social peers constantly adding new "needs," Porfirian consumers found themselves devoting considerable time to educating themselves as consumers. As we shall see, department stores helped Porfirian consumers with this education at the same time as they kept the cycle going.

Many modernizers saw department stores as creating a common set of cultural values, reference points, and categories. An analogy could be made between the function of department stores and state projects such as public education in inculcating values, behaviors, and identities. The main difference is that business arguably did a better job than the state. The values they promoted were those of a capitalist economy and culture and they applied not only nationally but globally. The simultaneous rise of the gente decente, mass consumption, and the Porfirian-era vogue of cosmopolitanism was not a coincidence. A common international culture as a mark of modernity is exactly what Auguste Genín is speaking of in his *Notes sur le Mexique* when he describes the modernizing function of department stores and the disappearance of distinct indigenous societies and cultures under the inexorable attraction and education of the goods and values of a culture of Western capitalism. In other words, department stores pleased Porfirians by promoting a cultural and economic system comfortingly familiar to the gente decente, on whose values the Porfirian development program was based.

Nearly every aspect of the department store served both an educational and entertainment function, but perhaps the most consistent blend of these two goals was the store's expression of the nineteenth-century belief in progress into which the whole gente decente value system was tied. In Mexico William Beezley has termed this widespread yet somewhat fuzzy faith in progress as the "Porfirian Persuasion." The most prominent ideologies of the nineteenth century—whether Comte's Positivism, Marx's and Engel's Communism, or assorted Utopian movements such as that of Saint Simonianism—expressed this seemingly unstoppable betterment of society thanks to the technological and productive advances achieved by humanity. Located in the heart of an urban center, the department store was constantly transforming itself, dramatically enacting and making tangible this belief system. The building, the inventory, the displays, and the advertising were all in a constant state of transition. It replicated the bourgeois cultural imperative of novelty, fashion, change—of improvement for the self, family, and nation.

The Palacio de Hierro: Mexico's First Department Store

The first department store in Mexico, the Palacio de Hierro, opened its doors for business on July 1, 1891. Its origins date back to 1860, when Alexandre Reynaud and V. Gassier—two Frenchmen from the Barcelonnette region—opened Las Fábricas de Francia under the Portal de las Flores.[2] In 1876 they received an offer to sell from their senior employees Joseph Tron and Joseph Leautaud.[3] Also Barcelonnettes, Tron and Leautaud were cosmopolitan men of their age who regularly traveled to the United States and Europe, mixing pleasure with business.[4] They kept up with new fashions in clothing as well as retailing structures and admired Boucicault's Bon Marché and stores such as Marshall Field's in Chicago. Over the next decade they planned the expansion of their store.

They recognized the limitations of their market, in terms of both disposable income and population; in 1892 Mexico City housed a mere 330,000 souls while Paris exceeded 1.5 million residents by the 1870s.[5] Raising capital would also be difficult, as the limited liability corporation did not exist in the Mexican commercial code at the time. Nonetheless, in 1888 they bought land down the street from their current store. Located on the northwest corner of San Bernardo and the Callejuela, the plot covered a modest twenty-five square meters, or just over fifty-six hundred square feet, and backed up against the Palacio Municipal (city hall) building that faced onto the Zócalo.[6]

Construction commenced the same year. Architectural plans came from Paris, while a Mexican architect directed the project. Using Gustave Eiffel's Bon Marché as their inspiration they employed an iron framework instead of traditional concrete.[7] The exponentially increased load-bearing capacity of iron allowed the owners to parlay a framework of thin iron columns into a more spacious, airy interior in which large quantities of goods could be displayed to an equally sizeable clientele. Dispensing with interior load-bearing walls was truly revolutionary. It also permitted Tron and Leautaud to maximize costly land prices by expanding vertically. The building stretched to an unprecedented five stories that towered over the Palacio Municipal. The iron came from the Paris foundry at Moisan, while granite stones from the Chiluca quarry covered the store façades.[8] Popular legend holds that the daily crowds of onlookers at the site, not knowing its purpose, dubbed it "El Palacio de Hierro," or "The Iron Palace." The street *chisme* held and the owners adopted it in place of the original "Fábricas de Francia."[9] Totaling twenty-five thousand square feet, the Palacio already exceeded the twenty thousand square feet later constructed in 1900 by Casa Boker, the largest of the German hardware/ department stores.[10]

Within a decade the Palacio began a string of expansion projects. By the late 1890s sufficient success, combined with competition from the enlarged Puerto de Veracruz (1897) and Puerto de Liverpool (1898), compelled the ownership to expand. In 1898 they became the first commercial house in Mexico to incorporate, changing from J. Tron y Compañia to El Palacio de Hierro, S.A., raised a staggering capital of four million pesos, and purchased neighboring properties.[11] The new building, at over fifty thousand square feet, was more than double the size of the original and stretched the full length of the block on San Bernardo.[12] It completely dwarfed city hall. Then, in 1900, the board approved the purchase of land and construction of a workshop several blocks south on Monterilla Street, now 5 de Febrero Street. Nearly 25,000 square meters, or 225,000 square feet in size, the shop employed approximately six hundred workers, mostly female, who produced articles in high demand, such as shirts, umbrellas, and furniture.[13] A smaller yet symbolically significant expansion occurred in 1905. In a vivid demonstration of the ascent of commercial interests and the political weakness of the ayuntamiento (which in 1903 had lost most authority to the governor of the newly formed Federal District) the Palacio sought to expand into the building that housed the city government.[14] In September 1905 Henri Tron confidently wrote Finance Minister Limantour asking to set up a meeting to discuss the issue, which had recently been passed on to him by the Secretaría de Gobernación.[15] Tron succeeded, and soon workers tore down the rear portion of the Palacio Municipal in preparation for the Palacio de Hierro expansion. Four years later, in 1909, the Palacio opened across the street their "Annex"—featuring the first basement in a Mexico City business house—which housed their furniture and home furnishings (*tapiceria*) departments. Meanwhile, in preparation for their final expansion during the Porfiriato, the board arranged for the purchase of its neighbor and competitor, El Importador, and began enlarging and remodeling the original building, concluding with much fanfare in the grand reopening inauguration of 1911.

Tron and Leautaud realized that what distinguished department stores from the preceding retailing structures was the context in which they placed the goods of modern society. They used the visual appeal and vast space of this revolutionary purpose-built building as their platform to develop fully the display and marketing strategies previously restrained by the spatial limitations of available retail structures. They highly publicized the high-volume, low-margin sales model with their slogan "Bueno, barato, y bonito," loosely translated as "Good, cheap, and beautiful."[16] The Puerto de Veracruz soon adopted a similar slogan, "Sell cheap to sell often."[17] The design of the store allowed them to maximize the use of show windows, seasonal expositions, color, and natural and artificial light. Although earlier stores had claimed to have instituted a "department system" the Palacio possessed the room to separate distinctly the various categories of goods. Each passing year brought heavier advertising in the commercial press and elsewhere and the institution of regular sales.

The instant success of the Palacio sparked a department store construction boom that transformed the skyline of downtown Mexico City.[18] The new stores towered over neighbors in a city dominated by two-story and the occasional three-story structures. Whether the five stories of the Palacio and Fábricas Universales or the four of the Puerto de Liverpool,

Puerto de Veracruz, or Ciudad de Londres, department stores stretched the city vertically in ways previously achieved only by cathedrals and churches. They expanded previous conventions of commercial space horizontally as well as vertically, stretching whole blocks in the case of the Centro Mercantil, Fábricas Universales, and the later Palacios (figure 14). More than just massive, they were elegant. Equally impressive was their distinctiveness; each possessed an easily identifiable style and became a landmark not only on the streets of the city but also in newspaper publicity that often paired text advertisements with a visual of the store itself. Unlike earlier stores, the building itself now became an attraction.

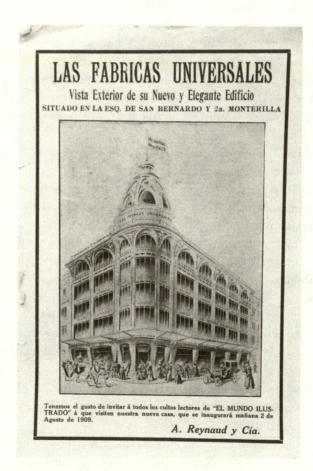

Figure 14. Advertisement announcing the inauguration of Las Fábricas Universales, one of numerous commercial buildings that transformed the Mexico City skyline and the downtown streetscape. Source: *El Mundo Ilustrado*, August 11, 1909, 260.

Showcases of Technological Prowess and Abundance

Leading retail establishments were evolving into showcases of the technological prowess and material achievements of modern society and industry. Besides their size and ability to move goods in mass quantities, they shared a number of parallels with the model factories of the age. Externally, the most obvious feature was the public clock. The Palacio de Hierro and the jeweler La Esmeralda possessed the largest, located at the top of their corner turrets. These clocks joined those of the El Buen Tono factory and other leading industrial plants along with dozens in town plazas in strikingly expressing the importance of time discipline in the culture of capitalism.[19] Of course, the Palacio's did not advise consumers of their "punching in" time, but it did help orient them to tram schedules, social engagements, business meetings, and a myriad of other episodes of daily life increasingly bound by the tyranny of the clock. Inside the stores customers encountered dazzling technologies such as pneumatic tube systems, elevators, in some cases escalators, water tanks, electric lights, indoor plumbing, and undoubtedly a host of other marvels. Several of these features, such as indoor plumbing and electric lights, helped popularize products that would become necessities in the homes of those pursuing a modern lifestyle.[20] The popularity of these fixtures paled in comparison to the most commented on attribute of department and many other stores: the exterior display windows.

Display windows and the goods behind them became both metaphors for modernization and important benchmarks of urban progress. Business owners in the central commercial district scrambled to acquire, publicize, light, and decorate their street-front displays. No business could be described without a mention of its display windows. New products catered to the artistic presentation of these displays. For example, Micro-Flora Garces advertised its artificial flowers for "houses in which there is good taste" by touting the appearance of its arrangements "in many of the most elegant window displays of this capital."[21] By the turn of the century newspapers announced the arrival of the latest fashions or seasonal items "in the windows of the great stores of Mexico."[22] From its inception the Palacio had promoted the practice of inviting customers to educate themselves through window shopping. Typical were ads such as the one from April 1892 announcing the latest arrival of silks from France, listing articles of this "most elegant and newest selection" and encouraging readers that "it is necessary to go and see our Shop windows. Note closely the prices."[23] A journalist for the monthly

Modern Mexico typified this intertwining of consumerism, modernity, and urban renewal in the popular mindset when he bullishly observed, "All through the business center of the city houses are being repaired, renovated, and enlarged. . . . A dozen years ago there was not a plate glass window on San Francisco Street; now it is lined with them; and behind them are displayed goods from every part of the world."[24]

Why were these windows such a powerful emblem of modernity? The answer lies in both the technology and the process used to create them in addition to their enhancement of the visual appeal of displayed goods. The Egyptians crafted opaque decorative glass before 1300 BC. Clearer glass appeared over the next millennium.[25] Improvements continued, and by the eighteenth century pane-glass windows could be found in the shops of aristocratic modistes in Paris.[26] Not until the mid-nineteenth century, however, did the technology of high-temperature furnaces and the use of arsenic oxide and antimony oxide become available to rid glass of carbon dioxide bubbles and create flawless sheets of glass.[27] In the ads in Eugenio Maillefert's 1867 commercial directory of Mexico the display windows are large but are still of the pane-and-frame variety.[28] Europeans first succeeded with the technique while American firms located from New York to St. Louis lagged behind, suffering three decades of financial failure. Mexican retailers most likely imported the majority of their windows, and the directory cites a tariff of 50 percent on window glass.[29] Further on in its pages it describes the dimensions, qualities, and sources of clear glass display windows, citing the best originating in England, followed by Germany, France, and finally Mexico. The United States is not even mentioned.[30] The directory notes dimensions of thirty-seven by forty-two inches, probably comparable to those illustrated in the ads. American producers achieved financial and technical success around 1880. Mass-manufacturing dropped the cost of flawless plate glass by 50 percent.[31] By the mid-Porfiriato Mexican firms purchased glass from both European and American suppliers. The famous interior decorating firm of Claudio Pellandini imported from France, while the firm of E. Heuer received American products. An 1897 contract between the Palacio de Hierro department store and Heuer reveals that while windows were not cheap they also were not exorbitantly priced. Four custom-cut windows measuring ten feet by twelve feet—over triple the dimensions of those three decades earlier—cost 330 pesos, a price including tariffs, transport on the Mexican Central Railroad, and all insurance in case of breakage.[32]

Displays became points of pride for businesses that competed for the most "luxurious" arrangements of "the best taste" that could "call the attention of the multitude that daily flowed along the main thorough-fares."[33] They sought to attract the mass of pleasure-seeking spectators and potential consumers who made up the phenomenon of the "urban crowd."[34] And they did so, spurring on perhaps one of the most popular urban entertainments of the Porfiriato: the leisure pursuit of window shopping. L. Frank Baum, the widely acknowledged father of display window art, may not have published his magazine *Show Window* until 1897, but by then Barcelonnette retailers had already moved past the crude display forms of piling goods in windows, as attested by the attention they received.[35] Such was the perceived and real importance of this crowd as a mass consumer market that not only did stores frequently portray it in their advertising but other consumer-goods manufacturers targeted window shoppers with their own publicity campaigns. The most memorable of these was Electric Man of the cigarette manufacturer El Buen Tono who, in the midst of nightly crowds of window shoppers, lit up his evening wear with lightbulbs spelling out the names of the latest brands (see chapter 1). Making window shopping an evening event required joint private- and state-driven urban improvements such as electrification. Mexico City began replacing its turpentine and hydrogen streetlamps with electricity in the early 1880s and department stores, beginning with the Palacio, installed electric lights. Other cities upgraded as well, allowing families to spend their evenings strolling down city streets gazing at the latest displays. In Guadalajara by 1900, for example, one commentator described the scene outside the Nuevo Mundo department store: "Profuse electrical illumination presents the store with a magical aspect at night, when its various articles of silk, millinery, perfume, parasols, lingerie, and countless others sparkle in its displays and windows, and when the ladies and girls [*señoras y niñas*] of Guadalajara—whose beauty and grace is famous—gather in large groups to visit that true exposition of fashion."[36] Buildings and display windows were far more than repositories for goods. They vividly displayed the material abundance and leisure opportunities afforded to society by nineteenth-century progress. And, of course, they demonstrated how that good life should be lived.

Interior displays drew on the same techniques as those used in exterior windows. New architectural technologies converged with new attention to display to create the space and atmosphere of these establishments. The spatial and aesthetic possibilities offered by new iron frameworks (as discussed earlier) were but one innovation found in the new stores. Eiffel's work in Paris had also paired iron with different forms of glass to maximize the use of natural light as a way to both better display goods and further an illusion of space in the store.[37] In advertising its week-long spring sale, the Palacio emphasizes this point, stating that after much preparation "newness prevails throughout. Departments have been rearranged to give us more light, more room, and to allow you to do your shopping and sight-seeing more comfortably. When you come, visit every Department on the different floors and see the many beautiful novelties on the market for the first time this season."[38] Plate-glass display windows were only one way that the stores used glass. Stained-glass windows added color and light; perhaps the most famous specimen was that in the great hall of the Centro Mercantil that included the monogram of the store. The wooden mostrador gradually changed to glass during the 1890s and display cases separate from the counters became commonplace. Electric light replaced turpentine and kerosene lamps, improving the light and air quality and reducing the cleaning requirements. Incandescent lamps were quite weak at first, often fifteen or twenty watts each. This helps explain the emphasis placed by early owners on natural light. The unreliability of the Mexico City grid also compelled stores to purchase their own direct-current electrical generators to cover during frequent black- or brownouts. Electricity also allowed for the installation of elevators to carry both people and goods up to higher floors, although the grand staircase tended to carry most of the human traffic. Mannequins, appearing in the early twentieth century in Mexico, were a further complement to new display techniques (figure 15).[39]

Department stores revolutionized the use of interior retail space not only for the display of goods but also the movement of customers. They created a new social space with their size and policies allowing free entry and browsing, a social space privatized and constructed with gente decente sensibilities yet also retaining the ability to impart a frisson of excitement through both the crowd and the displays of goods. Although separated from the streets, the stores seemed to create a new public sphere. The interior layout broke up space to create a grid system, not unlike the streets outside. Significantly, in most cases department stores in Mexico did not follow the American and French retail path of leaving goods out on shelves, tables, and racks for customers to touch and feel unaided by staff.[40] In this sense they followed the British model.[41]

Figure 15. Mannequins in the windows of La Suiza clothing store.
Mannequins became a common sight in downtown stores in the last
decade of the Porfiriato and were one of the many new display technologies
adopted by retailers during the era. Source: *El Mundo Ilustrado*, July 5, 1908, 22.

Sales were an exception to this rule, when tables were set out to let
crowds battle over merchandise.

The abundant space of these new stores allowed for the first true (and
much heralded) implementation of the department principle in Mexico.
This meant expanded product lines and distinctly separate classifications
of goods. In 1900 the Palacio boasted seventy-four departments, ranging
from gloves, umbrellas, towels, curtains, perfumes, furniture, artificial
plants, and toys to articles for church, cycling, travel, and the dining table
(figures 16 and 17).[42] Certain departments were undoubtedly bigger than
others, but the point is that the stores were organizing, categorizing, and
separating goods that displayed both the abundance of modern society
and the modern penchant for quantification and categorization. In other
words, department stores brought the bourgeois love of order and rationalization to the often chaotic display of goods typified by "backwards"
retailing forms such as markets. By no mere coincidence did the rise of

Figure 16. Interior of the Palacio de Hierro department store.
Men's hats, umbrellas, and travel necessities were three of the
seventy-four departments in the Palacio. Note the male clerks and
male customers. Source: *El Mundo Ilustrado*, September 18, 1904, 63.

department stores parallel that of museums and expositions. Hence the
comments such as that in an 1889 edition of *Le Courrier du Mexique* that
David Zivy's ultra-luxurious emporium of *articles de Paris*, La Parisiense
(located on the trendy first block of Plateros), "was not a store but a
museum" where "one could discover a *bibelot* [knick-knack] capable of
pleasing a friend, or an *objet d'art*, or buried in a corner a perfect gift
for the holidays."[43] At the same time (and barely preceding the department store), much in vogue were "industrial and commercial museums"
such as Le Comptoir in Mexico City, owned by A. Zaccarini. Located in
the fashionable Centro, this museum displayed and sold imported goods
from "top houses" in France.[44] International exhibitions preceded and
probably inspired the department store concept. The first exhibit took
place in 1851 at the Crystal Palace in London.[45] Commentators noted that
crowds were drawn to the abundance and spectacle of finished goods

Figure 17. This image of the ground floor in the Palacio de Hierro
illustrates the discrete departments and compartmentalized space typical
of Porfirian department stores. Note also the male clerks congregated on
both sides of the glass counters on the right side of the photo while several
female customers sit at the counter and inspect merchandise on the left.
Source: *El Mundo Ilustrado*, September 18, 1904, 63.

displayed in the massive glass and iron structure far more than to the
machinery or displays of agricultural and mining production. The next
exhibition took place in Paris in 1855. The French, whose commentators had focused on the good taste and beauty of the goods displayed in
London, emphasized the consumer over the producer categories of the
exhibition. This fit with the larger French aim under Louis Bonaparte to
establish Paris as the center of European civilization and culture. Legend
has it that Aristide Boucicault, then owner of a *magasin de nouveautés* in
Paris, found that he had lost his way in the middle of the exhibition.
The experience instilled not a sense of fear or confusion but enthrall-
ment. Captivated by "the spectacle of the goods on view and delighted
in the surprises that met his every turn," Boucicault supposedly used the

encounter to imagine a new marriage of retailing and display that would lead to the construction in 1869 of his Bon Marché.[46]

Spatial abundance and categorization did permit the ordering not only of goods but also of people. The department store may have ushered in a "democratization of luxury" but it also catered to—as well as reproduced—Mexican social hierarchy in its organization of interior space. The ground floor typically geared toward mass consumption, with fabrics, accessories, and ready-made clothing dominating the space. In the Palacio the second floor housed furniture until the annex opened in 1909, as well as rugs, tapestry, umbrellas, and those goods that fell under the catchall luxury term "articles de Paris." The third floor was exclusively a feminine domain, occupied by modistes who created outfits for Mexico's polite society so that they could attend in style church, horse races, banquets at the Casino Español, dances at the Club Français, theater at the National, or a kermesse at the Tivoli. It also sold lingerie and—as its 1900 agenda stated—"in a word, the feminine *toilette*."[47] The fourth and fifth floors held, as mentioned earlier, housing and dining facilities for employees.

From Laborious Task to Leisure Opportunity: A New Way to Shop

The retail policies of department stores added to their progressive image. Some were Barcelonnette policies, in force at almacenes de novedades as well as grandes almacenes. Free entry, home delivery, and product returns fell in this category.[48] In-store tailoring and couture design with fabric bought in the store had their beginnings in the earlier stores but now reached a much broader clientele.[49]

The most revolutionary department store policy in Mexico was the implementation of fixed prices and the abolition of bargaining (*regateo*). The Palacio led the charge in 1891 while the Puerto de Veracruz did so by 1894.[50] Along with fixed prices came the novel practice of writing the actual price on tags attached to the article.[51] This departed from the tradition of labeling ready-made garments and other articles not with numbers but with a series of letters. This code originated from the counter-bargaining days of the earlier cajones de ropa and almacenes de novedades when the code gave salesclerks instructions on the range of bargaining permitted on the item. Thus later department stores and newspaper stories covering them often wrote of the consumer breakthrough achieved by "fixed prices and numbers known to the public" (precios fijos con números conocidos del público).[52] Bargaining, of course, was the unquestioned norm prior to the first decades of the nineteenth century, when English drapers and Parisian magasin owners instituted the radical notion of fixed prices. Barcelonnettes did import the policy into their Mexican stores by the 1850s.[53] The transplant did not take, as indicated by the perception that the department stores were leading this practice four decades later. In fact, the economic inefficiencies and backwardness of the bargaining system received criticism from the business press long before and after the Palacio opened its doors. *La Semana Mercantil*, *La Semana en el Hogar*, and other papers pointed out that the time and labor wasted on earning a few centavos more on a sale could have been used to conclude several more sales that would have earned the store higher profits in the end. They viewed the bargaining system not just as a waste of time but also as instilling distrust between seller and buyer, as the former always inflated his price while the latter always offered a pittance. Each article described the social rituals—the poetry of the purchase—embedded in transactions but saw these as impediments to a progress whose time had come.[54] Not surprisingly, fixed prices did not plant deep roots in Mexican retailing, particularly outside of the most modern stores and even more so beyond the capital. In 1909 *La Semana Mercantil* still railed against the minimal adoption of fixed prices and known numbers in the country and berated the enduring popularity of the "flirtation at the counter" between clerk and customer.[55]

One crucial aspect of modern retailing rejected by Mexican department stores was the cash-only sales policy that was central to the new retail models emerging in Western Europe and the United States because it freed businesses from ponderous account burdens and allowed them to put capital into new inventory and hold down prices.[56] Mexico's merchants bowed instead to the reality of the country's credit tradition, which permeated all levels of society, from an aristocrat pawning the family jewels at the Monte de Piedad to cover the expenses of attending a fiesta presidencial to an urban worker visiting his neighborhood *casa de empeño* for a loan to tide him over through the expenses of Holy Week.[57] Evidence of department store credit extension as a norm comes from the fact that during sales events advertisements specifically stated the use of a cash-only policy for the duration of the occasion.[58] In addition, the Palacio account books noted bad customer debts (see chapter 3), and archival records of personal bankruptcies included debts to department stores and other major business houses that ran into the thousands of pesos.[59] Still unknown is whether stores extended this credit only to certain classes of customers and, if so, what the cutoff point was for that credit.

Adding to these strategies was the element of surprise and unexpectedness with which owners regaled customers. Whether distributing savings coupons, weighty agendas combining a daily planner with useful information on the store and the city, color lithograph calendars, or a host of other *regalitos*, department stores engaged in classic gift exchange rituals that reached back to earliest human civilization as well as the ultramodern practice of offering constant novelty to keep customers coming back for more.[60] These gifts joined the usual fashion cycle, the expositions, sales, and gargantuan exhibits such as the "White Sale" described by Zola in his *Au bonheur des dames* in which thousands of meters of white cloth and clothing blanketed the entire store interior to promote a one-time buy of that essential component in the Victorian/ Porfirian wardrobe: *ropa blanca*, or white undergarments and beddings. Zola based his description of the famous white sale on that mounted by Boucicault and his successors every year in late January. On sale days, revenues typically tripled.[61] Boucicault's competitors, such as the Louvre and Le Printemps, used these strategies to great effect. So, too, did storeowners in America. Gifts and surprises—in a word, novelty—succeeded, along with displays and other marketing strategies, in drawing customers back to the store far more often than their "basic needs" required. Going to the store became a consuming pleasure unto itself.

More than ever before, department stores made shopping a sensual experience. Marshaling a variety of retailing innovations that had evolved over the preceding decades in the revolutionary purpose-built building, the new stores provided a sensory setting to maximize the allure of their commodities. The visual appeal offered by the above techniques was, of course, predicated on an abundance of goods.[62] Major advances in production and transportation brought about by the Industrial Revolution in both Mexico and abroad ensured that Mexico City stores had goods to exhibit. Moreover, the rise of the ready-made clothing industry allowed for the visual appeal of a variety of designs, shapes, textures, and color.[63]

Color was particularly important. Just as new colors revolutionized print advertising, store owners used color to great effect in store décor, stained-glass windows, and especially in the display of the most colorful items of all: the goods themselves. The new science of textile dyes added a whole new dimension and depth to the world of fashion that benefited all consumers. The last half of the nineteenth century saw a revolution in the production of synthetic dyes that were cheaper, more colorfast, and covered a far broader range of the color spectrum than traditional organic dyes. In 1826 a German chemist created the first synthetic dye, aniline. By 1856 Henry Perkins had patented an aniline mauve, while in 1859 a French chemist discovered fuchsia, touching off a vogue of bright colored woolens. Synthetic blacks, blues, and greens followed in the next couple of years. These gains made by the application of empirical methods received another boost with the rise of organic chemistry in the late 1850s. This led to a colorfast aniline red suitable for wool and cotton in the 1870s and 1880s, which destroyed the cochineal industry and drove down prices.[64] The conspicuous display of this new rainbow of colors on an abundance of goods powerfully conveyed an impression of an embarrassment of material riches, which resonated in the popular imagination of limitless progress that gripped many transatlantic societies.

Sales—price reductions to turn over inventory quickly—were very much a modern invention and essential to the business model of department stores. Sales or price reductions had once been illegal, as they undermined the guild policy of uniform pricing that served—at least in theory—to provide artisans with a respectable income befitting their skills and social station. This system began to crack in the eighteenth century and truly crumbled in the nineteenth, in part due to the new retailing model of the magasins de nouveautés but also from guild members seeking to increase sales.[65] The 1850s saw the rise of special great sales in Paris and by the 1860s sales—often called expositions—had become "a semi-regular feature."[66] When the first publicly advertised sale occurred in Mexico remains unclear, but by the 1890s with the department stores they became a regularly announced feature in the press and undoubtedly beyond.

Sales served an undeniable economic and business function for stores operating on lean margins and high volumes by both injecting fresh capital and freeing up space for the purchase of the latest novelties. But they also meant much more. They brought controlled chaos to the order of the gente decente shopping experience, a sense of a store turned upside down. They were a break in normal time or routine, a spectacle, a transition point offering an element of controlled surprise for those living in a culture that sought ever-increasing levels of rationalization. Sales became a consumer holiday with a suspension of normal rules of retailing.

From an anthropological point of view, they brought Carnival to the
world of consumption.[67] One can see this assertion in the print advertising of sales. First, advertising images created the crowd and provided
a visual text for the excitement. The Palacio proved most adept at this
kind of graphic advertising. It generally followed the formula set by its
image for the July sale for 1908, which displayed a diverse and considerable crowd swarming about the store. Wives and husbands, girls and
boys, all were either jostling to peer into the windows or walking across
the street in the foreground to do so. Mixed in with the crowd of shoppers flowing onto the street were bicycles, automobiles, carriages, and in
the foreground a delivery vehicle for the store.[68] Two ads provide written
texts that encompass the suspension of normal rules and heighten a sense
of excitement and anxiety by alluding to the limitations of supply (which
strangely contrasted with the visual reality of material abundance displayed at these sales) and the competition with other shoppers for those
scarce goods. The first, from the Palacio de Hierro in 1906, announces
an end-of-season (*fin de estación*) clearance event for fabrics, ready-made
clothing, and "an infinity of other articles."[69] Promising "we will sell for
less than half price," the ad continues, "All articles on sale are rigorously
for cash only and will not be loaned for consultation." A list of accompanying sample prices joins an illustration of a crowd of women jam-
ming into the front door. The second ad belongs to El Surtidor in 1904.
Dangling the claim of 80 percent savings at this "Gran Exposición de
Barata," the store laid down two terms of sale: one, "In order to avoid lost
time for our clientele, all articles on sale will be put on tables with prices
marked"; and two, "Due to the low prices of all the merchandise . . . no
samples will be given, nor will any merchandise be loaned for viewing,
and we do not guarantee that stock will remain from one day to the
other. All exhibited goods will be cash only."[70]

These are just two ads but they illustrate regular sales strategies
adopted by modern Porfirian retailers: the suspension of credit, samples,
and loans; the use of tables on which to pile goods in contrast to the usual
counter service; and the display of an image of how a store and its consumers—always a crowd—would appear during a sales situation. Carnival is
a time of excess in anticipation of personal denial; in a sense sales may be
seen in this way, as an occasion of accelerated consumption in anticipation
of "regular" pricing, or perhaps instead as a convoluted way of marking
scarcity—of hording—before the return of fat, regular abundance. The
social sciences provide little guidance on this topic; surprisingly, while

anthropologists embraced the study of consumption far earlier than historians they have so far overlooked the Carnivalesque qualities of sales.

In addition to straightforward clearance sales, stores also transformed their time and space with the use of expositions. The Palacio held semiannual expositions in February or March and September or October after their equally significant semiannual clearance sales.[71] The early spring exposition celebrated the arrival of summer fashions; the fall exposition, winter fashions. Expositions involved special decorations for the store and usually a fashion show. The 1900 agenda for the Palacio de Hierro noted that these allowed visitors to examine and know exactly "the latest creations in fashion." These fashions for women arrived from France, the center of feminine luxury. Male fashions came from England.[72] The agenda continued that, while these were the big events of the year, "with each steamship arrival we bring to you the novelties that arise over the course of the year, all of which makes EL PALACIO DE HIERRO the center of Parisian Fashion."

The Palacio did not hold a monopoly on expositions, nor on clothing. The Puerto de Veracruz furniture and objet d'art exhibition of November and December 1906 is one example of this diversity.[73] Furthermore, it demonstrates that Porfirians paid as much attention to their home furnishings as they did to their clothing.[74] As the holiday season approached the Puerto de Veracruz transformed its third floor into an exposition of "French Industrial Art." They imported a decorator from the Paris School of Arts with a knowledge of "ancient and modern styles from the Byzantine and Gothic to Louis XVI and *art nouveau*" with the object of transforming the store interior space into a showcase of ready-to-buy room sets. The store advertised that customers who had visited Paris would be transported back to the galleries of the great stores of Paris such as the Bon Marché and the Louvre. Imported furniture, rugs, and artwork served to compose bedrooms, dining rooms, and game rooms, among others. The store offered fixed prices for the sets with the option of picking out bronzes and other fashion accessories á la carte with fashion assistance from employees. At least four bedroom displays ranged in price from 3,000 pesos down to 875 pesos (the Salon Doré Louis XV), suitable for different members of the family, such as the Laquée de Blance style created with a young girl or lady in mind (1,400 pesos). A Louis XVI ensemble was described as "two tonnes of perfect taste" and included a bed, two night tables, one toilette table, and an armoire with three doors, featuring one large panel of glass and two smaller lateral panels. One

article, touching on the department store trademark of affordable luxury, commented that "despite its fineness and elegance the set price is
a very modest $1,600." Appealing to the power of emulative consump-
tion the articles mentioned that several sets of the Louis XVI bedroom—
which had won first prize for artistic value at the Lyon Exposition—had
been purchased on the first day of its installation "by persons of the best
taste" and that "two of our best clients" had already acquired two pairs
of marble and bronze statues valued at 2,800 pesos and inspired by a set
found in the Louvre museum. Just so readers who had missed these fine
specimens could see what their betters had bought, the store promised
an exposition of similar art for ten days only starting on December 20.
In reality, most Mexicans could not afford this furniture, but keep in
mind this was imported furniture that cost considerably more than
quite decent domestic manufactures produced by the Palacio de Hierro
and Jorge de Unna (located in San Luis Potosí but marketed in the capital), often in American or French styles that offered attainable prices for
the respectable classes of the republic.[75] Finally, in a display of the fairly
sophisticated marketing strategies and "synergies" pursued by leading Porfirian retailers, in the same newspaper edition carrying articles
describing the exposition the Puerto de Veracruz bought full-page advertisements describing the store, the art, and the entertainment inside.[76]

Stepping back for a moment, consider the significance of packaged,
ready-to-buy room sets. The system radically departs from the tradition
of decorators customizing furniture to the interior space of each home.
It also relieved the housewife of the burden—or challenge—of selecting
a decoration scheme for the home in her charge. Nevertheless, the aristocracy and elite of the capital would probably not be caught dead buying "two tonnes of perfect taste," so who did this selection, arrangement,
and display of domestic scenes really appeal to? It undoubtedly targeted
the nouveau riche, who were rich in cash but poor in cultural capital.
Ready-made interiors facilitated the acquisition of respectability for this
group, who may have felt uncomfortable demonstrating their lack of
education to interior designers catering to the elite. But beyond appealing to a clientele who could purchase these ensembles, these displays
attracted the less financially endowed members of the gente decente.
For them, these displays offered an aspirational allure, an image of how
they *should* live, a glimpse inside the houses of their social superiors that
remained closed to them.

A Modern Way of Living:
Department Stores as Cultural Primers

Department stores were far more than economic institutions, they were cultural primers for Porfirian society. Department stores offer a window on how business and non-state institutions disseminated the idea of modernity and development to a broad swath of Mexican society. They sold more than goods: they sold a lifestyle. As Michael Miller observed in Paris, this lifestyle was an idealized one: "How the bourgeoisie like to conceive of their lives, what they expected of their lives, the minimum baggage they felt they could carry along with them in their lives all comes into focus in the pages and pictures of the Bon Marché."[77] Adding another level of complexity in Mexico and other "peripheral" nations was the fact that this image of modernity was an imported one that had to be reconciled and fitted within a Mexican reality. Critically, department stores were not mere reflections of gente decente values but also centers of gente decente cultural production. They made material the gente decente worldview in their architecture, inventory, and displays and in the pages of their seasonal catalogs and annual agendas.

Agendas and catalogs vividly illustrate Mexican gente decente culture during the Porfiriato. Their pages unify written and visual texts that present an idealized society of respectability, order, and progress centered on the family and its life and social rituals. They address the wife as the head of household consumption and management and the family agent in a relationship with the store. While they reflect a gente decente self-image, they also create that image. In their pages they construct a family of leisure segregated from work. Departments appear solely for these bourgeois leisure pursuits, offering goods such as parlor games, beach gear, traveling equipment, and cycling wear. Inside the home, rooms must possess a certain amount and type of furniture and decoration while meals must be served at the proper tables with correct silverware. Family members must not only be clothed but provisioned with the right attire for every occasion. Clothing for making and receiving social visits, church, shopping, tea, Sunday paseos, and evening strolls coordinated with attire specifically for morning, afternoon, dinner, evening, and bedtime. Children were not exempt from this, and boys in Porfirian Mexico were often dressed in the sailor suits so in vogue in France and England.[78] Department store agendas and catalogs covered every aspect of life, addressing the needs of newborns, children, schooling, *quinceañeras*, and most definitely marriage. One of the larger departments in the store was that of trousseaux, or the collection of clothing, lingerie, china, and other accessories prepared for a wedding day, night, and beyond. Usually these were gifts from the bridegroom to the bride (with an emphasis on slinky attire and material for the *sábana santa*—the much-giggled-at sheet used to prove virginity and demonstrate consummation) but the Palacio packages include such a variety of goods as to suggest it was more of a kit for setting up a home. In any case, Porfirian society turned what was once a fairly simple affair into a much-feared financial burden. A selection of trousseau sets in an early twentieth-century Palacio catalog notes anywhere from four to seven categories, including wedding attire and accessories, lingerie, menswear, dinnerware, and house attire.[79] The catalog offered five different packages, beginning near 1,000 pesos and ending at 3,000 pesos.

The agendas and catalogs—like the goods depicted on their pages—were shipped throughout the republic. They reached their destination by mail or via a network of traveling salesmen and commission agents. Inspired by the agendas of the Bon Marché and the catalogs of Sears Roebuck, they found ready adoption in Mexico not just by Barcelonnette department store owners but also by the Casa Boker hardware store, *El Imparcial* newspaper, and the El Buen Tono cigarette company. Agendas were modified almanacs whose history precedes the Porfiriato by many decades in Mexico, but it is during this time that the first commercial almanacs and agendas appeared and were rapidly disseminated.[80]

The Palacio published the largest and most widely distributed agenda, comprising 401 pages, in 1901.[81] The store distributed them free of charge as Christmas gifts to its customers in December and early January. What set the agenda apart from others was its sheer size, the scope of its information, and that unlike the publications of El Buen Tono and *El Imparcial* it was intended for matrons of the middle class. Interspersed throughout its pages were descriptions of the seventy-four departments and other store services and benefits such as fixed-price policies and store expositions. In addition, it provided copious lists of government offices and officials, public institutions, train and tram schedules, mail rates, and other information pertinent for personal and family negotiation of the budding local and national communication network and the enlarged role of the Porfirian state in daily life. Moreover, for the management of the home the agenda offered extensive information on the care of the family's health, clothing, and furniture as well as advice on food preparation ranging from jams to twelve-course meals that would leave one's guts groaning from excess. To help manage this domestic economy the agenda provided helpful tools, including daily planners, daily expense lists, and tables for calculating the payment of domestic servants and laundresses. To uplift, educate, and entertain in line with Porfirian standards for middle-class women the agenda provided religious calendars as well as romantic or moralistic short stories and poetry by Mexican, French, and Spanish authors under the heading "Agenda Recreativa." Its "Agenda Instructiva" tables informed readers how to convert Fahrenheit to Celsius, calculate the depth of the oceans, and understand the meaning of Mexican place-names and offered "for singing aficionados: some rules for pronouncing Italian."[82]

Throughout its pages this veritable consumer's bible weaves consumption and the Palacio de Hierro into the daily fabric of the lives of its readers. Its introduction notes that "this volume can constitute for families an album of memories, for the housewife a compendium of notes and appointments, and for the forgetful a powerful mnemonic aid." It continues, pointing out the lined page at the end of each month to note "the birth of a child, the day of his baptism, the date of his first communion, and his first triumphs at school." It mobilizes a discourse centered on the home, Porfirian sentimentality, and practicality—all cultural notions readily understood and embraced by its target audience. This discourse is epitomized at the close of its introduction: "In conclusion, we have endeavored to compile in this book all that is related to the order of a home as well as the well-being of a family; because of this we invite all the clients of 'El Palacio de Hierro' to make frequent use of this agenda whose utility is endless."[83]

The agendas were a great vehicle for store advertising and identity. Department stores piggybacked on the popularity of almanacs in Mexico and guaranteed themselves a wide market for this kind of publicity. At the same time the agenda helped to identify the Palacio as part of the gente decente way of life. By pairing the store with so many institutions and activities it presented itself as another indispensable establishment for respectable society.

The Palacio and other retailers deepened this relationship by inserting themselves into the social rhythm of respectable society, which, coincidentally, also happened to mark moments of increased consumption expenditures. Stores advertised heavily during holidays such as Christmas, Day of the Dead, New Year's, and Holy Week. By the twentieth century the Palacio was already depicting Santa Claus as the icon of Christmas for children. In one memorable ad, Saint Nicholas is riding a burro carrying a *cañasta* basket full of toys while flanked and followed by throngs of neatly dressed children (figure 18).[84] They also announced promotions and fashions for the social calendar of the capital. These included horse races at Peralvillo, Flower Wars during Holy Week, the fiestas presidenciales commemorating the reelections of Díaz, balls at the Casino Español, and a number of functions coinciding with expatriate holidays such as the American July 4, the French Bastille Day, the Spanish Fiestas de Covadonga, and an assortment of Italian, Basque, and German events. Religious events were also social events and stores advertised heavily for All Saints' Day and Day of the Dead in addition to maintaining a permanent department selling religious articles and modistes tailoring the latest tastes for high-society Sunday Mass at the Cathedral or La Profesa.[85]

Agendas, catalogs, and other store advertising provided a way for the gente decente, especially those recently arrived, to educate themselves in proper behavior that marked them as a distinct class—the self-described class of national progress.[86] These texts, like the store shelves, interweave consumption with social hierarchy and cultural differentiation. They display lower-priced or introductory-level goods that signify the minimal degree of respectability and then goods of ascending levels of prestige exhibiting for consumers the material goals to which they should aspire. Definite parallels exist between the purpose of this commercial propaganda and the manuals of etiquette that were so popular in the nineteenth and twentieth century. These manuals, such as those of Manuel Antonio Carreño, La Condesa de Tramar, or José Rosas Moreno instructed aspirants and recently arrived members of the gente decente across Latin America how to comport themselves and their families.[87] In the code of conduct and belief that they promoted—in their culture—they helped the socially insecure of post-Independence Mexico both to define themselves as members of respectable society, as citizens of the new Mexican nation-state, and to differentiate themselves from their social inferiors. The difference between these manuals and the department store agendas is that store publicity identified and injected these developmentalist values into the goods by which the gente decente defined themselves both individually and as a class.

Department store philanthropy and holiday participation further reinforced their position as a modernizing gente decente institution. Beyond their usual cultivation of benevolence in providing gifts to

Figure 18. A Mexicanized Saint Nicholas in a Palacio de Hierro advertisement for
toys and other gift items for the Christmas season. Although today many in
Mexico believe that Santa Claus is yet another recent cultural influence from the
United States that threatens the gift-giving tradition surrounding Epiphany and
the Three Kings on January 6, in fact his introduction long predates the apogee
of U.S. cultural influence in Mexico and suggests as much a European as a
U.S. origin. Source: *La Semana Ilustrada*, December 24, 1909, 2.

customers and benefits to workers the stores engaged in highly publicized charity works. One example was a banquet for the poor at which
the Palacio de Hierro and the Centro Mercantil joined tobacco companies and major newspapers in donating money and staff toward a feast
for several hundred of the capital city's destitute.[88] Store owners, as leading members of the community, shared the sense of noblesse oblige held

by elite and respectable society toward their social inferiors. In addition, as citizens of the most cultured nation of the world, Barcelonnette owners compounded this sentiment with a powerful faith in their civilizing mission toward less-developed peoples.

The placement of the stores in the downtown core between the Zócalo and Alameda Park ensured them a high degree of exposure during parades and other public festivals. National and political holidays such as Independence Day, the birthdays of Juarez and Díaz, and the quadrennial fiestas presidenciales were among those that afforded department stores the opportunity to express their patriotism and progressive spirit.[89] Owners adapted their display techniques for goods to that of the stores themselves. Store façades were completely transformed under banners, lights, and other decorations relevant to the event celebrated. Store goods added to the effect, such as the draping of enormous Oriental rugs from upper-floor balconies.[90] Display windows changed their educational function as images of Porfirian political mythmaking (paintings of patriotic heroes and other paraphernalia) replaced garments and other goods as the desired objects of public consumption. In addition, department stores entered the most magnificently decorated allegorical cars in patriotic and other parades (such as the Flower War during Holy Week), which drew rave reviews from journalists. Finally, stores dressed up, advertised heavily, and offered major sales during holidays celebrated by the foreign colonies.[91] At French-owned enterprises the Bastille Day festivities on July 14 received particular attention, as stores contributed not only money for the event organization but also an abundance of merchandise for the French community's charity auctions.[92] They typically displayed these donations in their show windows for weeks in advance.[93]

Anchors of Urban Transformation

In their prominent public role—whether in the streets, in their advertising messages, in their transformation of urban architecture, or in their infusing of retailing customs with gente decente values—we see how these stores were the latest stage of a historic process in Mexico: the fight over social space and dominant cultural values that reached back to the colonial period. This struggle found expression in continuous urban transformation and renewal projects undertaken in the capital that had the cumulative effect of ushering in an increasingly secular and commercial city conducive to the consumer culture represented by department stores. If we accept an anthropological conception of the city as a production of social and political goals and Sam Bass Warner's thesis that urban dwellers construct their city in competing "multiple urban images," then the agency of commercial interests in the shaping of urban areas deserves consideration as much as that of the state, popular organizations, and other historical actors.[94]

In its orderly, spacious, hygienic, and well-illuminated ideal, the department store offered an idealized capsule of the well-regulated city and society pursued since the colonial period. The city has always played an important cultural role in Iberian society, perceived not merely as a marketplace and a concentration of political, economic, and religious power but also as an island of civilization and, by the mid-nineteenth century, modernity in a sea of rural barbarism.[95] Attempts to civilize, modernize, and hopefully assimilate or at least control rural migrants entering the city have a long history in Mexico. They took on heightened importance during the Porfiriato because of the accelerated urban migration caused by a number of push-pull variables, ranging from Porfirian land policies favoring large economic interests over those of small communities to the promise of jobs and excitement offered by the city.[96]

The Bourbons had made the first concerted and sustained attempts to transform the physical and behavioral landscape of the capital to mirror Enlightenment ideals of order and rationality.[97] Viceroy Bucareli's creation of the Paseo Bucareli or his remodeling of the Alameda Park into its distinctive diagonal and cross pattern as a suitable place of leisure for respectable residents matched other Bourbon reforms, such as the institution of administrative arrondissements and ordinances requiring clear signs at street corners and on commercial establishments.[98] Campaigns to transform the moral matched the physical as prohibitions on popular forms of recreation, behaviors, and vices sought to clear an orderly public space for respectable society.[99] During the Early Republic an empty treasury combined with civil and political disorder blocked any serious urban renewal programs, but efforts to control public space and popular behavior mounted.[100]

It is the liberalizing economic changes of the Júarez regime during the War of the Reform in the 1850s that literally created an opening for commerce and private capital to transform the face of the city. In particular, the secular vengeance of the Ley Lerdo accelerated the physical transformation of the city. Convents and churches lost portions or all of their land in the name of straightening or widening central avenues

to match the urban reform projects that had already occurred in 1830s
Newcastle or were contemporaneously pursued in Haussman's Paris of
the 1850s.[101] While originally undertaken partly to inscribe Liberal cultural values on the city as well as to increase the state's capacity for public vigilance (or to make it harder for the rabble to erect barricades, in
the case of Paris after 1848), these changes generated considerable commercial benefits. A still small yet burgeoning affluent class (benefiting
in a variety of ways from the sale and development of once economically dormant ecclesiastical lands) flocked to the cafés, theaters, and
stores slowly being established along these new boulevards. Continuing
economic and political instability acted as a drag on this development in Mexico City but considerable physical change still took place.
Importantly, the French Intervention and installation of Maximilian by
Conservatives did little to slow these changes, as demonstrated by the
laying of the Paseo de la Reforma.[102] These actions set the stage for the
ascent of a secular and commercial urban society that germinated during the Reforma, Intervention, and Restored Republic before blossom-
ing during the Porfiriato.

Curiously, the historiography of the period has overlooked the
impact of commercial architecture in favor of that of the state. A great
deal of excellent work has analyzed the imprint of the modernizing state
on the physical transformation of the city: drainage works, electrification and illumination, street and sidewalk paving and widening, and the
erection of public monuments.[103] An equally rich parallel vein of research
has shown the ongoing Porfirian regulation of behavior and morality,
the pragmatic spatial marginalization of enduring popular mores and
modes of life.[104]

Yet in focusing on the rise of the centralizing state historians have
missed the role of commercial architecture in expanding and solidify-
ing an urban social space for the gente decente. Department, jewelry,
and hardware stores along with insurance and other companies commissioned purpose-built buildings that became landmarks in the capital for foreigners and residents alike and a testament to the triumph
of the Porfirian policy of trade liberalism, laissez-faire economics, and
social order. Unlike in the colonial and Early Republic periods, the once-
dominant architecture of church and state gave way to the preeminence
of the architecture of commercial capitalism. In 1891, while the Palacio
de Hierro was under construction, many thought that its size and novel
iron-girder framework signaled that it must be a new cathedral or palace.

A year later, in his *Practical Guide of the City and Valley of Mexico,* Emil Riedel noted that the five-story Palacio de Hierro loomed over city hall as "Mexico's highest building" and that already "little shops have given way to luxurious modern stores such as this one."[105]

Photographs of downtown Mexico City wordlessly record this transformation. First, consider the change in the appearance of the Portal de las Flores, one of the city's most important shopping zones from colonial times up through most of the Porfiriato.[106] In a photo from 1855 the two-story arcade buildings look uniformly dingy, with a single, impossible-to-read sign hanging over one of the portals. Thin shoots of trees line the walkways that converged on the kiosk in the center of the plaza, a beautification project with unsure success achieved sometime after the destruction of the Parián market in 1843 by Santa Anna. Overall, not a promising sight for the center of national political, religious, and commercial power. Twenty-five years later the trees are tall and lush; public lighting illuminates the kiosk and walkways. The transformation of the portal is even more remarkable. Given that Díaz had just turned over the presidency to Manuel González after a mere four years in power, the commercial development of the arcade clearly predates the "Porfirian miracle." Now different colored paint along with large, clear signs differentiate each of the clothing and accessories stores (almacenes de novedades) that monopolize the portal. The stores have grown, with most of the stretch now sporting a third-floor level. Claims of department store status and cachet advertised by the title grandes almacenes reach out to customers from Sebastian Robert's La Valenciana, which spans four of the arches along the arcade. Equally large are the signs of his French compatriots in La Ciudad de México and El Correo Francés that dominated the Portal de las Flores, while Al Progreso of Michel Bellon, located between Las Fábricas de Francia on the corner of Callejuela and La Valenciana, breaks the uniformity of this vertical expansion.[107] Émile Chabrand in 1892 confirmed this Gallic influence as he observed the near exclusivity of Barcelonnette (French) ownership of the portal shops (figure 19).[108]

The second nominee for considering the change in commercial structures and prominence belongs to the Puerto de Liverpool store over a span of almost forty years. The first image is a drawing from 1860.[109] A small, adobe, one-story corner building with recessed doors and windows reminds one of the architecture common in small-town Mexican shops today. At this point it is nothing more than a cajón de ropa but still commands a clientele derived from the better classes of Mexico City society.

Figure 19. The Portal de las Flores on the south side of the Zócalo,
circa 1901–1905. French-owned stores continue beyond view on the left side
of the image. The two-story building on the extreme right is the Palacio
Municipal (municipal palace), home of the ayuntamiento and other government
offices. The tall building in the background with lettering on its roof is the
Palacio de Hierro department store. Source: Archivo General de la Nación,
Fondo Instrucción Pública y Bellas Artes, Colección C. B. Waite, exp. 68.

The next image is a photo taken in 1872.[110] Still at the corner of Callejuela
and San Bernardo, the store has modernized with a large store sign with
raised lettering. Underneath the sign, pane-glass windows allow for display while an awning helps protect goods and window shoppers from
the sun and offers refuge from rainy season downpours. The third and
final image comes from the late 1890s, when Puerto de Liverpool owners
Ebrard and Fortolis transformed their establishment into a true department store by moving into a new, four-story, purpose-built structure.[111]

These time-lapse accounts represent a broad and insistent trend in
urban Mexico. Their images reveal the gradual yet increasing strength,
vitality, and importance of retailing and consumption in capitalino life
and culture. As a final note, consider the architectural contributions to

Mexico City from different historical eras. From the colonial period remain religious structures, palatial residences, and institutions of the state. Porfirian contributions from the church are negligible, while the state counts an assortment of monuments and a few buildings such as the post office and the Bellas Artes. What continues to define the urban core of the city are the commercial buildings that remain from the age of Díaz. Some continue in their original function, such as the Palacio de Hierro and the Puerto de Liverpool, while others have changed not only owners but businesses, such as the bottom floor of Casa Boker, now a Sanborn's restaurant, and the building for the life insurance company La Mutua, now a record store. Also remaining are architectural gems of the La Esmeralda jewelry store, the Centro Mercantil, the Fábricas de Francia, and the Puerto de Veracruz, among others. Strolling through downtown Mexico City between the Zócalo and Alameda Park one cannot help but experience an aesthetic frisson from the architectural beauty handed down from the Porfiriato. For all their faults, the Porfirian gente decente achieved in their buildings the solidity and grandeur to which they aspired to as a class.

A Celebration of Certitude

By 1910 the Barcelonnette owners of Mexico's department stores had plenty of reason to see themselves in a positive light. They saw themselves as they saw their stores: as powerful modernizing and civilizing agents in the republic. They had just ridden out the worst of the 1907 depression and were gearing up for the Centennial celebrations that would showcase the modernizing advances achieved by the Porfirian state and its pro-business policies. Through their stewardship of textile production and dry-goods retailing they had assisted greatly in expanding the historically weak domestic market. To many, the department store had fulfilled the Porfirian motto of Order and Progress, a perfect wedding of economic and cultural progress combined with a representation of a stable social hierarchy.

These icons of modernity marked the achievements and arrival of the gente decente in Mexico and of a global bourgeoisie more generally. They anchored and breathed new life into a sputtering urban modernization project into which the state and business had invested so heavily. To visitors and residents alike, they demonstrated that when it came to material progress capitalinos were as civilized as the residents of Paris, London, New York, and other centers of modernity.

Unbeknownst to the store owners, the sudden collapse of the Porfirian regime was less than a year away. But the department store and the consumer world that it promoted were far more durable. They were part of a larger economic and cultural global transformation that ran much deeper than the political currents of Mexico. The stores would survive the privations forced by the Mexican Revolution and World War I. They survived with adaptive strategies such as advertising and selling military uniforms to factions engaged in the national conflict before achieving new glories in the 1920s.[112]

In light of its material and moralizing contributions to the republic, should not business have its own day during the Independence celebrations? The French Chamber of Commerce in Mexico, dominated by the Barcelonnettes, thought so. They proposed the idea to the National Chamber of Commerce, who passed the resolution.[113] After negotiations with the centennial organizers they set September 4, 1910, as the date for "Dia de Comercio." By June the chamber had elected the organizing committee. Presided over by Santiago Arechiderra, a Basque and member of the Centro Mercantil executive, the committee included heavy French and Barcelonnette representation. This included members from the Palacio, Fábricas Universales, El Importador, the Puerto de Veracruz, El Paje, El Nuevo Mundo, and the Puerto de Liverpool, while Eugène Roux of the Ciudad de Londres served as one of the vice presidents. Other famous consumer retail manufacturers included El Buen Tono, the jewelers of La Esmeralda and La Perla, and several others. Representatives of banking, mining, and other industries served on the committee, but retailers still dominated.[114]

The fiestas were to demonstrate the progressive force of commerce in the making of a modern Mexico. As one newsmagazine describing the event wrote, "It cannot be denied; it was essential that since commerce is the life spirit for modern peoples that Mexico's should take part in this month's festivities."[115] On the morning of September 4 the festivities began. A congregation of several dozen allegorical floats formed at the Colón monument on the Paseo de la Reforma. Committees representing the economic sectors of commerce, agriculture, mining, industry, and banking joined ten workers' groups, including mutualist societies and "peons from neighboring haciendas" in entering floats. The most numerous and ostentatious vehicles, however, were from stores in the capital or tobacco and beer companies.[116] Firms spent lavishly on these allegorical themes; the Palacio would thrill crowds with its Middle

Ages motif, complete with knights and pages escorting the float.[117] Other department stores receiving special mention were those of the Centro Mercantil, the Fábricas Universales, and the Sorpresa y Primavera.[118] At 10:00 a.m. the procession began. Heading north, they turned east onto Avenida Juárez and continued directly to the Zócalo along San Francisco and Plateros. Judging by the photos taken along this first leg of the journey several thousand onlookers gathered to watch, leaving only a narrow passage on the street for the floats to pass. Entering the Zócalo the line of vehicles passed before the National Cathedral and the National Palace, where President Díaz, Vice President Ramón Corral, and the diplomatic corps viewed the procession from the balconies.[119] They continued around the plaza past the municipal hall and then headed back west past the Centro Mercantil along September 16 Avenue. Several blocks later they headed north, then switched back along Cinco de Mayo and finally returned east along Tacuba and stopped at the Alameda Park after completing a zigzag tour of all the streets in the commercial heart of the city between the Zócalo Plaza and the Alameda.[120] The vehicles were not the only ornaments along the route: nearly all the stores—particularly the department stores—had transformed their façades and show windows with patriotic colors, banners, and an assortment of other decorations, such as the ubiquitous shields with slogans such as "Peace," "Order and Progress," and "1810–1910." At night stores lit up their exteriors with thousands of bulbs supplied by the Mexican Light and Power Company (which had offered free bulbs to private residences wishing to illuminate their homes).[121] The National Cathedral and National Palace accommodated the most—sixteen thousand and eighty-nine hundred—but the Palacio followed closely with six thousand while the Importador, Centro Mercantil, and Francia Marítima each attached over one thousand lights in artistic arrangements.[122]

After the parade the participants and invited guests of the government and foreign diplomatic corps removed to the more secluded space of the gardens of the Chapultepec Restaurant. There they held a charity kermesse, complete with a variety of foreign dance style contests, assorted games, cinema exhibits, flirtatious "confetti battles," and the usual beer and cigarette company *puestos* where consumers could enjoy a drink under the shade of tall trees and take in the air. By late afternoon the "Garden Party" dispersed and gave way at six o'clock to the exclusive ball and banquet held in the Crystal Room in the restaurant. At eleven the party concluded with a fireworks display.[123]

The day had been a great success, with much champagne consumed while toasting the president, national progress, and the important role of business and right-thinking gentlemen in the continued modernization of the republic. To commemorate their role during the day and the broader centennial festivities the organizing committee spent an amazing 52,000 pesos to publish ten thousand copies of a luxurious photographic tome—the *Álbum oficial del Comité Nacional del Comercio: Premier centenario de la independencia de Mexico, 1810–1910*. Nearly two hundred pages, and measuring eighteen by fourteen inches, the album includes images of not only the parade, festivities, and leading stores but also government officials, foreign dignitaries, and photo after photo of commercial and industrial enterprises throughout the republic. Although it was an expensive project, the business community did not hesitate to produce such a magnificent record of the world they had helped to create. In their experience such capital investments had always delivered ample returns.

Table 1

DEPARTMENTS OF THE PALACIO DE HIERRO DEPARTMENT STORE

1. Departamento de Modas (Especialidad en trajes para doñas)
2. Departamento de Sastrería
3. Departamento de Sedas
4. Departamento de Telas de Lana y Lana y Seda
5. Departamento de Generos de Algodón para Vestidos
6. Departamento de Casimires
7. Departamento de Cambrays, Nansoucks, Batistas, y Organdis Blancos (Nuestro surtido se renueva á la llegada de cada vapor)
8. Departamento de Generos Blancos y Calicots
9. Departamento de Telas de Puro Lino
10. Departamento de Artículos para Forros de Todas Clases
11. Departamento de Lonas para Catres y Tiendas de Campaña
12. Departamento de Driles, Holandas, y Algodones
13. Departamento de Modas y Sombreros
14. Departamento de Modas y Costuras
15. Talleres de Confecciones
16. Departamento de Confecciones para Señora
17. Departamento de Batas y Matinés
18. Enaguas para Calle

19. Departamento de Bramantes de Algodón y de Lino y Cotines para Colchones
20. Departamento de Vestidos para Niñas
21. Departamento de Trajecitos para Niños
22. Departamento de Sombreros para Niñas
23. Departamento de Formas, Sombreros, y Adornos
24. Departamento de Corbatas para Caballeros
25. Departamento de Sombreritos y Fallas para Niñas
26. Departamento de Ropa Interior para Señoras y Niñas
27. Departamento de Corsetería
28. Departamento de Bonetería
29. Departamento de Pañuelos y Mascados
30. Departamento de Guantes
31. Departamento de Camisas, Cuellos, y Puños
32. Departamento de Paraguas
33. Departamento de Manteles y Servilletas
34. Departamento de Sombrillas y Encás
35. Departamento de Impermeables, Mangas, y Zapatos de Hule
36. Artículos para Ciclistas
37. Sombreros y Cachucas para Caballeros
38. Abanicos
39. Bastones (plumeros)
40. Departamento de Toallas, Sábanas de Baño, y Telas para Toallas
41. Alemaniscos y Servilletas
42. Artículos para Mesa
43. Hules para Mesas, Pasillos, y Escaleras
44. Departamento de Chales y Tapalos de Seda
45. Departamento de Ponchos, Plaids, etc.
46. Cobertadores y Edredones
47. Departamento de Colchas, Cojines, y Sábanas
48. Departamento de Tiras, Bordadas, y Encajes
49. Departamento de Listonería
50. Departamento de Adornos para Vestidos
51. Departamento de Paños, Astrakanes, Peluche, y Pieles para Confecciones
52. Departamento de Layettes, Ropones, y Pelisses
53. Departamento de Artículos Diversos
54. Departamento de Artículos para Viaje
55. Artículos de Devoción
56. Artículos para Desposadas
57. Trousseaux

58. Juguetería

59. Artículos de Paris

60. Departamento de Perfumería

61. Artículos de Mercería

62. Plantas Artificiales

63. Departamento de Muebles Finos Fantasia

64. Magnífico y Suntuoso Departamento de Muebles de Salón

65. Juegos de Comedor y Recámara

66. Departamento de Alfombras y Pasillos

67. Tapetes

68. Departamento de Cortinas, Visos, Transparentes, y Cortinaje de Todas Clases

69. Departamento de Brocateles, Bourets, Cretonas, Felpas, etc.

70. Departamento de Tul y Punto

71. Departamento de Flecos, Cordones, y Pasamanería para Muebles

72. Carpetas y Pantallas

73. Departamento de Talleres

74. Departamento de Mayoreo

Source: *Grandes almacenes de "El Palacio de Hierro." Obsequio a nuestros favorecedores. Agenda para el año 1900* (Mexico City: Tip. El Lápiz de Aguila, 1900).

Table 2

DEPARTMENT STORES AND IMPORTANT *ALMACENES DE NOVEDADES*
IN LATE PORFIRIAN MEXICO CITY

STORE NAME	STORE OWNER(S)	OTHER INFORMATION
1. El Palacio de Hierro, S.A.	J. Tron y Cia. (Tron family—Joseph, Jules, and Henri—and other shareholders).	Founded 1860 as Fábricas de Francia, opened as first department store in nation in 1891 with several expansions by 1910. Located on Calle Bernardo behind city hall. Branch store in Paris.
2. El Puerto de Liverpool, S.A.	J. B. Ebrard y Cia, Sucs. Located at San Bernardo and Callejuela, across the street and east of the Palacio de Hierro. Established in 1847. 1893 business reorganization added Antoine and François Proal, Alphonse Michel, and Honoré Béraud as partners. Expanded into a purpose-built department store in 1898. Incorporated as a sociedad anónima in 1907.	Branch store in Paris.
3. Las Fábricas Universales	A. (Alexandre) Reynaud y Cia. Hippolyte Donnadieu, the original owner, died in 1895 and was. buried in the French cemetery in Mexico City.	Established 1893. Originally at the corner of the Portal de las Flores and Callejuela, moved across the street (south) from the Palacio (Bernardo and Monterilla) for its expansion to a five-story department store in 1909. Branch store in Paris.
4. Al Puerto de Veracruz	(Léon) Signoret, (Léon and Maurice) Honnorat y Cia.	Located kitty-corner from the Palacio at Capuchinas and Monterilla (southwest corner). Branch store in Paris.
5. El Centro Mercantil/La Valenciana	Originally incorporated as a sociedad anónima with José de Teresa y Miranda as president. Sebastián Robert, owner of La Valenciana, bought the whole Centro building in 1901 and continued to lease out office space on the upper floors while maintaining a department store on the bottom three floors.	Located on the southwest corner of the Zócalo, the Centro Mercantil occupied approximately one-third the width of the Portal de Mercaderes and the entire length of Tlalpaleros. Today the Gran Hotel. S. Robert et Cie. operated a branch store in Paris.

Table 2 continued

6. La Ciudad de Londres	J. Ollivier y Cia., made up of Joseph and Marius Ollivier.	Located at the corner of Monterilla and Capuchinas; underwent major renovation and expansion in 1909. J. Ollivier y Cia. also owned the almacén de novedades El Sol and the Cristaleria Moderna, which sold domestic as well as imported crystal, porcelain, crockery, and silverware. In 1906 they purchased, renovated, and expanded the Sorpresa y Primavera Unidas.
7. La Francia Maritima	Donnadieu, Veyan y Cia.	Located on the corner on Angel and Capuchinas (southeast corner).
8. La Reforma de Comercio	A. (Adolphe) Richaud y Cia., Sucs.	Empedradillo y Tacuba, across from the back of the cathedral. Also owned El Nuevo Mundo.
9. La Sorpresa y Primavera Unidas	After 1906, J. Ollivier y Cia. Prior, owned by A. Fourcade y Cia. until Fourcade died and store experienced credit problems briefly. Originally founded in 1878 by Victor Goupil, a non-Barcelonnette Frenchman from Bordeaux, when he merged his La Sorpresa with neighboring Primavera. This was *the* store of the early Porfiriato.	Located on the first block of Plateros, stretching down La Palma. Probably shared a wall with the Centro Mercantil after the latter was built. Renovated to a five-story building by Ollivier.
10. El Importador	Max Chauvet.	San Bernardo no. 19.
11. El Correo Frances	M. Lambert y Cia.	Portal de las Flores nos. 6–7.
12. Fábricas de Francia et Novedades	Ailhaud Hnos.	Monterilla and Diputación.
13. El Progreso	Michel Bellon y Cia.	
14. El Surtidor	Primitivo Pérez y Cia.	Located on the first block of Plateros, nos. 3 and 4. One of the successful non-Barcelonnette stores. Gave itself a needed facelift between 1904 and 1906 that improved its image.
15. El Nuevo Mundo	A. Richaud y Cia., Sucs.	Same owners as La Reforma de Comercio.

Table 2 continued

16. El Paje (De la Ciudad de Bruselas, before 1903)	Jauffred y Audiffred until 1903, when purchased by the Mexican citizen Carlos Arellano (Carlos Arellano y Cia.).	Arellano moved the store from the corner of Empedradillo and the south side of the first block of Plateros (opening onto the Zócalo, part of the Portal de Mercaderes) to the north side and expanded the retail space considerably.
17. El Progreso Mercantil	A. Martin Levy.	Second block of Monterilla, nos. 10 and 11. Just south of the Puerto de Veracruz. Four stories, but not a corner lot.
18. El Gran Sedería	Jules Albert y Cia.	First block Plateros, no. 4.
19. New England	Armand Bugnot.	Claimed branches in the United States and Europe.
20. La Samaritana	García, Pérez, y Cia.	Empedradillo 3. To the west of the cathedral.
21. La Ciudad de Hamburgo	German.	
22. Korff y Honsberg	German.	
23. Casa Boker	Boker family. German.	Corner of Espíritu Santo and Cadena (today Isabel la Católica and Venustiano Carranza).
24. La Suiza	Deutschler y Kern. German.	First block Plateros, no. 1.
25. Al Zafiro	F. Sanche y Cia. Sucs. Spanish.	Located on the second block of Plateros and Palma.

Chapter 5

AN ALL-CONSUMING PASSION

Desire, Department Stores, and the Modernization of Crime

One of the manifestations of today's progress is,
as they say, the refinement of vice.
—*El Diablito Rojo*, July 13, 1908, 2.

TWO IMPECCABLY DRESSED YOUNG WOMEN WALKED INTO THE PALACIO de Hierro and took seats at the counter of the cashmere department. This was not an ideal moment for leisurely shopping. The clock neared six, marking the middle of the early evening shopping rush hour, when capitalino society left work and flooded the main traffic arteries in carriages and on foot. This crush of humanity had many often overlapping aims: some to purchase needed household items, others to window shop or browse the aisles, many to see and be seen on the boulevard, and of course, a good number simply yearning for the tranquility of home after a day at the office. Moreover, with New Year's just days away, the larger-than-normal crowds of customers in the Palacio examined merchandise in search of gifts and the perfect accessories and dress material for parties to welcome in another year of prosperity.

Within moments a clerk in the department—an impeccably groomed young man—introduced himself to Juana Rojas and María Victoria

Villanueva. As they exchanged the usual salutations that prefaced commercial transactions he sized up his new customers. Well-dressed, versed in the etiquette of the store counter, and quite attractive—not too dark—they offered the potential of not only a decent commission but also an agreeable opportunity for flirtation. He mentioned that he had not seen them before, noting that he would have remembered such a beautiful sight. They replied that their families had recently moved from Morelia and that they looked forward to the wonderful shopping and entertainment offered by the capital. And so the conversation went, with the clerk bringing more and more pieces of cashmere for inspection. He seeking to charm them into purchasing as much as possible and perhaps even into seeing him some other time outside of the store; the young ladies, showering him with "flattery and smiles," hoping perhaps for a "special discount" that clerks often informally granted loyal or particularly attractive members of their personal clientele. The Palacio was not the only store where the sensuousness of the goods and the store atmosphere merged with the rapport between many young male clerks and their female customers.

Unfortunately for the clerk, the two ladies had sized him up while he did the same with them. They determined him an easy mark. As shoplifters, Juana and María were looking for more than a discount on their purchases that night.

After a period of time the cashmere had accumulated into a considerable pile that threatened to topple onto the merchandise being viewed by the customers on either side. The ladies asked the clerk to bring down one more shawl, one located on the top shelf of the tarima behind him. Rapidly becoming disenchanted, he mulled over a woman's inability to make decisions while he turned to climb the ladder for the item. As he turned, Juana quickly whisked two of the shawls from the middle of the soft mountain and stuffed them into the pocket of the long coat that protected her from the icy December winds. Although sizeable, the pieces of material easily fit into the pocket; Juana had installed "kangaroo pouches," ripping out the stitching at the base of the pocket and then sewing on extra material to extend its capacity. Returning with the top-shelf cashmere the clerk received an unwelcome response. The ladies apologized and said they were too exhausted to decide. They promised to return tomorrow and make a decision. Only after they had left and merged into a throng of shoppers did the clerk notice the missing pieces as he sorted, folded, and returned the merchandise. Feelings of anger mixed with a realization of his gullibility as he called the department manager to inform him of the deception. After passing the word and calling the store detectives the personnel might have caught Juana and María and sent them to Belén prison. More likely, those seemingly solid members of respectable society had slipped into the protective anonymity of the boulevard crowd. The only decision left was whether to keep their goods or to visit their favorite pawnshop and pocket the sixty or eighty pesos they would receive. Shoplifting in Mexico could be lucrative indeed.[1]

Analyzing how Mexican society and its press reacted to—and interpreted—criminality in the new department stores offers an untried approach to understanding the profound impact of modernization and the harder to quantify influence of modernity on crime itself.[2] This chapter begins with an overview of how shoplifters operated, how store management responded, how the press reported the crimes, and how these compared to similar activities in other contemporary societies. Following that is a consideration of how the manipulation and transgression of cultural assumptions by shoplifters threatened the safety of Porfirian categories of social order. A summary of other forms of department store criminality completes an evidential background for the chapter. At this point an outline of the traditional elite model of crime will serve as a starting mark from which to observe how radically department store crimes departed from its premises. The extensive press coverage and public fascination with property thefts such as shoplifting signaled the ascent of a new, modernizing theory of criminality that helped explain this phenomenon of criminals heretofore considered ill-fated now adopting modern skills and values to successfully prey on symbols of Mexican progress. The final section of this chapter will observe the transatlantic nature of this theory of crime before concluding how it served to illuminate both the contradictions and tensions within the Porfirian vision of orderly progress in a modern society as well as to provide a comforting explanation for the larger social changes that department store crime represented.

A Few Specifics

What we know about shoplifting and other department store criminality as a historical subject is limited. Historians such as Elaine Abelson, Patricia O'Brien, and—to a lesser degree—Michael Miller have written on its significance in the United States and France at the end of the nineteenth century.[3] Bill Lancaster comments briefly on its presence in London stores during the same time period.[4] Among Mexican historians shoplifting remains to be investigated. Despite this, we can still make some general observations on the modus operandi of Porfirian shoplifters and the cat-and-mouse game they played with store personnel as well as offer a few initial comparisons to their contemporary North Atlantic counterparts.

Accounts of shoplifters at Mexico City department stores and *magasins de novedades* began to appear regularly in the mid-1890s. Although I am sure that they began earlier, the first accounts that I found occurred in 1896, and by April 1897 the French colony's *L'Echo du Mexique* could opine that "very often the press in the capital registers thefts committed by women in the *magasins de novedades*" as a preamble for its account of how a woman stole fourteen meters of black cashmere from the store El Correo Frances.[5] Given the quantity of fabric (over forty feet), one must wonder where she hid it and how she made her escape so quickly.

Robberies could be made by individuals although often teams of two or even three cooperated in same- or opposite-sex combinations. Although the press reported frequent thefts committed by men and, to a far lesser extent, children, the majority of acts were those by women. While the scene introducing this chapter involved both ladies seated at the counter, often shoplifters working in teams left one member—the mark—at some distance from the counter. In this approach the individual charged with the initial snatch departs from the counter and passes off the goods to the unknown mark, who may pass the goods to yet another before exiting. In so doing the individual making the initial grab may plead innocence in case of capture. If working alone or if all members worked the counters, the usual plan was to follow the strategy of Juana and María described above. A variation or amplification of this may be found in this description of the shoplifter offered by the tabloid newspaper *La Gaceta de Policía*: "Dressed elegantly, she has polite manners [*ademanos correctos*] and endless kind smiles for the employees from whom they request to see measures of expensive silk, they use an opportune moment to hide the pieces in their clothing whereupon they exit from the establishment saying that the object did not please them, or that it was too expensive, or that they'll 'come back later.'"[6] No matter the strategy, shoplifters often altered their clothing to hide their contraband. Such alterations included the kangaroo pouches described in the introduction or other hidden pockets as well as secret compartments in the crowns of gentlemen's hats.[7]

The gender of the shoplifters often determined their tactics. Since the overwhelming majority—if not all—of a store's clerks were male, women tended to charm the salesclerks into complacency. They followed the model of Otilia Salazar, described as dedicated to robbing clothing stores by "distracting the employees with flattery and smiles in order to slip away with numerous objects."[8] Even more devastating were the likes of Amelia Serrano and María Soledad Ajuvita, who "have hypnotized with their looks and refined manners the unsuspecting employees of clothing stores."[9] Men often employed an upper-class attitude of entitlement to bully the clerk into handing over the goods. Both sexes relied heavily on diversionary tactics. Take, for example, the elegantly dressed man who, while inspecting a half-dozen cashmere scarves, had an accomplice run in and steal his watch; then he ran out in pursuit while carrying the merchandise, never to return.[10]

Shoplifters, like pickpockets, preferred large crowds in which to operate and chose favorable business hours. These conditions led to distracted employees and greater cover while fleeing the store. For this reason heightened shoplifting activity occurred during the hours between 11:00 a.m. and 1:00 p.m. and then 5:00 p.m. and 7:00 p.m.[11]

Mexican retailing traditions shaped the nature and tactics of shoplifting. Two of these customs stand out. The first was the policy of giving out merchandise to potential customers *á vistas*. This allowed a client to take the item—whether a length of fabric or ready-made items—home for consultations with family and friends.[12] While suggesting the high degree of sociability involved in Porfirian consumer rituals—particularly among women—its potential for abuse stands obvious. No serious effort developed to end this custom, although some editorials complained that it caused owners undue hardship given the amount of capital loaned out and the damaged goods that occasionally returned or the stolen goods that never did.[13] Certainly department store criminals must have exploited this generous policy, and edgy store clerks would occasionally presume a client's criminality prematurely.[14]

The second and most influential custom affecting the dynamics of shoplifting was the retention of most goods behind long rows of polished wood counters called mostradores. If made out of glass, as they increasingly were, they began to take on the more general name for display cases: *aparadores*. The mostrador made shoplifting a considerably more challenging task than merely snatching merchandise off of a rack. Despite the opportunities presented at certain sales with goods piled on tables either inside or outside the store, most of this crime appears to have been over-the-counter shoplifting. Elaine Abelson confirms this pattern even in American department stores, which displayed their goods more accessibly than their Mexican counterparts did.[15]

Pawnshops were one of the most common places for shoplifters and other criminals to convert their goods into cash. The reputation of pawnshops as fences for stolen goods predates the Porfiriato and reaches far back into the colonial period. Marie Francois has described the organization, contents, and criminal connections (unwitting or not) of both the Monte de Piedad and smaller, private casas de empeños from the Bourbon period until 1920.[16] She notes the stricter criteria of the Monte de Piedad and the constant calls and occasionally action for better regulation. Still, in 1895 *La Semana Mercantil* considered pawnshops the weak link in the fight against property theft and ridiculed the current regulations that prohibited only the receiving of weapons and items belonging to the nation.[17] The journal pointed out that those shop owners who did not question the origins of goods, particularly brand-new items, were just as guilty as those who committed the crimes. As in any profession or economic sector some actors were less scrupulous than others. *Empeñeros* who did accept stolen goods knowing they could pay less to thieves needing quick cash often knew their limits on certain high-profile items. For example, the bicycle craze in Mexico City in the 1890s precipitated a crime wave on the new and popular technology.[18] If they were stolen from a store, police would immediately go to the pawnshops and tell them not to buy.[19] Owners knew they could be financially liable if police found stolen merchandise in their stores.

In 1905 department and other clothing store owners demanded and achieved tougher regulations against pawnshops. Store owners directed the National Chamber of Commerce to push Governor Landa y Escandón to institute closer surveillance and tougher penalties on pawns. In a populist spirit, Landa y Escandón also reduced the usurious interest tax that empeñeros charged on goods.[20]

Pawnshops were not the only places to unload stolen goods. The street sale of cheap, stolen merchandise was another. Reselling of items to competitors of the victims also occurred.[21] One of the most talked about and therefore probably overrated places for the sale of stolen goods was the Mercado de Volador, often dubbed the Thieves' Market. Supposedly what thieves stole during the week showed up for sale on Sunday. Foreign visitors with plans of writing a book about their journey made obligatory pilgrimages to this market. They titillated their readers with images of "picturesque crowds of ragged vendors" acting as fences and repeated how "many instances are told by foreigners who were robbed, and, in a few hours, found their property exposed for sale in this market. They were obliged to pay considerable sums to recover their own property."[22] Even the French colony's *Le Courrier du Mexique* thought that the Parisian paper *Globe Trotter* had exaggerated the market for its readers' benefit and blackened the reputation of Mexican society with such claims as "the vagabonds of Mexico are perhaps the greatest thieves in creation."[23] Despite its high profile, the Volador had become little more than a tourist trap flea market by the mid-Porfiriato.

Stores did not leave themselves defenseless. They marshaled a variety of defenses against shoplifting. Store employees caught shoplifters and held them until police arrived. Managers watched both customers and employees. Larger retailers such as department stores appear to have emulated the French, British, and Americans and hired store detectives to nab shoplifters and pickpockets. These detectives also served as another level of surveillance against employees who—as will be discussed later in this chapter—were not unknown to supplement their incomes at the expense of their employers. Electric lighting and glass merchandise cases also helped, furnishing what Elaine Abelson calls "still another view of the continual dichotomy between display and protection."[24] Light and glass, in concert with color, the creation of the crowd, and other devices, were two of the most prominent ways in which the department store heightened sensory stimulation and created a desire for the merchandise. At the same time, light and glass assisted in ordering and surveilling that desire and minimizing the number of items leaving the store unpaid-for. The installation of electricity generators by the big stores and the regular complaints against the patchy service of the electric company by groups such as the National Chamber of Commerce were in equal parts addressing concerns of merchandise protection and public order, as well as providing proper display conditions.[25]

Surprisingly, Porfirians did not really have a specific term for shoplifting or shoplifters. *Ládron* and *ratero* applied to more general theft but were employed for store theft as well. The most common label, *cruzador* or *cruzadora*, was adopted into common usage from street slang (*calo*). Almost unknown today, the term receives a concise—and one of the few—published definition as follows: "A woman who robs retail stores and is often accompanied by another, often handing off to her what she has stolen."[26] In press and police reports, shoplifters could be men, women, and children, but tellingly this definition focuses on feminine criminality. Because these shoplifters often dressed to fit the image of a respectable client they also attracted the label of *elegantes*, a more general term for men and women that covered actors beyond retail stores who, in the eyes of respectable society, had committed the added transgressive crime of exceeding class boundaries. The label *elegante* was a contemptuous one and should be considered a criminalized version of *lagartijo*, or lizard. This latter term was commonly used to describe the well-dressed and often dandified young men of indeterminate social background who hung out in the downtown commercial zone, often lounging against display windows like lizards seeking to catch the eye of a young lady passing by in a carriage or on foot.[27]

But what about the kleptomaniac? While widespread in France and the United States, the term found occasional usage in Mexico but more often as a description of the act—kleptomania—than the actors—kleptomaniacs. The term *kleptomania* first entered common usage in Europe during the first half of the nineteenth century to describe individuals (mostly women) who stole compulsively from stores selling clothing, fabrics, and accessories. It received its first lengthy and scientific treatment in 1840 France.[28] Originally focused on the pathology or eccentricity of the individual, the study of kleptomania changed as the century drew to a close. Studies increasingly emphasized the social milieu in which kleptomania took place. They noted the connection between the development of department stores and the dramatic rise in the incidence of kleptomania. The "Palaces of Consumption," with their irresistible—some would say seductive—display techniques, seemed capable of turning ladies of respectable society into inveterate criminals against their will. Many worried that department stores might lead to the mass criminalization of middle-class French women; they expressed the confusion experienced by many on how department stores, as bourgeois institutions, "were expected to uphold the moral order, not threaten it."[29]

The concept of kleptomania was, of course, rife with assumptions of class. Ladies could not be called criminals, so the medicalization of shoplifting offered a palatable option and allowed for the retention of respectability among the deserving.[30] Making shoplifting a medical condition for those within a certain social station made "I couldn't help myself" a sufficient alibi, one that, along with a donation to charity and perhaps a promise never to enter the store again, often proved sufficient

to shield the offender from criminal prosecution or public humiliation. As Abelson makes clear, store managers often turned a blind eye
to shoplifting among their better clientele until it became too blatant
and preferred to hush up rather than publicize any infractions so as to
protect the store's valued customer base and its public image as a safe
and morally irreproachable place for respectable ladies to congregate.[31]
Despite this public hand-wringing about middle-class women, Miller
compels his readers to remember that much of the crime committed
in the Bon Marché was the work of "professionals or common shoplifters."[32] Presumably this means individuals of a lower class or criminal
class, but I wonder if this barrier between kleptomaniac and mere shoplifter, between respectable and criminal, is perhaps more porous than
Miller allows.

This ambiguity strikes at the heart of one of the key questions in
this chapter: who were the shoplifters in Mexico City? An unexpected
divergence exists between Mexican newspapers and those of the United
States and France when it comes to the coverage of store theft. Abelson's
and O'Brien's sources demonstrate that the press did not share the com-
punction of store managers to hush-up shoplifting by respectable ladies
and made information readily available about these women. Name,
age, address, occupation of husband, and other data helped place these
women in their social context.[33] In Mexican newspapers no such coverage existed; reports of gente decente shoplifting were largely hushed up.
Even the French colony press—as the voice of the largest retailing interests and therefore an advocate of tougher punishment—abstained from
publishing full names when it did occasionally report on gente decente
shoplifting in the early years of the media mania related to the crime.
L'Echo du Mexique represented this style in one of its 1896 crime reports:
"Two young ladies, M.M. and P.A., belonging to the bourgeoisie, were
surprised yesterday morning in Jules Albert's store on 1a. Monterilla at
the moment when they hid under their skirts several scarves that they
had come to steal. They were escorted to the police station."[34] Such
reports in Mexico involving middle-class ladies were rare, exceedingly
so for those "escorted to the police station."

Thus shoplifters reported in the Mexican press were rarely "kleptomaniacs" from respectable society but rather "cruzadoras" and "elegantes" purported to originate from a far less honorable class of people. These
were people assumed and sometimes confirmed to have experienced multiple arrests, to belong to a lower socioeconomic standing, and to compose

a "criminal class" that preyed on respectable society, threatened public order, and retarded national progress. The public crime narratives built on their actions and presumed motives form the foundation of this chapter.

Transgressions and Concerns of Proper Consumption

In executing their crimes, department store shoplifters crystallized the insecurities of Porfirian respectable society. Many of these insecurities reflected a common transatlantic belief among elites that their societies were in a state of decay and moral decline despite the dramatic material and intellectual achievements achieved in the nineteenth century.[35] Shoplifters not only broke criminal laws against theft of property but also manipulated and defied elite assumptions about social space, race, class, gender, and proper consumption. Report after criminal report created an impression that the societal danger of shoplifters was less their economic predations than their social effrontery and threat to "moral order." Undoubtedly the cumulative economic cost of shoplifting must have been considerable for store owners; nonetheless, in the narrative created by the press the frequent recitation of the value of stolen merchandise often comes across as a frustrated and inadequate attempt to quantify the extent of the greater crime against society.

Penetrating and disrupting the orderly social space of the *gente decente* stands as the first transgression. Historians of both the colonial and national periods of Mexico have marked out the ongoing struggle between ruling and popular classes to stake their claim to public space and define the character of the cities. Concerns of moral safety served as a central justification for expelling lower class recreations and individuals from urban centers. Physically marginalizing or outright banning activities such as gambling, begging, prostitution, and cockfighting or popular institutions including *pulquerías* and sidewalk cinemas were just a few of the state-directed strategies enacted by the *gente decente* to reduce crime and immorality in order to create an orderly, moral social space that made tangible their vision of modern urban living.[36] Sweeping police reforms and the stationing of thousands of new gendarmes in the capital served to administer and enforce these laws. Results were mixed in the city centers that were the focal point of these sanitization efforts.

Department stores set a new stage in this conflict. They reflected the influence and impact of commercial capital on Mexican society. The construction of these enormous stores—the quintessential institution of respectable society—established a new hybrid space both public and private: private in that it was both enclosed and on private property; pub-lic in that it was a market moved inside, governed by the new consumer culture mantra touting the "democratization of luxury" and its policies of free entry and the serving of an economically ecumenical clientele. This new space had the potential to realize an ordered and surveilled "public space" for respectable society. Most galling to social observers was that the audacity of shoplifters and other lawbreakers brought dis-order to the hoped-for order.

Manipulating Porfirian stereotypes and assumptions of race, class, and gender was essential in this disordering of social space. Consider first class and race, two categories of social distinction so closely intertwined in Mexican society. While department stores now allowed most anyone in, the best service as usual went to those who appeared best able to afford it. On the most superficial level, the employee's calculations took into account the color of skin and manner of dress. A perusal of the pho-tos published in the "Página negra" section of the *Gaceta de Policía* reveals shoplifters with skin tone ranging from the medium-brown mestiza to olive and what appears quite pale.[37] Proper attire and a full purse often lightens one's skin socially in Mexico; the women in the photos dressed in a range from tasteful to extremely fashionable, with not a single *zar-ape*, rebozo, or hair braid among the lot. The jolting distinctiveness of the few reported exceptions to this rule makes the point.[38]

Newspaper reports of shoplifting regularly noted that the culprits were "well-dressed" or "elegantly dressed" or "appeared honorable" and had thus fooled the employee. But as the Mexican *dicho* goes, "A monkey dressed in silk is still a monkey."[39] For that reason, an accomplished con artist had to possess not only shopping etiquette to lull an employee into complacency but also the constellation of manners and knowledge that marked one as one of the better members of society. This made *elegantes* such as the con artist who robbed the famous Labadie jewelers in 1903 so dangerous: claiming he was the son of a "comfortable family from the interior," he was an "individual correctly presented, wore suits of fine cashmere, and changed morning and afternoon conforming to the demands of the most rigorous fashion."[40] Or Berta Gutiérrez and Rosa Rubio, "very dangerous *cruzadoras* who, elegantly dressed, entered dry-goods stores where they've committed numerous ingeniously executed robberies. They are now free and the public must be alert because their distinguished manners and attire can easily surprise the good faith of the public."[41]

In this way the manipulation of societal assumptions by shoplifting and swindling elegantes was a classic "crime of passing." This status misrepresentation cut to the quick of Porfirian society's obsession with social hierarchies and the need to make them visible through such markers of personal consumption as clothing. In a society so concerned with maintaining visible social boundaries and order, little wonder Porfirians sought to transform the character of—or outright ban—popular Carnival celebrations for both their "world-turned-upside-down" nature as well as the masks and costumes—the public disguises—that marked this holiday.[42]

But a worrying thought must have tugged at newspaper readers if they considered that shoplifters could replicate not only the material trappings of class but also the much more difficult niceties of etiquette and behavior. Were the perpetrators of these crimes really social impostors? Might a considerable number be class traitors instead? Could the deeply ingrained and comforting belief in a neat division between respectable society and a criminal class recruited from the lower socioeconomic stations remain intact? Many undoubtedly did grapple with this, given the appearance of kleptomania as a category to medicalize and decriminalize property theft by middle-class ladies. Such threats to the received wisdom of social classification must have only compounded fin-de-siècle angst about the stability of society.

Equally disturbing as the manipulation of class and race attributions was that of gender. Women shoplifters—cruzadoras—were often young and attractive, and they used Porfirian notions of chivalry and gender distinctions to their fullest advantage. An 1897 editorial in *El Imparcial* attacks the double standard used by society in judging male and female thieves.[43] Titled "Thefts by the Fair Sex: Hearts and Lace" and written in the midst of what the press called a crime wave perpetrated by petty criminals, the editorial begins by castigating readers who assumed such a title would lead to a tale of how a dark-eyed beauty had robbed the editorialist of his heart. He lays out his argument that those "dedicated to the betterment of society to the detriment of crooks" need to carefully consider the typical societal response to "crime *performed* by smooth and white hands."[44] A description of a recent clothing store theft in which the gendarmes arrested two young ladies with unpaid goods sets the scene. Next he states that the perpetrators undoubtedly "started to cry" and that women were far better at such crime than "individuals of the stronger but ugly sex." He continues, "When a thief is caught in the act he doesn't start to cry, but starts to run. The indignant public shouts 'Catch the thief! Catch the thief!' When a young, female elegante cries, the public is moved. 'Poor little girl! Who can be sure that the unfortunate thing didn't steal the lace *OUT OF NECESSITY!*'" (italics in original). The editorialist notes that those who scold the thief invariably get the following response from the public: "Man, don't be such a brute! How can you be so insolent as to accuse this young lady of the crime of robbery? Don't you see that it is a sin against chivalry?" Other onlookers, "more generously," make the following offer: "I will pay for the lace. What's the charge?" Before going on to a much longer diatribe against mothers who are delinquent in the raising of their children, he urges readers to apply the law regardless of sex and commends most gendarmes for applying the law despite the misguided thoughts of the surrounding crowd.

Although in the stores cruzadoras could use Porfirian notions of gender to their advantage, in the daily press those same cultural assumptions about a woman's relationship to society and its morality were used to reprove her actions. Cruzadoras drew the most ire from commentators and received the most coverage in *La Gaceta de Policía* because they tapped into a deep-running fear in Mexican society about the moral dangers associated with the public woman. Construction of gender and class in Mexico converged in a belief system among the gente decente based around contrasting notions of femininity, what William French has called "prostitutes and guardian angels."[45] The association of the public sphere with moral danger and the private with safety formed the "cult of domesticity," the foundation of Western society's middle-class worldview and self-definition. Social and economic realities of market societies usually conflict with cultural ideologies, and this was no exception. In chapter 1 we saw an eruption of this in the public discourse over the use of cigarette girls (*cantineras*) by El Buen Tono during the Unión Mercantil boycott and the attack and defense over the moral honor of these girls on the streets. These could be rationalized away because they were working-class girls and were forced by circumstance into the public sphere. The perceived moral dangers encountered by middle-class women—often sallying forth without a male chaperon—wandering downtown and being served by young, male clerks in department stores, as mentioned in chapter 3, proved more difficult to dispel.

An illustrative distillation of this gender construct and the threat posed to it by cruzadoras comes from the "Página negra" section just before Christmas in 1905 (it also parallels the diatribe in the 1897 *El Imparcial* editorial quoted above):

> Depressing to one's spirit is the idea that among the feminine sex there are more than just a few who dedicate themselves, in their pursuit of making a living, to taking on the completely alien form of the ratero [thief].

> How many considerations have been made to explain the fact of the abundance of cruzadoras! If the act of robbery is repugnant in a man, it is even more reproachable in a woman.

> The woman is the director of education in the home, and no one can obscure the influence that the habits, vices, and criminal behaviors of the mother, the older sister, the woman of the house, must exercise in the moral environment of a family.

> We have said many times in the past that [shoplifters range from] girls of just a few years to old women; shabbily dressed and shoeless to women of middle-class attire, with hat, fine shoes and the general appearance of decent persons.[46]

For the *Gaceta* and the language of respectability it employed, females who committed criminal acts were an abomination of the natural order. As women served the role of both biological and social reproduction in modernizing societies, their aberrant behavior threatened not only their own health and stability but also that of their family and their country. As Robert Buffington and Pablo Piccato have noted, in the international competition among nation-states prior to World War I, such acts by women amounted to treason against the state.[47]

Finally, although the *Gaceta* warned that shoplifters originated from most ranges of the social spectrum its greatest contempt and most photographic coverage were not for the poorest-looking criminals but rather for those passing as members of the gente decente. This leads to the final transgressive act of shoplifters, so increasingly central in the modern world: a crime of consumption. This concern, too, should be approached as part of the larger transatlantic elite concern with the decline of national vigor and morality.

Shoplifting threatened the precarious logical foundations of Porfirian progress. For Porfirian society consumption was inextricably connected with modernity. The flood of commodities, new institutions of leisure and consumption, and a higher material standard of living for many coincided with the rapid and wrenching social, economic, and cultural changes associated with modernity sweeping Mexico. Understandably, the mixed impact of these transformative influences resulted in the ambiguous feelings toward "progress" so well documented by cultural and social historians of Mexico in the past two decades.[48] This ambiguity found expression in public commentary on consumption or, more often, on its contemporary synonym, "luxury." Like the notion of progress itself, Porfirians did not outright condemn consumption but rather, like their counterparts to the north and across the Atlantic, they sought to manage consumption, to harness it in the service of the national drive to modernize both the economy and culture. Participation in a budding consumer society became a duty of citizenship in the nation-state. In Mexico the constant criticism of Indians as nonconsumers and therefore a drag on both economic and cultural progress starkly expresses this reality of the consumer-citizen identity in the modern nation.[49]

Fears of the impact of consumerist values in Mexico mirrored those held by much of the European bourgeois class. These included perceptions of national and class moral decay as well as the ghastly possibility of blurred social distinctions threatened by the so-called democratization of luxury. Thus we see in Mexico a version of what Warren G. Breckman has described in the Wilhelmine German context as a distinction between productive and unproductive consumption. This vision held that in order to be good, "consumption of the individual should balance his productive power"; if it did not, such consumption became "luxury" and therefore should be labeled socially undesirable.[50] In the worldview of the gente decente the survival of a modern nation required that a new consumer ethic be balanced by a work ethic.

Public diatribes on property theft in Mexico City reveal this ideology in the rawest form. Besides the usual calls to whip thieves, journalists decried the fact that such criminals passed "short vacations" in jail, eating better inside than out.[51] Turning these unproductive leisured consumers into productive members of society became the rallying cry of criminal reformers. Reformers and eventually lawmakers decided that forced work offered the solution. In 1904 new legislation in the Penal Code changed the penalty for theft from three days in Belén prison to five or six months of hard labor, often in the dreaded Valle Nacional and other insalubrious agricultural zones.[52] In *El Imparcial* a columnist noted that crime had dropped considerably after one month under the new law, with a dramatic decline among those "dressed respectably."[53] He continued that the usual poor and dirty criminals did not have much to worry about forced labor, being accustomed to such a condition in their miserable lives. Rather, the "ratero elegante, he that commits robberies to sustain a life of dissipation, almost of opulence, has almost completely disappeared because for him the punishment of the new Code is too hard." Although overly optimistic on the decline of the elegante, the columnist and his glee represent the common sentiment among his class toward those committing the paired transgressive crimes of status misrepresentation and illegal consumption.

Writ large, this worldview insisted that the advancement of the nation-state required the balancing of national and personal consumption with production capabilities. Consumption in a natural equilibrium, what I would call "proper consumption" or consumption proper to one's place in society, could serve the interests of an abstract nation as well as social harmony by maintaining class distinctions.

Excessive consumption could be disastrous. The great fear of nineteenth-century bourgeois society was the threat to the stability of social identities and to larger issues of hierarchy and order in society. First of all, by the second half of the nineteenth century the bourgeoisie became preoccupied by the precariousness of its position within society. In Europe a work ethic had historically distinguished this class from the aristocracy. Their economic power had yielded the eventual social, political, and cultural clout that made them the dominant social class of the nineteenth century and their interests, for all intents and purposes, synonymous with those of the nation-state. But this ethic brought the money that led not only to the possibility of higher consumption to express conspicuously their social position but also the danger that subsequent generations might become the same unproductive, dandified rentier class, indistinguishable from the early aristocracy, from which they had distanced themselves.[54] This same anxiety circulated through Mexican social circles even though in Mexico the social dynamics were far different. There the middling classes were far smaller and weaker, less independent, and considerably more dependent on government rather than business for their elevated social station. Although public discourse occasionally positioned the middling classes as the productive backbone of the nation, many of the ruling elite looked upon them contemptuously compared to their European counterparts. Most telling is President Díaz's description of this class and what he considered their excessive consumption: "They wake up late, being public employees with patrons of influence, attend their work without punctuality, call in sick often . . . never miss bullfights, seek endless diversions . . . they marry young and have unlimited numbers of children, spending more than they earn and indebt themselves to usurers to pay for holiday celebrations and birthday parties [saint's days]."[55] This internal conflict over self-definition—as primarily leisured consumers or as producers—infused bourgeois concerns internationally.

Secondly, the middling classes feared the working classes from which many of them were no more than a generation or two removed and by no means permanently so, depending on their economic fortunes. In Mexico the comparatively small size of the gente decente and the fear of the *población flotante*—the floating population of migrant labor that flowed into cities and traveled throughout the republic on the rail system—made these fears even more disturbing.[56] Besides fears of physical harm, the concern of blurring the lines between classes occupied top billing in the list of middle-class anxieties. Emulative consumption, or the copying of one's "betters," was not a new phenomenon. In fact, the bourgeoisie of early centuries had experienced public humiliation and often prison sentences mandated by sumptuary legislation passed by the aristocracy that prohibited the upstart merchant and professional class from displaying certain commodities, such as the color purple. Changes in attitude, liberal legal codes, and the "democratization of luxury" promoted by leaders of retailing made such de jure sanctions impossible. Whether or not the emulative consumption of the Porfiriato was an exercise in social climbing through imitation or more of a challenge remains debatable. In any case, gente decente society sought to institute a de facto class distinction in consumption as it patrolled the boundaries of proper consumption through articles in the press about gauche interlopers and in innumerable daily encounters between individuals passing spoken and unspoken judgment on those who crossed invisible lines of sartorial acceptability. In *El Mundo Ilustrado* one such public denouncement comes from a writer recounting his recent train trip with a companion. He describes the boarding of a young women "attired in a magnificent toilette" whose ruse crumbles as soon as she speaks, at which point "we noted that her education did not correspond to her dress." Continuing, he relays that he found out that she was a seamstress going to the house of a relative where she was to be the *madrina* (godmother) at a baptism. This remark "obliged us to exchange among ourselves an ironic smile" because her toilette was not at all appropriate for the occasion, as "it was not in relation to her resources; it was truly the toilette of a duchess." He concludes with this advice or warning to his readers: "When it comes to clothing, it is necessary not to depart from the following rule: Dress yourself according to your age and position."[57]

Family and particularly women served as the connective links for class, consumption, and the nation-state in the dominant cultural framework of nineteenth-century bourgeois society. As outlined previously in an excerpt from the *Gaceta*, certain particular characteristics of women made them the soul of family life. They provided the love, moral education, household economic administration, and increasingly, the consumption requirements of the home. Women in Mexico and elsewhere, therefore, possessed a weighty social role, given that bourgeois society considered the family the building blocks of the nation.[58]

The dark side of the feminine character was its supposed taste for luxury. For centuries women have been viewed as more susceptible to luxury and, more recently, to the ever-changing dictates of fashion. By the Porfirian era in Mexico the average household, particularly the urban one, had cast off home production in favor of the ease, quality, and abundance offered by the market. Women, in charge of the household economy, were required to enter this public realm to fulfill their domestic duties.[59] Consumption hardened as a feminine trait while productive activities solidified as masculine. Nowhere is this Porfirian language of gendered consumption more transparent than in the press, which offered up as regular fare the trope that men were incapable of shopping. In articles such as "The Purchase of Fabrics" a social observer notes that sometimes men, "out of gallantry or to help their spouse," take it upon themselves to purchase the fabrics required by the house, but few understand the task at hand and "it can be almost guaranteed that their purchase is always expensive and of poor quality." A woman, on the other hand, "educated in such niceties, makes a better and less expensive purchase."[60] In one of the many contradictions found in the Porfirian social vision, this praise for feminine skill and thrift butted against women's assumed weakness for luxury. This weakness, combined with the

emergence of department stores, boutiques, and commercialized entertainment districts in urban centers, led to the vociferously expressed fear
that their desire and capacity to consume might imperil their ability to
manage the household economy.

Only a strong moral core could prevent the love of finery and consumption from ruining a woman and her family both economically and
morally. Such concerns preoccupied writers of widely purchased etiquette and religious manuals as well as those for the prominent newspapers in the capital.[61] Ironically, these newspapers counseled restraint on
one page while on the next they actively promoted the latest clothing
or home-furnishing styles. What served to unify this apparent contradiction was the emphasis on proper, class-specific consumption. "The
clothing that family members wear must be in harmony with their
means and with their social position," sternly warned one article before
focusing blame on the core of the family turned rotten, namely mothers
"who excite the vanity of their daughters, instilling pernicious needs,
fomenting in them a passion that can drive them towards vice."[62] A parallel theme of feminine vanity was that of the newlywed couple. Brides
received constant admonishment in the press to not exceed the budgets
of their husbands as they furnished their new homes. In "The Selection
and Arrangement of the Home" an expert in home decoration advises
and warns readers to beware easy credit payment options and the desire
for excessively luxurious furniture. "Preferable is a modest set of furnishings representative of your resources which can be improved as your
husband's fortunes improve."[63] Porfirian literature echoed this theme
with cautionary tales such as "La mujer económica," in which a man
recounts how his bride and mother-in-law tricked him into believing her
thrifty, but the new wife now seeks to match the conspicuous consumption of her other married friends. Another example is "Un secreto de
casada," concerning the plight of a young housewife who nearly runs
her husband into debt by her slavish devotion to fashion, encouraged by
a Jewish-French modiste who supplies her vanity.[64]

Throughout this internal discourse of the gente decente the themes
of consumption, class, gender, and morality interweave. An essential fragility of the morality and socioeconomic fortunes of the individual and
family underpins the conversation and underscores the insecurity felt
by much of respectable society. Women are presented as the linchpins
of this social and moral order and therefore the weakest link.

Shoplifting became such a lightning-rod issue for Porfirians because it realized these fears of the gente decente. Discussion of the topic allowed anxieties to surface over the shape of society that they were creating. Onto shoplifters, especially cruzadoras, Porfirians projected their fears about the place and morality of women, the stability and distinguishability of social classes and order, and the precariousness of public space for "civilized" society, seemingly threatened and surrounded by forces of chaotic backwardness. That these concerns should focus on the act of consumption and in locations such as the department store only makes sense for a class so proud of their material culture and the goods that made their values concrete. If one accepts that the nineteenth-century state—like the department store—reflected the values and goals of respectable society, then the act of shoplifting may be seen as questioning the assumptions of the whole national modernization project. The Porfirian motto of Order and Progress manifested the gente decente ideal; that shoplifters successfully hijacked the commodities, cultural education, and institutions of this progress and brought disorder to order deeply threatened those who believed in the perfectibility of modern society.

Death by a Thousand Cuts

Shoplifters were not the only threats to department stores. They delivered but one of a thousand cuts by which these institutions of the gente decente suffered injury to their financial bottom line and public reputation.[65] Many of the thefts illustrate how criminals adapted to the world of Porfirian progress.

The practice of home-delivery service coupled with COD (cash on delivery) or deferred payment provided numerous opportunities for the crude theft or clever swindle. Among the former were the two men who overheard a delivery order, raced to the house on Avenida Juárez, greeted the female employee bringing the goods, then stole the clothes, valued at nearly 500 pesos.[66] An example of the latter comes from the swindle conducted against the Centro Mercantil in 1906. "Two men of industry, extremely elegant in dress and bearing, with ostentation and sumptuous jewelry" selected 700 pesos worth of bronzes and other objets d'art and asked that they be delivered to a hotel on Independencia whereupon they would pay for the goods. An employee brought the sculptures to the men in the hotel lobby, at which point one offered to guard the goods

while the other ordered the boy to accompany him to his office, where
he would be paid. En route to the fictitious office the swindler separated
from the employee in the boulevard crowd. Returning to the hotel, the
employee found the goods and the customers gone.[67]

The considerable value of goods in transport throughout the city
proved irresistible not only to thieves preying on the delivery agents
but often even to those agents themselves: stories of licensed *cargadores*
(porters) commissioned by department stores never arriving at their
destination were not unusual.[68] Assaults on *cobradores*, or collectors,
who traveled to the homes of customers throughout the city collecting
payments stung establishments of all sizes. These collectors, often well
known, were out in force on Saturdays and on the fifteenth of every
month and made easy targets. Since they received payments in cash they
often carried thousands of pesos in banknotes in their pocketbooks.
As a response stores encouraged the use of checks to reduce the attrac-
tiveness of their employees as targets.[69]

Warehouses located in the city were another point in the distribution pipeline besides stores themselves from which thieves could siphon
off goods. Employees at the warehouses often supplemented their incomes with bonuses in kind, much the same way that dockworkers and
others regularly pilfered the goods that passed through their workplace.
More spectacular and newsworthy were the cases such as the crime
committed at the warehouses of the Centro Mercantil in the spring of
1901. Two friends recently fired from their department store jobs formed
the nucleus of the gang involved. One, Margarito Reyes, had just lost his
job at the Centro Mercantil warehouse and the other, Vicente Jay, left
the employ of the Oriental clothing store located under the Portal de
las Flores. They invited a maintenance technician from the telegraph
office and another man to join them in a heist of thousands of pesos'
worth of merchandise from Reyes's former employer. After taking a
coach to the warehouse they gained admittance upon telling the guards
that they were looking for a broken telegraph wire on the roof. The
telegraph technician's uniform had "served to inspire confidence," and
the other three accomplices merely posed as assistants. Once on the roof
they broke the locks on the roof door. Gaining access to the merchandise areas, they stole seven crates of silk ties, shirts, cashmere goods,
and other costly items. Eventually caught more than two months later,
the four revealed where they had sold many of the goods, including the
Merced and San Juan markets. A significant portion of the goods were

recovered in the possession of Jay, who, it turned out, had been stealing from his employer for some time and hoarding the items with the idea of opening his own clothing store.[70]

Inside the department stores con artists and other thieves teamed up with employees to fleece owners. Illustrative is the case of one swindler described as twenty-five years old with the appearance of a "gentleman of industry, dressed with tasteful elegance and fine jewelry" who robbed department stores with the help of employees. On holidays, when stores closed at noon, he would plan for an employee to let him in through a service door, whereupon he would select and then carry out "pieces of the finest silk" and boxes of handkerchiefs, ties, scarves, and other items under a large Spanish cape worn for the occasion. Authorities finally caught him not in a department store but for chatting up and then robbing ladies of their travel bags on Pullman rail cars between Orizaba and the Federal District. Such information reinforces the suspicion that these "modern" criminals possessed both ample talents and an ability to adapt to—and exploit—the new technologies of progress.[71]

External threats to stores did not blind owners to the fact that their own employees embezzled with alacrity and needed little outside assistance. Singly or in groups, employees stole quantities ranging from the relatively insignificant, like the 50 pesos Margarito Gútierrez stole from the Puerto de Veracruz in 1896, to the considerable—3,000 pesos lifted and pawned by four staff members at the Cajón de Sol in 1898.[72] Collaboration among employees could reach staggering numbers not only within department stores but also at other retailers, such as the famous La Profesa pharmacy, where twenty-five employees were arrested for pawning both medical supplies and more typical consumer goods.[73] Nor were these necessarily new or seemingly disgruntled personnel; high-level employees possessing both seniority and trust from management betrayed this confidence. Cobradores, the bill collectors mentioned earlier, occasionally decided that the receipts of the day offered an early and comfortable retirement and disappeared from town. In two representative examples, the Centro Mercantil lost 1,650 pesos and La Valenciana scrambled to recover 8,000 pesos.[74]

Store management obviously kept an eye on their staff and frequently caught dishonest employees, who faced instant job termination, imprisonment, and likely blacklisting among not only clothing stores but all retail employment opportunities offered by the tight-knit and influential French community. Two examples illustrate the surveillance techniques used by store managers. At the Palacio de Hierro Antonio Reynaud noticed that a number of objects on display were disappearing in his department. Suspecting employee involvement, he instituted a system of surveillance. Within days he had caught the employees Porfirio Galán and Nieves Reyes in the act, called for a gendarme, and sent them off to jail. A sweep of pawnshops recovered high-end wallets, cigar boxes, and silk scarves, which made up only a small portion of the overall theft believed to have been conducted over a period of months.[75] At the Nuevo Mundo store a young Spaniard named Eloy Castillo parlayed a number of glowing letters of reference into a job as counter clerk. Within days his supervisor suspected him of giving out á vistas (items loaned for home inspection) to unknown persons, which did not return to the store. Furthering the suspicions of his boss, Castillo rapidly upgraded his clothing and "appeared to be spending considerable sums which surely exceeded his salary." The supervisor then caught him in the act of hiding thirteen expensive scarves between several shirts to fill an á vistas order in which Castillo had documented only the shirts. Upon interrogation Castillo maintained his innocence until another employee informed on him.[76]

Despite the efforts of supervisors, the losses to employee theft continued. Clearly the much-vaunted and generally valid reputation of family unity in Barcelonnette stores had disappeared by the last decade of the Porfiriato. Perhaps Thomas Edison's invention in 1910 of an automated salesclerk to replace human employees in clothing stores best reflected the international extent of frustration in an age when technology promised to address and solve the problems of the day.[77]

Breaking the Mold: *Violence au Vol*

The public fascination and frustration with department store theft must be placed in the context of contemporary thinking about national development in Mexico. As in the North Atlantic nations such as the United States, France, Germany, and Britain, which served as global models for economic and cultural emulation, Mexican respectable society possessed the sense that its modernizing efforts were beset on all sides by destabilizing and backward elements of society. National and, indeed, general human progress entailed a cultural war. Criminal activity, perceived as welling up from traditional elements of society, served as one of several focal points for these concerns of social instability.

By 1890 Porfirian leaders and social commentators believed Mexico was in the midst of a crime wave. The 1895 census provided statistical grist for a budding Mexican criminology publishing mill that shrilly pronounced that homicide rates in Mexico dwarfed those experienced by European societies.[78] Equally disturbing was the quadrupling of property crime rates between 1885 and 1895.[79] The press echoed comments like those of *La Semana Mercantil* in 1891, noting the "marked and perceptible worsening of criminality in the capital."[80] Those concerned viewed pockets of respectability and urban progress like downtown as besieged on all sides by criminal elements from the lower classes. This perspective envisioned the worst elements of traditional Mexico trying to destroy a budding modern Mexico. In response, Díaz's government reformed and reinforced the police forces, prison institutions, and the penal codes.[81] Government leaders such as Finance Minister José Yves Limantour stocked their libraries with books on the subject with the hope of finding a solution.[82]

It was not supposed to be this way. Since the Restored Republic under Benito Juárez and Sebastián Lerdo de Tejada liberal idealism had combined with the influence of positivism in offering the hope that crime could be abolished as a result of the inexorable forward march of humanity. Crime was supposed to be antithetical to the world of progress, as irreconcilable a combination as oil and water. By the Porfiriato this utopian idealism had morphed into the colder utilitarianism of social Darwinism to provide the dominant elite foundation for understanding crime.

Herbert Spencer developed social Darwinism by adapting Charles Darwin's evolutionary theories to fit human society. He popularized the phrase "survival of the fittest," offering a theory attractive to many Mexican rulers for justifying their program of laissez-faire economic development, social differentiation, and disdain for the lower classes and Indian populations. "Survival of the fittest" granted them a convenient lens through which to view the abject poverty and misery of the popular classes as an example of natural selection, of populations with weak traits genetically destined to perish for their inability to adapt to new conditions.

Mexican leaders' criminological model embodied these social Darwinist beliefs. Despite the statistical fact that, historically, criminal behavior in Mexico had cut across social and ethnic lines, criminologists such as Miguel Macedo, Julio Guerrero, and Carlos Roumagnac knit together criminology theories from Europe and the United States to provide social and hereditary explanations for lower-class criminality in the capital. The argument ran as follows: members of the lower classes committed the vast majority of crimes due to their depraved moral character, influenced by broken homes, disease, alcohol and drug abuse, and promiscuous sexuality. Characteristically they carried out their crimes spontaneously when they were drunk, passionate, and desperate; they acted with little foresight. Moreover, according to Macedo, "personal experience" teaches that violent crimes "are almost all committed by individuals of the lower class against individuals of the same class." Julio Guerrero perceived criminals to represent the pathetic failures in the Darwinist struggles for life, "unable to resist the continuous, enervating influences of the physical and social milieu . . . who finally become obstacles for the other members of society. In their weakness they have lost any sense of collective action or responsibility."[83] In short, the typical Mexican criminal was imagined as male, lower class, Indian or mestizo, of low intelligence, and acting alone. He was often inebriated and in a moment of passion he committed a violent act, usually "over a woman or a centavo," as one newspaper opined.[84]

This model, already under assault, reached a critical point by the mid-1890s with the establishment of department stores and the ascent of shoplifting as a central narrative in the mass-circulation press. The spotlight on department store criminality in turn held attention on the fragility of this conventional, elite model of crime. Nonviolent, sober, and premeditated, crimes such as shoplifting involved the acquisition of goods and material wealth. With characteristics, causation, and aims completely different from a violent crime against an individual, a sophisticated property crime committed against a business institution appeared to represent a society in transition.

Crime seemed to be reflecting the economic, social, and cultural changes facilitated by the policies of the national governments since the Restored Republic. Crime patterns reflected the fact that criminals go where the money is. During the Porfiriato this increasingly transferred the bulk of property crime incidence from the countryside to the city. Díaz used the laying of a national transportation and communication infrastructure to enforce a crackdown on rural banditry.[85] At the same time, Mexico City's historically central commercial, political, and religious role in national life was only elevated by trends of urbanization, industrialization, and the rise of a consumer society, with its greater emphasis on material goods as social and cultural markers. Together this concentration of accessible wealth in the windows and behind the counters of stores made rising property crime an obvious eventuality.

Following another trend, these criminals appeared to be organizing. Cruzadoras and elegantes often acted in teams. Newspapers warned of the appearance of organized gangs of such thieves. In 1904 *El Imparcial* fretted in an editorial titled "Criminal Industries" that these gangs were formed by individuals "who appeared well dressed, well-mannered and who can easily have access to locations frequented by distinguished people, which makes them even more dangerous."[86] This organizing and—equally important—professionalizing of the trade may have merely reflected the fears of the press. Even so, it projected an impression of a modernizing world of crime that duplicated the organizing trends in labor (unions) and in business (trusts, oligopolies) that dominated business news and social critiques of the late nineteenth century in Mexico as well as the United States and Europe. The fear of an organized class of thieves also reflects the larger economic and cultural trend toward professionalization and specialization. If industrial standardization and assembly-line business models could have an impact on blue-collar and white-collar jobs, why not a modernizing criminal class?[87]

The image of so many women shoplifters mirrored social changes as well as stereotypes. Women during the Porfiriato became increasingly public, not only in their capacity as consumers in the commercial and entertainment zone of the city but also by filling the ranks of factory workers (whether working the cigarette-rolling machines at El Buen Tono or the sewing machines at the Palacio de Hierro workshops) and low-level white-collar positions such as telephone operators and typists. Conventional wisdom held that they were better suited than men for tasks that involved repetition, patience, and attention to detail. It only made sense that within the criminal world shoplifting—with its requirement of finesse, forethought, and a dose of captivating charm—would naturally appear most suitable to the fairer sex.

Finally, the issue of clothing and class transgression by shoplifters signaled a profound social conflict and shifting within the attitudes of the Mexican public. The outrage expressed by social commentators (and the thrill likely experienced by many readers) suggests the remarkable sense of fragility many Porfirians perceived in the traditional social order and visible social boundaries. Shoplifting became a lightning rod for this issue. Perhaps this mimics democratic trends in European (and North American) societies such as France, where many refused to participate in proper rituals of deference to their social superiors.[88] In addition, the rise of ever-larger cities raised the question of how to mark one's place in society for public consumption. This question took on added consequence for a city such as Mexico's capital in which heavy immigration of rural populations rendered a homogenous population impossible. To accomplish this task of social distinction required a heavy reliance on external markers such as etiquette, bearing, and particularly clothing. But as the cruzadoras and elegantes so amply demonstrated, clothing could be easily copied and shifting fashions faithfully followed even by those without unlimited funds. More disturbingly, etiquette and bearing could also be hijacked. In this light, shoplifters were so wildly fascinating to the broader public because they showed just how fluid society had become and how easily alternate identities could be assumed in relatively anonymous modern urban zones of the nation.

Beyond these departures signaled by department store crimes, the characterization of the average criminal as violent and feeble-minded seemed to clash with a series of audacious property crimes that reached the highest echelons of the Porfirian regime. President Díaz himself suffered the theft of a sizeable quantity of jewels from his house in 1894. Other notable crime victims included Secretary of War Bernardo Reyes (check and signature forgery); Julio Limantour, prominent businessman and brother of the finance minister (burglary of home); and chief of the Rurales police force José Benavides, the latter falling victim to a pickpocket at a police banquet given in honor of President Díaz. Even the chief of the secret police, Miguel Cabrera, had to resort to chasing down a thief who stole his horse's saddle from his home.[89]

By the beginning of the twentieth century a competing crime narrative was developing. Famous academics spurred this new narrative, not least the startling observation made in 1895 by French sociologist Émile Durkheim that crime is normal in society, "an integral part of all healthy societies."[90] In Mexico this new explanation of crime linked the nation's economic and social modernization with a refinement of crime defined most notably as a shift of *violence au vol*, from violent crime to property crime.[91] In 1904 the newspaper *El Imparcial*, responding to a slickly executed store robbery, noted, "In the good old days, robbery was generally accompanied by violence. . . . Now robbery has been civilized and has shed itself of its once brutal character."[92] Another paper described how, as Mexico's wealth increased, violent robberies diminished, having given way to "the ingenious and subtle robbery common in affluent societies that distinguishes the progress of nations."[93] The article continues in this vein, depicting Mexico City as a veritable candy store for the crafty criminal and attributing the capital's social importance, immense wealth, and profusion of commercial establishments as the cause of Mexico's new immigration of "crime artists." The penny press paper *El Diablito Rojo* summed up this new vision best when it wrote, "One of the manifestations of today's progress is, as they say, the refinement of vice."[94]

Newspapers now trumpeted how criminals seemed to adopt the latest technology and turn it against society. Using headlines such as "New Form of Robbery" and "New Genre of Theft," the press informed the public about how criminals used chloroform, the telephone, and even the camera to commit ever more daring crimes.[95] Cinemas in the city catered to the public's appetite for the subject, screening films such as *The History of Crime*.[96]

An indicator of how much the Mexican elite and press embraced this new notion of modernizing crime came in their reporting of similar crimes abroad. Reflecting their identity as a postcolonial society with extraordinarily intense pretensions of "catching up" with the most advanced global civilizing nations, they often sought to compare events at home with those taking place in Europe and the United States. Comparisons of transportation systems, fashions, shopping venues, financial institutions, and sports events now made room for those on crime.[97] International reports of spectacular crimes or crime trends found their place in Mexican newspapers as a comforting indication that—although vexing—the "modernization" and increase in property crime at home merely demonstrated that national progress continued in lockstep with global leaders. Thus dispatches from New York on department store shoplifting not only informed Mexican readers that these criminals stole over US$500,000 annually and that police estimated that the "weaker sex" made up over 95 percent of their ranks, they also subtly paralleled similar reports on domestic affairs.[98]

Now the press adopted a bifurcated approach to crime reporting. While it sensationalized modern crimes (thefts of property and crimes that were premeditated and required modern behaviors and often technologies) it treated as ordinary the random and violent criminal acts—murder, drunkenness, assaults—that were considered representative of "Old Mexico." This new model of crime reporting achieved a two-tiered vision of crime that mirrored the elite social Darwinian vision of society: modern versus traditional; evolving and advancing versus stagnating and dying. In essence, this new narrative patched the cognitive dissonance experienced by respectable society as the press increasingly reported crime that departed from the received wisdom of conventional criminal behavior, crime that often embodied and employed the values, skills, and technologies that progressive Mexicans believed in. It involved discarding the notion that one day society would progress beyond crime, but then celebrity academics like Durkheim had already paved the way for that. Most importantly, it permitted elites to retain their cherished social Darwinian perception of national development.

This chapter urges historians to rethink previous assumptions of crime and crime narratives in Porfirian Mexico. This is not to say that earlier interpretations have not linked crime with Porfirian modernization, but usually the modernization involves government responses to the problem (police, legal, and institutional reforms) or else readings of public narratives surrounding famous cases that offer a window into the tensions that rapid social change inflicted.[99] Building on these earlier works and approaching the subject through the lens of consumer institutions and the values they promoted and represented, I have forwarded the idea of a modernizing crime narrative developing by the turn of the century that mirrored a broader vision of Mexican society divided into traditional and modern categories. Department store criminality and the public narratives it inspired revealed the tension if not contradiction within the Porfirian motto of Order and Progress: Porfirian elites wished for rapid economic and cultural modernization while retaining rigid social hierarchies that those changes, by necessity, threatened. Elite public responses to increasing property crime—often near-hysterical and apocalyptic—undoubtedly contained a valid and genuine concern. At the same time, however, a careful reading suggests a parallel message conveyed in these narratives. For all of the concern that department store criminality and its social transgressions threatened Porfirian society, below this surface of hysteria lay a comforting perception that this trend in criminal behavior signaled the profundity of national progress. Keeping in mind that Porfirian Mexico was a postcolonial society whose elites drew on foreign economic and cultural trends as benchmarks for their own efforts to "civilize" their nation, the belief that Mexican criminality increasingly copied European and North American trends allowed for a positive interpretation. In short, such sophisticated and nonviolent property crime offered solid proof of the modernization of national society and culture. If Mexican criminals—believed to be drawn from the lowest segments of society—could modernize, then there could be no doubt that Mexican society was advancing in concert with the civilizing nations of the world.

Finally, this chapter has offered a basic overview of the modernization of crime in Mexico and the economic and cultural changes that shaped the new narrative. Mostly it portrayed the narrative of Mexico's rulers while hinting at the transgressive appeal of department store criminality for a much broader segment of society. Concerns over the social consequences and messages of shoplifting and other property crime were fears of the elite in Mexico as well as Europe and the rest of North America. These intense fears of national decay amid material and technological abundance were historically specific to fin-de-siècle elites of the modernizing world. Eugen Weber, in his studies of France at this time, notes that the majority of society did not share these fears.[100] Instead, broad democratic trends and freedoms influencing political, social, and cultural spheres offered a sense of personal liberation unheard of in the past. Urbanization assisted this trend, and the proliferation of goods, technologies, and labor-saving machinery and devices made life far easier than rural existence had ever offered. Despite their considerable problems, city life and city jobs beckoned to many.

How to examine this in a Mexican context remains a challenge when the historiography of the period has relatively recently expanded beyond viewing the Porfiriato exclusively as a prelude to Revolution to perceive it more as a pivotal historical moment in the national transition to modernity. The work of Luis González offers historians an entrance into how modernization and modernity seeped into rural Mexico. In his micro-history *San José de Gracia: Mexican Village in Transition* he notes the increasing recognition and immense appeal of Porfirian Mexico City and its spectacles, inventions, and conveniences to a rural village's residents. Equally importantly he describes how the new rail system and the newspapers and goods it brought transformed expectations of village residents—particularly the young—and steadily expanded their worldview and range of experience.[101] While this study has sought to retain this line of inquiry throughout, the next chapter engages it most tightly. It considers how a robbery-murder committed at the La Profesa jewelry store in Mexico City in 1890 provides a case study not only of Mexican crime on the cusp of modernization and the contesting elite and popular narratives constructed to interpret it but also of how members of the lower and lower-middle class arrived at and negotiated this modernizing urban world.

Chapter 6

HOT DIAMONDS, COLD STEEL

The La Profesa Jewelry Store Robbery

Very fashionable just now are pearls . . .
— PRINCE FORTUNATUS, JOURNALIST, *TWO REPUBLICS*, MAY 19, 1891, 4

Among other brilliant toilettes . . . were those of Mrs. Sánchez Navarro (one of the finest in the room—ingénue dress of green and pink broche, and old point lace—wonderful jewels).
— *TWO REPUBLICS*, MAY 20, 1891, 4,
REPORTING ON A BALL AT THE MEXICO CITY JOCKEY CLUB

A vixen sneered at a lioness because she never bore more than one cub. "Only one," she replied, "but a lion."
— AESOP

ON THE NIGHT OF FEBRUARY 20, 1891, FIVE MEN, WEARING FIVE FINELY tailored suits and carrying one sharp knife, slashed through the patina of order and progress that Mexican elites and social reformers had cultivated and polished over the preceding fifteen years of rule by President Porfirio Díaz. By brutally killing and robbing the jeweler don Tomás Hernández

Aguirre in his own store, Gerard Nevraumont, Nicolas Treffel, Anton Sousa, Jesús Bruno Martínez, and Aurelio Caballero laid bare the social and cultural tensions and intellectual currents of the rapidly modernizing Porfirian society. Although they committed only one crime together, their crime, the ensuing manhunt, the trial, and the media coverage of the event offer a vivid and comprehensive window into the relationships among crime, commodification, and modernization in Porfirian society.[1]

Hernández undoubtedly prided himself on his and his store's place in Porfirian society. Through his ownership of—and identification with— La Profesa, he became a well-known and well-respected family man in the community, and his nephew had even taken up his trade in Guanajuato. La Profesa was not a large store, attached both physically and commercially to the enormous La Esmeralda jewelry store next door (figure 20). Nevertheless, it displayed some of the finest pieces of jewelry in the city, and with La Esmeralda it helped to bedeck in sparkling wealth the most elegant ladies of Mexico City society for their appearances at the balls of the Jockey Club and other elite institutions. La Esmeralda, too, had endured since the beginning of the regime of Porfirio Díaz, sparkling as the symbol of an increasingly materialistic and commodified culture. Other large stores existed at this time, like the Spanish-run La Elegancia dry goods two blocks to the northwest and the French-owned Palacio de Hierro—the first department store in Mexico—that opened later that year; yet few came close to the sheer opulence and concentrated retailing capital that La Esmeralda and La Profesa possessed.[2]

Together, the two establishments housed not only watches by Longines, necklaces of pearls, and bracelets of diamonds but also, in these commodities, the hopes, assumptions, and philosophies of the ruling members of Porfirian society, who looked to Western Europe and North America for economic and cultural inspiration. Located on the trendy streets of Plateros and San Francisco, where many of the city's wealthiest citizens lived and major businesses resided, the stores acted as a center point of the social space Porfirian reformers sought to carve out for the middling and upper classes, the gente decente. In this space grew an image of society as perceived by its respectable members: a rationally ordered consumer paradise free of the dangerous and criminal lower class. Here they could liberally enjoy the fruits of social order and material progress that now seemed ripe after fifteen years of cultivation by the Díaz government. La Profesa and La Esmeralda represented all of this, and in 1891 they metaphorically held their place as one of the finest jewels in the Porfirian crown.[3]

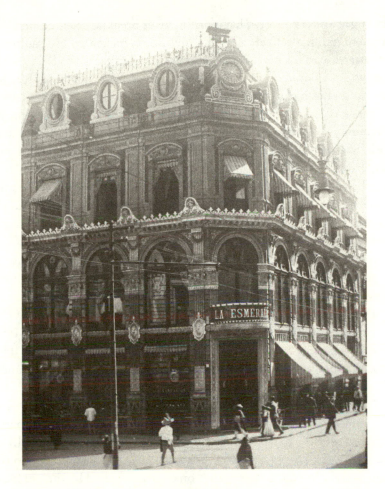

Figure 20. The famous La Esmeralda jewelry store, located next door to
the smaller La Profesa jewelry store. Source: Archivo General de la Nación,
Fondo Instrucción Pública y Bellas Artes, Colección F. Miret, exp. 37.

The Crime

That certainty of personal safety, social order, and linear national progress was rattled on the night of February 20 when the five robbers threatened to destroy this oasis of civilization. Planning had begun six months
before, but that afternoon they took care of last-minute details. The dapperly dressed Martínez, Caballero, and Treffel lounged on benches in
the Zócalo gardens, watching the street life pass the Monte de Piedad
pawnshop and the cathedral, waiting for Nevraumont and Sousa to finish

dressing at Sousa's house. That morning over breakfast Nevraumont had agreed to join the robbery. He and Sousa then picked up Nevraumont's cigarette case at his hotel before purchasing a knife, dark glasses, and a bit of wig at a *tlapalería*, or general corner store. Afterward they lunched at Sousa's, put on suits, then pasted on false beards that Sousa's mistress, Concepción (Concha) Peña, had fashioned from the wig fragment. For Nevraumont, Peña molded a piece of *chicle*, or gum, to fill in a missing tooth. She then ordered a coach and the two men picked up their partners, drove several blocks down Cinco de Mayo, turned down La Palma past the offices of the newspaper *El Universal*, and stopped at a small figone, a sidewalk stand selling food and drink, to have a glass of pulque. At six o'clock they then walked the last block and a half to La Profesa. Nevraumont had already arranged an after-hours appointment with Hernández, having visited with him previously to discuss a purchase, so the store owner thought little of unlocking the door and letting inside the well-dressed Nevraumont.[4]

But Hernández quickly suspected a trap. He realized his error when Martínez entered the humid shop and asked to purchase a silver timepiece at the same time as Treffel stepped inside and closed the door, leaving Sousa and Caballero to maintain watch outside. Hernández told the men that they were not there to buy watches, that they were not "gente buena," drew a revolver from his belt, and tried to shoot Nevraumont. The cartridge in his gun failed to explode, allowing Nevraumont time to wrestle him to the floor and drag him to the living quarters in the rear of the shop. With the help of Martínez he bound, gagged, and placed the storeowner on a sofa. Worried by the old man's labored breathing, Nevraumont propped him up with several pillows for greater comfort.[5]

Although joining the team only that very day, Nevraumont now took charge. He told Martínez and Treffel to guard Hernández for few moments while he returned to the showroom. He walked straight to the show window "looking out onto the street and took a diamond bracelet that passersby had seen for days and had stirred their greed and covetousness." He hid the magnificent piece, all twenty-five diamonds set in gold and surrounding a "very clear" single diamond of "great dimensions," then returned to the back room and called out to Treffel and Martínez to help him in front. Martínez reached for a display of watch chains, but Nevraumont restrained him, pointing out that they were only gold-plated. Martínez returned to the bedroom to guard

Hernández. As the two remaining thieves pilfered the showcases and any strongboxes that they could open, Nevraumont went to investigate the strained breathing of Hernández, only to see Martínez wielding his knife "like a picador," plunging with his full weight the last of three fatal wounds into the shop owner, whom one newspaper described as "the unfortunate old man [*infeliz anciano*]." No kidding. Nevraumont and Treffel, distraught at the turn of events, asked him why he did it. Martínez allegedly replied, "Dead men tell no tales" (Los muertos no hablan). They quickly stripped Hernández of his watch and emptied his wallet, left the body where it lay, and fled the building after a total of fifteen minutes.[6]

Moments later they flagged down a coach, drove to a pulquería, had several glasses, and then headed back to Sousa's house to divide the spoils, approximately 4,000–8,000 pesos in diamonds, pearls, jewelry, and cash. The diamond bracelet and a blue diamond solitaire were the most impressive acquisitions, later appraised at 800 and 400 pesos each. Nevraumont kept these for himself, never telling the others that he had stolen them on his first forage through the showroom. The rest of the jewelry consisted of loose diamonds, "clear, like drops of water"; diamond and gold rings; watches; watch chains; pearl necklaces; and black pearl, diamond, emerald, gold, and platinum earrings, pins, broaches, and other assorted pieces. Over the next four weeks much of this would be melted down, pawned, or sold on the street—a ready market in Mexico City. The value of the taking in this robbery placed the five among the criminal elite, as they exceeded the common parameters of the criminal code. The code outlined prison sentences for crimes of 50–1,000 pesos, with criminals who surpassed that amount receiving one and a half years plus one extra month for every 100 additional pesos.[7]

A short time later, at a quarter to eight, the night watchman for La Esmeralda stopped short in front of La Profesa. The main door gaped open, demanding immediate attention from the watchman, who duly investigated with his lantern. He found that "the interior of the store was in disorder" and quickly notified the local gendarme, number 605, and the employees of La Esmeralda. Within minutes journalists from the newspaper *La Voz de México* arrived and notified the police station by way of telephone from their shop on nearby Santa Clara Street. Little did the night watchman know that he had just set in motion the investigation of what some have called the first modern crime in Mexico.[8]

Large rewards may or may not have helped to capture the thieves, but they definitely suggested the importance that prominent members of Mexican society attached to this event. Within days President Díaz himself was offering 2,000 pesos to the person who captured the criminals, and the district governor offered 500 pesos to the gendarme who apprehended them. Díaz broke with his usual role of noninvolvement in police duties and took an active interest in this case; *La Voz de México* noted on March 3 that he "had ceaselessly pushed" district authorities to capture the criminals.[9] The robbery of La Profesa was no ordinary case, a fact that newspapers and public opinion soon made clear. By March 3 police had captured Caballero, Treffel, and Sousa. On March 6 Martínez fell prey to the secret police when an agent lured him into a sombrero shop where authorities awaited him. Nevraumont escaped the police until March 14, when they found him in Tuxpan, Veracruz, cursing the bad weather that had delayed his steamship trip to Havana.[10]

The La Profesa robbery and trial offer a remarkable snapshot of Porfirian society in the throes of rapid economic and cultural modernization. Through the broadsheets of the famous popular graphic artist José Guadalupe Posada and the reports of two newspapers—the American colony's *Two Republics* and the Catholic *La Voz de México*—the trial comes alive. The effects of modernization on daily life, the commercialization and spectacles of urban society, the living conditions and survival strategies of the urban poor, the social discourse of criminality, and the intersection of class, gender, and ethnicity in society all surfaced during this case. La Profesa represented one of the rare crimes that threatened the "common knowledge" canons of belief held by a society, and the intense public interest and participation in the investigation and trial during the ensuing ten weeks suggested that this robbery was deeply impressed on the psyche of Porfirian society.

The Transgressions

When Nevraumont walked over the threshold of La Profesa, he crossed class and ethnic boundaries both set by Porfirian society and shaped by positivist and social Darwinian intellectual currents. He and his gang committed a transgressive crime. Hernández had opened his door to him because he fit the social typecast of a wealthy, respectable person of reason: well dressed and French, not cotton-clad, Indian, and poor. By betraying this trust, he pierced many of the social Darwinian beliefs that influenced the thoughts of Mexican ruling elites.[11]

Carefully planned, soberly executed, and thoroughly brilliant in its daring, the robbery and its architects challenged conventional thinking about criminals and their place and future within a modernizing society. Baffled commentators spoke for the public as they wondered just how the thieves had seamlessly carried out this crime during the busiest time of the day, under the bright artificial lights of the streets, "without the notice of any authorities or passers-by." Moreover, Sousa and Caballero, along with a woman believed to be Concha Peña, watched store owner Hernández and his habits every day for six months. The crime's perpetrators dressed not in the clothes of poverty but those of prosperity. For some Mexicans, this sartorial sleight of hand hearkened back to the days of Jesús Arriaga—popularly known as Chucho el Roto (Chucho the Dandy)—the first famous urban bandit of the Porfiriato, who robbed prominent citizens and establishments, including La Profesa, in the early 1880s while wearing the attire of archbishops or elite women. The La Profesa robbers also targeted a social class superior to their own and could do so disguised not only by dress but also by ethnicity: Treffel was French, and Nevraumont and Sousa had a French father and mother, respectively. They granted followers of the case a window of opportunity to consider the less-than-desirable consequences of the foreign cultural and social traits that Porfirian rule had unquestionably ushered into Mexico. Most damning to the Mexican criminological model, these thieves showed no signs of succumbing to the social milieu and wallowing in solitary self-destruction. Instead they engaged it, adopting its rules of competition, and most disturbing, bonded together in collective action to acquire wealth.[12]

Stealing the luxuries of the Porfirian elite marked the La Profesa robbery as a direct personal attack on Mexico's rulers. The Mexican elite fetishized precious stones and jewelry, investing them with the power and values of their class. The charity balls of the Jockey Club, the Casino Español, and other socialite functions seemed to exist only for men of the capital city's leisure class to display the latest finery of their women. Newspaper reports explained in great detail each woman's toilette, her French fashions, and her jewelry. Silver brocade and strings of pearls cascaded off dresses, while diamonds, emeralds, and gold highlighted creamy-skinned throats, cleavages, fingers, ears, and wrists, not to mention the beautifully coiffed obsidian hair for which they acted as a foil. Diamonds symbolized the Porfirian lady. By robbing La Profesa, Nevraumont and the others metaphorically stole the wives and daughters of society's powerful males.[13]

Their attack on La Profesa also threatened the common belief in the progressive function and social reform opportunity provided by urban spaces that the respectable members of Mexican society shared with their counterparts in Europe. In the nineteenth century social commentators closely related the city and the positivist beliefs of order and progress developed by Auguste Comte. In Victorian England the middle classes saw that the growth and quality of their cities depended on technological and material achievements. Never before had the possibilities for controlling the environment appeared so attainable. Yet the new cities that grew so fast and glittered with more wealth than any society had ever known also stank of poverty as abject as any society had ever suffered. But Victorians, like Porfirians, believed that the forward march of progress in physical conditions would lead inevitably to the eradication of social evils and criminal behavior.[14]

This philosophy applied in Mexico, but in an altered form. Because of social Darwinian ideas, Mexico's rulers did not believe that Indians and those of obvious Indian descent—meaning the majority of the popular classes—could ever be redeemed, and therefore they sought to marginalize these groups in urban areas. They undertook this project of social spatial segregation in full force by the end of the 1880s, enacting financial and zoning regulations to push tenements, brothels, cantinas, and gambling establishments outside of a budding urban core constructed in their image of a modern, progressive, capitalist city.[15] Here they could build an efficient infrastructure, with sidewalks, paved streets, transportation networks, and sewage systems. On this infrastructure the wealth of a capitalist economy would construct parks for leisure pursuits, offices for productive purposes, or consumer palaces— great showcases to announce the products of material progress and industrial technology, the commodification of social value. In front of these glittering displays to material culture, members of respectable society could mimic their social equivalents in North America and Western Europe, especially France. The French had invented a peculiar leisure activity involving these exhibits, an activity known as window-shopping but one that the French in their inimitably descriptive way called *leche-vitrine*, literally "licking the window." The supposed existence of this safe, ordered, urban social space allowed criminologist Miguel Macedo to declare that "among the middle and upper classes there exists a firmly rooted sense of personal security that manifests itself in an extraordinary liberty of action."[16]

Therefore, not only did the five robbers steal the elite's luxuries and transgress class and ethnic assumptions, they also transgressed on the urban space of respectable society. From the first editorial two days after the crime until a final analysis on April 28, the journalists and editors of *La Voz de México* affected a constant, shrill sense of outrage against this spatial transgression. They likened the crime to the sword of Damocles hanging over "the lives, interests, and security of those who live in Mexico." La Profesa should have received protection not only from its location but from the street lighting and the "thousands of men, women, and children" returning home after their daily labor. After the crime many residents of the city could not resist making pilgrimages to the site "in the heart of the city," and by February 24 a group of "curious onlookers, vagrants, and unemployed contemplated the closed door" of La Profesa.[17]

For many of these onlookers who claimed membership in respectable society, it was absolutely astonishing to discover that criminal elements had found a way to prey on progress and indeed to carry out a crime against one of the most prominent symbols of Porfirian material culture. The slick, transgressive style and French influence on the heist suggested that the elimination of crime might not be an inevitable consequence of forward-marching behavior. Crime, then, might not result from social or hereditary conditions, a revelation that did not sit well with contemporary social Darwinian and positivist models of societal improvement.

Prior to the La Profesa robbery, many members of the gente decente may have wished for this idealized vision of progress, but they also recognized nagging inconsistencies between their social theories and the social realities of life in the capital; the La Profesa robbery and homicide merely provided a forum in which to express their concern. An example of the already existing queasiness, often caused by the effects of modernization itself, may be found within a stone's throw of Hernández's business. Businessmen along the street complained of the sore eyes and throats caused by the fine dust circulating from the laying of the new street pavement, a project that reached Hernández's store on January 25. The reticence of many proprietors to sweep their sidewalks only worsened the situation. Hernández probably sympathized with his colleagues, given his penchant for stepping outside for a cigarette and some street watching. Public opinion questioned the merits of this pavement project, wondering if the blocks would retain shape or stay in place. Moreover, while rain kept the dust from rising it made the pavement impassable for equestrian traffic. It frequently led to careening coaches and sometimes even to death caused by skittish steeds. Those who could not afford the cost of even a third-class coach apparently took great pleasure in spotting these spills: The American colony newspaper, *Two Republics*, disapprovingly noted how after a rain shower "the street gamins [urchins] watched with unholy joy the frantic effort of the coach horses to keep themselves from falling down. . . . As many as three horses were seen within a distance of one block, all in more or less advanced state of prostration."[18]

Popular traditions and crime continued to undermine the gente decente's efforts to mold central Mexico City in their image. Police tried to enforce regulations seeking to push popular behaviors outside of this central zone, regulations such as the one prohibiting enchilada makers from cooking in the doorways of shops "or where the spattering grease may soil the clothes of the passers-by." Hernández's corner attracted a significant crowd of undesirables, leading Hernández to place a placard in his show window "forbidding idlers to stand on that corner by order of the governor of the Federal District." The corner, "famous . . . for dudes and mashers," could now be deemed respectable space for "the ladies having occasion to pass." Even the habitations of citizens reflected this social mélange, where colonial mansions regularly neighbored a tenement, or *casa de vecindad*. In 1890 the social segregation and rationalization of urban space in Mexico City had begun, but it was far from complete.[19]

More than anything else, the perceived crime wave in the city must have shaken the faith in progress held by Hernández and other members of the gente decente in early 1891.[20] True, Díaz had instituted a number of police reform measures in 1879 to provide a safe and investor-friendly environment. He replaced the hated Resguardo Diurno and Nocturno with the gendarmes and a mounted police force, concentrating the resources of the eight police districts in the main commercial areas. Foreign commentators noted as early as 1883 that police stood within one hundred yards of each other, and in 1888 William E. Curtis wrote, "At every street corner there is a patrolman night and day." And yet by 1891 newspapers reported daily the latest crimes against establishments or persons on Plateros and San Francisco, whether by longtime employees, construction workers, burglars, or pickpockets imposing their version of wealth redistribution on window-shoppers.[21]

Hernández had intimately experienced crime before the final, fatal robbery. Only eight days before his murder, thieves stole several rings.

This theft duplicated another recent minor heist at the store. Six or seven years previously he had suffered a major robbery. After the two latest heists, he invested in an electric alarm-bell system for his display cases that drew on new technology entering the market from New York City. His store appeared to attract famous crimes and criminals. Approximately a decade previously Chucho el Roto ravaged his display cases between robbing the National Bank, the Frizac business house, and the famous dry-goods store La Sorpresa y Primavera. Thus, on the night of February 20, 1891, the impression of Porfirian progress and policing abilities held by Hernández and his gente decente brethren likely mixed anxiety amid a hopeful view of the future.[22]

Attacks on police ineptitude immediately followed the crime. *Two Republics* generally approved of the police efforts and efficiency, but the editorials of *La Voz de México* alternated between begrudging support and blistering charges of incompetence. The day after the crime it noted the "insecurity that increased daily" and claimed that "if the police do not redouble their vigilance quickly," scandals like La Profesa would continue to plague the city. *La Voz* continued its attacks three days later, charging "the ineffective vigilance of the police" for "the bandits that swarm among us . . . mocking with notorious nerve."[23]

The lethargic Inspector General Luis Carballeda and the ruthless Miguel Cabrera—Carballeda's second in command and head of the secret police formed in 1890—were likely the targets of much of this enmity. Carballeda, like many of the inspectors general, took an active part in the revolt of Tuxtepec in 1876 that placed Díaz in power. Beyond a brief flurry of reform measures coinciding with Díaz's in 1879, Carballeda filled the inspector's chair for seventeen years—1877 to 1880 and 1884 to 1897—with remarkable mediocrity. Cabrera, the de facto head of the secret police (Comisiones de Seguridad), commanded a most unloved institution that many viewed as both too intrusive and a complete waste of money. (A sign of their ineffectiveness was that while secret police agents wore civilian attire to preserve their anonymity, uniformed gendarmes still saluted them in the street.) Not surprisingly, then, Concha Peña charged Cabrera during trial with threatening her and treating her poorly, a charge elaborated on by Treffel, who received significant support in the press for his claim that Cabrera had tortured him for a confession.[24]

These were not the men to tackle a new breed of criminal that Mexicans believed to be invading the nation. The La Profesa robbery was only the most outstanding of a series of urban crimes carried out by organized, professional criminals who composed a criminal class in society—or so the newspapers believed. "Police investigations in connection with the Hernández murder" uncovered an unrelated union of malefactors, "a regularly-organized band of swindlers" who made scamming inheritances their specialty. Three weeks later news broke of an "organized gang" of pickpockets in the city, a group that one journalist dubbed "the light-fingered gentry of Mexico." Although speaking facetiously, this journalist in fact came closer to the truth than he might have wanted to admit, as pickpockets had become professional, belonging to a class of young thieves of superior skills and intelligence, the most successful ones rarely drawn from the poorest of the poor. To accentuate the international threat posed by this seemingly new "criminal class," stories ran on the spread of the Mafia in the United States and beyond. Testimony from the La Profesa trial only fueled fears that this organized group of professionals lurked just below the surface of respectable society. Treffel freely admitted that they planned their heist based on a series of spectacular jewelry store holdups recently executed in Paris.[25]

Contemporaries of the crime must have wondered what prompted this sudden rush of criminality or, more accurately, high-profile attacks on the institutions and persons of respectable citizens in Mexico City. The answer lay in economic and social developments transforming Mexico during the Porfiriato that led to the closing of the rural frontier of banditry and the opening of a new frontier of spectacular urban thievery.

The disorder and limited extension of the state in the aftermath of independence in 1821 permitted an environment of countryside lawlessness that marked an age of rural banditry. Domestic factionalism between Liberals and Conservatives caused nearly a half century of internecine warfare among Mexicans, marked by military interventions and wars with foreign powers such as Spain in 1829, the citizens of the United States in 1836 over Texas, the country itself in 1846, and France in several engagements. The last of these engagements with France began in 1862 when the emperor Napoleon III imposed his nephew, Austrian archduke Ferdinand Maximilian, on the throne of Mexico and ended with Maximilian's execution in 1867 in front of a firing squad of Liberals under the leadership of Benito Juárez. Serious political disputes ended in 1867, but the economic situation remained grave. Unworked mines had flooded, foreign and domestic capital had fled the unstable economy, federal coffers were empty, and the transportation infrastructure consisted of little more than bandit-plagued carriage and mule trails. Bandits faced few threats of state control in this world, and their brazen exploits expressed this confidence. Starting in 1876 with the rise to power of Porfirio Díaz the heyday of rural banditry began to subside.

Although the legendary Rurales (the reorganized rural police corps first established by Juárez and patterned on the Canadian Mounties and the Texas Rangers) received much credit for the restoration of order in the countryside, it was the railroads that struck the greatest blow to bandit freedom. Díaz instituted an aggressive track-laying program with the help of foreign technology and capital. Less than six hundred kilometers of railroad tracks existed in Mexico prior to Díaz; by 1910 nearly nineteen thousand kilometers crisscrossed the nation. Railroad engines not only transported consumer and industrial goods to markets but also permitted quicker responses of security forces to suppress rural banditry and the mythology surrounding it. With the lone example of Santanón in 1906, no rural bandit after the capture of Ignacio Para in 1892 fired the Mexican imagination during the remainder of the Porfiriato.[26] As Paul Vanderwood explained, "gone were the great bandit gangs of the past"; the social and political streambeds that had spawned them now lay dry, for "development had shunted them aside."[27]

The closing of the rural frontier coincided with the opening of an urban frontier of celebrated crime. On the material level, the expanding areas of the Porfiriato offered far greater opportunities, given the inclination for thieves to join together in pursuit of larger windfalls. New branches of criminal opportunities also developed in the urban setting, namely embezzling and counterfeiting. Thieves could not help but be attracted and tempted by the accumulation of goods in confined areas like the jewelry, silversmithing, and shopping drags of Plateros and San Francisco in Mexico City.[28]

These, then, were some of the social and cultural issues swirling about the preparation for the trial. In addition to committing armed robbery and murder, the La Profesa perpetrators had also transgressed class, ethnic, and urban spatial boundaries, not to mention metaphorically stealing the women of the elite. The fallibility of social Darwinian and positivist models of society was also at issue in the public discourse that struggled over the apparent modernization of crime in Mexican society. Impotency among the law enforcement authorities in the face of an apparent urban crime wave provided an easy target and lightning rod for public criticism of the Porfirian regime.

The Trial

On April 15 *Two Republics* presaged the importance and popularity of the upcoming trial, set to start five days later. Judge Lic. Salvador Medina y Ormacchea—the brother of the judges Antonio and Carlos who ten years earlier had published one of the first proposals for Mexico's federal penitentiary—had already heard the charges from chief prosecutor Victoriano Pimentel, former editor of the major newspaper *El Universal*, that would condemn all five of the accused to death if found guilty. He ordered that admission to the trial be restricted to special invitation. Chairs would be placed between the benches in all twenty rows of the large hall in the Palace of Justice, thus expanding the seating capacity from four hundred to six hundred. Furthermore, he decreed that police place a strong guard in the salon and that "a company of soldiers will occupy the court to keep order." On trial day neither the seating arrangements nor the security detail proved sufficient.[29]

At nine o'clock on the morning of April 20, 1891, thirty-seven days after the police finally caught Nevraumont, the crowd on Cordobanes Street outside the courts presented quite the sight to onlookers and headaches for the police. *La Voz* likened the "multitude of people from all social classes" to an invasion. The street was so crowded by people "struggling to get into the court room" that General Carballeda sent for a troop of mounted police "to clear the mob away." But as the police cleared Cordobanes Street, the throng flowed into parallel and perpendicular streets. When officials sought to disperse these areas "the mob swayed back into Cordobanes again." Onlookers would not be denied their day in court. Eventually, Carballeda called in more mounted police to control the crowds on all three converging streets, especially the front of the Justice Palace, which "every man and woman was evidently trying his and her best to reach."[30]

Given the state of pandemonium inside the hall, those outside would have achieved negligible results even if they had gained admittance. Police and soldiers maintained a reasonable semblance of order, allowing the galleries to fill "till not another man or woman could find room." The description of the crowd revealed both a cross-section of society and telling examples of the journalist's view of social order. He noted that "men of all classes and grades" made up much of the crowd, including lawyers, merchants, traders, shopkeepers, politicians, military officers, newspaper reporters, "and many nondescripts." Many of the "gentler sex" rubbed shoulders with the men, including a healthy contingent of "ladies well-known in the best of Mexico's fashionable society." These women enjoyed the company of numerous members of Mexico's power structure, most notably Julio Limantour, brother of Mexico's finance minister, José Yves Limantour, and one of the great investors and land speculators of the capital, who also sat on the executive board of several major companies.[31]

Reporters from all the major newspapers pressed into the galleries. Since the trial began, the newspapers, whether Spanish-, French-, or English-language, Catholic or Liberal, elite or popular, all fanned—and were fanned by—the insatiable fascination of their reading public for information on this gruesome, shocking, yet highly titillating crime. Twenty-one reporters from eleven major newspapers attended the trial itself, including such notables as Carlos Roumagnac, who represented El Tiempo and would later become one of the Porfiriato's greatest criminologists. Whether José Guadalupe Posada, the famous popular graphic artist of the Porfiriato, attended the trial is uncertain, yet he produced no less than ten broadsheets on the La Profesa affair, including two on the trial itself.[32]

Ironically, in the midst of this press of flesh seeking to catch a glimpse of these now-famous robbers, the onlookers needed only to pay attention to their own watches and purses to observe equally skilled thieves in action. Pickpockets knew a prize venue when they saw one, and they attended in force. Secret police agents played cat and mouse with the "light-fingered gentry," nabbing one man in the act. Further examination of the suspect revealed seven watches on his person. Numerous other catches rewarded officers with two or three watches per arrest. Entertainment and excitement—a carnivalesque atmosphere—emanated throughout the hall and the outside streets. In a wonderful bit of understatement, the Two Republics journalist commented that "today and every day until the conclusion of the trial, there will be an absorbing interest felt in the proceedings of the case."[33]

La Voz de México spoke the truth when it promised to pass along the robbers' personal testimonies to its readers because they were "the most interesting part of this cause célèbre."[34] Besides the testimonies of Nevraumont, Martínez, Caballero, Treffel, and Sousa, readers pored over the stories of Sousa's mistress, Concha Peña, and two part-time fences—Vicente Reyero and Clemente Corona—as well as several forensic experts, the owners of La Esmeralda next door, the coach driver, jewelry agents, and numerous others. The details of these testimonies not only cut through generalizations and myths about criminality, modernization, and social transformation but also describe—often in wrenching detail—the diverse paths that lead people to crime.

From the beginning of their declarations the five accused quickly dispelled the idea that they represented a unified, long-term, professional gang as they each sought to minimize their culpability in the organization of the crime and execution of the murder. Carlos Sousa claimed Caballero was the "soul of the affair," and Caballero blamed "el francés," meaning Treffel. Martínez first fingered Nevraumont as the "alma principal" but then changed his statement to say that Caballero was his boss and Nevraumont took command during the actual crime, an argument that the prosecution finally adopted.[35]

Previous prison time brought these men together. Every one of them had spent time in the Mexico City jail of Belén, known as the national prison before becoming the municipal prison in 1886. The prison, a former convent, was the antithesis of restrictive penitentiary architecture. Every day the prisoners packed the main patio. They talked, played cards, or sunned themselves after bathing in the patio's fountain. Little had changed from 1879, when Francisco G. Cosmes described the prison: "Gathered together in a patio, without doing absolutely anything . . . the prisoners improve themselves in all secrets of crime through a system of mutual education that would cause the envy of the Lancastrian Company."[36] Here, in Belén, Caballero envisioned and planned the robbery.[37] He met Sousa there in 1887. At a later date they both met Treffel. Having served three sentences at Belén, Treffel forged a lifetime bond with Sousa when he saved Sousa's life. When Sousa lay ill in the prison infirmary and had to take medicine, Treffel found out that someone had switched the labels on his two bottles. As Sousa concluded, "It was a prison friendship" (Era una amistad de cárcel). Treffel also edited a newspaper in prison titled *La Verdad* and signed his name "Fray Patricio" because Caballero called him "padre."[38] Martínez knew all of his accomplices except Nevraumont from prison, although he was never an intimate friend with any of them during his seven-year sentence for robbing a store with his brother. He attained the position of president in Belén, although Sousa intimated that Martínez earned the title from his ability to handle a weapon, not from democratic elections.[39] At least in the case of La Profesa, prison did breed crime.

Techniques to capture criminals also advanced with the larger Porfirian modernization project, often piggybacking on technologies primarily designed to expand a growing consumer market. One example was the use of the fledgling telephone network in Mexico City to help inform the police station of the crime. Another was photography. Carballeda used prisoner photographs collected in Belén prison's special registration book to positively identify Martínez. After police captured Caballero, the prisoner claimed the still-at-large Martínez as one of his accomplices. To verify this, Carballeda showed the photos to Treffel, Sousa, Reyero, and Corona, who all identified Martínez. This use of photography by law enforcement considerably predates the findings of earlier studies but sources indicate it had become standard practice: in September 1891 the city council provided funding for the photographing of over fifteen hundred convicted criminals.[40]

The story of Nevraumont's flight and capture reveals the dramatic changes wrought by modernization on Mexican daily life during the Porfiriato. After the crime Nevraumont set a path for Havana, Cuba. Dressed as dapperly as ever, he traveled by train to Puebla, then Zacapoaxtla, and finally to Veracruz, selling jewels along the way. There he walked up the coastline to Papantla and onward to the port of Tuxpan, where eight days later he planned to set sail by steamship to Havana. He did not raise suspicion in the towns he walked through, "for his suit, manners, and general comportment did not betray that of an assassin." Townspeople thought he was merely the son of a good family (*buena familia*) or else a traveling salesman hawking merchandise for one of the merchant houses of the capital.[41]

His chances for escape seemed likely, having quickly escaped Mexico City, but the equally rapid distribution of mass-circulation newspapers foiled his escape. The March 6 edition of *El Universal* reached Tuxpan on March 11, and one local resident identified Nevraumont as the man in the portrait on the cover page. Local police telegraphed Mexico City for verification, as reports had placed Nevraumont as far north as Ciudad Juárez. Inspector Miguel Cabrera of the secret police wired back that he would arrive soon. Nevraumont planned to sail on the day of Cabrera's arrival, but high winds prevented the departure of his boat, the USS *Orizaba*. Police tracked him down at the clothing store of Sres. Díaz y Lorenzo, where they found him leaning against the shop window and complaining about the bad weather. Two days later authorities sent him under guard by steamer to Veracruz and from there by train to Buenavista station in Mexico City, where he arrived on March 23. Along the way, crowds and journalists sought to catch a glimpse of him. One reporter from the French newspaper *Le Trait d'Union* tried to board the ship from Tuxpan to Veracruz to gain an interview, but police stopped him. Nevraumont's flight and apprehension incorporated many of the aspects of modernization transforming Mexico: the train, steamship, telegraph, mass-circulation newspapers, photography, commercial zones, and the anonymity provided by a fluid labor force that Nevraumont benefited from in his presumed role as a traveling salesman.[42]

The fluidity of labor also revealed itself in the personal testimonies of the accused. Their diverse job and educational backgrounds muddied the clear belief of many in society that there existed professional criminals who dedicated their lives to crime. Their birthplaces reflected the cosmopolitanism of Mexico City and its role as a destination to make a fortune: Caballero was born in Michoacán, Sousa in Veracruz, Treffel in Lorraine, France, and Nevraumont grew up in San Luis Potosí, while the birthplace of Martínez remained unclear. Trial records told little of Martínez's history beyond his criminality, a significant omission that may have tied into his being the most Indian of the group and thus fitting the description of the positivist and social Darwinian criminal. With his elementary school education, Caballero worked for a number of years in two jobs, the latter of which he alleged he lost when a fellow night watchman spread rumors about him to their boss.[43]

After he left prison in 1887 Treffel sought work while he lived off the 20 pesos he received from Belén, presumably for his work during the final *libertad preparatoria* phase of his sentence, and the 300 francs that his dead mother had left him.[44] He traveled about the area in search of work before returning to Mexico City with hopes of gaining employment with the Barcelonnettes, the Frenchmen who dominated the clothing retail business in the republic as well as other large businesses as varied as dynamite making, beer brewing, and cigarette manufacturing (see chapter 3). According to Treffel, a number of them also dabbled in smuggling operations. In a demonstration of the famed regionalism of the Barcelonnettes, when Treffel told them that he came from Lorraine they replied, "Ah! Then there is no work." Trained as a plasterer, he could not find employment elsewhere. He tried unsuccessfully to obtain a construction job at La Esmeralda. Ironically, he would later bury his jewels at the construction site of the new La Esmeralda building. His last effort at legal employment failed: he lost his job as a cargador at the customs house before accepting, out of sheer desperation, Sousa's offer to participate in the robbery.[45]

More than any of the accused, Sousa and Nevraumont proved that the line between honest laborer and criminal was a fine one indeed, one that Mexicans of all classes crossed more often than the gente decente would like to believe. Rather than opposing the legal system, the two of them actually participated in it before their crime; at different times both had found employment as court secretaries (*secretarios de juzgado*) in Veracruz.[46] Sousa achieved his position through ties made "with several well-informed people in the state government" during his schooling. Later he moved to Tamaulipas as a watchman but lost his job when a powerful smuggler had him transferred to Veracruz for reporting him. Back in Veracruz he amassed 3,000 pesos as a consignment dealer and then traveled to Mexico City to make his fortune. A string of fish, pulque, and *aguas frescas* businesses failed; "in every one he lost money and brought misery to him."[47] As for Nevraumont, he attended college with his future fence in Mexico City, Vicente Reyero, and later received his job as court secretary in Veracruz. He fell prey to the fickleness of the city *jefe político* who, in an "arbitrary decision" impressed him into the army. Nevraumont served briefly in the Twenty-third Battalion before being discharged owing to his bouts of epilepsy. On February 18, two days before the crime, he arrived in Mexico City.[48]

Nevraumont and Sousa both served in the Porfirian military, a topic to which historians have only begun to warm.[49] Responding to the prosecution's final argument to the jury, Nevraumont's lawyer asked the jury to consider his client's respected position of court secretary in Veracruz and to remember not only his service but also his father's sacrifice in the military. Colonel D. Fernando Nevraumont died in Veracruz of yellow fever while defending ex-president Juárez, implying that the senior Nevraumont fought against Díaz in the failed Plan de Noria in 1871.[50] In Sousa's case, after the robbery he fled to the military thermal baths at Santa Clara outside of San Cristóbal Ecatepec in the state of Mexico. He told the colonel in charge, Genaro Soberanis, that Minister of War General Pedro Hinojosa had recommended him to the baths, as he was a rheumatic war veteran. After the baths cured him, he said, he would be sent to Sonora to fight in the campaign against the Yaqui Indians. The police eventually captured him during his stay at the baths.[51]

The testimony of Concepción (Concha) Peña weaves the survival strategies of a lower-middle-class woman with the fabric of popular traditions blended with new cultural forms in urban Mexico. Peña did not fit the bipolar "prostitutes or guardian angels" gente decente stereotype of the Mexican woman.[52] Contradicting the prosecution's insinuations about his "relaciones ilícitas," Sousa stated that although they lived together for six months, she was not dependent upon him and, if anything, the opposite was true. They had met when a friend of Sousa's invited him to her home to sing some songs from Veracruz.[53] To move to Mexico City she had sold a plot of land in Morelos, and with that money she traveled to the capital, bought jewelry and other items from pawnshops, and then sold them to other pawnshops for a higher price. She noted that she would sometimes entrust Sousa with this work, "and with the earnings from this business I support myself." She knew that Sousa lacked employment but supported him in court by pointing out that he was looking for work and at various times he had showed her letters of recommendation (*cartas de recomendación*).[54]

On the court's request she described her home. She and Sousa lived in a tenement, a casa de vecindad, within two blocks of where the family of Hernández lived. The apartment comprised four small rooms, including a small entrance room, a dining room and kitchen, a main living room, and a bedroom. The bedroom connected to the main room by means of a partition consisting of a frame with India paper (thin, tough, opaque printing paper) on one side and lace curtains on the other. Through tears in the paper she had observed the robbers dividing up the spoils on the night of the robbery and homicide.[55]

By way of elaborating on how she met Nevraumont for the first time on February 20, Peña served up a slice of daily customs and diversions for the urban working class. Responding to the prosecutor Pimentel's question of whether she expected Nevraumont at lunch that day, she responded negatively. Sousa had annoyed her because he had mentioned that since it was Friday, he wanted her to prepare a little bit of fish "al estilo de Veracruz." Pimental, in an effort to play on socioeconomic divisions, noted that she had earlier mentioned that Nevraumont had a decent aspect and fine clothing and then asked her, "Weren't you mortified that a person like that would eat in your company?" Peña deftly countered this affront to her honor, replying that her cooking may not be "sumptuous" (*opípara*), but neither was it humble. He then moved on to her role in disguising Nevraumont and Sousa, but she claimed not to have helped except by preparing the glue that Sousa had requested for the beards. After arranging his beard, Nevraumont apparently said, "Watch where the jewel falls" (Mire ud. se le cae la piocha), mimicking a circus trick. Puzzled, she asked Sousa what he meant, receiving a smile and the reply, "Perhaps we're in Carnival, eh?" (Acaso no estamos en Carnaval?). Peña, clinging to her innocence, claimed that she thought he was talking about "some latest entertainment" (algún diversion de la época) in town.[56]

Peña's efforts to minimize her role illustrated a general effort by each of the accused to save him- or herself by utilizing assumptions of gender, class, and ethnicity. Despite overwhelming evidence to the contrary provided by Nevraumont and others, Peña sought to avoid guilt by wrapping herself in the mantle of the "guardian angel," the innocent and pure woman merely following her man. Earlier testimony had identified her as the woman helping to stake out the store and to disguise Nevraumont and Sousa, yet she clung to the story that she knew of the crime only after the five men returned with the jewels.[57] At that point she claimed to have kicked Sousa out of the apartment, saying that she wanted no part of this shameful act. Her specious claims received little sympathy from *La Voz*, which followed her comment with the disclaimer "that, at least, is what Concha has declared."[58]

The prosecution continually sought to link sexual immorality with criminality, not only with Peña's relationship to Sousa but also with that between Treffel and his mistress, Taurina Pérez. Treffel's testimony stands as one of the few examples of honor, loyalty, and defiance of the court during the trial. Asked why he did not bring his jewels to his house but instead buried them at the La Esmeralda construction site, Treffel answered that he did not wish to compromise his Pérez. He did not wish to involve her because he loved her for her "noble heart" and because he "owe[d] her many favors and respect[ed] her." Pimentel, sensing a bit of juicy revelation for the court and his audience, pressed Treffel on what type of favors he owed her. Treffel cut short this line of questioning with a curt response: "No señor; I come here for the crime of robbery, and as those favors have absolutely no connection to this crime, I believe your whole point is a useless one."[59]

Treffel's refusal to cower before the courts may have stemmed from his image as a well-dressed and well-mannered Frenchman and reveals yet again the importance of class and ethnicity in the trial. Before the trial began two pulque-dealer associates of Caballero named Gerardo and Timoteo Wesche were released from custody after protesting their innocence, a claim *La Voz* unquestionably accepted, "knowing, as we know, that Wesches belong to an honorable family in Puebla." Their father helped arrange loans with the Germans and was "so respected that despite German citizenship [he was] named citizen of the State of Puebla."[60]

Defense lawyers for both Treffel and Martínez attempted to gain freedom for their clients using strategies that reflected class and racial criteria, although their approaches were polar opposites. Treffel's lawyer, Joaquín Carbajal, referring to a letter from the French legation vouching for the good conduct of Treffel, asked the psychologist Dr. Maldonado y Móron if his client, given his known mental and physical constitution, could have suffered a "descomposición" in his moral faculties and sense when he committed the crime.[61] Martínez did not have the resources of the French legation or the social status to suggest that his transgression amounted to a mere temporary lapse. Instead his lawyer, Maximiliano Baz, sought protection in social Darwinian theories and the new science of phrenology, asking Dr. Fernándo Ortigoso to examine the head of Martínez to clarify whether his client was micro- or macrocephalic and if his cerebral organs were underdeveloped.[62]

Martínez was obviously no fool, and he readily recognized that his position as the most Indian left him susceptible to the role of scapegoat. On April 27, the penultimate day of the trial, during which Martínez and Nevraumont verbally sparred over who committed the actual murder, Martínez broke from the dialogue and with "viveza y energia" addressed the court: "It seems to me that I am accused of murdering Mr. Hernández because I am Indian and ugly." He fought a losing battle, however, and when the prosecution decided to charge him alone for the murder of don Tomás Hernández, "an applause was heard; the judge banged his gavel prohibiting any such demonstration."[63] The La Profesa robbery was the perfect modernizing crime with one flaw: the violent murder of Tomás Hernández. The inevitability of attributing this excess to the lone phenotypically Indian defendant in order to preserve the narrative of cultural progress appeared preordained.

The tension of the trial and the stakes involved clearly took their toll on the accused, although in telling instances the reports of the middle-class *Two Republics* and *La Voz de México* (a more explicitly sensationalistic tabloid) sharply contrasted with the broadsheets produced by José Guadalupe Posada and targeted for a popular audience. Articles in *Two Republics* were replete with accounts of the beaten, docile, and resigned demeanor of the prisoners, while *La Voz* occasionally noted instances of confidence, like those of Nevraumont's "elegantly dressed and smiling" fence, Vicente Reyero.[64] On March 7, while Caballero, Treffel, Sousa, and Martínez were in custody, a journalist from *Two Republics* declared that all of the prisoners appeared "demoralized. There is none of the bravado, so common among criminals, displayed by them." "Nervousness and fear" gripped Treffel. Martínez had threatened suicide. Upon his capture, Nevraumont reportedly revealed a "sullen demeanor," having "given up all hope of escaping his doom." Entering the courtroom, Nevraumont appeared agitated, mopping his beaded brow with a handkerchief. His distressed behavior elicited soothing comments from the judge telling him to calm himself.[65]

On April 29 the judge read the verdict of the jury, which led to the final collapse of Martínez. Salvador Medina y Ormacchea sentenced Martínez and Nevraumont to death for murder, the execution to take place at Belén, while the others received punishments to be served at the dreaded presidio at San Juan Ulúa in Veracruz.[66] This ruling in and of itself illustrates the threat that Mexican society considered the crime to represent. Before 1900 Federal District judges rarely sentenced an accused to death, limiting those eligible to traitors in foreign wars, bandits, patricides, and "murderers who acted with perfidy, *premeditation or a desire for profit.*"[67] Moreover, the Federal District did not transport criminals to Ulúa because of the high daily expense. For example, in 1885 the presidio held only seven civilian prisoners. This number continued to decline.[68] Nevraumont, after appealing his death sentence, had the sentence commuted to nineteen years and 1,000 pesos in fines; Caballero, Sousa, and Treffel accepted sixteen years of hard labor and a similar fine. Peña would spend five years at Belén. All of the five main participants would die in prison except Treffel, who eventually became a successful businessman in Puebla.[69] *Two Republics* reported that immediately after hearing his sentence Martínez "completely lost his reason" and "thinks he is a green parrot." He supposedly spent the remainder of the hearing repeating words and phrases spoken by others.[70]

Posada's broadsheet graphics diametrically opposed the characterizations of *Two Republics*, which had most maligned Martínez. His focus on Martínez as both the killer and the most Indian defendant sought to—and likely succeeded in—appealing to his popular audience, comprised mostly of lower- and lower-middle-class mestizos and those of Indian descent. Occasionally at odds with the accompanying text written by the broadsheet publisher-owner Antonio Vanegas Arroyo, Posada invariably portrayed Martínez as confident and defiant after the trial, a real macho. Confined in Belén, Martínez briefly escaped by climbing over the walls; not the typical actions of a broken man. Furthermore, he declared his hatred for, and resolve to kill, his arresting police officer,

Miguel Cabrera. He scratched into his prison cell wall, "Soon they are going to kill me, but I don't care. I will kill Cabrera." Not long after, guards discovered a knife blade in his room.[71] On the day of his execution Martínez would take one last swipe at Cabrera. Escorted into the patio for his execution, he asked permission to speak with Cabrera. They were speaking in low voices when suddenly Martínez pulled out another knife and wounded Cabrera in the arm. Pandemonium broke out in the courtyard but eventually the guards recaptured Martínez. He cried out for one last time that Nevraumont was the assassin, not him. Defiant to the end, he ordered the riflemen to aim and fire. They needed three finishing shots (*tiros de gracia*) to end his life.[72]

The La Profesa heist was arguably the first modern robbery in Mexico. In its aftermath the government significantly strengthened and reorganized the secret police force, while jewelry store owners discussed the early closing of their shops to avoid the fate of Hernández.[73] Not only did the crime's technical and organizational elements mark a new level of illicit finesse, but they also opened a window onto Porfirian society and brought together a realization of the related developments of crime, commodification, and modernization. Porfirian society could separate the violence that marred the perfect modernizing crime by attributing the act to Martínez, the only member whose skin color, clothing, and cultural orientation were those of traditional Mexico. In doing so, they preserved and reinforced the modernizing crime thesis developing at the time: that a progressing Mexico was ineluctably—if slowly—moving from a "violence to theft" model of crime. In addition, throughout the trial social assumptions regarding class, gender, ethnicity, and race intersected with the public discourse on these transformations, not only in discussions about the trial but also in the actions of the accused themselves.

La Profesa broke open public discussion on changing perceptions of crime in modern society. It laid the foundation for the narratives surrounding shoplifting and the modernizing theory of crime discussed in the previous chapter. Sensational crimes have long received sensational press coverage, but La Profesa occurred as the Mexican mass-circulation press was diversifying and expanding rapidly.[74] The crime and its trial became a spectacle in the press, a commodity to be packaged and sold to "the public." Journalists sought to provide readers with a comprehensible and comprehensive narrative of the crime, the trial,

and the eventual demise of the criminals. They added to an increasingly rich urban narrative in which residents could imagine themselves
as omniscient viewers and integral parts of this incongruous realization of competing social visions known as Mexico City.[75] Journalists
received assistance and authority from voices of the rising science of
criminology who wielded their scientific authority in an effort to provide an incontrovertible account of the actions of individuals as well
as those of the larger society in the midst of rapid social and cultural
change. This mixing of science and journalism blended into a new and
extremely profitable popular criminology peddled by the likes of Julio
Guerrero, Federico Gamboa, and Carlos Roumagnac, who covered the
La Profesa trial for *El Tiempo* and would parlay this experience into his
widely acclaimed *Los criminales en México: Ensayo de psicología criminal*
in 1904.[76] But for all the talk of morality, penitence, and head measure-
ments, perhaps the greatest public attraction of the crime remained the
jewels and their immense value.

The crime became a touchstone for the commodification of Porfirian
society and its changing material culture. In his pathbreaking study of
the town of San José de Gracia in the state of Michoacán, Luis González
illustrates how this emphasis on materialism pervaded far beyond the
urban zones of the republic. The news and allure of the technological
wonders in Mexico City joined increased trade ties with the outside to
encourage young town members to strive to improve their material
status. Social and community bonds remained strong but loosened as
the values of individualism and competition gained moral currency. As
González concluded, "It became fashionable to be rich."[77]

With the shifting directions of social values, so follow the myths
that society creates. A society that treasured its material progress and
culture could not help but mythologize and deify those who operated in,
and yet threatened, this milieu. The cosmopolitan flavor of wealth and
exoticism added by Treffel, Nevraumont, and Sousa reflected the increasing influence of international culture on Mexico City. Moreover, the robbers of La Profesa were not the social bandits of the past. Not once does
any mention of any social redistribution of the jewels and cash appear
in newspaper accounts nor in their actions. This is a sharp break from
the myths of Chucho el Roto, who robbed to avenge the actions of certain elites against him. The shift to materialism should not be exaggerated, as in 1900 the next urban bandit, Jesús Negrete—El Tigre de Santa
Julia—again exemplified the beneficent bandit pushed to criminality

because of social conditions.[78] Nevertheless, like the changes in San José de Gracia, the values of Mexico City society noticeably shifted toward materialistic individualism while retaining a significant grounding in traditional notions of social justice and solidarity.

Neatly dividing this struggle between popular and elite views does not do justice to the impact on society of crime and criminality. After the trial rumors spread that Nevraumont and Sousa had begun to write a novel based on their crime, a novel that likely would find a readership among the gente decente and the elite, not the readers of Posada's broadsheets.[79] Moreover, the descriptions of the crowd at the trial suggest that Mexico's progress-oriented "respectable" society took an intense interest in both the robbers and the crime. The sizable contingent of ladies from fashionable families implies a certain romantic allure possessed by Nevraumont and the others, perhaps the fantasy that those who stole them away from their families metaphorically might do so in reality. Maybe the attendance and fascination of the trial watchers account for a peculiar ambivalence toward the general type of crime this represented. On the one hand it was feared, despised, and vociferously condemned. Yet it was also secretly, and not-so-secretly, admired by Mexicans eager to hear any fresh details about this sensational criminal exploit.

Perhaps, then, the La Profesa robbers should be defined not as protesting but rather embracing the norms of their society. Like so many others, they merely came to terms with the value placed on material wealth achieved through acquisitive capitalism in the manner most readily available to men without property or little means. Sousa, after a long string of business failures, looked for a new infusion of capital. Nevraumont appeared to choose the route of the leisure class by attempting to flee to Havana to spend his recently earned wealth. By violating elite social space and ransacking a bastion of material progress, they had come to the realization that crime does pay. U.S. prison investigator Richard Dugdale stated in 1877 that "we must dispossess ourselves of the idea that crime does not pay. In reality it does." Ten years later Italian criminologist Napoleone Colajanni argued crime paid better than honest labor.[80]

Although each of the accused participated in the job for different reasons, perhaps Nevraumont, Caballero, Sousa, and Treffel aspired to the rank and status of a new body of professional criminals who preyed on the material progress of the age. They could choose their inspirational models from a host of international locales: maybe the Parisian jewelry thieves that Treffel had mentioned during the trial; or George White and Mark Shinburn, who for two years prepared for their eventual theft of US$2.9 million from the Ocean Bank of Chicago; or even the great Edward Pierce, who spirited away 12,000 English pounds' worth of gold bullion in the famous Great Train Robbery of 1855. The point is that these were intelligent, professional men who committed the crimes they did for both the challenge and the financial gain. Train robber Pierce spoke for them all when, asked why he committed the crime, he shrugged his shoulders and explained, "I wanted the money." Later Pierce escaped custody and fled with two accomplices and the stolen cash, never to be found again.[81]

Whatever the case may be, the La Profesa jewelry store robbery and homicide temporarily threatened the day-to-day assumptions of Mexican respectable society and its members' faith in Porfirian order and progress. This window on Porfirian society revealed the disturbing revelation of the inseparable development of property crime with the consumerism and modernization that were transforming urban Mexico materially and culturally. At stake was the psychological investment in materialism as a concrete expression of progress, of an orderly, criminal-free future utopia. Like Aesop's lioness at the start of this chapter, the business relationship between Gerard Nevraumont, Nicolas Treffel, Jesús Bruno Martínez, Anton Sousa, and Aurelio Caballero may have borne only one crime, but its roar shook the whole of Mexico City society.

CONCLUSION

THIS STUDY HAS SHOWN THE MEXICAN EXPERIENCE OF A GLOBAL PHE-
nomenon during the presidency of Porfirio Díaz: the rise of a modern
consumer culture. To be sure, the cultural and economic processes that
gave it form long preceded and outlived the political periodization of
the Porfiriato. That said, during the Porfiriato those processes accelerated rapidly, and consumption assumed the modern forms and scope of
today—of mass consumption and highly visual advertising, a core component of an urban and increasingly national mass culture and its symbolic universe. Moreover, this study demonstrates a society fully aware
of and fascinated by the ascent of this consumer culture and its significance to daily life, even if historians after the Revolution failed to
share their appreciation. Filtered through Mexican traditions and practices and focused most intensely on the capital and urban areas, the
changes wrought by these new patterns and practices of consumption
transformed the material culture of the city, including the food, clothing, housing, architecture, entertainments, and physical landscape. The
Mexico City of 1910 bore little resemblance to that entered by a trium-
phant General Porfirio Díaz thirty-five years earlier. People used goods
and the language of goods along with the physical spaces of consumption (department stores, commercial entertainments, etc.) to construct
individual and group identities to situate themselves and others in the
rapidly changing context of daily urban life. Goods and the language of
goods were also used both to define and to challenge social hierarchies
and boundaries. Mexican society, in other words, became increasingly
reliant upon consumption as a means of communication, as a medium
through which to express, contest, and negotiate meaning.

This book is part of a new trend in Latin American history that emphasizes the study of material culture and urban history. It follows on the heels of Marie Francois's and Jürgen Buchenau's recent studies of the Mexico City pawnshop and German-owned hardware store, respectively.[1] Through the selection of various aspects of urban material culture, such as the cigarette industry and its marketing, diverse forms of advertising, department stores, and modernizing property crime, this study has sought to extract a number of themes with which to introduce consumption as a category of historical analysis. These selections serve as snapshots that often engage ongoing debates in Mexican historiography and that demonstrate the usefulness of viewing Mexican history through the lens of consumption for more established research methodologies. Studying the growth of the domestic market, domestic manufacture, and imported goods serves to remind historians that the export orientation of the Porfirian economy did not preclude the development of a domestic consumer market and industrial base. This is the implicit conclusion of much traditional economic historiography and is only recently receiving reassessment.[2] Connected with this development is the rise of the New Institutional Economics (NIE) school of thought in Latin American economics. NIE adherents eschew the structural approach and economic determinism of dependency and world systems theorists. Instead, they analyze Latin American economic development through a prism of social and cultural as well as economic lenses, considering not just external and macroeconomic factors but also the experience and strategies of individual firms, entrepreneurs, and other domestic components that shaped national economies and financial systems.[3] This study, with its original work on the tobacco industry and particularly the department store and French Barcelonnette community, adds to this growing field of knowledge. Incorporating consumption into the construction of modern categories and conceptions of criminality intersects with a growing corpus of work on the subject.[4] Considering how consumption helped to construct categories of gender and class strengthens an already dynamic and substantial field of research.[5] As a subfield of this, research connecting prostitution, notions of the body politic, and the Mexican state could benefit from incorporating elements of consumption, drawing on the considerable body of European historiography on the prostitute, linking the commodification of women with that of modern society.[6] A refresher reading of the Porfirian novel *Santa* will quickly demonstrate how members of the gente decente linked prostitution, consumption, modern morality, and social health.[7]

The most significant insight of this study is its reconceptualization of Porfirian modernization. For too long, historians of Mexico have considered modernization as a top-down imposition, as a veneer applied by the Porfirian leadership to Mexican society. For some, the culture of consumption described in this study should be included in this thin façade. Such a perspective falls into the false perception that modernization is a foreign import, a quality not embraced by the majority of the Mexican public. And yet the Mexican Revolution did not return Mexico to an earlier time; most of its leadership came from the most economically dynamic region of the republic, the north, and most of those leaders were staunch modernizers. The cigarette companies, breweries, and department stores all survived and attained greater levels of profitability and significance in the 1920s. The danger of the traditional interpretation is in its confusion of the more superficial currents of politics in history with the deeper flows of economic and cultural processes. While the Porfirian regime may have crumbled, the many material and cultural changes wrought by a global process and its local creators remained.

A view of Porfirian society through the lens of consumption helps to explain the durability of these changes as it brings to light the popular and participatory nature of modernization. To be sure, modernization had a top-down component. This study reveals that the rise of a consumer culture was central to the Porfirian project of modernization and political centralization. For Porfirian leaders and many citizens, economic modernization and political centralization were merely the means to the ultimate end proof of national progress: cultural modernization along the models represented by North Atlantic societies. Yet this study also introduces actors generally absent or weakly represented in the Mexican historiographical discussion of state formation and modernization. As demonstrated in the chapters on the cigarette industry, department stores, and advertising, one such group is the business community and its role in transmitting and negotiating the meaning of modernity and progress.[8] Even this, however, could be argued as the state building alliances with nonstate actors such as the business community in order to extend its reach. Less debatable and more consequential is this study's identification of widespread marketing toward and participation of urban working-class consumers. By doing so, it directly challenges traditional interpretations that have argued for the incapacity and unwillingness of this important social group to engage in consumption activity and to embrace a modernizing material culture. Contrary to received scholarly wisdom, urban workers did embrace the notion of progress and the material culture that provided its tangible evidence. What they did not share was their superiors' belief that social and political inequalities were normative in a modern Mexico. This new perspective on working-class consumer identity challenges the standard condemnation of the Porfirian regime's emphasis on material progress as a causative factor for the Mexican Revolution that began in 1910.

Another insight concerns the salient role of the French contribution to Mexican modernization and consumer culture. Although popular and scholarly histories of the Porfiriato have long mentioned the *afrancesamiento* of Mexican society in the decades prior to the Revolution, work on the French community and its influence on consumption patterns has only recently begun among French and Mexican scholars. In the English-language historiography U.S. economic and cultural influence has long held sway, to the detriment of studies on the French and more general European influence on Porfirian Mexico. Studies on the American community by John M. Hart and William Schell have swung the pendulum to the extreme of the arc, emphasizing the impact of U.S. capitalism in Mexico and minimizing the role of native and European contributions.[9] Julio Moreno goes so far as to argue that a consumer culture developed in Mexico only with the entrance of Sears Roebuck and the J. Walter Thompson advertising agency in the 1940s.[10] While it is true that the United States dominated sectors such as mining and transportation and became the single-largest foreign investor, its economic and cultural dominance would not reach its apogee until after World War I. To balance this interpretation, every chapter in this study demonstrates how the French community capitalized on its cultural cachet and assumed a salient role in creating a Mexican consumer culture. In particular, its members dominated the dry-goods retail sector in the capital and many provincial cities as well as developed domestic industrial capacity for the production of consumer goods (especially textiles and certain comestibles) capable of meeting internal market demand. Rather than focusing on one group as the sole creators of a Mexican consumer culture, "becoming a consuming people" was a cultural, economic, and political process forged by national and international players representing all classes, genders, and races.[11]

A final word on the scope of this project and the possibilities for future research. Although this study has focused on the capital, Mexico City is not representative of the entire republic. Perhaps most pressing of all in the study of Porfirian consumption is a move beyond the metropolis, beyond Mexico City and into the states to consider not only the cities but also smaller population centers. Such work may revolutionize the way we understand Porfirian material culture and modernization. Understanding and tracking the agency system would provide great insight into the modernizing products available to clients in a small town's consumer catchment area. To give a specific example, Eduardo Maynez of Parras, Coahuila, served as the exclusive agent in his town for the following services and products: a savings bank in Monterrey, patent medicines, French perfumes, candies, Spanish and French novels, scientific and business books, music and instruments from Mexico City's famous Wagner and Levien, wines and *aguardientes* of the Carmen distillery, and pasta for the manufacturer La Diana.[12] Finding and mining the archives of the Administración de Rentas y Contribuciones for each state in which traveling salesmen and peddlers were required to register would prove a gold mine for tracking the extension of a national market. Further work on mule trains would also aid this effort. By studying the way in which modern consumer goods and consumption patterns and practices influenced everyday life in rural areas, historians could fully grasp the national and long-range consequences of creating Mexican consumer culture in the age of Porfirio Díaz.

The preface of this book ended with the remark by José Arcadio Buendía that "incredible things are happening in this world." Turning from that fictional and mythic account of village life in late nineteenth- and early twentieth-century Colombia, this study now concludes with one Mexican historian's insight into how these "incredible things" changed daily life in his childhood village during roughly the same time period. The similarities are remarkable. In the third chapter of *San José de Gracia: Mexican Village in Transition*, Luis González discusses the changes that occurred between 1900 and 1910. He introduces don Gregorio, a prominent local merchant and liaison with the larger world who took local products to Mexico City once a month. As trade increased, new stores opened and a greater number of goods arrived. New competition sprang up but don Gregorio remained the champion importer and exporter. He was also the best storyteller and brought back tales of the city, of don Porfirio, and of new inventions like the train and electric light. In 1906 the first of a flood of newspapers from the capital arrived. Residents were astonished not by politics, strikes, and other national events but, as González writes, "by the news of seemingly incredible inventions. There were flying machines with wings, the wireless telegraph, the telephone, the automobile, motion pictures, electric streetcars, photographs, the phonograph, the incandescent light, the submarine, aspirin, and other medicaments and artifacts of modern life."[13] The chapter continues, describing the arrival and impact of new goods on the town, the growing wealth, social divisions, and expenditures to make life more comfortable. With a transforming material culture and the ideas that came with it, González describes a shift in mentality, particularly among the young, to embrace change.[14] He notes the expansion of the residents' worldview beyond the patria chica, the recognition of a budding nationalism, and the identification of San José with the Mexican fatherland.[15] Although he does not say it directly, González captures the interconnection between material culture and mentality as he traces the diffusion of modernity into his childhood town.

Perhaps the distance between Porfirian Mexico City and San José de Gracia was not so great as we have imagined.

NOTES

Preface

1. Gabriel García Márquez, *One Hundred Years of Solitude*, trans. Gregory Rabassa (New York: Alfred A. Knopf, 1998).
2. Ibid., 40.
3. Ibid., 12.

Introduction

Abbreviations Used in the Notes

AACM: Archivos del ex-Ayuntamiento de la Ciudad de México, Mexico City

AGN: Archivo General de la Nación, Mexico City

APH: Archivo Palacio de Hierro, Mexico City

JYL-CEHM: Archivo José Yves Limantour, Centro de Estudios de Historia de México Carso, Chimalistac, Mexico City

Nineteenth Century, PyM-AGN: Nineteenth-century century patents, in Patentes y Marcas (Cajas Negras), Grupo Documental 218, Fondo Secretaría de Comercio y Fomento Industrial, AGN

PyM-AGN: Twentieth-century patents, in Patentes y Marcas (Grises Grandes), Grupo Documental 218, Fondo Secretaría de Comercio y Fomento Industrial, AGN

1. J. Figueroa Domenech, *Guía general descriptiva de la República Mexicana*, 2 vols. (Mexico City: Ramón de S. N. Araluce, 1899), 1:254.
2. Perhaps the most well-known of this genre is Justo Sierra, *México, su evolución social: Síntesis de la organización administrativa y military y del estado economic de la federación Mexicana* . . . 2 vols. (Barcelona: J. Ballesca y compañia, successor,

1900–1902). In addition to works by Mexicans, dozens of publications by foreigners sought primarily to entice foreign investment. Among these are Mrs. Alec Tweedie, *Maker of Modern Mexico, Porfirio Díaz* (New York: J. Lane, 1906); Percy F. Martin, *Mexico of the Twentieth Century*, 2 vols. (London: Edward Arnold, 1907); William E. Carson, *Mexico: The Wonderland of the South* (New York: MacMillan, 1909); and Auguste Génin, *Notes sur le Mexique* (Mexico City: Imprenta Lacaud, 1908–1910).

3. The work that marks the beginning of this more balanced scholarship is Daniel Cosío Villegas, ed., *Historia moderna de México*, 9 vols. (Mexico City: Editorial Hermes, 1955–1973). A few examples of the studies that followed include François-Xavier Guerra, *México: Del antiguo regimen a la revolución*, 2 vols. (Mexico City: Fondo de Cultura Económica, 1988); Edward Beatty, *Institutions and Investment: The Political Basis of Industrialization in Mexico Before 1911* (Stanford, CA: Stanford University Press, 2001); and Mauricio Tenorio-Trillo, *Mexico at the World's Fairs: Crafting a Modern Nation* (Berkeley: University of California Press, 1996).

4. Emilio Kourí, *A Pueblo Divided: Business, Property, and Community in Papantla, Mexico* (Stanford, CA: Stanford University Press, 2004). For a similar emphasis on autonomous popular response to modernization, see William H. Beezley, *Mexican National Identity: Memory, Innuendo, and Popular Culture* (Tucson: University of Arizona Press, 2008).

5. Editorial by Alfonso Luis Velasco in *El Avisador Comercial*, May 12, 1889, 2.

6. For an explanation of the etymology and methodology of this approach to history, see Alf Lüdtke, "Introduction: What is the History of Everyday Life and Who Are Its Practitioners?" in Lüdtke, ed., *The History of Everyday Life: Reconstructing Historical Experiences and Ways of Life*, trans. William Templer (Princeton, NJ: Princeton University Press, 1995).

7. Eric Van Young, "The New Cultural History Comes to Old Mexico," *Hispanic American Historical Review* 79, no.2 (May 1999): 211–47.

8. One of the earliest works considering modernizing material culture and national identity in a Latin American society is Jeffrey D. Needell, *A Tropical Belle Epoque: Elite Culture and Society in Turn-of-the-Century Rio de Janeiro* (Cambridge: Cambridge University Press, 1987). See also Benjamin Orlove, ed., *The Allure of the Foreign: Imported Goods in Postcolonial Latin America* (Ann Arbor: University of Michigan Press, 1997); and Marie Eileen Francois, "The Products of Consumption: Housework in Latin American Political Economies and Cultures," *History Compass* 6, no. 1 (2008): 207–42. Fernando Rocchi offers a brief but excellent consideration of the rise of an Argentine consumer culture and market within his larger study of industrialization, *Chimneys in the Desert: Industrialization in Argentina During the Export Boom Years, 1870–1930* (Stanford, CA: Stanford University Press, 2006).

9. Alan Knight, "Patterns and Prescriptions in Mexican Historiography," *Bulletin of Latin American Research* 25, no. 3 (2006): 348.

10. Jeffrey Pilcher, "Fajitas and the Failure of Refrigerated Meatpacking in Mexico: Consumer Culture and Porfirian Capitalism," *The Americas* 60, no. 3 (January 2004): 411–29; Steven B. Bunker, "'Consumers of Good Taste:' Marketing Modernity

in Northern Mexico, 1890–1910," *Mexican Studies/Estudios Mexicanos* 13, no. 2
(Summer 1997): 227–69; Víctor M. Macías-González, "The *Lagartijo* at *The High
Life*: Masculine Consumption, Race, Nation, and Homosexuality in Porfirian
Mexico," in Robert McKee Irwin, Edward J. McCaughan, and Michelle Rocío
Nasser, eds., *The Famous 41: Sexuality and Social Control in Mexico, 1901* (New
York: Palgrave Macmillan, 2003), 227–50; William H. Beezley, "The Porfirian Smart
Set Anticipates Thorstein Veblen in Guadalajara," in William H. Beezley, Cheryl
English Martin, and William E. French, eds., *Rituals of Rule, Rituals of Resistance:
Public Celebrations and Popular Culture in Mexico* (Wilmington, DE: Scholarly
Resources, 1994), 173–90; Jürgen Buchenau, *Tools of Progress: A German Merchant
Family in Mexico City, 1865–Present* (Albuquerque: University of New Mexico
Press, 2004); Susie S. Porter, *Working Women in Mexico City: Public Discourses and
Material Conditions, 1879–1931* (Tucson: University of Arizona Press, 2003).

11. For the first narrative and historiographic review of consumption and material
culture over the course of Mexican history, see Steven B. Bunker and Víctor M.
Macías-González, "Consumption and Material Culture from Pre-contact through
the Porfiriato" and "Consumption and Material Culture in the Twentieth Century,"
both in William H. Beezley, ed., *A Companion to Mexican History and Culture*
(Malden, MA: Blackwell, 2011), 54–82, 83–118. An excellent study of inconspicuous
consumption and the changing material culture of Mexico City during the long
nineteenth century is Marie Eileen Francois, *A Culture of Everyday Credit:
Housekeeping, Pawnbroking, and Governance in Mexico City, 1750–1920* (Lincoln:
University of Nebraska Press, 2006). For a superb history of consumer culture
along the U.S.-Mexican border, see Alexis McCrossen, ed., *Land of Necessity:
Consumer Culture in the United States–Mexico Borderlands* (Durham, NC:
Duke University Press, 2009). For the twentieth century, see Julio E. Moreno,
*Yankee Don't Go Home!: Mexican Nationalism, American Business Culture, and the
Shaping of Modern Mexico, 1920–1950* (Chapel Hill: University of North Carolina
Press, 2003); Eric Zolov, *Refried Elvis: The Rise of the Mexican Counterculture*
(Berkeley: University of California Press, 1999); and Anne Rubenstein, *Bad
Language, Naked Ladies, and Other Threats to the Nation: A Political History of
Comic Books in Mexico* (Durham, NC: Duke University Press, 1998).

12. Denise Hellion, *Exposición permanente: Anuncios y anunciantes en* El Mundo
Ilustrado (Mexico City: INAH–Universidad Autónoma Metropolitana-
Azcapotzalco, 2008); Nora Pérez-Rayón, "La publicidad en México a fines del siglo
XIX: Expresión del progreso económico y la modernidad porfirista, transmisora
de nuevos valores y modelos culturales," *Sociológica* 9, no. 1 (September–December
1994): 195–226; Berta Tello Peón, "Intención decorativo en los objetos de uso
cotidiano de los interiores domésticos del Porfiriato," in *El arte y la vida cotidiana*,
ed. Elena Estrada de Gerleso (Mexico City: UNAM Instituto de Investigaciones
Estéticas, 1995), 139–54; Thelma Camacho Morfín, *Imágenes de México: Las
historietas de El Buen Tono de Juan B. Urrutia, 1909–1912* (Mexico City: Instituto
Mora, 2002); Julieta Ortiz Gaitán, *Imágenes del deseo: Arte y publicidad en la prensa*

ilustrada Mexicana (1894–1939) (Mexico City: UNAM, 2003); *México, ¿quieres tomarte una foto conmigo? Cien años de consumo* (Mexico City: PROFECO/ Editorial Gustavo Casasola, 1996); Asociación Mexicana de Agencias de Publicidad, *Crónica de la publicidad en México: 1901–2001* (Mexico City: Editorial Clío, 2002).

13. Pilar Gonzalbo Aizpuru, director, *Historia de la vida cotidiana en México*, 6 vols. (Mexico City: El Colegio de México–Fondo de Cultura Económica, 2004–2006).

14. Neil McKendrick, John Brewer, and J. H. Plumb, *The Birth of a Consumer Society: The Commercialization of Eighteenth-Century England* (Bloomington: Indiana University Press, 1982).

15. Michael B. Miller, *The Bon Marché: Bourgeois Culture and the Department Store, 1869–1920* (Princeton, NJ: Princeton University Press, 1981).

16. The literature is too vast for a note. A good place to start is the best early edited volume, John Brewer and Roy Porter, eds., *Consumption and the World of Goods* (London: Routledge, 1993). Following closely in influence is Victoria de Grazia and Ellen Furlough, eds., *The Sex of Things: Gender and Consumption in Historical Perspective* (Berkeley: University of California Press, 1996). For the seminal text in U.S. scholarship on consumption, see Richard Wightman Fox and T. J. Jackson Lears, eds., *The Culture of Consumption: Critical Essays in American History, 1880–1980* (New York: Pantheon, 1983). Review essays surveying the landscape of the historiography and identifying deficiencies include Mary Louise Roberts, "Gender, Consumption, and Commodity Culture," *American Historical Review* 103, no. 3 (June 1998): 817–44; Peter N. Stearns, "Stages of Consumerism: Recent Work on the Issues of Periodization," *Journal of Modern History* 69 (March 1997): 102–17; and Frank Trentmann, "Beyond Consumerism: New Historical Perspectives on Consumption," *Journal of Contemporary History* 39, no. 3 (July 2004): 373–401. Two intriguing recent studies are Krista Lysack, *Come Buy, Come Buy: Shopping and the Culture of Consumption in Victorian Women's Writing* (Athens: Ohio University Press, 2008); and S. Jonathan Wiesen, *Creating the Nazi Marketplace: Commerce and Consumption in the Third Reich* (New York: Cambridge University Press, 2011).

17. See, for example, Stearns, "Stages of Consumerism," 117.

18. Arnold J. Bauer, *Goods, Power, History: Latin America's Material Culture* (New York: Cambridge University Press, 2001), 129–64.

19. Christine Ruane, "Clothes Shopping in Imperial Russia: The Development of a Consumer Culture," *Journal of Social History* 28 (Summer 1995): 765–82; Timothy Burke, *Lifebuoy Men, Lux Women: Commodification, Consumption, and Cleanliness in Modern Zimbabwe* (Durham, NC: Duke University Press, 1996); Jeremy Prestholdt, "On the Global Repercussions of East African Consumerism," *American Historical Review* 109, no. 3 (June 2004): 755–81. A synthesis is Peter N. Stearns, *Consumerism in World History: The Global Transformation of Desire* (London: Routledge, 2006). For two excellent studies on China and Japan, see Karl Gerth, *China Made: Consumer Culture and the Creation of the Nation* (Cambridge, MA: Harvard University Press, 2003); and Penelope Francks, *The Japanese Consumer: An Alternative History of Modern Japan* (New York: Cambridge University Press, 2009).

20. For a Catholic critique of fashion cycles and increased consumption, see R. P. V. Marchal, *La mujer perfecta*, trans. S. P. Vicens y Marco (Barcelona: Gustavo Gili, 1908). For a concise intellectual history of the varying Porfirian discourses on the market (and, by extension, the social impact of commerce and consumption), see Richard Weiner, *Race, Nation, and Market: Economic Culture in Porfirian Mexico* (Tucson: University of Arizona Press, 2004).

21. In addition to the Domenech volume cited in note 1, two examples of photographic albums documenting the material progress of the capital and the nation (with a heavy emphasis on commercial architecture or commercial images such as advertising on city streets) are Guillermo Kahlo, *Mexiko 1904* (Mexico City: Universidad Iberoamericana, 2002); and *Álbum oficial del Comité Nacional del Comercio: Premier centenario de la independencia de México, 1810–1910* (Mexico City: Gómez de la Puente, 1910).

22. Andrés Molina Enríquez, *Los grandes problemas nacionales* (Mexico City: Impr. de A. Carranza e hijos, 1909), esp. 227–34; Miguel Macedo, *La criminalidad en México: Medios de combatirla* (Mexico City: Oficina tip. de la Secretaría de Fomento, 1897), 7–8, 16, 19; Julio Guerrero, *La génesis del crimen en México: Ensayo de psiquiatría social* (Mexico City: Imprenta de la Vda. de Ch. Bouret, 1901).

23. Adam Smith, *The Wealth of Nations* (Amherst, NY: Prometheus Books, 1991), 444.

24. Domenech, *Guía general descriptiva*, 1:254.

25. *Modern Mexico*, January 1897, 12.

26. *La Semana Mercantil*, July 1, 1895, 305.

27. Carson, *Mexico: Wonderland of the South*, 206; William Henry Bishop, *Old Mexico and Her Lost Provinces* (New York: Harper and Brothers, 1883).

28. The perceived excesses or demands of modern life in the capital may be found in *El Mundo Ilustrado*, April 27, 1902, 1. The article editorializes on the expense and time involved in an urban toilette and social life, listing all the items required and concluding that "urbanity is like the corset, like the English collar, like the cravat of a uniform . . ."

29. *El Imparcial*, December 2, 1902, 1; *El Avisador Comercial*, May 12, 1889, 2.

30. *La Semana Mercantil*, April 10, 1893, 175; March 9, 1891, 114; *El Economista Mexicano*, February 21, 1891, 31.

31. *El Imparcial*, August 24, 1900, 1, condenses the latest argument of economist J. B. Say, who favored a utilitarian economic approach to consumption that frowned upon luxury consumption and favored consumption that benefited major domestic industries. For perhaps the earliest and most famous entrant into this debate, see Bernard Mandeville, *The Fable of the Bees; or, Private Vices, Publick Benefits*, published in 1714. For an analysis of Mandeville and other participants in this debate, see Roger Mason, *The Economics of Conspicuous Consumption: Theory and Thought Since 1700* (Cheltenham, UK: Edward Elgar, 1998).

32. *Le Mexique*, October 5, 1908, 276.

33. *La Victoria*, May 29, 1877, 1.

34. Pablo Piccato, *City of Suspects: Crime in Mexico City, 1900–1931* (Durham, NC: Duke University Press, 2001), 21–22.

35. Beatty, *Institutions and Investment*, 40.

36. Piccato, *City of Suspects*; James Alex Garza, *The Imagined Underworld: Sex, Crime, and Vice in Porfirian Mexico City* (Lincoln: University of Nebraska Press, 2007).

37. Beatty, *Institutions and Investment*, 32.

38. Piccato, *City of Suspects*, 23; Porter, *Working Women in Mexico City*.

39. For Veracruz, see Andrew Grant Wood, *Revolution in the Street: Women, Workers, and Urban Protest in Veracruz, 1870–1927* (Wilmington, DE: Scholarly Resources 2001), esp. 1–20; and for Tampico, see Marcial E. Ocasio-Meléndez, "Mexican Urban History: The Case of Tampico, Tamaulipas, 1876–1924" (PhD diss., Michigan State University, 1988).

40. Mary Kay Vaughan, "Primary Education and Literacy in Nineteenth-Century Mexico: Research Trends, 1968–1988," *Latin American Research Review* 25, no.1 (1990): 31–66, esp. 42–43. For the Federal District, see *Estadísticas históricas de México* (Mexico City: INEGI, 1984), 92.

41. Bunker and Macías-González, "Consumption and Material Culture, Pre-contact through the Porfiriato," 54.

42. For a synthesis of this whole period, see ibid.

43. José María Luis Mora, *Obras completas*, vol. 4, *Obra historica* (Mexico City: Secretaría de Educación Pública–Instituto de Investigaciones Dr. José María Luis Mora, 1987), 110.

44. I borrow this phrase from Orlove, *Allure of the Foreign*.

45. Mary Nolan, *Visions of Modernity: American Business and the Modernization of Germany* (New York: Oxford University Press, 1994), 9.

46. Moreno, *Yankee Don't Go Home!*, locates the origins of a modern Mexican consumer culture in the importation of U.S. business practices in the decades after World War I. William Schell, *Integral Outsiders: The American Colony in Mexico City, 1876–1911* (Wilmington, DE: Scholarly Resources, 2001), and John Mason Hart, *Empire and Revolution: The Americans in Mexico Since the Civil War* (Berkeley: University of California Press, 2002), are two studies that emphasize the American influence in Mexico during the Porfiriato, a perception that tends to imbue much of the English-language historiography of the period. Recent studies presenting the European influence include Buchenau, *Tools of Progress*; and Paul H Garner, *British Lions and Mexican Eagles: Business, Politics, and Empire in the Career of Weetman Pearson in Mexico, 1889–1919* (Stanford, CA: Stanford University Press, 2011).

Chapter 1

1. *Le Courrier du Mexique*, December 25, 1907, 3; *El Mundo Ilustrado*, January 5, 1908, 3.

2. The phrase is from Sally West, *I Shop in Moscow: Advertising and the Creation of Consumer Culture in Late Tsarist Russia* (DeKalb: Northern Illinois Press, 2011), 96.

3. On individualization, see William French, "Living the Vida Local: Contours of Everyday Life," in Beezley, *Companion to Mexican History*, 17; and Colin Campbell, *The Romantic Ethic and the Spirit of Modern Consumerism* (Oxford: Basil Blackwell, 1987).

4. The finest and most comprehensive study of the colonial tobacco monopoly is Susan Deans-Smith, *Bureaucrats, Planters, and Workers: The Making of the Tobacco Monopoly in Bourbon Mexico* (Austin: University of Texas Press, 1992). It includes information on Antonio Charro and the predominance of cigarettes and cigars (12, 149–52).

5. Deans-Smith, *Bureaucrats, Planters*, 7.

6. Rosa María Meyer Cosío, "La ciudad como centro commercial e industrial," in *El corazón de una nación independiente. Ensayos sobre la Ciudad de México*, ed. Isabel Tovar de Arechederra and Magdalena Mas (Mexico City: Universidad Iberoamericana-Departamento del Distrito Federal, 1994), 47–67.

7. Deans-Smith, *Bureaucrats, Planters*, 144–45.

8. Fanny Calderón de la Barca, *Life in Mexico During a Residence of Two Years in That Country* (London: E. P. Dutton, 1917), 33, 55.

9. Ignacio Cumplido, ed., *El álbum mexicano*, 2 vols. (Mexico City: Imp. de Ignacio Cumplido, 1849); *Los mexicanos: Pintados por si mismos, por varios autores* (Mexico City: Casa de M. Murguia, Portal del Aguila de Oro, 1855); Luis G. Inclán, *Astucia: El jefe de los hermanos de la hoja; ó, Los charros contrabandistas de la rama* (Mexico City: Librería de la vda. de Ch. Bouret, 1908). See also María Concepción Amerlinck, *Historia y cultura del tabaco en México* (Mexico City: Tabacos Mexicanos, 1988).

10. Luis Nicolau d'Olwer et al., *El Porfiriato: La vida económica*, vol. 7 of Villegas, *Historia moderna de México*, 82–85.

11. Ibid., 362–63; Stephen H. Haber, *Industry and Underdevelopment: The Industrialization of Mexico, 1890–1940* (Stanford, CA: Stanford University Press, 1989), 51, 99. For the Porfirian conditions that favored import substitution and helped provide a stable, supportive business environment for aggressive companies like El Buen Tono, see Beatty, *Institutions and Investment*, particularly 46–48, on incorporation laws.

12. D'Olwer et al., *El Porfiriato: La vida económica*, 362–63.

13. Carson, *Mexico: Wonderland of the South*, 65.

14. Carson, *Mexico: Wonderland of the South*, 124; *El Mundo Ilustrado*, March 20, 1900.

15. Percy F. Martin, *Mexico of the Twentieth Century* (London: Edward Arnold, 1907), 1:197.

16. Beatty, *Institutions and Investment*, 39–43.

17. Domenech, *Guía general descriptiva*, 1:186; caja 46, exp. 1788, November 11, 1885 (máquina para encajillar cigarros de papel), Nineteenth Century, PyM-AGN.

18. Moisés González Navarro, *El Porfiriato: La vida social*, vol. 4 of Villegas, *Historia moderna de México*, 294–97; Porter, *Working Women in Mexico City*, 73–95. Newspaper articles concerning new machinery, wages, and work conditions of female cigarette employees include *La Semana en el Hogar*, July 29, 1895, 1–2; August 5, 1895, 1–2; *El Imparcial*, October 17, 1900, 1; and *La Clase Media*, November 21, 1909, 3.

19. González Navarro, *El Porfiriato: La vida social*, 295.

20. John Lear, "Mexico City: Popular Classes and Revolutionary Politics" in *Cities of*

Hope: People, Protests, and Progress in Urbanizing Latin America, 1870–1930, ed. Ronn Pineo and James A. Baer (Boulder, CO: Westview Press, 1998), 55–57.

21. For summaries of Pugibet, see his obituary in *Le Trait d'Union,* March 6, 1915, 1; *Diccionario Porrua: Historia, biografía y geografía de México,* 5th ed. (Mexico City: Editorial Porrua, 1994), 2366–77; and Camacho Morfín, *Imágenes de México.* For information on the high rate of interlocking directories among the Mexican industrial elite (not unlike the United States at the time), see Haber, *Industry and Underdevelopment,* 67.

22. Camacho Morfín, *Imágenes de México,* 17–18, interprets a more active role for Portilla. For more information on the Portilla y Garaycoechea family background, see Víctor Manuel Macías-González, "Apuntes geneológicas de la elite porfiriana" (unpublished manuscript, ca. 1994–1999). *L'Echo du Mexique* discussed the transfer of title by Sra. Guadalupe Portilla de Pugibet to the incorporated company on February 18, 1894, 2, and February 20, 1894, 2, wishing Ernesto Pugibet the same good business relations with the new society members as he enjoyed with his wife. On a final note of Pugibet's indebtedness to the Portilla family's political and economic resources, *L'Echo du Mexique,* January 30, 1896, 2, comments on the Portilla family occupying two of the four top posts within the administrative council of Pugibet's San Ildefonso textile mill and hydroelectric power facility, indicating that family money assisted in this enterprise.

23. Juan Manuel Aurrecocchea and Armando Batra, *Puros cuentos: La historia de la historieta en México* (Mexico City: Editorial Grijalbo, 1988), 1:120; Reginald Tower, "General Report on Mexico for the Year 1908," Mexico City, to Sir Edward Grey, Foreign Office, London, January 1, 1909, doc. 262, in George Phillip, ed., *British Documents on Foreign Affairs: Reports and Papers from the Foreign Office Confidential Print,* pt. 1, *From the Mid-nineteenth Century to the First World War,* ser. D, *Latin America, 1845–1914,*vol. 4, *Mexico, 1861–1910* (Bethesda, MD: University Publications of America, 1998), 326, BDFA-Mexico.

24. *L'Echo du Mexique,* April 15, 1893, 2; *Le Courrier du Mexique,* December 30, 1900, 2; February 6, 1906, 3; April 2, 1909, 3; *El Imparcial,* December 11, 1904, 4.

25. *Le Courrier du Mexique,* December 13, 1908, 3; *El Imparcial,* February 4, 1909, 2.

26. For examples, see Pugibet to JYL, Paris, July 28, 1899, Pugibet to JYL, Lucerne, August 9, 1899, and JYL to Pugibet, Mexico City, June 6, 1899, CDLIV 1883–1899, roll 11, carp. 42, JYL-CEHM; JYL to María Teresa Iturbe, Mexico City, March 5, 1907, CDLIV 1907, roll 45, carp. 17, JYL-CEHM.

27. Upon leaving for Europe Pugibet sent Limantour one of the first fine-grade traveling shawls made by the factory. Pugibet to JYL, Mexico City, March 18, 1907, CDLIV 1907, roll 46, carp. 21, JYL-CEHM.

28. JYL to Pugibet, Mexico City, November 22, 1907, CDLIV 1907, roll 45, carp. 16, JYL-CEHM. See also Joaquin Nuñez de Prado to JYL, Mexico City, March 29, 1901, CDLIV 1901, roll 9, carp. 15, JYL-CEHM; and José Vázquez to JYL, October 16, 1907, CDLIV 1907, roll 48, carp. 25, JYL-CEHM.

29. Pugibet to JYL, March 14, 1906, and JYL to Pugibet, March 16, 1906, CDLIV 1906,

roll 40, carp. 13, JYL-CEHM. An interesting aside—given the recent and ongoing lawsuits surrounding the tobacco industry's supposed duping of the public as to the health risks of tobacco—is that nicotine was already considered a dangerous substance during the Porfiriato: "for it is well known, nicotine is most injurious to smokers." *Mexican Herald*, January 28, 1906, 9. In fact, El Buen Tono processed it out of tobacco and marketed it for home use against mites and for agricultural use against parasites in sheep. On the toxicity of nicotine and how it was extracted, see the *Mexican Herald*, January 28, 1906, 9. Mexican hacendados commonly used the toxin on their flocks, and the son of Porfirio Díaz was no exception, as described in *El Imparcial*, March 1, 1906, 2. On how this health concern affected advertising, see *El Imparcial*, November 7, 1907, 7, for the launch by the Tabacalera Mexicana of its luxury brand Monograma. The company noted that the cigarette contained a cardboard mouthpiece and cotton filter, "which blocks the passage of nicotine."

30. Pugibet to JYL, Mexico City, May 23, 1903, CDLIV 1903, roll 21, carp. 15, JYL-CEHM.

31. JYL to Julio Limantour, Paris, July 5, 1906, CDLIV 1906, roll 38, carp. 4, JYL-CEHM.

32. *Le Mexique*, June 20, 1907, 156; *Le Courrier du Mexique*, September 23, 1904, 3; February 11, 1906, 3; June 16, 1907, 2; June 22, 1907, 3; Pugibet to JYL, May 20, 1908, CDLIV 1908, roll 54, carp. 20, JYL-CEHM.

33. Although the brand name uses *cigarros* or cigars, all descriptions of the actual product refer to it as *cigarillos*, or cigarettes. The ceding of Mexican patent rights for Decouflé machines to both Pugibet and Portilla receives a paragraph in Agustin Verdugo, Jorge Vera Estañol, and Manuel Calero y Sierra, *El Buen Tono y la "Bonsack Machine Company." Sentencia de la Suprema Corte de justicia de la Nación y otras piezas relativas al juicio seguido entre "El Buen Tono" y el Sr. W. H. Butler* (Mexico City: Imprenta de Ignacio Escalante, 1900), 8. On the registration of the new brand, see *El Economista Mexicano*, April 16, 1892, 4. *L'Echo du Mexique*, May 6, 1892, 4, offers one instance where the press extolled the hygienic and gustatory virtues of the new process and noted that the French tobacco monopoly used the same equipment.

34. For the initial incorporation, see *L'Echo du Mexique*, October 4, 1894, 1. The number of rolling machines increased to 104 in 1898, 190 by 1904, and over 200 by 1906. *Le Mexique*, May 20, 1898, 1; May 3, 1904, 4; *Le Courrier du Mexique*, December 6, 1906, 3; Raoul Bigot, *Le Mexique moderne* (Paris: Pierre Roger, 1910), 119. On the forms of organization available to businesses in Porfirian Mexico, see Aurora Gómez-Galvarriato and Aldo Musacchio, "Organizational Choice in a French Civil Law Underdeveloped Economy: Partnerships, Corporations, and the Chartering of Business in Mexico, 1886–1910" (Harvard Business School Working Paper No. 05–024, Harvard University, 2004).

35. Capital and investment information regularly appeared in the newspapers. Examples supporting these statistics include *Le Mexique*, May 20, 1898, 1; April 5, 1909, 113–115; March 20, 1910, 91–93.

36. For an excellent work on this subject and the fusing of art and advertising in the making of a modern Mexican visual culture, see Ortiz Gaitán, *Imágenes del deseo*, esp. 109–62, on Mexican artist biographies.

37. Cited in Barros, *Crónica gráfica de la Ciudad de México en el centenario de la independencia* (Mexico City: Departamento del Distrito Federal, Secretaría General de Desarrollo Social, Comité Interno de Ediciones Gubernamentales, 1988), 62. This is a reproduction of the 1910 *Álbum gráfico de la República Mexicana* compiled and authored by Eugenio Espino Barros. The French economic analyst Raoul Bigot sought to improve the state of French imports to Mexico and reverse their steady decline in the face of German, American, Belgian, and British competition. He attacked the arrogance of French producers for resting on the supposed world renown of their products instead of aggressively marketing on the terms of each host society and economy. For him, El Buen Tono stood out as an ideal wedding of French quality and luxury with savvy advertising and distribution. Bigot, *Le Mexique moderne*, 119. For another description, see Domenech, *Guía general descriptiva*, 1:179–80.

38. Domenech, *Guía general descriptiva*, 1:179–80.

39. *Le Courrier du Mexique*, June 21, 1907, 3; Génin, *Notes sur le Mexique*, 127–28.

40. Ortiz Gaitán, *Imágenes del deseo*, 13.

41. Porter, *Working Women in Mexico City*, 22; Haber, *Industry and Underdevelopment*, 48–51; d'Olwer et al., *El Porfiriato: La vida económica*, 693–94.

42. Luis C. Cerda González, *Historia financiera del Banco Nacional de México: Porfiriato, 1884–1910* (Mexico City: Fomento Cultural Banamex, A.C., 1994), 2:249; d'Olwer et al., *El Porfiriato: La vida económica*, 235; Alexander Saragoza, *The Monterrey Elite and the Mexican State, 1880–1940* (Austin: University of Texas Press, 1988), 57–59. Information on Basagoiti's funeral in Morelia, including the accompanying eight urban railcars and numerous private carriages, may be found in *El Imparcial*, January 6, 1905, 2.

43. Haber, *Industry and Underdevelopment*, 70–71.

44. *El Imparcial*, July 22, 1900, 2; October 17, 1900, 1; November 12, 1900, 3; September 9, 1903, 2.

45. *El Imparcial*, November 12, 1900, 3; *Le Courrier du Mexique*, November 13, 1900, 3.

46. This view persists even in the otherwise excellent work of Mexican historians working on subjects related to Porfirian consumer culture. See, e.g., Camacho Morfín, *Imágenes de México*, 27; Ortiz Gaitán, *Imágenes del deseo*, 277; and Nora Pérez-Rayón Elizundia, *México 1900: Percepciones y valores en la gran prensa capitalina* (Mexico City: UAM-Azcapotzalco, 2001), 35–36, 335, 343.

47. Haber, *Industry and Underdevelopment*, 50–51; Tower, "General Report on Mexico, 1908," doc. 264.

48. Stephen Haber calculates (conservatively, I think) that the market for consumer goods in 1895 totaled five million individuals based on the assumption that two million workers engaged in nonagricultural wage-earning sectors each supported approximately 1.5 other people. Haber, *Industry and Underdevelopment*, 27.

The Porfirian cigarette packet contained between twelve and fourteen cigarettes. *Le Courrier du Mexique*, August 1, 1908, 2; Bigot, *Le Mexique moderne*, 117.

49. For the monthly expenses of semiskilled workers in 1913, see box 55, exp. 8, Fondo Ramo Trabajo, AGN. I am indebted to John Lear for this reference. As for the budgets of unskilled workers, see González Navarro, *El Porfiriato: La vida social*, 391.

50. For the growth of domestic industrialization, see Haber, *Industry and Underdevelopment*; and Beatty, *Institutions and Investment*.

51. *Le Courrier du Mexique*, January 12, 1906, 3.

52. Flipping through any newspaper in the country would likely yield advertisements for one or more cigarette brands. Occasionally certain advertisements or articles listed a number of brand names. For the brands of La Cigarrera Mexicana, see *El Imparcial*, May 20, 1907, 6; for El Buen Tono, consult the wonderfully graphic advertisement in *El Mundo Ilustrado*, April 15, 1906, 4.

53. See, for example, *El Imparcial*, March 17, 1907, 3, for the Royal Concession from Alfonso XIII to Pugibet; *Frivolidades*, May 22, 1910, 4, for the launch of Cigarros El Centenario; *Le Courrier du Mexique*, December 25, 1907, 3, for the tour of El Buen Tono and Mexico by Mme. Calvé; and *Le Courrier du Mexique*, February 10, 1890, 3, and *El Periódico Oficial* (Oaxaca), April 24, 1887, 1, for mention of the brands named after Mazzantini and Judic.

54. West, *I Shop in Moscow*, 114–15. West describes this marketing as the making of "The Vicarious Elite."

55. Examples of these goods and services are as follows: for furniture, see *La Palanca*, November 6, 1904, 4; for watches, see *La Cagarruta*, December 20, 1906, 4; for aluminum beds, see *El Diablito Bromista*, July 10, 1904, 4; for photographs, see *El Chango*, May 28, 1905, 1; and for phonographs, see *La Guacamaya*, December 5, 1902, 3.

56. *El Diablito Bromista*, October 26, 1905, 5; November 26, 1905, 1.

57. The El Buen Tono cartoon appears in *El Heraldo Obrero, Defensor de los Obreros*, June 11, 1905, 4. The Tabacalera picture riddles appear in *El Diablito Bromista*, October 1, 1905, 1; October 8, 1905, 1; and November 12, 1905, 1. The possible Posada riddle appears in *El Diablito Bromista*, September 25, 1905, 1, with his signature in the bottom right. In this riddle the top line consists of seven segments. The first is an upside-down sun, second a small *e* over a large *M*, third a small *o* in the crook of a large *J*, fourth a bull, fifth three cigarettes, sixth an *el* inside a large *D*, and seventh an image of the earth. This translates into "Los [*sol* backward] mejores [*res* is the steer] cigarros del mundo."

58. María Elena Díaz, "The Satiric Penny Press for Workers in Mexico, 1900–1910: A Case Study in the Politicisation of Popular Culture," *Journal of Latin American Studies* 22, no. 3 (October 1990), 518. Díaz argues that the albures demonstrate the utilization of folklore as a vehicle for transmitting ideas of social and political protest, but given that approximately half of the paper consisted of advertisements— many of which employed albures—the same claim could be made for popular customs being used to transmit the values of the market and consumerism.

59. "La Mansión de Luzbel" appears in *La Guacamaya*, February 8, 1906, 3. These stories by Tabacalera appear regularly in this paper, including the dates of November 30, 1905, 2–3; December 28, 1905, 2; January 11, 1906, 2–3; January 18, 1906, 3; January 25, 1906, 3; and February 1, 1906, 3. Similar stories appear in *El Diablito Bromista* throughout the autumn of 1905, including October 8, 1905, 3.

60. *El Imparcial*, November 16, 1905, 4.

61. Camacho Morfín, *Imágenes de México*, 32.

62. For example, *La Clase Media*, February 6, 1910, 4, concludes with the middle-class mantra "Those who do not smoke save their health, time, and money."

63. Patience Schell, "Teaching the Children of the Revolution: Church and State Education in Mexico City, 1917–1926" (PhD diss., St. Anthony's College, Oxford University, 1998), 144–45.

64. Porter, *Working Women in Mexico City*; William E. French, "Prostitutes and Guardian Angels: Women, Work, and the Family in Porfirian Mexico," *Hispanic American Historical Review* 72, no. 4 (November 1992): 529–52; Carmen Ramos Escandón, "Señoritas Porfirianas: Mujer e ideología en el México progresista, 1880–1910," in *Presencia y transparencia: La mujer en la historia de México*, ed. Carmen Ramos Escandón (Mexico City: El Colegio de México, 1987), 143–62.

65. *L'Echo du Mexique*, March 11, 1893, 2; *El Imparcial*, September 5, 1902, 4. The *El Imparcial* article supported the ban, pleaded the case of fire safety, then took a castigatory tone in noting that recently over fifty spectators and actors had been detained and fined from five to twenty pesos. The shrillness of the article suggests the mass public opposition to, and futility of, the antismoking decrees.

66. Carlos Tejeda to Ayuntamiento, November 20, 1900, exp. 1054, Diversiones Públicas 1899–1900, AACM.

67. *El Imparcial*, July 28, 1899, 1.

68. *El Imparcial*, October 29, 1905, 2.

69. Despite these pleas I have found no evidence that Pugibet officially sought a retraction of the decree. One of the letters to Pugibet may be found in *Le Courrier du Mexique*, March 10, 1909, 3.

70. *Actualidades*, March 15, 1909, 13.

71. *El Anunciador Mexicano: Organo de Comercio e Industria*, November 22, 1877, 3. On La Poblana see *La Victoria* (Oaxaca), February 1, 1878, 4.

72. *Modern Mexico*, January 1897, 10, and again in June 1897, 13.

73. William Curtis, *The Capitals of Spanish America* (New York: Harper and Bros., 1888), 37.

74. Martin, *Mexico of the Twentieth Century*, 1:196.

75. Carson, *Mexico: Wonderland of the South*, 165.

76. For cartoons advertising the El Buen Tono brand Gardenias, see *Le Courrier du Mexique*, December 31, 1909, 8; and the *Mexican Herald*, October 9, 1904, 3. For an example of Tabacalera depicting female desire for cigarettes, see *El Diablito Bromista*, October 1, 1905, 3.

77. For examples, see *El Mundo Ilustrado*, January 1, 1906, 8; and January 7, 1906, 4.

78. *El Imparcial*, May 2, 1908, 8.

79. See chapter 2 for information on the blurred line between advertising and editorial in Porfirian newspapers.

80. On urban spectacles and mass culture, see Vanessa Schwartz, *Spectacular Realities: Early Mass Culture in Fin-de-Siècle Paris* (Berkeley: University of California Press, 1998), esp. 2–5.

81. For more information on early hot air balloon ascensions, see Gary Kuhn, "Fiestas and Fiascoes—Balloon Flights in Nineteenth-Century Mexico," *Journal of Sports History* 13, no. 2 (Summer 1986): 111–18. For an earlier flight for tobacco publicity purposes, see Tony Morgan, "Proletarians, Politicos, and Patriarchs: The Use and Abuse of Cultural Customs in the Early Industrialization of Mexico City, 1880–1910," in Beezley, Martin, and French, *Rituals of Rule*, 154.

82. The following articles provided the information for the inaugural flight: *El Popular*, January 7, 1907, 1; *Le Courrier du Mexique*, December 12, 1906, 3; December 15, 1906, 3; December 18, 1906, 3; January 8, 1907, 3; *El Imparcial*, December 9, 1906, 3; December 16, 1906, 3. For a list of aircraft specifications, see *Le Courrier du Mexique*, December 22, 1907, 3.

83. *Le Courrier du Mexique*, January 22, 1909, 3; December 29, 1908, 3; December 2, 1907, 3; *El Imparcial*, January 30, 1908, 1.

84. *El Imparcial*, January 30, 1908, 1; *Le Courrier du Mexique*, November 30, 1907, 3; December 2, 1907, 3; December 8, 1907, 2; December 15, 1908, 2; January 31, 1908, 3.

85. *El Imparcial*, January 30, 1908, 1; *Le Courrier du Mexique*, January 31, 1908, 3.

86. *Le Courrier du Mexique*, January 22, 1909, 3; January 25, 1909, 3; January 29, 1909, 3.

87. *Le Courrier du Mexique*, September 4, 1910, 2; February 8, 1910, 3; February 23, 1910, 2; April 21, 1910, 3. For Raoul-Duval's advertisements of his champagne and Perrier stocks, see *Le Courrier du Mexique*, February 26, 1910, 5; April 23, 1910, 3; and April 24, 1910, 3. Note how the dates of his ads coincide with his flight dates. For pictures and the story of Braniff's flight, see *La Semana Ilustrada*, December 31, 1909.

88. *El Imparcial*, April 19, 1908, 7.

89. *El Imparcial*, April 26, 1908, 3. Further specifications of Electric Man come from the patent filed for the invention. Although invented by Y. D. Arroyo, El Buen Tono held the patent. His official name was "El Hombre Luminoso." Legajo 209, exp. 17, pat. 7894, April 9, 1908, PyM-AGN. Months earlier a similar invention received a provisional patent. A British inventor, Donald George Kennedy Turnbull, who was represented (as many budding innovators were) by the Agencia Internacional de Patentes Julio Grandjean, filed for the protection of a much bulkier form of the El Buen Tono device. This contraption involved a box strapped to the chest with lights illuminating the advertising message within. Legajo 209, exp. 11, pat. 7318, September 25, 1907, and Legajo 207, exp. 24, pat. 8423, September 30, 1908, PyM-AGN.

90. A representative sample of this genre is Hilarión Barajas, *Pequeño manual de usos y costumbres de México, y breve colección de algunas frases y modismos figurados, de*

varios refranes y de muchas otras frases latinas, impuestas unas por el buen gusto é introducidas las otras por el uso y modo común de hablar (Mexico City: Tip. Guadalupana, de Reyes Velasco, 1901), esp. 25–30 for fashion advice and 26 on walking sticks.

91. *Le Courrier du Mexique*, December 25, 1907, 3.

92. On Paris advertising carriages, see H. Hazel Hahn, *Scenes of Parisian Modernity: Culture and Consumption in the Nineteenth Century* (New York: Palgrave MacMillan, 2009), 152–53.

93. Advertising patents help to flesh out photos and news stories. Three representative samples of advertising coaches that received patent protection are: Legajo 207, exp. 5, pat. 5284, January 25, 1906 (Carro anunciador "Alerta"); Legajo 207, exp. 14, pat. 6918, May 31, 1907 (Un carro anunciador); and Legajo 207, exp. 15, pat. 7080, July 19, 1907 (Un carro anunciador denominado "A. Jauregui"), all in PyM-AGN.

94. For information on fires in cinemas, consult Aurelio de los Reyes, *Los origenes del cine en México (1896–1900)* (Mexico City: Fondo de Cultura Económica, 1983), 78–80. The worst of these Porfirian conflagrations took place in Acapulco, where three hundred spectators died in a theater fire in February 1909.

95. *Le Courrier du Mexique*, December 30, 1900, 2; Lucien Leroy, *Mexico: Ses colonies française, suisse et belge et l'etat économique, politique et financier du Mexique en 1898* (Mexico City: Imprimerie Bouligny y Schmidt Sucs., 1898), 50.

96. *Le Courrier du Mexique*, December 28, 1907, 2. For photos of the mixed fleet, see Génin, *Notes sur le Mexique*, 7.

97. *El Imparcial*, April 19, 1908, 7; May 2, 1908, 8.

98. Génin, *Notes sur le Mexique*, 293; *Le Courrier du Mexique*, December 20, 1903, 2.

99. On the distrust of bicycles, see William H. Beezley, *Judas at the Jockey Club and Other Episodes of Porfirian Mexico* (Lincoln: University of Nebraska Press, 1987), 13–66. For the widespread hatred of the electric trams through the work of popular artist José Guadalupe Posada, consult Patrick Frank, *Posada's Broadsheets: Mexican Popular Imagery, 1890–1910* (Albuquerque: University of New Mexico Press, 1998), 187–91.

100. *El Imparcial*, December 7, 1906, 2. Photos of the three vehicles offered in 1907 exist in *Le Courrier du Mexique*, January 30, 1907, 4; and *El Imparcial*, January 26, 1907, 6. The lotteries, which ran from April 2, 1906, through the end of the regime, will be discussed later in this chapter. I have analyzed the rolls of winners, and the number of those who won ten pesos or more averages one thousand for each lottery. Again, this does not include the substantial number who won lesser prizes or nothing at all.

101. Lisa Singleton, "Economic Origins of the Mexican Welfare State, 1840–1890" (PhD diss., Tulane University, 2011), provides an excellent history of the lottery in nineteenth-century Mexico.

102. See Beezley, *Mexican National Identity*, 34. For a hoax committed against El Buen Tono, falsely claiming it was running a lottery on terms that would have bankrupted the company, see *La Paz Público*, February 18, 1894, 1.

103. For Tabacalera, see the full-page ad in *El Imparcial*, December 21, 1905, 6; El Buen Tono's draw dates and lottery information are in *El Imparcial*, February 4, 1906, 3.

104. *El Mensajero: Revista Mensual de la Loteria de la Compañia de Tranvias Electricos, S.A.*, November 1906, 1.

105. For information on the first official civic celebration of Díaz's birthday in 1891, see Beezley, *Mexican National Identity*, 80.

106. *Le Courrier du Mexique*, April 3, 1906, 3; April 2, 1907, 3.

107. *El Imparcial*, June 23, 1906, 2.

108. This last, largest number comes from the April 2, 1909, draw as the company escalated its giveaway beyond previous limits. As the article states, "For the next drawing the great company will invest $30,000, with a grand prize of $15,000. Get ready, reader." *El Imparcial*, January 9, 1909, 2.

109. For example, see *El Imparcial*, January 1, 1906, 3.

110. El Buen Tono cars noted in *El Imparcial*, January 26, 1907, 6; exhibition in the Trutz windows, *Le Courrier du Mexique*, March 22, 1907, 3; the Tabacalera house, *El Imparcial*, January 27, 1907, 8.

111. *El Imparcial*, December 21, 1905, 6; *El Mundo Ilustrado*, April 8, 1906; Gustavo Casasola, *Seis siglos de historia gráfica de México, 1325–1925* (Mexico City: Editorial Gustavo Casasola, 1968), 1325.

112. For out-of-town grand-prize winners for both companies, see *El Mundo Ilustrado*, April 8, 1906 (Miguel Ramos, San Blas, Tepic, 5,000 pesos, El Buen Tono) and July 15, 1906 (David Samuel Maceda, Puebla City, 5,000 pesos, El Buen Tono); and *El Imparcial*, July 10, 1906, 2 (Antonio Vicente, Merida, 1,000 pesos, Tabacalera Mexicana). Further information on the national aspect of these lotteries will be covered later in this chapter.

113. On charity, see *El Imparcial*, June 8, 1906, 6; on letters verifying reception of prize money after the first three lotteries, see *El Imparcial*, May 16, 1906, 6; July 11, 1906, 5; and September 29, 1906, 6. For the thoroughly suspicious, see the correspondence between Pugibet and José Yves Limantour discussing company annual expenses (comparing the years 1906 and 1907), in which Pugibet states that they paid out 24,000 pesos in prize money for the December 31, 1906, lottery. Pugibet to JYL, January 18, 1908, CDLIV 1908, roll 54, carp. 20, JYL-CEHM.

114. *El Imparcial*, June 24, 1906, 6.

115. This statistic is based on my analysis of the posted winners of four El Buen Tono lotteries occurring between April 1906 and December 1907. Of a total of 3,175 participants earning ten pesos or more, 87.7 percent were men, 11.7 percent women, 0.4 percent boys, and 0.2 percent girls. For the lists, see *El Imparcial*, April 6, 1906, 5–6; July 3, 1906, 5–6; September 18, 1906, 7–8; January 2, 1908, 3.

116. *El Imparcial*, July 19, 1906, 6; *Le Courrier du Mexique*, September 19, 1907, 2.

117. *El Imparcial*, June 29, 1906, 2. The term "guardian angel" comes from William E. French and refers to the construction of the Mexican middle-class female identity in terms of thrift, selflessness, and moral education of the family conducted in the private sphere of the home. The guardian angel developed against the foil of the "prostitute," or public woman, supposedly given to maximizing ostentation and

self-interest at the expense of morality and the fundamental unit of the Mexican nation: the family. William E. French, *A Peaceful and Working People: Manners, Morals, and Class Formation in Northern Mexico* (Albuquerque: University of New Mexico Press, 1996), 87–108.

118. For more on this process, see French, *Peaceful and Working People*, 3–107.

119. See ibid., 4–6, for a definition of the gente decente and the centrality of culture in class formation.

120. *Le Courrier du Mexique*, December 27, 1906, 2; January 4, 1907, 3.

121. On the importance of Mexico as a market for the Lumiére company, see Richard Abel, *The Ciné Goes to Town: French Cinema, 1896–1914*, updated and expanded ed. (Berkeley: University of California Press, 1994), 11. For opening night in 1896, see Felipe Garrido, *Luz y sombra: Los inicios del cine en la prensa de la ciudad de México* (Mexico City: Consejo Nacional Para la Cultura y las Artes, 1997), 44–45. On the decline of the cinema in Mexico City and its early years in the provinces, see de los Reyes, *Los origenes del cine*, 141–63.

122. Moulinié is a fascinating character in early Mexican cinema and commercial viewing venues. He left his children in France and emigrated to Mexico with his wife to make his fortune. Beginning in 1897 in the city of Puebla he presented shows of his own work and that imported from the three major studios in France. (The three studios were those of Georges Méliès, Louis Lumière, and the Pathé brothers. The origins, output, and impacts of these three are described at length in Abel, *Ciné Goes to Town*). Traveling throughout the republic, he exhibited shows in Guadalajara, San Luis Potosí, Chihuahua, and other urban centers with electricity. Somehow he even found electricity sources in small towns, where spectators either sat on the ground or brought their own chairs. Eventually he settled in the capital and opened El Palacio Encantado, located across the street from the National Theater. His establishment exhibited not only cinematic views but also a wax museum and an exhibition of optical illusions imported from the United States. For more on Moulinié, consult Juan Felipe Leal, Eduardo Barraza, and Carlos Flores, *El arcón de las vistas: Cartelera del cine en México, 1896–1910* (Mexico City: UNAM, 1994), 35–36. Moulinié's mixture of attractions suggests that he adopted the idea for his business from the famous Parisian wax museum the Musée Grévin, which by 1900 had incorporated the cinema to bolster ticket sales for its main attraction of wax displays. Schwartz, *Spectacular Realities*, 89–148, 177–204.

123. Morgan, "Proletarians, Politicos, and Patriarchs," 155.

124. The municipal archives—the Archivos de ex-Ayuntamiento de la Ciudad de México (AACM)—contain many successful and unsuccessful requests for projected advertisements, including the following: Antonio Garcia and Luis Gardimo to Ayuntamiento, February 27, 1895, exp. 77, Policía, Letreros (1847–1895); Francisco Roqueta and Roberto Díaz de León to Ayuntamiento, March 19, 1897, exp. 96, Policía, Letreros (1896–1915); Alberto Juaregui to Ayuntamiento, June 19, 1900, exp. 117, Policía, Letreros (1896–1915); and Mario Vázquez to Ayuntamiento, January 17, 1902, exp. 144, Policía, Letreros (1896–1915).

125. For one of several descriptions of the crowd, see *El Imparcial*, May 2, 1908, 8. On film sourcing, French film production dominated the global market prior to World War I. Many of the films advertised in Porfirian Mexico match those mentioned in Abel, *Cine Goes to Town*. Even in the United States, Pathé Frères dominated the silver screen until 1908 due to the low productivity, slipshod quality, and slow adoption of new film technologies by Edison, Biograph, Lubin, and other American producers. See Richard Abel, *The Red Rooster Scare: Making Cinema American, 1900–1910* (Berkeley: University of California Press, 1999).

126. Luis G. Urbina, cited in Manuel González Casanova, *Los escritores mexicanos y los inicios del cine* (Mexico City: UNAM, 1995), 41. For examples of an El Buen Tono film listing in the newspaper, see *El Imparcial*, September 24, 1905, 3. Known Mexican film productions between 1896 and 1910 total 370 (Juan Felipe Leal, Eduardo Barraza, and Alejandra Jablonska, *Vistas que no se ven: Filmografía mexicana 1896–1910* [Mexico City: UNAM, 1993], 37–120), while the number of all productions shown is conservatively marked at 1,100 (Leal, Barraza, and Jablonska, *El arcón de las vistas*, 55–318).

127. For the first illuminated kiosk in Paris, see Hahn, *Scenes of Parisian Modernity*, 149–51. In Mexico City, see Ildefonso Estrada y Zenea to Ayuntamiento, August 21, 1875, exp. 17, Policía, Letreros (1847–1895), AACM.

128. The best photo of the kiosk that I have seen is in the Gertrude Fitzgerald Photography Collection, box 1, folder 1, Special Collections, University of Texas–El Paso.

129. *El Mundo Ilustrado*, May 20, 1906. El Buen Tono bought clocks for this kiosk and its factory from the famous La Esmeralda jewelry store, located just a few blocks away and owned by the Swiss company Hauser and Zivy. See the company ad in *El Imparcial*, January 26, 1908, 8, for the location of all its public clocks throughout the republic.

130. Ernesto Pugibet to Ayuntamiento, June 2, 1903, exp. 1101, Alumbrado 1902–1905, AACM.

131. These fears of urban crowds were justified and grounded in experience. One of the most destructive displays of crowd violence in the capital during the Porfiriato occurred in November 1884, when a crowd swept through the central streets destroying property, including over two thousand streetlamps (hydrogen gas, not electric, at this point) in the Zócalo, along Plateros, Cinco de Mayo, and other thoroughfares. The city council agreed to pay the streetlamp company not out of contractual obligation but because street lighting was an essential public service. Interestingly, they changed the company's description of the event from "public manifestations" to "manifestaciones populares" and "manifestaciones del pueblo," thus implicitly shifting blame solely onto the lower classes. Exp. 603, Alumbrado 1884–1888, AACM.

132. On French celebrity culture during this era, see Hahn, *Scenes of Parisian Modernity*, 161–82.

133. Leal, Barraza, and Jablonska, *Vistas que no se ven*, 56. For cartoon strips following the same plot, see *El Imparcial*, February 17, 1907, 3 (man run over by a car,

smoke blown into his mouth) and October 16, 1904, 3 (rural family run over by steamroller, again revived by cigarette smoke).

134. For actresses, see, for example, *El Mundo Ilustrado*, January 7, 1906, 3–4. The case of Bombita demonstrates the common nature of cross-marketing by El Buen Tono. For example, on one side of a page in the newsmagazine *El Mundo Ilustrado* (December 24, 1905, 8) readers read the story and saw action photos of the bullfighter Bombita and his exploits of the previous day; on the opposite side of the page ran a full-page advertisement by El Buen Tono featuring text and a picture of Bombita in a tuxedo, smiling as he holds a packet of Canela Pura brand cigarettes. Although no direct evidence links films to this advertisement, a strong likelihood remains that several of the numerous films made of Bombita and later Gaona included direct references to a sponsoring cigarette company. Citations for these films figure prominently throughout the lists in Leal, Barraza, and Jablonska, *Vistas que no se ven*, esp. 96–119. El Buen Tono also immortalized Bombita in its cartoons, one of the funniest appearing in *El Mundo Ilustrado*, February 11, 1906, 3. For information on the author of these cartoons that appeared between 1903 and 1912, consult Camacho Morfín, *Imágenes de México*; an analysis of their images is in Bunker, "Consumers of Good Taste." For information on Ricardo Bell and his business relationship with El Buen Tono, see Steven B. Bunker, "More Popular Than Pulque: Ricardo Bell, Porfirian Payaso Extraordinaire" (paper presented at the XIII Reunión de Historiadores de México, Estadounidenses, y Canadienses, Querétaro, Mexico, October 30, 2010).

135. An example of the persistent belief in the limited or nonexistent participation of most Mexicans in Porfirian consumer culture, even in works on consumption, is the otherwise exceptional study by Ortiz Gaitán, *Imágenes del deseo*, 277.

136. For the descriptions of Independence Day in 1905 and 1906, see *El Mundo Ilustrado*, September 24, 1905, 8; and *El Imparcial*, September 11, 1906, 6. A concise listing of several such events, including El Buen Tono's exhibits in Veracruz, is found in Morgan, "Proletarians, Politicos, and Patriarchs," 155. The Tabacalera's parry in Veracruz comes to light in *El Imparcial*, December 30, 1905, 3. Information on pricing structures for theaters may be found in a description of La Cigarrera Mexicana's cinema exhibit at the Riva Palacio theater in mid-1907, in Garrido, *Luz y sombra*, 114–15; and also in the description of Tabacalera's Independence Day festivities, *El Imparcial*, September 11, 1906, 6. Seating capacity information comes from Emil Riedel, *Practical Guide of the City and Valley of Mexico with Excursions to Toluca, Tula, Pachuca, Puebla, Cuernavaca, etc.* (Mexico City: I. Epstein, 1892), 217–18; and "Informe de la Comisión de Diversiones Públicas," 1898, exp. 909, Diversiones Públicas, 1891–1898, AACM.

137. Martin, *Mexico of the Twentieth Century*, 1:118. Illuminating descriptions of tobacco advertising forms and locations may be found in *La Gaceta de Policía*, February 11, 1906, 6; and February 18, 1906, 6.

138. *Le Courrier du Mexique*, March 25, 1909, 2.

139. Examples of these inventions with confirmed public use include Legajo 207, exp. 33,

pat. 9131, May 10, 1909 (revolving three-panel billboard); Legajo 207, exp. 18, pat. 8085, June 8, 1908 (automatic advertisement dispenser); and Legajo 209, exp. 13, pat. 7013, June 26, 1907 (cigarette sample dispenser), all in PyM-AGN.

140. Hazel Hahn traces theater curtain advertisements in Paris to 1840 and notes their frequent adoption in *Scenes of Parisian Modernity*, 32, 139. A photo of an advertising theater curtain can be found in *México, ¿quieres tomarte una foto conmigo?*, 31. Visual and textual descriptions of more advanced stage curtain advertising technologies can be found in successful patent applications such as Legajo 207, exp. 20, pat. 8180, July 17, 1908 ("Telón anunciador sin fin"); and Legajo 207, exp. 22, pat. 8221, July 21, 1908 ("Un mecanismo aplicable a los telones anunciadores para espectáculos"), both in PyM-AGN.

141. Anita Brenner noted this common sight in *The Wind That Swept Mexico* (Austin: University of Texas Press, 1971), plate 10.

142. Nearly any photo of a drinking establishment or grocery store reveals these posters. Two excellent photographs of the interiors of tienda de abarrotes—one unnamed and servicing a working-class clientele, the other the famously posh Ultramarinos Finos, provisioning the bon ton of the capital—exist in a postcard collection compiled by Victor Alfonso Maldonado, *México: A principios de siglo* (Mexico City: Agualarga Editores, 1996). Porfirian writer Ángel de Campo based his novel *La rumba* on the working-class barrio circling the plaza of the same name. In his description of the *cantina de barrio* he noted the "cigarette ads glued to the wall." De Campo, *Ocios y apuntes y* La rumba (Mexico City: Editorial Porrua, 1995), 210. The size and composition of the posters come from two in this author's personal collection of Mexican advertising. Both advertise El Buen Tono brands, one for Mejores, the other listing a number of premium brands next to a tuxedo-clad smoker. The first is older, the second newer, as reflected in its superior graphics and technical finish.

143. See the photos of the Verbena de los Angeles in *La Semana Ilustrada*, August 12, 1910, 12.

144. A smattering of examples of this Christmas largesse includes *L'Echo du Mexique*, January 4, 1896, 2; and *Le Courrier du Mexique*, December 24, 1899, 3; January 1, 1902, 3; January 3, 1903, 2; December 23, 1904, 3; and December 27, 1904, 3.

145. Three dozen of these cards are part of this author's personal collection. The collection includes those distributed by tobacco companies other than the big three and also by other companies, such as La Manita chocolate factory. Tobacco companies in the United States and Europe used this same marketing tool, and in fact some of the images used in card series distributed in Mexico were probably French in origin.

146. This last clause is paraphrased from West, *I Shop in Moscow*, 121.

147. For a description and history of the Bonsack machines, see W. Hamish Fraser, *The Coming of the Mass Market, 1850–1914* (Hamden, CT: Archon Books, 1981), 70. The Spanish-, French-, and English-language newspapers all covered the case by printing lengthy articles, usually produced by one side or the other. A smattering of

stories printed includes *El Imparcial*, September 22, 1899, 2; December 22, 1899, 2; April 19, 1900, 3; April 29, 1900, 6; May 2, 1900, 3; May 4, 1900, 3; May 7, 1900, 3; May 9, 1900, 3; May 11, 1900, 3; May 19, 1900, 3; November 24, 1900, 3; *Le Courrier du Mexique*, November 28, 1900, 3; January 30, 1901, 3; and the *Mexican Herald*, May 7, 1900, 5.

148. *El Imparcial*, December 26, 1905, 2; January 3, 1906, 2; January 19, 1906, 2.

149. My favorite Tabacalera advertisement features a sandal-wearing Indian named Doroteo dressed in a modern jacket and pant combination sitting on a bench smoking a Flor de Canela and declaring the controversy ridiculous ("Todo eso son papas!!"). *El Imparcial*, January 12, 1906, 6. As for its defense that the package designs and colors completely differed, see *El Imparcial*, December 27, 1905, 2; and December 31, 1905, 2. *La Gaceta de Policía*, February 11, 1906, 6, announced the placement of Tabacalera advertisements comparing the two sets of brands.

150. For one example of Tabacalera touting its pay and labor relations see *El Imparcial*, February 5, 1906, 3. For two examples of El Buen Tono worker testimonials, see *Le Courrier du Mexique*, January 17, 1906, 2; and January 21, 1906, 2. For a study of women workers protesting their work conditions in the tobacco industry and other industries, see Porter, *Working Women in Mexico City*, 73–95.

151. *L'Echo du Mexique*, September 12, 1894, 2. Significantly, the Unión recognized the national reach of El Buen Tono's market and voted in March "to extend the propaganda, publishing a manifesto and sending circulars to the states of the Republic." *El Imparcial*, March 20, 1906, 2.

152. *La Gaceta de Policía*, February 11, 1906, 14.

153. *El Mundo Ilustrado*, March 4, 1906. See versions of this in *El Imparcial*, February 22, 1906, 6; and February 25, 1906, 8.

154. For a listing of the establishments, see *El Imparcial*, March 1, 1906, 3.

155. For one of the many accounts of company sales, see *El Imparcial*, June 6, 1906, 6, which includes the percentage of sales made by the ambulatory vendors.

156. In a long-running cartoon that reached beyond the capital, Tabacalera titled its first shot "The First Defeat of the Sandwich Army." *El Correo de Chihuahua*, June 23, 1906, 4. El Buen Tono's retort came in *El Imparcial*, March 16, 1906, 3.

157. *El Correo de Chihuahua*, April 18, 1906, 4.

158. *El Imparcial*, March 4, 1906, 2.

159. For two examples of "our numerous consumers" quotes, see *El Imparcial*, February 20, 1906, 3; and *Le Courrier du Mexique*, March 1, 1906, 4. For the "circle the wagons" image, see *El Imparcial*, March 16, 1906, 3.

160. Published simultaneously in *Le Courrier du Mexique*, February 23, 1906, 3; and *El Imparcial*, February 24, 1906, 2.

161. *Le Courrier du Mexique*, November 1, 1906, 3, details the sale. *Le Courrier du Mexique*, December 29, 1907, 3, announces the transfer of the factory.

162. See two sources on the sale of Tabacalera: *Le Courrier du Mexique*, February 21, 1908, 3; and *La Semana Mercantil*, March 2, 1908, 117. The fact of this merger has been erased in official tobacco history today in Mexico. Tabacalera Mexicana is

the name of the only large Mexican cigarette manufacturer remaining, although it is in reality owned by British American Tobacco. In the company's official history of tobacco in Mexico it tells of El Buen Tono's absorption by foreign tobacco interests in the 1930s but says nothing of the 1908 purchase or its own ascent as a front for foreign capital. See Amerlinck, *Historia y cultura del tabaco*.

163. For a good account of the image and illusion of the Porfirian regime, see Víctor Manuel Macías-González, "The Mexican Aristocracy and Porfirio Díaz, 1876–1911" (PhD diss., Texas Christian University, 1999), 142–202, 236–84.

164. Tobacco has a long history as a global commodity. Two fine works on its popular adoption in England and colonial British America are Carole Shammas, *The Preindustrial Consumer in England and America* (Oxford: Oxford University Press, 1990); and Shammas, "Changes in Anglo-American Consumption from 1550 to 1800" in Brewer and Porter, *Consumption and the World of Goods*, 177–205.

165. For visuals of El Buen Tono advertisements featuring the main factory and its machinery, see Bunker, "Consumers of Good Taste," 234–36.

166. Beezley, *Judas at the Jockey Club*.

Chapter 2

1. Ildefonso Estrada y Zenea to Ayuntamiento, August 21, 1874, exp. 17, Letreros (1847–1895), AACM. The first illuminated kiosk in Paris appeared in 1857. Hahn, *Scenes of Parisian Modernity*, 147.

2. See chapter 1 for a description of the particularly elaborate kiosk of El Buen Tono. The cover photo of Kahlo, *Mexiko 1904*, displays two kiosks on the western side of the Zócalo.

3. Three scholarly studies stand out for their analysis of Porfirian advertising images: Ortiz Gaitán, *Imágenes del deseo*; Camacho Morfín, *Imágenes de México*; and Hellion, *Exposición permanente*. Pérez-Rayón Elizundia, in her chapter "La publicidad," in *México 1900*, 325–44, approaches advertising as a transmission agent for cultural values and analyzes categories of advertising published in four upscale Porfirian publications. The glossy newsmagazine *El Mundo Ilustrado* serves as the sole source for Hellion and Ortiz Gaitán. Pérez-Rayón Elizundia analyzes four sources, *El Imparcial*, *Diario del Hogar*, *El Tiempo*, and *El Pais*, while Camacho Morfín draws her comic advertisements from *El Imparcial* and the newspapers of the French and Spanish colonies.

4. Ortiz Gaitán begins in 1894, Pérez-Rayón Elizundia focuses on 1900, Camacho Morfín emphasizes the last series of Urrutia's comics beginning in 1909, and Hellion's images are from 1904 onward, although she provides historical context dating back to the 1890s in several cases.

5. Within the scholarship, Florence Toussaint gave legitimacy to this view when she concluded that the readership of newspapers remained limited to the middle and upper classes, as workers could not afford them. *Escenario de la prensa en el porfiriato* (Mexico City: Fundación Manuel Buendía, 1989), 67–71. Hellion, Ortiz

Gaitán, and Pérez-Rayón Elizundia all reference Toussaint. Hellion accepts this restricted readership (and by implication consuming class), while Ortiz Gaitán and Pérez-Rayón Elizundia offer minor caveats but generally support this notion of limited participation in the print and consumer culture of the capital and nation. Hellion, *Exposición permanente*, 22; Pérez-Rayón Elizundia, *México 1900*, 35–36, 335, 343; Ortiz Gaitán, *Imágenes del deseo*, 277–78.

6. Yolanda Zamora Casillas, "Alacena publicitaria," *Revista Mexicana de Ciencias Políticas y Sociales* 109 (1982): 48.

7. *El Eco Nacional*, January 1, 1857. Half of page 1 is devoted to advertising, including an illustrated ad for La Veracruzana Tabacos. Page 4 also contains ads. An ad for a clothes store (*cajón de ropa*) called La Industria Francesa provides an example of a single ad covering half of one page in *El Eco Nacional*, June 10, 1857, 1.

8. William H. Beezley links popular performance culture to commerce and national identity formation in his *Mexican National Identity*.

9. Non-rhyming popular sayings, or *dichos*, could also be employed to encourage consumption. One such example comes from a New Year's ad for the home and office furnishing company Mosler, Bowen and Cook: "An old saying says that to put a good foot forward in the New Year one should exhibit something new, such as adorning a home with an object of relative value as a demonstration of prosperity and well-being." *El Imparcial*, December 29, 1903, 4.

10. Salvador Novo, *Apuntes para una historia de la publicidad en la Ciudad de México* (Mexico City: Organización Editorial Novaro, 1967), 81–85. See pages 83–84 for an exchange between *criollo* and *peninsular* merchants in the Parián market. On décimas and their broader context, see Frank, *Posada's Broadsheets*, 169–70.

11. Novo, *Apuntes*, 129.

12. West, *I Shop in Moscow*, 21.

13. West, *I Shop in Moscow*, 21–22; Hahn, *Scenes of Parisian Modernity*, 17.

14. Novo, *Apuntes*, 103–5.

15. The text of this law appears in Comisión de Policía to Ayuntamiento, May 6, 1871, exp. 6, Letreros (1847–1895), AACM.

16. For an early Porfirian example, see Inspector de Letreros to Ayuntamiento, September 15, 1877, exp. 22, Letreros (1847–1895), AACM. For later reports from inspectors, see Regidor Carballeda to Ayuntamiento, January 14, 1890, exp. 58, Letreros (1847–1895), AACM; and Thomas Moran to Ayuntamiento, October 16, 1891, exp. 62, Letreros (1847–1895), AACM.

17. Thomas Moran to Ayuntamiento, October 16, 1891, exp. 62, Letreros (1847–1895), AACM.

18. Barbara A. Tenenbaum, "Streetwise History: The Paseo de la Reforma and the Porfirian State, 1876–1910," in Beezley, Martin, and French, *Rituals of Rule*, 127–50; and Bunker and Macías-González, "Consumption and Material Culture, Pre-contact through the Porfiriato," 65.

19. Bunker and Macías-González, "Consumption and Material Culture, Pre-contact through the Porfiriato," 65–66.

20. Zamora Casillas, "Alacena publicitaria," 50–51. The agency is the sole listing under advertising in Eugenio Maillefert, *Directorio del comercio del Imperio Mexicano para el año de 1867* (1867; reprint, Mexico City: Instituto Mora, 1992), 244.

21. Ortiz Gaitán, *Imágenes del deseo*, 52–53.

22. Simón López e hijo to Ayuntamiento, September 9, 1875, exp. 18, Letreros (1847–1895), AACM.

23. Sally West identifies this same phenomenon and timing in Moscow. West, *I Shop in Moscow*, 28.

24. On N. W. Ayer & Son and the rise of the modern advertising agency, see Stephen J. Eskilson, *Graphic Design: A New History* (New Haven, CT: Yale University Press, 2007); and Ralph M. Hower, *The History of an Advertising Agency: N. W. Ayer & Son at Work, 1869–1949* (Cambridge, MA: Harvard University Press, 1949). On its appearance in Mexico, see Moreno, *Yankee Don't Go Home!*, 85.

25. The listing came from Domenech, *Guía general descriptiva*, 1:651. On José D. Gayosso, see *L'Echo du Mexique*, June 14, 1894, 2. David Camacho established his company in 1892 and operated an advertising newspaper titled *Oferta y Demanda*. See *L'Echo du Mexique*, March 18, 1897, 2. On his correspondence with Finance Minister José Yves Limantour regarding the department stores the Palacio de Hierro and the Puerto de Veracruz, and the brewery Cervecería Cuauhtémoc, see Camacho to JYL, Mexico City, n.d., CDLIV 1883–1899, roll 3, doc. 2214, JYL-CEHM; and Camacho to JYL, Mexico City, November 21, 1899, CDLIV 1883–1899, roll 3, doc. 2221, JYL-CEHM.

26. *The Massey-Gilbert Blue Book of Mexico: A Directory in English of the City of Mexico* (México: Massey-Gilbert, 1901), 189, lists five such businesses. Additional firms include José Bianchi, Artículos Anunciadores (*El Imparcial*, August 17, 1904, 1), and Wright Bros. Novedades para Anunciantes (Wright Brothers to JYL, Mexico City, September 2, 1908, CDLIV 1907, roll 48, carp. 26, JYL-CEHM).

27. John H. Greaves & Co., *Mexican Herald*, May 6, 1900, 3; Compañia de Anuncios Mexicanos, S.A., J. R. Southworth to JYL, Mexico City, March, 1904, CDLIV 1904, roll 28, carp. 20, JYL-CEHM; Empresa Explotadora del Anuncio de Movimiento sobre Vehiculos, *La Clase Media*, July 1, 1908, 3; and the Publicity Company, *Mexican Herald*, January 1, 1906, 3; January 21, 1906, 12; May 27, 1906, 23.

28. All patents are located in the Fondo Secretaría de Comercio y Fomento Industrial in the Archivo General de la Nación. Twentieth-century patents are from Patentes y Marcas (Grises Grandes), Grupo Documental 218 (PyM-AGN). Nineteenth-century century patents are from Patentes y Marcas (Cajas Negras), Grupo Documental 218 (Nineteenth Century, PyM-AGN).

29. Five broad categories of marketing patent ideas characterize submissions to Fomento. The first two are improvements to interior retail space, such as hanging display counters so that customers could better see the products and improvements in exterior store signs. The third is customer promotion gifts with company labels, such as soaps, calendars, and postcards. Vending machines make up a fourth category, selling everything from nuts to theater glasses and shaped from

the mundane box to a bird that would dip for cigarettes in exchange for centavos. A final group—and the focus of this section—is general advertising systems seeking to better attract the attention of the consumer in public spaces.

30. Examples include Saltillo, Legajo 209, exp. 36, pat. 10,338, April 4, 1910; Puebla, Legajo 207, exp. 14, pat. 6918, May 31, 1907; and Morelos, Legajo 207, exp. 19, pat. 8175, July 6, 1908, all in PyM-AGN.

31. Examples include: Legajo 209, exp. 11, pat. 7318, September 25, 1907 (Grandjean); Legajo 209, exp. 6, pat. 4946, September 28, 1905 (Sepúlveda); Legajo 207, exp. 28, pat. 8791, January 23, 1909 (General C.H.M. y Agramonte), all in PyM-AGN.

32. Legajo 197, exp. 49, pat. 6168, October 11, 1906 (pharmacist); Legajo 207, exp.7, pat. 4070, October 20, 1904, and Legajo 206, exp. 151, pat. 4442, November 26, 1912 (commission agents); Legajo 203, exp. 51, pat. 12,328, November 8, 1911 (store owner); Legajo 198, exp. 49, pat. 9407, July 20, 1909, (War and Navy Secretary employee), all in PyM-AGN

33. Company patents include those by office equipment retailer Mosler, Bowen and Cook (Legajo 207, exp.3, pat. 3546, February 27, 1904, PyM-AGN) and cigarette manufacturer El Buen Tono (Legajo 140, exp. 27, no pat. number, November 14, 1910 PyM-AGN).

34. Sally West does not include public advertising space brokers (but does include newspaper brokers) in her excellent study of nineteenth-century advertising in late Tsarist Russia. West, *I Shop in Moscow*, 34–40. Julio Moreno's brief review of Porfirian advertising also focuses on advertising in the press. Moreno, *Yankee Don't Go Home!*, 85. The practice of space brokering began in 1842 in Pennsylvania when Volney B. Palmer bought up large blocks of discounted advertising space in newspapers and resold it. By serving as a centralized broker, he saw himself saving advertisers the time and confusion of corresponding with multiple editors with their varying conditions of sale. See Donald R. Holland, "Volney B. Palmer: The Nation's First Advertising Man," *Pennsylvania Magazine of History and Biography* 98, no. 3 (July 1974): 353–81.

35. *Mexican Herald*, May 6, 1906, 19; January 21, 1906, 12.

36. See the top left corner of every edition of *El Imparcial* for the notice of the relationship between the Goetschel agency and the newspaper. See also José Alberto Villamil Duarte, *Publicidad Mexicana: Su historia, sus instituciones, sus hombres* (Mexico City: Demoscopia, 1971), 110. For Tablada's informative and hilarious account of his relationship with the Sánchez Juárez automobile agency and garage, see José Juan Tablada, *Las sombras largas* (Mexico City: Consejo Nacional para la Cultura y las Artes, 1993), 255–58.

37. Advertising contract, Copiador 1889–1903, p. 34, APH.

38. Caja 39, exp. 1617, February 4, 1889, Nineteenth Century PyM-AGN.

39. Legajo 209, exp. 10, pat. 6583, February 15, 1907, PyM-AGN.

40. Francisco Neugebaner, representative for the Siemens & Halske Company, to Ayuntamiento, January 14, 1898, exp. 106, Letreros (1896–1915), AACM. Neugebaner asked for and received permission to enter into a contract with an unspecified

advertising agency to rent out space on its boxes. The contract lasted for four years.

41. Views of the Zócalo, for example, are fairly easy to come by in photo collections or in the weekly illustrated magazines published during the Porfiriato. One example is *La Semana Ilustrada*, April 8, 1910, which reveals the tram kiosk in the plaza (across from the La Opera bar) to be covered in advertising, even on the tower housing the public clock.

42. Legajo 207, exp. 28, pat. 8791, January 23, 1909, PyM-AGN.

43. Legajo 209, exp. 37, pat. 10,430, April 23, 1910, PyM-AGN.

44. Legajo 207, exp. 9, pat. 6096, September 22, 1906, PyM-AGN.

45. Legajo 207, exp. 1, pat. 3273, October 20, 1903, PyM-AGN.

46. Legajo 209, exp. 6, pat. 4946, September 28, 1905, PyM-AGN.

47. Ayuntamiento records include several successful licensing applications for mobile advertising projection, the earliest of which is Ignacio Alarcón to Ayuntamiento, March 8, 1889, exp. 52, Letreros (1847–1895), AACM. Provisional patent applications for these kinds of systems include Legajo 207, exp. 15, pat. 7080, July 19, 1907, PyM-AGN.

48. *La Clase Media*, July 1, 1908, 3.

49. *El Imparcial*, December 17, 1899, 1, described the new Plaza de Toros "Mexico" and its attention to advertising space: "In the upper part of the plaza they have constructed several large overhangs [*copetes*], or so we have heard, that are not very artistic but they will serve as space for advertising posters. What an innovation."

50. See "Bombita and El Buen Tono," *El Mundo Ilustrado*, December 24, 1905, 6; and figure 5 in chapter 1.

51. Legajo 206, exp. 6, pat. 4074, October 18, 1904, PyM-AGN.

52. Legajo 209, exp. 34, pat. 9851, November 19, 1909, PyM-AGN.

53. Legajo 209, exp. 10, pat. 6583, February 15, 1907, PyM-AGN.

54. Legajo 200, exp. 31, pat. 6504, January 22, 1907, PyM-AGN.

55. See an example of such a curtain in *México, ¿quieres tomarte una foto conmigo?*, 31.

56. Legajo 207, exp. 20, pat. 8180, July 7, 1908, PyM-AGN.

57. Legajo 206, exp. 2, pat. 3297, October 31, 1903, PyM-AGN.

58. For a concise summation of the ambivalence toward Porfirian modernization represented by the tram, see Piccato, *City of Suspects*, 24–26.

59. See, for example, the photograph of the kiosk in *La Semana Ilustrada*, April 8, 1910, 5.

60. For example, Martin, *Mexico of the Twentieth-Century*, 1:235. This includes a photograph of a tramcar interior filled with ads.

61. Legajo 209, exp. 36, pat. 10,338, April 4, 1910, PyM-AGN.

62. Legajo 207, exp. 8, pat. 6005, August 18, 1906, PyM-AGN.

63. Wolfgang Schivelbusch, *Disenchanted Night: The Industrialization of Light in the Nineteenth Century*, trans. Angela Davies (Berkeley: University of California Press, 1988), esp. chapters 2 ("The Street") and 3 ("Night Life"). For the Mexican experience, consult Lillian Briseño Senosiain, *Candil de la calle, oscuridad de su casa. La iluminación de la ciudad de México durante el Porfiriato* (Mexico City: Tecnológico de Monterrey, Instituto Mora, 2008); and Diana Jeaneth Montano,

"Electrifying Mexico: Cultural Response to a New Technology, 1880s–1960s" (PhD diss., University of Arizona, forthcoming).

64. González Navarro, *El Porfiriato: La vida social*, 694.

65. The earlier version of the Anunciador Standard is Legajo 207, exp. 27, pat. 8733, January 5, 1909, PyM-AGN. Both inventions were likely used in practice, given the support of the application by the El Buen Tono cigarette company and one of the largest drugstores in the city, J. Labadie.

66. See *El Imparcial*, October 23, 1904, 3, for a sample.

67. Eduardo H. Barreira to Ayuntamiento, March 29, 1889, exp. 53, Letreros (1847–1895), AACM; and Michael Ximénez to Ayuntamiento, June 21, 1892, exp. 65, Letreros (1847–1895), AACM.

68. Electric Man's patent is Legajo 209, exp. 17, pat. 7894, April 9, 1908, PyM-AGN. The other definite patent is Legajo 207, exp. 25, pat. 8423, September 30, 1908 (Un aparato para anunciar ambulantes), PyM-AGN; the third patent application is Legajo 209, exp. 11, pat. 7318, September 25, 1907, PyM-AGN.

69. Ernesto Pugibet, [illegible] Tron, and [illegible] Martin to Ayuntamiento, October 1, 1901, exp. 132, Letreros (1847–1895), AACM.

70. For examples of licenses received for magic lantern commercial entertainment ventures, see J. Martínez Castaño to Ayuntamiento, February 23, 1902, exp. 1197, Diversiones Públicas, AACM; and [illegible name] to Ayuntamiento, June 4, 1902, exp. 1171, Diversiones Públicas, AACM. For a description of the magic lantern, see *Le Mexique*, July 20, 1902, 11. For its vogue in France, see Hahn, *Scenes of Parisian Modernity*, 131–37.

71. Juan H. Purdy y Cia to Ayuntamiento, October 27, 1882, exp. 29, Letreros (1847–1895), AACM.

72. Enrique Angulo, Caja 39, exp. 1609, January 31, 1889, Nineteenth Century PyM-AGN.

73. Ignacio Alarcón to Ayuntamiento, March 8, 1889, exp. 52, Letreros (1847–1895), AACM.

74. Alfonso Rodríguez to Ayuntamiento, April 20, 1896, exp. 88, Letreros (1896–1915), AACM.

75. Examples include Legajo 207, exp. 5, pat. 5284, January 25, 1906, PyM-AGN; and Legajo 207, exp. 15, Pat. 7080, July 19, 1907, PyM-AGN.

76. Legajo 207, exp. 14, pat. 6918, May 31, 1907, PyM-AGN.

77. A sample of approved magic lantern–type licenses for a variety of locations and surfaces include Antonio Garcia and Luis Gardimo to Ayuntamiento, February 27, 1895, exp. 77, Letreros (1847–1895), AACM; Francisco Ramírez to Ayuntamiento, May 24, 1901, exp. 131, Letreros (1896–1915), AACM; and Wagner & Levien, Sucs., to Ayuntamiento, February 17, 1902, exp. 45, Letreros (1896–1915), AACM.

78. For approval of the Alameda license, see José Ketchum to Ayuntamiento, June 4, 1897, exp. 94, Letreros (1896–1915), AACM. For the Teatro Nacional, see Francisco Roqueta and Roberto Díaz de León to Ayuntamiento, November 30, 1897, exp. 97, Letreros (1896–1915), AACM.

79. Alberto Jauregui to Ayuntamiento, June 19, 1900, exp. 117, Letreros (1896–1915), AACM.

80. Mario Vázquez to Ayuntamiento, January 17, 1902, exp. 144, Letreros (1896–1915), AACM.

81. Schwartz, *Spectacular Realities*, 149–76.

82. Emilio Bellan to Ayuntamiento, April 7, 1902, exp. 135, Letreros (1896–1915), AACM.

83. Alberto Díaz to Ayuntamiento, November 18, 1892, exp. 62, Letreros (1847–1895), AACM; emphasis in original.

84. Vicente Moyano to Ayuntamiento, September 19, 1892, exp. 64, Letreros (1847–1895), AACM.

85. Federico Bodet y Cia. to Ayuntamiento, April 23, 1895, exp. 75, Letreros (1847–1895), AACM; Alberto Jauregui to Ayuntamiento, June 19, 1900, exp. 117, Letreros (1896–1915), AACM; José Gastaldi to Ayuntamiento, July 19, 1899, exp. 109, Letreros (1896–1915), AACM; and Alfonso Hermann to Ayuntamiento, March 29, 1898, exp. 102, Letreros (1896–1915), AACM.

86. Mario Vázquez to Ayuntamiento, January 17, 1902, exp. 144, Letreros (1896–1915), AACM.

87. Comisión de Policía to Ayuntamiento, May 6, 1871, exp. 9, Letreros (1847–1895), AACM. See Hahn, *Scenes of Parisian Modernity*, 11, 42–44, for early bill posting and publicity regulations in France, 1791–1852.

88. Comisión de Policía, April 5, 1875, exp. 15, Letreros (1847–1895), AACM.

89. Quoted from León Gómez to Ayuntamiento, February 14, 1890, exp. 59, Letreros (1847–1895), AACM, with additional information from Felix Garcia Relaño to Ayuntamiento, June 9, 1879, exp. 24, Letreros (1847–1895), AACM.

90. For example, Felix Garcia Relaño to Ayuntamiento, June 9, 1879, exp. 24, Letreros (1847–1895), AACM; José Christian y Socios, June 2, 1995, exp. 41, Letreros (1847–1895), AACM; Juan H. Delgado to Ayuntamiento, November 1, 1888, exp. 50, Letreros (1847–1895), AACM; Enrique Roldán y Cia. to Ayuntamiento, March 7, 1889, exp. 57, Letreros (1847–1895), AACM; and Alberto Díaz to Ayuntamiento, November 18, 1892, exp. 62, Letreros (1847–1895), AACM.

91. José Gayosso to Ayuntamiento, June 8, 1894, exp. 67, Letreros (1847–1895), AACM.

92. Federico Bodet y Cia. to Ayuntamiento, April 23, 1895, exp. 75, Letreros (1847–1895), AACM.

93. Francisco Gutiérrez Solórzano to Ayuntamiento, September 11, 1882, exp. 28, Letreros (1847–1895), AACM. Another example is Michel Ximénez to Ayuntamiento, June 21, 1892, exp. 65, Letreros (1847–1895), AACM.

94. Crescencio Salazar and Carlos Gual to Ayuntamiento, November 26, 1890, exp. 61, Letreros (1847–1895), AACM. See also J. Navarro to Ayuntamiento, May 26, 1897, Letreros (1895–1915), AACM; and Andrés Eizaguirre (vice director of El Buen Tono) to Ayuntamiento, January 31, 1902, exp. 136, Letreros (1895–1915), AACM.

95. José Gastaldi to Ayuntamiento, July 19, 1899, exp. 109, Letreros (1896–1915), AACM.

96. Eduardo Barreira to Ayuntamiento, March 29, 1889, exp. 53, Letreros (1847–1915), AACM.

97. See Schwartz, *Spectacular Realities*, for the transition of the Parisian crowd and the rise of mass culture during this same time period.

98. José Mariano Crespo to Ayuntamiento, October 6, 1896, exp. 83, Letreros (1896–1915), AACM.

99. Daniel R. de la Vega to Ayuntamiento, May 15, 1899, exp. 111, Letreros (1896–1915), AACM.

100. For example, Pérez-Rayón, "La publicidad"; and Phyllis Smith, "Contentious Voices amid the Order: The Porfirian Press in Mexico City, 1876–1911" (PhD diss., University of Arizona, 1996). Exceptions exist, such as William Beezley's "Porfirian Smart Set."

101. Benedict Anderson, *Imagined Communities: Reflections on the Origin and Spread of Nationalism*, 2nd ed. (London: Verso, 1991), 35.

102. Ibid., 62.

103. Pérez-Rayón, "La publicidad."

104. Smith, "Contentious Voices," 195.

105. *El Anunciador Mexicano: Organo del Comercio e Industria*, November 22, 1877, 1.

106. For an account of Reyes Spíndola and his newspaper empire, see Antonio Saborit, *Como marmól recién lavado: El Mundo Ilustrado de Rafael Reyes Spíndola* (Mexico City: Ediciones Sin Nombre; CONACULTA, 2006).

107. Rafael Reyes Spíndola to JYL, Mexico City, December 5, 1902, CDLIV 1902, roll 14, carp. 13, JYL-CEHM.

108. Moisés González Navarro, *Estadísticas sociales del Porfiriato, 1877–1910* (Mexico City: Dirección General de Estadística, 1956), 7; *Estadísticas históricas*, 24.

109. Karl Polanyi, *The Great Transformation: The Political and Economic Origins of Our Time* (Boston: Beacon Hill Press, 1957).

110. Schwartz, *Spectacular Realities*, 27.

111. Anderson, *Imagined Communities*, esp. 23–25. Anderson implicitly makes this case when he counterposes the medieval world, "in which the figuring of imagined reality was overwhelmingly visual and aural," based on religious icons, art, and oral traditions, with the modern world, in which the imagining of time as well as self and group identity found structure in "two forms of imagining which first flowered in Europe in the eighteenth century: the novel and the newspaper." More broadly, his concentration on textual narratives and his silence on even the increasing visual element of newspapers reinforces this oversight.

112. Schwartz, *Spectacular Realities*, 2.

113. Reyes Spíndola to JYL, Mexico City, September 22, 1893, CDLIV 1883–1899, roll 12, carp. 44, JYL-CEHM.

114. Reyes Spíndola to JYL, Mexico City, December 5, 1902, CDLIV 1902, roll 14, carp. 13, JYL-CEHM.

115. El Duque Job was Gutiérrez Najera's pseudonym and the title of one of his most famous poems.

116. *Le Courrier du Mexique*, February 20, 1901, 3; *El Imparcial*, February 20, 1901, 1; *El Mundo Ilustrado*, February 23, 1901, 1. For the most interesting crowd illustration,

see the one on the front page of *El Imparcial*, February 20, 1900, 1, for the almanac distributed the year before.

117. Vaughan, "Primary Education and Literacy," esp. 42–43. For the Federal District rate, see *Estadísticas históricas*, 92.

118. Luis González, *San José de Gracia: Mexican Village in Transition*, trans. John Upton (Austin: University of Texas Press, 1974), xxvii.

119. Reyes-Spíndola to JYL, Mexico City, December 5, 1902, CDLIV 1902, roll 14, carp. 13, JYL-CEHM.

120. *La Semana Mercantil*, December 25, 1893, 616–17.

121. *La Semana en el Hogar*, July 23, 1895, 1.

122. *El Anunciador Mexicano*, November 22, 1877, 1.

123. *Le Courrier du Mexique*, February 16, 1906, 2; *El Imparcial*, September 14, 1899, 1.

124. *Don Cucufate*, August 20, 1906, 4.

125. *Mexican Herald*, May 20, 1906, 21.

126. Pérez-Rayón, "La publicidad," 196.

127. Leora Auslander, *Taste and Power: Furnishing Modern France* (Berkeley: University of California Press, 1996), 257.

128. Shammas, *Pre-industrial Consumer*, 1.

129. Frank, *Posada's Broadsheets*, 10. Frank makes a convincing argument for the similarities between Arroyo's broadsheets and the French *canards* and how the format arrived in Mexico.

130. Díaz, "Satiric Penny Press."

131. Lizbeth Cohen, "The Class Experience of Mass Consumption: Workers as Consumers in Interwar America," in Richard Wightman Fox and T. J. Jackson Lears, eds., *The Power of Culture: Critical Essays in American History* (Chicago: University of Chicago Press, 1993), 135–62. See page 138 for an explanation of moral capitalism.

132. William R. Leach, "Transformations in a Culture of Consumption: Women and Department Stores, 1890–1925," *Journal of American History* 71, no. 2 (September 1984): 320.

133. Like their counterparts in the capital, these papers varied in their level of independence. *Heraldo de Morelos: Semanario Político-Mutualista* was one paper that relied on government subsidies and other support in return for a pro-regime stance. A copy can be found attached to the correspondence between José M. Espinosa y Cuevas (honorary president of the Patriotic Committee of Morelos) and José Yves Limantour, CDLIV 1906, roll 41, carp. 19, JYL-CEHM.

134. *El Diablito Bromista*, April 26, 1903, 1. The editors printed this information below the title header on every edition.

135. *Don Cucufate*, September 10, 1906, 4.

136. Reyes Spíndola to JYL, CDLIV 1902, roll 14, carp. 13, JYL-CEHM.

137. *El Moquete*, July 10, 1904, 4.

138. See, for example, "La Fabrica de Metepec," *La Palanca*, December 18, 1904, 2; and "Todo en contra del pobre: Los comerciantes de carnes en los mercados," *El Chile Piquín*, February 2, 1905, 1–2. For much more extensive coverage of this subject see Díaz, "Satiric Penny Press."

139. *El Diablito Bromista*, May 31, 1903, 4.

140. Examples of these categories include: *El Duende*, November 15, 1904, 4; *El Moquete*, February 16, 1905, 4; *El Diablito Bromista*, April 12, 1907, 2 (for the Gran Salon Cuauhtémoc, a modern restaurant and café serving "exquisite national dishes" whose motto was "SELL EXCELLENCE in order to acquire a large clientele"); and *La Guacamaya*, July 18, 1906, 3 (for La Mascota restaurant, "served by young ladies").

141. *El Duende*, November 15, 1904, 3 (a combined cantina and grocery store, or *almacén de abarrotes*, also advertised in *El Pinche*, April 28, 1904, 2); *El Chango*, June 16, 1905, 3 (La Balanza de Comercio, a combined "gran tienda y cantina"); and *La Guacamaya*, June 9, 1904, 3 (El Nuevo Continente, Café Cantina y Restaurante, serving "exquisite beer"). Pulquerías stand out as the most frequently advertised, listing not only the brands and/or origins of their drinks but all the food offered as an accompaniment: the Gran Pulquería Los Pabellones, selling products from San Antonio, Ometusco, Tetepechilco, and Guadalupe (*El Moquete*, July 30, 1904, 3); Gran Pulquería La Batalla de Puebla (*El Moquete*, July 3, 1904, 3); El Aguila de Oro, offering pulque from the "famous haciendas" of S. Nicolás el Grande (*El Moquete*, February 5, 1905, 4; also in *El Pinche*, April 28, 1904, 2, in which it states it does not give out prizes and that its rewards to customers include "not adulterating the pulque, attending to its customers, and never increasing the price of its pulque to its consumers"); the Fonda Los Bebedores, featuring appetizing and succulent dishes to go with the "famous pulque El Aguila de Oro" (*El Moquete*, February 15, 1905, 4); and Gran Pulquería Las Cazadora, selling from the haciendas of Jalostoc and Tesoyo (*El Moquete*, February 16, 1905, 4).

142. Ads for liquor stores and manufactures include *La Palanca*, September 11, 1904, 1; *El Moquete*, June 10, 1904, 4 (tequila); *El Pinche*, April 28, 1904, 2 (groceries, wines, and liquors, domestic and imported); and *El Pinche*, April 28, 1904, 4 ("the best tequila in the world"). Regarding pulque, see *El Diablito Bromista*, May 31, 1908, 3. This particular vendor sold from six expendios around the city, including the middle-class Ribera de San Cosme, offering pulque at the fairly steep price of five centavos per bottle.

143. See *La Guacamaya*, June 2, 1904, 3; September 1, 1904, 3; and December 15, 1904, 3.

144. *El Diablito Bromista*, September 11, 1904, 1; October 1, 1905, 3.

145. See *El Diablito Bromista*, October 8, 1905, 3; November 19, 1905, 3–4; November 26, 1905, 3. See also *La Guacamaya*, November 30, 1905, 2–3; December 14, 1904, 3; January 4, 1906, 3; June 11, 1906, 2–3; January 18, 1906, 3; January 25, 1906, 3; February 8, 1906, 3; and March 5, 1906, 3.

146. Bullfights were advertised in *El Papagayo*, September 17, 1904, 3 (Plaza de Toros de Chapultepec); *El Diablito Bromista*, April 26, 1903, 2 (Plaza de Toros México); *El Diablito Bromista*, April 26, 1903, 3 (Chapultepec); *El Diablito Bromista*, May 31, 1903, 3 (Chapultepec); *El Diablito Bromista*, January 10, 1904, 1 (México); and *El Diablito Bromista*, January 31, 1904, 3 (México). Cinema ads appeared less frequently, but the best, which includes a list of titles (such as "The plebe without

a Pulman"), appears in *El Diablito Bromista*, August 7, 1904, 4. Theaters such as the Teatro Popular advertised such events as puppet shows, including one whose puppeteer (Federico Confreras) won prizes at the New Orleans and Chicago Expositions: *La Guacamaya*, July 2, 1903, 1.

147. Circus ads included those for the Gran Circo Gasca (Plazuela de la Aguilita), Circo Metropolitano (Calle de Matamoros), Gran Circo Bell, Gran Circo Treviño (Calzada de la Reforma), Gran Circo Metropolitano (Plazuela del Salto de Agua), Gran Circo Guerrero (11A Calle de Camelia), Gran Circo Lezama (Plazuela de la Aguilita), and Gran Circo Victoria. An ad for Ricardo Bell's Gran Circo Bell and its seventy artists appears in *Don Cucufate*, September 3, 1906, 3; and *La Guacamaya*, September 30, 1906, 1.

148. For Gran Circo Treviño, see *El Diablito Bromista*, January 24, 1904, 1; for Gran Circo Victoria, see *La Guacamaya*, November 26, 1903, 3, and *El Diablito Bromista*, February 14, 1904, 3; and for Gran Circo Guerrero, *El Diablito Bromista*, August 28, 1904, 4.

149. *La Guacamaya*, November 26, 1903, 3.

150. *El Diablito Bromista*, February 14, 1904, 3. The title of the ad offering this discount is headlined, "¡¡¡INTERESANTE A LOS OBREROS!!!"

151. *El Chango*, May 28, 1905, 1; *El Diablito Bromista*, July 10, 1904, 4; *La Guacamaya*, April 5, 1906, 1.

152. *El Duende*, January 12, 1905, 4.

153. *La Guacamaya*, February 18, 1904, 3.

154. *El Duende*, November 15, 1904, 4.

155. Irwin, McCaughan, and Rocío Nasser, *Famous 41*.

156. *La Cagarruta*, December 20, 1906, 4; *Don Cucufate*, August 5, 1906, 4.

157. *La Guacamaya*, February 18, 1904, 3; *El Pinche*, December 1, 1904, 4.

158. The sole exception was the Instituto Eléctrico Medico del Dr. S. S. Hall. *Don Cucufate*, July 29, 1906, 3.

159. *El Chango*, *El Moquete*, *Don Cucufate*, *El Diablito Bromista*, and *La Guacamaya*.

160. *El Moquete*, July 10, 1904, 4.

161. *El Papagayo*, August 7, 1904, 3–4; *La Guacamaya*, September 29, 1904, 3–4.

162. For an interesting description of these three levels of "care" and who patronized them, see *El Imparcial*, April 21, 1903, 1.

163. See, for example, *Don Cucufate*, July 29, 1906, 3; or *El Diablito Bromista*, November 19, 1905, 3.

164. *El Imparcial*, December 16, 1903, 4.

165. For example, the Gran Cereria el Sr. de Amecameca, established in 1889, whose factory and retail shop faces onto the Plaza de San Juan, home of the El Buen Tono cigarette factory. *La Palanca*, October 2, 1904, 4.

166. *El Diablito Bromista*, March 6, 1904, 1; January 6, 1907, 1; July 7, 1907, 1.

167. *El Diablito Bromista*, September 29, 1907, 4.

168. *El Diablito Bromista*, July 10, 1904, 4.

169. *El Diablito Bromista*, April 26, 1903, 2.

170. *El Duende*, November 15, 1904, 4.

171. *La Palanca*, October 30, 1904, 2. This ad appeared regularly.

172. *La Palanca*, October 16, 1904, 2. This ad appeared regularly.

173. For wallpaper, see *El Diablito Bromista*, August 21, 1904, 1; for *cristalerias*, see *La Palanca*, October 30, 1904, 2; for furniture producers other than those noted below, see Gran Muebleria of Pedro Gómez in *La Palanca*, November 6, 1904, 4, offering a variety of qualities (*muebles finos y corrientes*), tin beds, cotton and wool mattresses, an assortment of furniture styles, and promises that "it is the business that sells for the lowest price in all of the Republic."

174. *El Diablito Bromista*, July 10, 1904, 4.

175. Ibid.

176. *El Diablito Bromista*, February 11, 1906, 1.

177. For a discussion of the braiding of conspicuous consumption, politics, and gender during the Porfiriato, see Macías-González, "*Lagartijo* at *The High Life*." For a sample of three scholarly criticisms of Porfirian elite consumption, see Adolfo Gilly, ed., *Interpretaciones de la Revolución Mexicana* (Mexico City: Fondo de Cultura Económica, 1980); González Navarro, *El Porfiriato: La vida social*; and Juan Felipe Leal, "El estado y el bloque en el poder, 1867–1914," *Historia Mexicana* 23, no. 4 (April–June 1974): 700–721. A far less polemical and far more enlightening interpretation of Porfirian elite conspicuous consumption comes from Beezley, "Porfirian Smart Set." On Porfirian banquets, see Jeffrey M. Pilcher, *¡Qué vivan los tamales! Food and the Making of Mexican Identity* (Albuquerque: University of New Mexico Press, 1998), 64–65.

178. For information on one or several of these categories and the development of the domestic consumer market, see Mario Cerutti, *Burguesía, capitals e industria en el norte de México: Monterrey y su ámbito regional (1850–1910)* (Monterrey: Alianza Editorial, 1992); Barbara Hibino, "Cervecería Cuauhtémoc: A Case Study of Technological and Industrial Development in Mexico," *Mexican Studies/ Estudios Mexicanos* 8, no. 1 (Winter 1992): 23–43; Sandra Kuntz Ficker, *Empresa extranjera y mercado interno: El Ferrocarril Central Mexicano, 1880–1907* (Mexico City: El Colegio de México, 1995); and Aurora Gómez Galvarriato Freer, "Industrialización, empresas y trabajadores industrials, del Porfiriato a la Revolución: La nueva historiografía," *Historia Mexicana* 52, no. 3 (January–March 2003): 773–805.

179. Tello Peón, "Intención decorativo"; Auslander, *Taste and Power*; Whitney Walton, *France at the Crystal Palace: Bourgeois Taste and Artisan Manufacture in the Nineteenth Century* (Berkeley: University of California Press, 1996), 23–116.

180. *Le Courrier du Mexique*, September 16, 1904, 3. With the U.S. ambassador to Mexico present, Edison's representatives presented Díaz on his birthday with a phonograph specially constructed in Menlo Park. Entirely adorned with gold leaf, it bore a plaque with the following inscription: "Special phonograph presented by Thomas Alva Edison to his Excellence, General Porfirio Díaz, President of Mexico, September 15, 1904."

181. Both of the following approved petitions to set up public phonographs and charge one centavo per song: Mariano González to the Ayuntamiento, June 12, 1902, exp. 1186, Diversiones Públicas, AACM; and Francisco Granada to the Ayuntamiento, August 13, 1902, exp. 1191, Diversiones Públicas, AACM.
182. *L'Echo du Mexique*, April 24, 1895, 2.
183. See, for example, *El Diablito Bromista*, November 27, 1904, 4.
184. *La Guacamaya*, December 15, 1902, 3.

Chapter 3

1. The first significant contribution comes from the field of architecture: Patricia Martínez Gutiérrez, *El Palacio de Hierro: Arranque de la modernidad arquitectónica en la Ciudad de México* (Mexico City: Instituto de Investigaciones Estéticas, UNAM, 2005).
2. John Lear, *Workers, Neighbors, and Citizens: The Revolution in Mexico City* (Lincoln: University of Nebraska Press, 2001), 49–86; Aurora Gómez Galvarriato Freer, "The Impact of Revolution: Business and Labor in the Mexican Textile Industry, Orizaba, Veracruz, 1900–1930" (PhD diss., Harvard University, 1999).
3. Buchenau, *Tools of Progress*. Aurora Gómez Galvarriato Freer has achieved a similar goal indirectly through the investigation of the textile industry and its connection with department stores through their ownership. She is one of a number of economic historians in Mexico constructing a solid economic foundation for a historiography of daily and material culture that cultural historians have left untouched. For an overview of this movement, see Gómez Galvarriato Freer, "Industrialización, empresas y trabajadores industriales."
4. *El Imparcial*, July 4, 1900, 1.
5. An example is my attempt to access the archives of the Puerto de Liverpool department store, one of two remaining Porfirian-era department stores. Despite introductions from my contacts at the Palacio de Hierro and other connections, I was informed that a soon-to-be-released store history commemorating its 150-year anniversary (just under 100 years as a department store) would answer any questions. The resulting product, attributed to Anilú Elías, *150 años de costumbres, modas y Liverpool* (Mexico City: El Puerto de Liverpool, 1997), is nearly useless as a historical source. It is a largely fictional account of founding families, capitalino society, and the store that culminates in a bubbly outlook for the store's future. The account, with rambling, flowery prose reminiscent of an English garden, provides no citations, few dates, and a baffling narrative. The photos are, however, quite lovely. Unfortunately, the history fails to enlighten us to any degree on the actual workings, composition, or character of the store.
6. Most historians working outside of the United States, Canada, and parts of Europe understand the problem of not just document but also archival neglect. In specific consideration of department stores, the Palacio de Hierro suffered from a fire in 1914 that destroyed the store and most of its records. Even the remaining copiadores

to which I had access had singed leather casings. This fire began from an electrical short in one of the display windows, a fate suffered by other department stores. Similarly, La Valenciana, owned by Sebastian Robert, burned down in 1900, leading Robert to move into the Centro Mercantil in 1901. In the new building several years later another display-window electrical fire threatened the store once again. For the original fire, see *El Imparcial*, September 28, 1900, 1. On the later fire in the Centro Mercantil, see *La Semana Mercantil*, April 16, 1906, 182.

7. The earliest and still best cultural history of the department store is Miller, *Bon Marché*. Miller anchors his cultural analysis with a thorough consideration of the business and labor history of the store. The result is an enduring example of how cultural history should be written. Other contributions to the historiography include Geoffrey Crossick and Serge Jaumain, eds., *Cathedrals of Consumption: The European Department Store, 1850–1939* (Aldershot, UK: Ashgate Publishing, 1999); Bill Lancaster, *The Department Store: A Social History* (London: Leicester University Press, 1995); Susan Porter Benson, *Counter Cultures: Saleswomen, Managers, and Customers in American Department Stores, 1890–1940* (Urbana: University of Illinois Press, 1986); William R. Leach, *Land of Desire: Merchants, Power, and the Rise of a New American Culture* (New York: Pantheon Books, 1993); Rosalind Williams, *Dream Worlds: Mass Consumption in Late Nineteenth-Century France* (Berkeley: University of California Press, 1982); Elaine Abelson, *When Ladies Go A-Thieving: Middle-Class Shoplifters and the Victorian Department Store* (New York: Oxford University Press, 1989); and Cynthia Wright, "'Feminine Trifles of Vast Importance': Writing Gender into the History of Consumption," in *Gender Conflicts: New Essays in Women's History*, ed. Franca Iacovetta and Mariana Valverde (Toronto: University of Toronto Press, 1992), 229–60.

8. The first monograph of this field appears to be Patrice Gouy, *Pérégrinations des "Barcelonnettes" au Mexique* (Grenoble: Presses Universitaires de Grenoble, 1980). The best and least hagiographical is the most recent, a collection of essays and other contributions from sixteen historians and descendants of the Barcelonnettes: François Arnaud, Anselme Charpenel, Léon Martin, André Signoret, and Elie Borel, eds., *Les Barcelonnettes au Mexique: Récits et témoignages* (Barcelonnette: Sabença de la Valeia, 1994). A source for information but altogether hagiographical and uncritical of the French *mission civilisatrice* is Raymonde Antiq-Auvaro, *L'emigration des Barcelonnettes au Mexique* (Nice: Editions Serre, 1992). More useful is Maurice Proal and Pierre Martin Charpenel, *L'empire des Barcelonnettes au Mexique* (Marseille: Editions Jeanne Laffitte, 1986). This work has been translated, given a prologue by Mexican historian Jean Meyer, and slightly edited for its Mexican audience (note the change in title) as Proal and Charpenel, *Los Barcelonnettes en México* (Mexico City: Editorial Clío, 1998). Also available in Spanish is a condensed version of Gouy's book in the form of an article: Gouy, "Peregrinaciones de los Barcelonnettes a México," *Artes de México*, no. 39 (1997): 62–67. This issue, titled "Francia-México: Imágenes Compartidas," is part of a broader trend in Mexico and France to commemorate the cultural ties between

the two nations (something of a defense against American influence). Mexican historians—many with French ancestry—have contributed to this renaissance of "pan-Latinism," the most notable and worthwhile example being the collection of Javier Pérez Siller, coord., *México Francia: Memoria de una sensibilidad común, siglos XIX–XX* (Mexico City: Editorial Ducere, 1998).

9. This idea of an inclusive history, or *histoire totale*, is not an original one. For a recent and thoughtful consideration of this approach, consult Eric Van Young, "La pareja dispareja: Breves comentarios acerca de la relación entre historia económica y cultural," *Historia Mexicana* 52, no. 3 (January–March 2003): 831–72.

10. Beezley, "Porfirian Smart Set," 175. For an example of viceregal processions, see Linda A. Curcio-Nagy, "Giants and Gypsies: Corpus Christi in Colonial Mexico City," in Beezley, Martin, and French, *Rituals of Rule*, 1–26; for Porfirian charity events, see Macías-González, "Mexican Aristocracy," 80–141; and for commercialized Porfirian holidays, consult Bunker, "Consumers of Good Taste."

11. Tenorio-Trillo, *Mexico at the World's Fairs*.

12. Today the Centro Mercantil is the Gran Hotel. Unless otherwise cited, details of the following account may be found in *El Imparcial*, September 3, 1899, 2; *Le Courrier du Mexique*, September 5, 1899, 3; and Domenech, *Guía general descriptiva*, 2:760–61.

13. Photos and descriptions of the elevator and stained-glass window are in Proal and Charpenel, *Barcelonnettes en México*, 42–43.

14. On Díaz's stint in retailing, see Paul Garner, *Porfirio Díaz* (Harlow, UK: Pearson Education, 2001), 27.

15. Dawn Keremetsis, *La industria textil Mexicana en el siglo XIX* (Mexico City: SepSetentas, 1973), 123–24, briefly discusses the use of cheap percale fabric among the lower classes, particularly for women.

16. Émile Chabrand, *De Barcelonnette au Mexique* (Paris: Plon, Nourrit, 1892), 386–87.

17. "Indian" cloth refers to printed calico of the sort originally imported from India and then later taken over and industrialized by mills in Manchester and Rouen.

18. On the purchase of "whiteness" and the colonial caste system, see Colin M. MacLachlan and Jaime E. Rodríguez O., *The Forging of the Cosmic Race: A Reinterpretation of Colonial Mexico* (Berkeley: University of California Press, 1980), 199–201. For the light-skinned Porfirian ideal, see Macías-González, "Mexican Aristocracy," esp. 142–202; and Stacie G. Widdifield, *The Embodiment of the National in Late Nineteenth-Century Mexican Painting* (Tucson: University of Arizona Press, 1996). Today, skin-whitening creams are widely available. Pond's sells a popular version advertised throughout Mexico City, which claims that its product whitens the skin not for racial reasons but rather to repair the damage done by sun and air pollution to one's original skin tone.

19. For a great deal of information on calicot, including its manufacture and slang usage in the nineteenth century, consult the 1866 version of the *Larousse Dictionnaire Universel*, s.v. "calicot."

20. Génin, *Notes sur le Mexique*, esp. 108–12.

21. Ibid., 108.

22. The seminal work in understanding the concept of gender remains Joan Wallach Scott, "Gender: A Useful Category of Historical Analysis," *American Historical Review* 91, no. 5 (December 1986): 1067–75; and Joan Wallach Scott, *Gender and the Politics of History* (New York: Columbia University Press, 1988). For Porfirian Mexico, consult French, *Peaceful and Working People*, 87–139; Macías-González, "Mexican Aristocracy"; and Robert Buffington and Pablo Piccato, "Tales of Two Women: The Narrative Construal of Porfirian Reality," *The Americas* 55, no. 3 (January 1999): 391–424. For other useful works on gender in post-Independence (as well as colonial) Mexico, see Ramos Escandón, *Presencia y transparencia*; and Jean Franco, *Plotting Women: Gender and Representation in Mexico* (New York: Columbia University Press, 1989).

23. Thorstein Veblen, *The Theory of the Leisure Class* (1899; reprint, New York: Penguin Books, 1994). For a humorous application of Veblen's theory to literature, see Stephen Leacock, *Arcadian Adventures with the Idle Rich* (Toronto: Cromwell, 1914). Veblen's presence at the University of Chicago attracted Leacock, one of Canada's most famous humorists, to take his doctorate there in 1903.

24. The best collection of essays considering the gendering of consumption is de Grazia and Furlough, *Sex of Things*.

25. Macías-González, "Mexican Aristocracy," 116–41.

26. *El Imparcial*, September 3, 1899, 2.

27. *Le Courrier du Mexique*, September 5, 1899, 3.

28. The department stores were Palacio de Hierro, Puerto de Veracruz, Ciudad de Londres, Puerto de Liverpool, Francia Maritima, Centro Mercantil/La Valenciana, Las Fábricas Universales, La Reforma de Comercio, and La Sorpresa y Primavera Unidas. Other stores, such as El Importador, would follow before the Mexican Revolution began. German department stores emphasizing hardware but also incorporating to some degree product lines such as clothing and toys include Casa Boker, Ciudad de Hamburgo, and Korff-Honsberg.

29. *Le Courrier du Mexique*, October 15, 1899, 3.

30. For the opening of El Paje, see *El Mundo Ilustrado*, May 16, 1903, 14. For La Perla information, see *Le Courrier du Mexique*, January 13, 1903, 3; and *El Mundo Ilustrado*, January 18, 1903, 3.

31. On A. T. Stewart's claim to having the earliest department store with his New York "Marble Palace" in 1846 and his "Cast Iron Palace" in 1862, see Miller, *Bon Marché*, 29. On the origins of the Bon Marché and its distinctive business model, marketing practices, and retail policies, see ibid., 21–27. More generally, see Lancaster, *Department Store*, 1–5, for clearly defined terms and historiography. John Benson and Gareth Shaw, eds., *The Evolution of Retail Systems, c. 1800–1914* (Leicester, UK: Leicester University Press, 1992) offers a more economic and quantitative history of retail development in Germany, Britain, and Canada that thoughtfully analyzes the different development patterns of department stores in those countries with necessary reference to the United States and France.

32. Too often economic modernization and the concept of "modernity" are based on industrialization. Whitney Walton decouples modernity from industrialization as she considers how France achieved a leading global role in taste and fashion precisely from its emphasis on handcrafted and specialized products (with increasing machine inputs as technologies improved), in contrast to standardized, mass-industrial manufacture. See Walton, *France at the Crystal Palace*.

33. Information on Canada comes from Benson and Shaw, *Evolution of Retail Systems*, 190–91. For more on Canadian department store origins, see James Bryant, *Department Store Disease* (Toronto: McClelland and Stewart, 1977). On Selfridge's of London, see Benson and Shaw, *Evolution of Retail Systems*, 141. On the slow development of department stores in Germany, see ibid., 174, and Warren G. Breckman, "Disciplining Consumption: The Debate about Luxury in Wilhelmine Germany, 1890–1914," *Journal of Social History* 24, no. 3 (Spring 1991): 485–505, in which he dates the beginning of department stores in Germany to the 1890s.

34. On Chile, see Bauer, *Goods, Power, History*, 156. Regarding Argentina, James R. Scobie, one of the greatest urban historians of Latin America, provides an example of how recent the interest is in connecting department stores, shopping, and consumerism with urban development and modernity. He mentions the Gath y Chaves department store only once in passing in *Buenos Aires: Plaza to Suburb, 1870–1910* (New York: Oxford University Press, 1974), 34. Jeffrey Needell does not even mention department stores in his description of shopping habits and haunts in his pathbreaking *Tropical Belle Epoque*.

35. The Bon Marché, upon completion in 1887, covered almost five hundred thousand square feet between its main building and its annex across the street.

36. French, *Peaceful and Working People*, 63.

37. For a compelling historical anthropological view on the increasing importance of goods and their meaning in Western society, see Grant McCracken, *Culture and Consumption: New Approaches to the Symbolic Character of Consumer Goods and Activities* (Bloomington: Indiana University Press, 1988). The classic text on consumption, goods, history, and meaning remains the multidisciplinary compilation Brewer and Porter, *Consumption and the World of Goods*. An important monograph representing a movement to place consumerism and the heightened cultural significance of goods long before the advent of the Industrial Revolution is Lisa Jardine, *Worldly Goods: A New History of the Renaissance* (New York: W. W. Norton, 1996).

38. Miller, *Bon Marché*, 3.

39. "The dry goods trade of this country is almost exclusively in the hands of the French merchants." *Modern Mexico*, February 1901, 10.

40. A caveat is in order here. I am defining department stores as those whose interior space is distinctly compartmentalized and that carry diverse lines of merchandise with an emphasis on clothing, fashions, and accessories. Porfirian department stores actually offered much more than this, including a wide range of home

furnishings and services as well as luxury objects, toys, and a variety of other nontextile goods. Jürgen Buchenau, in his work on the Casa Boker, makes the compelling argument that the Boker store of 1900 was "the first department store that did not sell textiles." Buchenau, *Tools of Progress*, 64. The Germans dominated the hardware business in Mexico much as the Barcelonnettes controlled textiles and fashion, and certain of their stores, such as Korff y Honsberg, sold not only hardware but toys and garments as well. Nevertheless, for this study, while the German stores were technically department stores, only the French stores, which more closely resemble the transnational model, were called *los grandes almacenes* by residents and visitors alike.

41. Schwartz, *Spectacular Realities*, esp. 7–8. See also Walton, *France at the Crystal Palace*. At the same time that France held global leadership in many categories of taste and in feminine fashion, London firmly retained its position as the source of masculine fashion. David Kuchta makes a compelling argument for how this gendered polarization of fashion along national lines came to be in "The Making of the Self-Made Man: Class, Clothing, and English Masculinity, 1688–1832," in de Grazia and Furlough, *Sex of Things*, 54–78. Kuchta's work offers a refreshing reminder that gender history is not just about women but rather about the construction of masculinity and femininity.

42. Pablo Piccato, "'El Paso de Venus por el disco del sol': Criminality and Alcoholism in the Late Porfiriato," *Mexican Studies/Estudios Mexicanos* 11, no. 2 (Summer 1995): 203–41.

43. For a concise synopsis of the Barcelonnette social and economic system, see Gouy, *Pérégrinations*, 12, 59.

44. Buchenau, *Tools of Progress*, 64.

45. Gouy, *Pérégrinations*, 23–36.

46. For the fate of Jacques, see Arnaud et al., *Barcelonnettes au Mexique*, 110–11. The Arnaud brothers have played a central role in the history/myth of the Barcelonnettes in Mexico. Only one recent history has pieced together an account of the brothers based on family papers and other archival sources. This work places the brothers in Mexico before rather than after Independence as well as revealing that their point of origin was Louisiana, where the Arnauds and other Barcelonnette families had set up farming colonies during the first decade of the nineteenth century. See Pierre Coste, "Jacques Arnaud, ses frères et ses descendants," in Arnaud et al., *Barcelonnettes au Mexique*, 100–112.

47. Arnaud et al., *Barcelonnettes au Mexique*, 8, 20–21.

48. Ibid., 81.

49. Antiq-Auvaro, *Emigration des Barcelonnettes*, 34.

50. D'Olwer et al., *El Porfiriato: La vida económica*, 785.

51. Chabrand, *De Barcelonnette*, 406.

52. Ibid.; Arnaud et al., *Barcelonnettes au Mexique*, 33–35; Gouy, *Pérégrinations*, 54–58.

53. Lucía de Robina, *Reconciliación de México y Francia (1870–1880)* (Mexico City: Secretaría de Relaciones Exteriores, 1963). Pages 36 and 37 specifically describe

the resumption of relations on December 2, 1880, after eighteen years of official diplomatic silence.

54. Emilio Meyran to JYL, Mexico City, December 17, 1903, CDLIV 1903, roll 22, carp. 22, JYL-CEHM. Meyran, writing on Centro Mercantil letterhead, described the eagle "as a testament of respect and true affection."

55. The classic English-language text on the role of the railroad in this process is John H. Coatsworth, *Growth Against Development: The Economic Impact of Railroads in Porfirian Mexico* (DeKalb: Northern Illinois University Press, 1981). For the best summary of this view of the Mexican economy, see Benjamin Orlove and Arnold J. Bauer, "Giving Importance to Imports," in Orlove, *Allure of the Foreign*, 1–30.

56. Kuntz Ficker, *Empresa extranjera*; Gómez Galvarriato Freer, "Impact of Revolution." For an overview of the new economic historiography in Mexico, see Gómez Galvarriato Freer, "Industrialización, empresas y trabajadores industriales."

57. Beatty, *Institutions and Investment*.

58. Miller, *Bon Marché*, 57–58.

59. Arnaud et al., *Barcelonnettes au Mexique*, 20.

60. See Proal and Charpenel, *Barcelonnettes en México*, 28–34, for a French vision of the Mexican textile industry. For a good overview of the Mexican textile industry, consult Keremetsis, *La industria textil Mexicana*.

61. Proal and Charpenel, *Barcelonnettes en México*, 28–29. These were Joseph Tron y Cia. (*Cia.* is the abbreviation for *Compañia*) (Palacio de Hierro), J. B. Ebrard y Cia. (Puerto de Liverpool), J. Ollivier (Ciudad de Londres), Signoret y Honnorat (Puerto de Veracruz), and M. Lambert y Cia. (El Correo Francés). Arnaud et al., *Barcelonnettes au Mexique*, 44, lists the ownership and percentage of the shares owned. It contradicts the assertion that CIVSA formed out of Barcelonnettes excluded from CIDOSA. After Ollivier, Tron, and Ebrard, the largest shareholder was A. Richaud (El Nuevo Mundo, La Reforma de Comercio). A. Reynaud (Fábricas Universales) was the sixth-largest shareholder, Sebastián Robert (La Valenciana/El Centro Mercantil) was seventh, M. Lambert (El Correo Frances) was eighth, and M. Bellon (El Progreso) was ninth.

62. Proal and Charpenel, *Barcelonnettes en México*, 33–34. CIVSA founders included the owners of Fábricas Universales, La Valenciana/El Centro Mercantil, La Reforma de Comercio, El Nuevo Mundo, and large almacenes de novedades like El Progreso. For information on the division between the two Barcelonnette business groups, see Jean Meyer, "Les Français au Mexique au XIXème siècle," *Cahiers des Amériques Latines* 9–10 (1974): 62–64.

63. See the store façade illustrated in Sebastián Robert to Ayuntamiento, December 10, 1901, Portales 1559–1918, tomo I, AACM. Robert's store, La Valenciana, had burned down and his subsequent battle with the city over its replacement proved a catalyst to his purchase of El Centro Mercantil. He nevertheless rebuilt on the same site after winning over the city council with a little help from his friend José Yves Limantour.

64. See, for example, the photo of the Centro in Proal and Charpenel, *Empire des Barcelonnettes*, 39.

65. *Le Mexique*, June 20, 1907, 151.

66. *Le Courrier du Mexique*, April 16, 1901, 2.

67. J. Tron y Cia., contract with Bermejillo y Cia., no date (likely sometime in 1890), pp. 11–12, Copiador I (1889–1903), APH. The contract is with the mill La Magdalena, which the contract states is owned by Tron, J. B. Ebrard, J. Ollivier, Signoret Honnorat, Richaud, Aubert y Cia., Lambert Reynaud Cia., and Garcin Faudon y Cia.

68. Ollivier y Cia., J. Tron y Cia., J. B. Ebrard y Cia., Richaud Aubert y Cia., Signoret Honnorat y Cia., Lambert Reynaud y Cia., Garcin Faudon Cia., and S. Robert y Cia. to Sres. Watson Phillips y Cia. Sucs., January 28, 1891, p. 16, Copiador I (1889–1903), APH.

69. *Echo du Mexique*, January 15, 1897, 1.

70. See, for example, J. Tron y Cia. to Cia. Industrial de Orizaba, September 6, 1894, Copiador I (1889–1903), APH. In this entry the Palacio informs CIDOSA that it has received sixty-five shares worth 65,000 pesos, corresponding to an increase in CIDOSA's capitalization, and had received another thirty shares for Julio Tron. In another letter to CIDOSA, on February 11, 1895 (p. 74, Copiador I), the Palacio acknowledges receipt of 36,400 pesos for its 1894 dividend based on the 4,550 shares owned by J. Tron y Cia. and 2,400 pesos, corresponding to the 8 percent dividend paid on the three hundred personal shares of Julio Tron. As for ownership in other textile mills, see J. Tron y Cia. to Ernest Pugibet, February 4, 1898, p. 167, Copiador I (1889–1903), APH, for the additional purchase of one thousand shares in the San Ildefonso Mill (wool products). A later example is the letter from Henri Tron to the textile mill La Perfeccionada, S.A., December 31, 1904, Mexico City, p. 108, Copiador I (1889–1903), APH, as a dividend payment to Tron for his personal investment of 50,000 pesos in the company.

71. In the French press, consult *Le Courrier du Mexique*, May 12, 1890, 4; and *Le Courrier du Mexique*, January 17, 1903, 2.

72. JYL to Eduardo Noetzlin, Mexico City, September 22, 1900, CDLIV 1900, roll 1, carp. 1, JYL-CEHM.

73. See Arnaud et al., *Barcelonnettes au Mexique*, 42–46. For France as the fourth-largest importer, see *Le Mexique*, July 20, 1902, 1.

74. F. Bianconi, *Le Mexique á la portée des industriels, des capitalistes, des negociants importateurs et des travailleurs* (Paris: Imprimerie Chaix, 1899), 115. Eugen Weber, *France: Fin de Siècle* (Cambridge, MA: Belknap Press of Harvard University Press, 1986), 139, discusses the concern within the Parisian press for the failing of French business in the marketplace.

75. The various presses and commentators for each foreign community constructed a narrative of international trade warfare taking place on Mexican soil. They bemoaned the weaknesses of their commercial "troops" and fretted that market share would be lost to other competitors. The French press in 1892 talked of a "Commercial Conquest" as it berated the American control of transportation and the favoritism shown to American business. *L'Echo du Mexique*, September 9, 1892, 1.

French commercial commentators such as F. Bianconi worried over "our risking the total abandonment to our competitors a market of nearly 11 million souls" (Bianconi, *Le Mexique*, 115), while Gaston Routier described the Mexican market as an international battleground on which France must vanquish the British and Germans. Gaston Routier, *Le Mexique* (Paris: Lille Imp. L. Danel, 1891), 89–80.

76. Arthur W. Fergusson, *Mexico* (Washington, D.C.: Bureau of the American Republics, 1891), 137. The Barcelonnettes were not the only merchants who diversified their imported product sources. See Buchenau, *Tools of Progress*, 48, for the origins of goods sold by German-owned Casa Boker.

77. Gouy, *Pérégrinations*, 10.

78. An account of a Frenchman turned away from a Barcelonnette business because he was not from the valley appears in *La Voz de México*, March 6, 1891, 2.

79. Haber, *Industry and Underdevelopment*. For the latest criticism of Haber and information on a growing body of regional and industry-specific economic history demonstrating the problems with his overgeneralized analysis, see Gómez Galvarriato Freer, "Industrialización, empresas y trabajadores industriales."

80. "Ganancias y Perdidas 1896" and "Repartición de las Ganancias 1896," December 31, 1896, pp. 144–45, Copiador I (1889–1903), APH.

81. "Ganancias y Perdidas 1899" and "Repartición de Ganancias 1899," December 31, 1899, pp. 268–70, Copiador I (1889–1903), APH; "Ganancias y Perdidas 1901" and "Repartición de Ganancias 1901," December 31, 1901, pp. 334, 356, Copiador I (1889–1903), APH; "Ganancias y Perdidas 1902" and "Repartición de Ganancias 1902," December 31, 1902, pp. 482, Copiador I (1889–1903), APH; "Ganancias y Perdidas 1905" and "Repartición de Ganancias 1905," December 31, 1905, pp. 218, Copiador II (1903–1910), APH; and "Ganancias y Perdidas 1907" and "Repartición de Ganancias 1907," December 31, 1907, pp. 365–66, Copiador II (1903–1910), APH.

82. Gouy, *Pérégrinations*, 59.

83. *Modern Mexico*, March 1897, 6.

84. All of the Barcelonnette studies cover this subject. For example, see Gouy, *Pérégrinations*, 59. Information on this pattern in the city of Puebla may be found in Leticia Gamboa Ojeda, "Los Barcelonnettes en la ciudad de Puebla: Panorama de sus actividades económicas en el Porfiriato" in Pérez Siller, *México-Francia*, 171–94, esp. 181. The figure of 100,000 francs comes from Chabrand, *De Barcelonnette*, 399.

85. *Le Courrier du Mexique*, April 16, 1901, 2.

86. Fergusson, *Mexico*, 136.

87. Miller, *Bon Marché*, 54, 178; Lancaster, *Department Store*, 9.

88. *Modern Mexico*, November 1897, 9.

89. "Ganancias y Perdidas 1903," January 1, 1904, pp. 56–57, Copiador II (1903–1910), APH.

90. "Ganancias y Perdidas 1905," December 31, 1905, p. 218, Copiador II (1903–1910), APH; "Ganancias y Perdidas 1906," December 31, 1906, p. 333, Copiador II (1903–1910), APH; and "Ganancias y Perdidas 1907," December 31, 1907, pp. 365–66, Copiador II (1903–1910), APH.

91. Miller, *Bon Marché*, 99–105, discusses the use and purpose of pensions, provident funds (for funerals, disabilities, spousal benefits), and profit sharing at the Bon Marché. Miller discusses the paternalism of these programs as well as their cohesive role within a bureaucratic organization.

92. Arnaud et al., *Barcelonnettes au Mexique*, 67. No exact date is attributed to this letter, although Charpenel probably wrote it in 1910, the year that he arrived in Mexico after Centro Mercantil owner Sebastian Robert recruited him directly.

93. Balance de "El Palacio de Hierro" S. A., December 31, 1901, pp. 390–91, Copiador I (1889–1903), APH.

94. Ibid.

95. Paul Saint Marc came to Mexico with the first troops during the French Intervention. He was a low-ranking officer of the Third Regiment of the Zouaves but left the army before the fall of Maximilian. He immediately set up a perfume business and became an important member of the French community in Mexico. He died in 1906 at the age of sixty-eight. See his obituary in *Le Courrier du Mexique*, April 29, 1906, 1, for the most concise account of his life. See also Joseph Tron to Saint Marc, January 21, 1893, and August 16, 1893, pp. 36, 47, Copiador I (1889–1903), APH.

96. Unsigned letter to Louis Ollivier, December 31, 1895, p. 98, Copiador I (1889–1903), APH; and H. Tron to J. B. Ebrard y Cia. Sucs., June 17, 1904, p. 71, Copiador II (1903–1910), APH.

97. Remussat to El Buen Tono, S. A., January 28, 1903, p. 472, Copiador I (1889–1903), APH, acknowledging the receipt of a 50,000-peso check from Hugo Scherer y Cia. The rate of return was set at a lower-than-normal 4 percent, but funds would be made available with a short, eight-day advance warning.

98. See, for example, Remussat to Antoine Proal, January 4, 1906, p. 330, Copiador II (1903–1910), APH. Proal had retired and was living in Paris. Copiador III (1910–1914) lists extensively depositors living in France in 1910, whether Paris (pp. 15, 16, 17), Cannes (pp. 14, 39), Barcelonnette (pp. 17, 23), Aix en Provence (pp. 26, 27), Nice (p. 25), or Marseille (p. 17).

99. Unsigned to Victor Audiffred, Guanajuato, July 31, 1893, and unsigned to Lions Hnos., Puebla, August 19, 1893, pp. 46, 48, Copiador I (1889–1903), APH. For more on the Lions brothers, see Gamboa Ojeda, "Los Barcelonnettes en la ciudad de Puebla," 178.

100. In order, see pages 61 (Gallardo), 63 (Garcin), 67, 87 (de Caire), 100, 168 (Peker), 133 (Maupuy), 378–79 (Génin), and 35, 56, 77, 89, 113, 123 (Vda. de Teresa), Copiador I (1889–1903), APH.

101. Unsigned to Fortoul Chapuy y Cia., January 1, 1900, p. 246, Copiador I (1889–1903), APH.

102. Remussat to Mme. Vve. J. Chapuy, May 25, 1909, p. 423, Copiador II (1903–1910), APH.

103. Unsigned to Fortoul Chapuy de Guadalajara, April 1, 1899, pp. 217, 218, Copiador I (1889–1903), APH. Sent on the same day, the first letter acknowledged the receipt of 15,500 pesos for the widow of Emilio Gandoulf and the second of 8,000 pesos

for the widow Remigio. Both were on terms of 7 percent with a sixty-day notice of withdrawal.

104. For the 3,000-peso deposit, see Unsigned to Pedro Padral, August 19, 1894, p. 57, Copiador I (1889–1903), APH. See also, for example, Joseph Tron to Sras. Vda. de Teresa é Hijas, July 1, 1895, p. 89, and Joseph Tron to Alfonso Ebrard, July 15, 1895, p. 90, Copiador I (1889–1903), APH.

105. Remussat to Proal, January 4, 1906, p. 330, Copiador II (1903–1910), APH. Proal, now retired, was a partner in the Puerto de Liverpool. Based on the 82,500-peso balance noted in the entry Henri Tron to Proal, July 16, 1903, p. 3, Copiador II (1903–1910), APH, his account had grown by 17,500 pesos in less than three years.

106. See Miller's chapter "Selling the Store" in *Bon Marche*, 190–230. Also consult Lancaster's chapter "Behind the Counter: Workers and the Department Store," in *Department Store*, 125–57. Finally, William R. Leach provides an American treatment of paternalism and employee benefits during this time period in *Land of Desire*, 115–22.

107. The best extended description of the clerk's life in a traditional cajón de ropa or almacén de novedades may be found in Chabrand, *De Barcelonnette*, 375–99, or the translated and reprinted version, *De Barceloneta a la República Mexicana* (Mexico City: Banco de México, 1987), 193–208.

108. All the French accounts of the Barcelonnettes discuss this issue to some degree. For the indebtedness of immigrants to their new employers for the cost of the voyage, see Arnaud et al., *Barcelonnettes au Mexique*, 21. I strongly recommend two contributions to this volume that rely heavily on the letters of Barcelonnette clerks to reconstruct their life in the valley, recruitment, voyage, and experience in Mexican department stores: Anselme Charpenel and Yvonne Charpenel, "L'épopée des Barcelonnettes," 52–72; and Pierre Martin-Charpenel, "Léon Martin au Mexique: Lettres (1902–1905)," 73–92.

109. Chabrand, *De Barcelonnette*, 261; and Arnaud et al., *Barcelonnettes au Mexique*, 21. Prominent examples of Basques in French business include Andres Eizaguirre— who was Ernesto Pugibet's treasurer and right-hand man at El Buen Tono—and Santiago Arechiderra—the Centro Mercantil Administrative Council member and president of the organizing committee for the 1910 Mexican Commerce Festival (see the end of chapter 4).

110. Lear, *Workers, Neighbors, and Citizens*, 74–75.

111. Buchenau, *Tools of Progress*, 66.

112. Wallace Thompson, *The Mexican Mind: A Study of National Psychology* (Boston: Little, Brown, 1922), 57.

113. *Massey-Gilbert Blue Book*, 206, 250, 251.

114. The Puerto de Veracruz, for example, claimed that each department could attend to the needs of customers in English, French, German, Italian, and Portuguese in addition to Spanish. *El Imparcial*, July 3, 1899, 4. For a pre-Porfirian example, see the ad in Maillefert, *Directorio del comercio*, 67, for the famous Zolly Hermanos haberdashery under the Portal de Mercaderes, which advertised its command of German, Spanish, French, and Italian.

115. Miller, *Bon Marché*, 193; Lancaster, *Department Store*, 125–29, 138.

116. Jennifer Jones, "*Coquettes* and *Grisettes*: Women Buying and Selling in Ancien Régime Paris" in de Grazia and Furlough, *Sex of Things*, 25–53.

117. The obviously female *modistas* and the primarily female-owned silk shops (*sederías*) continued to thrive in the Porfiriato much as they had during the 1860s. See their listings in Maillefert, *Directorio del comercio*, 292, 297.

118. Domenech, *Guía general descriptiva*, 2:760. As might be expected, this spatial confinement of female employees closely resembles that of the Bon Marché and other Parisian stores on which Mexican stores patterned themselves. Miller, *Bon Marché*, 78.

119. Proal and Charpenel, *Barcelonnettes en México*, 12.

120. Copy of reference letter for Srita. Jeanne Colón, January 2, 1903, p. 464, Copiador I (1889–1903), APH.

121. *Mexican Herald*, May 13, 1906, 9.

122. Henri Tron to Emilio Pimentel, October 31, 1906, p. 317, Copiador II (1903–1910), APH.

123. Miller, *Bon Marché*, 78.

124. *La Mujer Mexicana*, March 1905, back cover.

125. Rosa Warin to JYL, Mexico City, November 15, 1909, CDLIV 1909, roll 63, carp. 30, JYL-CEHM. Warin is probably the "French artist ladies' tailor" mentioned by a Ciudad de Londres ad in the *Mexican Herald* prior to the centennial celebrations, touting "the Paris Touch," which "confers distinction upon these street costumes." August 28, 1910, 12.

126. For the Puerto de Liverpool, see *Mexican Herald*, July 3, 1910, 8. For the Palacio de Hierro, *Mexican Herald*, August 25, 1910, 6; and in its four-hundred-page almanac/agenda gift to its customers, *Grandes Almacenes de "El Palacio de Hierro" obsequio a nuestros favorecedores. Agenda para el año 1900* (Mexico City: Tip. El Lápiz de Aguila, 1900), 47.

127. *Actualidades*, March 15, 1909, 13. This cartoon montage, titled "El Feminismo" (note the masculine gendering of what should be a feminine, *la feminisma*), offered thirteen images of why feminism would be great. These included female counter clerks serving male customers along with women serenading men, wearing pants, and offering up their tramcar seats to men.

128. Carson, *Mexico: Wonderland of the South*, 56.

129. For example, Morgan, "Proletarians, Politicos, and Patriarchs."

130. *Le Mexique*, May 5, 1898, 20, cited in Gouy, *Pérégrinations*, 60–63.

131. *Massey-Gilbert Blue Book*, 206, 213, 230, 251, 266, 271 (Palacio de Hierro); 213, 242 (Ciudad de Londres); 214, 218, 230, 243 (Puerto de Veracruz); and 250, 266 (Centro Mercantil).

132. Charpenel and Charpenel, "L'épopée," 67.

133. Martin-Charpenel, "Léon Martin," 84–85.

134. Lear, "Mexico City," 60.

135. *Le Courrier du Mexique*, April 8, 1898, 3.

136. Miller, *Bon Marché*, 190–221.

137. For information on the Cercle Français, see Arnaud et al., *Barcelonnettes au Mexique*, 40–41; and for the YMCA, see Glenn Avent, "A Popular and Wholesome Resort: Gender, Class, and the YMCA in Porfirian Mexico" (master's thesis, University of British Columbia, 1996).

138. Miller, *Bon Marché*, 192–97. For the literary genre on the perils of consumption for women as consumers or clerks, browse through Emile Zola, *Au bonheur des dames* (Paris: Charpentier, 1883); Margarete Böhme, *The Department Store: A Novel of To-Day*, trans. Ethel Colburn Mayne (New York: D. Appleton, 1912); Theodore Dreiser, *Sister Carrie* (New York: Penguin, 1981); Paul Dubuisson, *Les voleuses de grands magasins* (Paris: A. Storck, 1902); and M. F. Honoré, *Les employés de commerce á Paris au point de vue social* (Paris: n.p., 1895).

139. One popular and widely read source for the sexual danger or license found between store personnel and their customers was the cheap and usually racy paperbacks offered by the *bibliotecas económicas*, or popular bookstores. As discussed in chapter 2, these printers and retailers possessed an impressive distribution network for their products as well as an avid reader base. Proof that these books did choose department stores as their setting comes in an article titled "Flirting at the Counter" in *El Imparcial*, December 18, 1897, 2. The article recounts the recent occurrence of an employee of a cajón making sexual advances toward a female customer trying on gloves. It blames "this commercial epidemic of flirting learned in the novels of the bibliotecas económicas."

140. González Navarro, *El Porfiriato: La vida social*, 350.

141. *Le Courrier du Mexique*, August 23, 1902, 2.

142. The society planned a new reunion center that opened late in 1910, including a café, billiards, library, and "all games permitted by law." *Le Courrier du Mexique*, October 31, 1906, 3.

143. *Le Courrier du Mexique*, January 12, 1905, 3.

144. González Navarro, *El Porfiriato: La vida social*, 288.

145. Ibid.

146. Both Anselme Charpenel and León Martin describe this in their letters as Barcelonnette clerks. Arnaud et al., *Barcelonnettes au Mexique*, 66, 81.

147. *La Semana Mercantil*, March 23, 1896, 157–58.

148. It is important to note that the press largely supported employee demands for Sunday as a day of rest under the umbrella of progress. A lively conversation among the newspapers in the capital ensued and lasted for at least four months. Employees of department and other stores carrying multiple product lines were joined by employees of the *camiserías* and *sederías*. Meetings attracted over five hundred attendees. See, for example, *Le Courrier du Mexique*, August 20, 1902, 3; August 21, 1902, 2; and August 23, 1902, 2. Additional articles can be found in *El Imparcial*, August 23, 1902, 2; October 6, 1902, 2; October 9, 1902, 3; and October 16, 1902, 3.

149. González Navarro, *El Porfiriato: La vida social*, 287.

150. Arnaud et al., *Barcelonnettes au Mexique*, 82.

151. González Navarro, *El Porfiriato: La vida social*, 288. Eugène Pottier wrote the lyrics to *L'Internationale* in 1870.

152. Arnaud et al., *Barcelonnettes au Mexique*, 83, 84, 85.

153. In his introduction, Michael Miller considers how the Bon Marché reflected these trends in French society. Miller, *Bon Marché*, 3–16.

154. Curtis, *Capitals of Spanish America*, 39.

155. Nevin O. Winter, *Mexico and Her People of Today: An Account of the Customs, Characteristics, Amusements, History and Advancement of the Mexicans, and the Development and Resources of Their Country*, rev. ed. (Boston: L. C. Page, 1923), 162–63; first published in 1907.

156. Miller, *Bon Marché*, 165–66.

157. Maillefert, *Directorio del comercio*, 193, 201.

158. See Chabrand, *De Barcelonnette*, 375–95, for the whole account of the store.

159. Buchenau, *Tools of Progress*, 57.

160. Chabrand, *De Barcelonnette*, 391, 392. Chabrand includes two accounts, one of Indian peons from the hacienda and another, on page 391, of "less-civilized" Indians whose backward state is made obvious by their lack of foot- and headwear.

161. Bianconi, *Le Mexique*, 116.

162. Ibid., 113.

163. *Catálogo de la biblioteca del Señor Licenciado don José Y. Limantour* (Mexico City: n.p., 1913).

164. French, *Peaceful and Working People*, 4–7.

165. In a 1906 Palacio de Hierro catalog in my possession, men's coats, shirts, and ties occupy pages 61–66 and 70–78. Unfortunately, the first pages are missing and, as a consequence, so too is the information on the exact season and product line emphasis.

166. Although ads for these two make obvious their clientele, one entry in the *Mexican Herald*, July 3, 1910, 3, states clearly, "We Deal Only in Clothing for Men and Boys."

167. Perhaps one of the most enlightening examples of Porfirian elite males as conscientious shoppers comes from a series of exchanges among Limantour, Díaz, and Carmelita (Díaz's wife). Limantour is on a lengthy vacation in Paris and the sea resort of Biarritz. He describes in detail his choice of diamonds and emeralds from three different Paris jewelers—Cartier, Morel, and Boucheron—and which jeweler will set those stones in a collar and tiara. He documents the plans of each house meticulously and explains his decisions in terms of "good taste" (*buen gusto*). He concludes his last letter to Carmelita with, "Believe me, Carmelita, I am your most addicted and sincere friend." See in particular, Porfirio Díaz to JYL, Mexico City, November 20, 1906, JYL to Carmelita, Paris, May 24, 1906, and JYL to Carmelita, Biarritz, August 4, 1906, CDLIV 1906, roll 37, carp. 1, JYL-CEHM.

168. For published work, see Macías-González, "*Lagartijo* at *The High Life*," 228–49.

169. See photo in Proal and Charpenel, *Empire des Barcelonnettes*, 39.

170. Domenech, *Guía general descriptiva*, 1:261.

171. Maillefert, *Directorio del comercio*, 192, 197.

172. Thompson, *Mexican Mind*, 57.
173. *Mexican Herald*, December 25, 1895, 8.

Chapter 4

1. Among others, see Mary Douglas and Baron Isherwood, *The World of Goods: Towards an Anthropology of Consumption* (New York: W. W. Norton, 1978); Chandra Mukerji, *From Graven Images: Patterns of Modern Materialism* (New York: Columbia University Press, 1983); and McCracken, *Culture and Consumption*.
2. "El Palacio de Hierro: Que hay detrás del nombre?" A copy of this single-sheet document, published probably in the 1980s, was given to me by one of the two caretakers of the Archivo Palacio de Hierro. A list of stores and addresses from 1864, in Arnaud et al., *Barcelonnettes au Mexique*, 28, confirms Las Fábricas' existence.
3. From "La Historia de nuestra empresa," n.d. This three-page document was also given to me at the Archivo Palacio de Hierro.
4. Elite Barcelonnettes traveled regularly, especially during the last half of the Porfiriato. Many maintained homes in Mexico, but I suspect many others followed Julio Tron of the Palacio, who lived with his family in a hotel while in Mexico City. See *Le Courrier du Mexique*, February 10, 1898, 2, announcing Tron and his family's return from Europe to the Hotel Sanze.
5. Chabrand, *De Barcelonnette*, 249; Miller, *Bon Marché*, 35. In 1895 the population of Mexico City was estimated to be between 330,000 and 340,000, with the whole federal district at just under 450,000. González Navarro, *Estadísticas sociales*, 7; *Estadísticas históricas*, 32.
6. "La Historia de nuestra empresa," 1.
7. Gouy, *Pérégrinations*, 61. For an excellent study of the architecture and significance of the Palacio, see Martínez Gutiérrez, *El Palacio de Hierro*.
8. Gouy, *Pérégrinations*, 61.
9. "El Palacio de Hierro: Que hay detrás del nombre?"
10. Buchenau, *Tools of Progress*, 62.
11. *Le Courrier du Mexique*, April 8, 1898, 3; April 14, 1898, 3.
12. Proal and Charpenel, *Empire des Barcelonnettes*, 35.
13. Ibid.; Buchenau, *Tools of Progress*, 59; Lear, "Mexico City," 74–75.
14. Ariel Rodríguez Kuri, *La experiencia olvidada. El Ayuntamiento de México: Política y gobierno, 1876–1912* (Mexico City: El Colegio de México, 1996), esp. 51–80.
15. H. Tron to JYL, September 27, 1905, Mexico City, CDLIV 1905, roll 36, carp. 22, JYL-CEHM.
16. Domenech, *Guía general descriptiva*, 1:261.
17. "Vender barato para vender mucho," *El Imparcial*, July 3, 1899, 4.
18. *Álbum oficial*, n.p. The introductory editorial section is paginated (twelve pages) but the subsequent two hundred pages (approximately) of photographs are not.
19. See the ad placed by La Esmeralda owners Hauser and Zivy in *El Imparcial*, January 26, 1908, 8. It lists the location and purchasers of all the public clocks that they

had installed across the republic. For the classic account of time discipline and capitalism, see E. P. Thompson, "Time, Work-Discipline, and Industrial Capitalism," *Past and Present* 38, no. 1 (1967): 56–97.

20. For Porfirian home interior decoration and organization, see Tello Peón, "Intención decorativa."

21. *El Entreacto*, March 8, 1908, 1.

22. *Le Courrier du Mexique*, November 29, 1902, 3.

23. *El Tiempo Ilustrado*, April 26, 1892, 12.

24. *Modern Mexico*, January 1897, 12.

25. Alan MacFarlane and Gerry Martin, *Glass: A World History* (Chicago: University of Chicago Press, 2002), 11.

26. Jones, "*Coquettes* and *Grisettes*," 33.

27. MacFarlane and Martin, *Glass*, 204. These new furnaces could reach temperatures of over fifteen hundred degrees Fahrenheit. The addition of soda or potash reduced the melting point of silica to just below nine hundred degrees Fahrenheit.

28. Maillefert, *Directorio del comercio*, 193, 201.

29. Ibid., 147.

30. Ibid., 156.

31. *Glass, Paints, Varnishes and Brushes: Their History, Manufacture and Use* (Pittsburgh: Pittsburgh Plate Glass Company, 1923), 31.

32. J. Tron to E. Heuer y Cia., Mexico City, April 20, 1897, Copiador 1889–1903, p. 153, APH. The cost of 330 pesos equaled roughly one year's salary for unskilled workers or beginning department store clerks in the capital and approximately four or five months' salary for a more senior clerk.

33. *El Mundo Ilustrado*, November 3, 1901, 11.

34. Gregory Shaya has offered an important way of looking at the urban crowd, viewing it as a cultural construction of the mass commercial press and a representation of contemporary cultural concerns. Shaya, "The *Flâneur*, the *Badaud*, and the Making of a Mass Public in France, circa 1860–1910," *American Historical Review* 109, no. 1 (February 2004): 41–77.

35. Leach, *Land of Desire*, 55–61.

36. Domenech, *Guía general descriptiva*, 1:242.

37. Miller, *Bon Marché*, 42.

38. *Mexican Herald*, March 11, 1906, 9.

39. A basic mannequin may be seen in a Ciudad de Londres ad in *El Mundo Ilustrado*, July 18, 1909, 12; much fancier, fully fleshed-out, and poised displays exhibiting the wedding trousseau of an elite Porfirian woman in the display window of an undisclosed store appear in the *Semana Ilustrada*, January 14, 1910, 14.

40. For information about open displays in the United States refer to Abelson, *When Ladies Go A-Thieving*.

41. For mention of the British system, see Lancaster, *Department Store*, 28. Perhaps the best way to conceive of this arrangement is to imagine the BBC comedy *Are You Being Served?* in a Porfirian Mexico context.

42. This number derives from a count of departments listed throughout *Grandes Almacenes de "El Palacio de Hierro."* The index on pages 395–99 offers a near-complete list. See table 1, at the end of this chapter.

43. *Le Courrier du Mexique*, December 30, 1889, 7.

44. One ad that lists many of the French companies represented by the museum is found in *Le Courrier du Mexique*, October 20, 1890, 4.

45. For an important way of looking at the 1851 exhibition through the eyes of consumption, gender, and different national meanings of modernity, see Walton, *France at the Crystal Palace.*

46. Lancaster, *Department Store*, 17.

47. The description of each floor comes from an account of the store inauguration found in Gouy, *Pérégrinations*, 62.

48. A full description of the Palacio return policy may be read in *Grandes Almacenes de "El Palacio de Hierro,"* 4.

49. Ibid., 47.

50. For both stores, see *La Semana en el Hogar*, July 22, 1895, 2. See also the approving, if not completely gushing, article noting the retailing advances made by the Palacio in *El Tiempo Ilustrado*, April 14, 1892, 16. Strangely, the Palacio's own brief historical account ("La Historia de nuestra empresa") places 1894 as the date at which the store switched over to fixed prices.

51. In *Grandes Almacenes de "El Palacio de Hierro,"* 3, a lengthy explanation of store policies ensues. Under the title "General Principles of this Department Store" the agenda states, "Our system of sales, marking the prices of *each merchandise* in known numbers and being INVARIABLY FIXED, has effectively contributed to the always growing reputation of this business that enjoys the reputation as the first of its class in the Republic." As this extract suggests, the Palacio and other stores took their adoption of fixed pricing extremely seriously and promoted it as a truly progressive act that saved both time and money for consumers. The Palacio never missed the opportunity to advertise that it was the first store in the republic to institute the policy.

52. A sample from editorials and advertisements: *La Semana en el Hogar*, July 22, 1895, 2; *Le Courrier du Mexique*, November 13, 1898, 3; and *El Imparcial*, September 25, 1899, 4.

53. See, for example, the ad for the Galeria de Ropa Hecha on Santa Clara Street, which repeats twice that its inventory (of a considerable fifty thousand articles of ready-made clothing) sells at fixed prices. *El Eco Nacional*, January 11, 1857, 4.

54. *La Semana Mercantil*, May 20, 1889, 299–300; January 29, 1894, 53–54. See also *La Semana en el Hogar*, July 22, 1895, 2.

55. *La Semana Mercantil*, March 22, 1909, 155–56.

56. Miller, *Bon Marché*, 54.

57. *México Gráfico*, November 25, 1888, 4; Francois, *Culture of Everyday Credit.*

58. *El Imparcial*, August 1, 1906, 6; *Mexican Herald*, April 29, 1906, 16.

59. See Emilio Sola (architect) to JYL, Mexico City, June 7, 1908, CDLIV 1908, roll 55,

carp. 25, JYL-CEHM; and JYL to Guillermo de Heredia (architect), Mexico City, November 5, 1909, CDLIV 1909, roll 61, carp. 19, JYL-CEHM. Sola owed a mere 1,700 pesos, including 283 pesos to the Palacio, over 300 pesos to jewelers, and over 350 pesos to clothing and crystal shops. Heredia owed over 30,000 pesos, including 12,000 pesos to various banks. Of the rest he owed over 1,000 pesos to the Puerto de Veracruz, lesser amounts to the Ciudad de Londres and the Puerto de Liverpool, and nearly 1,000 pesos each to the jeweler La Perla and the interior decorator Claudio Pellandini.

60. On the importance of gift exchange and the distinction between materialistic values and "a materials-intensive way of life, which may use goods as means to other ends," consult Michael Schudson, *Advertising, the Uneasy Persuasion* (New York: Basic Books, 1984), 135–43.

61. Miller, *Bon Marché*, 62, 70–71.

62. The image of abundance and plenty in Porfirian celebrations, marketing, and department stores marks an important use of longstanding popular culture imagery by producers, merchants, and the leadership of society to legitimize and normalize the current system of economic and social organization. T. J. Jackson Lears provides a thought-provoking treatment of this subject in *Fables of Abundance: A Cultural History of Advertising in America* (New York: Basic Books, 1994).

63. Miller, *Bon Marché*, 34, discusses the important of ready-made clothing in the rise of mass retailing. Lower prices and faster transaction times were two important qualities.

64. François Delamare and Bernard Guineau, *Colors: The Story of Dyes and Pigments*, trans. Sophie Hawkes (New York: Harry N. Abrams, 2000), 99–103; Stuart Robinson, *A History of Dyed Textiles* (Cambridge, MA: MIT Press, 1969), 33–36.

65. Cissie Fairchilds offers a portrait of this decline in "The Production and Marketing of Populuxe Goods in Eighteenth-Century Paris" in Brewer and Porter, *Consumption and the World of Goods*, 228–48.

66. Miller, *Bon Marché*, 27, 33.

67. Carnival, with its subversive, world-inverting role, enjoys a special position in cultural studies. A sampling of its evolutionary place in academic studies can be found in Mikhail Bakhtin, *Rabelais and His World*, trans. Helene Iswolsky (Cambridge, MA: MIT Press, 1968); Emmanuel Le Roy Ladurie, *Carnival in Romans*, trans. Mary Feeney (New York: George Braziller, 1980); and Joseph Roach, *Cities of the Dead: Circum-Atlantic Performance* (New York: Columbia University Press, 1996).

68. *El Imparcial*, March 17, 1907, 6. Another image was an all-female one. The Palacio ad in the *Mexican Herald*, July 29, 1906, 13, announced a summer closeout sale. An image of well-dressed women thronging into the store sits above a list of goods and prices. Between the two a paragraph of text hypes the sale and promises more than 50 percent savings, extra clerks, and extra delivery wagons. Finally, it reminds customers, "Positively no goods charged at these prices."

69. *El Imparcial*, August 1, 1906, 6.

70. *El Imparcial*, January 17, 1905, 5.

71. *Grandes Almacenes de "El Palacio de Hierro,"* 129.

72. An example of this is José Yves Limantour dealing directly with London shops for clothing for his son. He requested catalogs and material patterns for overcoats, Eton suits, tweed suits, and other items as well as requesting samples of material. On other occasions he sent sizing information and discussed fabrics with London tailors via mail correspondence. See the dialogue between Samuel Brothers of London and Limantour: Samuel Brothers to JYL, London, September 21, 1904, and JYL to Samuel Brothers, Mexico City, November 10, 1904, CDLIV 1904, roll 29, carp. 26, JYL-CEHM.

73. The best sources are in *Le Courrier du Mexique*, November 18, 1906, 3–4; and December 16, 1906, 4. Also see the preparations for this event and the offer of a Parisian "expert decorator" to help arrange every room in a house in preparation for a reception in *Mexican Herald*, July 8, 1906, 16. Four year later, in 1910, a commemorative album of the centennial celebrations noted its special displays exhibiting furnished rooms for every part of a home: "salons, boudoirs, bedrooms, dressing rooms, libraries, smoking rooms, etc." Eugenio Espino Barros, *Crónica gráfica*, 60–61.

74. Tello Peón, "Intención decorativa."

75. For an account of furniture and its cost at the Palacio, see *El Imparcial*, October 13, 1903, 2. Jorge de Unna regularly placed full-page ads. He effectively combined photos of his furniture and letters from government ministries thanking him for the tasteful furnishing of their offices. One example is that from the Secretaría de Justicia é Instrucción Pública describing the Louis XIV style used in the reception room as "elegant," "in good taste," and "equaling the best foreign work." *El Mundo Ilustrado*, January 25, 1903, 20. See also *El Mundo Ilustrado*, May 20, 1900, 14; July 8, 1900, 14; and August 26, 1900, 14.

76. See *Le Courrier du Mexique*, November 18, 1906, 8.

77. Miller, *Bon Marché*, 180.

78. An example of this dreadful image can be seen in an ad for the Puerto de Veracruz in the *Mexican Herald*, January 14, 1906, 4. See also *México, ¿quieres tomarte una foto conmigo?*, 83–84.

79. Palacio de Hierro catalog for 1906(?), pp. 3–9, copy in author's collection. A catalog for a store specializing in weddings is *Le trousseau: Gran casa de modas y artículos de lujo para señora*, owned by Victoria A. de Villa (Amador Trade Catalog Collection, New Mexico State University, Las Cruces). This catalog, addressed to gentlemen, stays closer to traditional bridegroom-to-bride gift arrangements. It includes only women's clothing and accessories, all made in France.

80. The most famous almanac in Mexico is that of Galván. For a brief history of agendas and almanacs in France, see Miller, *Bon Marché*, 187–89.

81. *Grandes Almacenes de "El Palacio de Hierro."* Other department stores undoubtedly followed, but when I cannot say with certainty. By 1908 Fábricas Universales offered one. *Le Courrier du Mexique*, January 3, 1908, 2. The Puerto de Veracruz continued to offer through 1904, at least, a calendar and aluminum ashtray as Christmas gifts for its customers. *El Imparcial*, January 17, 1904, 4.

82. These specific topics are covered in the "Agenda Instructiva" on pp. 214, 315, and 350.

83. *Grandes Almacenes de "El Palacio de Hierro,"* 1.

84. *La Semana Ilustrada*, December 24, 1909, back cover. See also *El Imparcial*, December 16, 1907, 8, for another Palacio Christmas ad for toys, featuring over fifty illustrations, including tennis sets, dolls and dollhouse furnishings, gun sets, billiard sets, automobile/chauffeur/garage sets, toy pianos, and a puppet theater featuring one character being hanged to death. Toys do tell a great deal about a society.

85. A sample: for a ball at the Casino Español (Palacio de Hierro), *El Imparcial*, April 27, 1909, 8; Flower Wars (Puerto de Liverpool), *El Imparcial*, May 2, 1909, 12; the Centennial (Fábricas Universales), *Mexican Herald,* August 26, 1910, 2; American Independence (El Importador, Palacio de Hierro, Puerto de Veracruz, Ciudad de Londres), *Mexican Herald*, July 3, 1910, 6, 7, 11, 16; and presidential fiestas (Puerto de Veracruz), *Le Courrier du Mexique*, December 30, 1900, 2.

86. For just two examples of this, see the comments of Luis G. Urbina in *El Mundo Ilustrado*, December 9, 1906, 1; and *El Imparcial*, October 22, 1907, 1, on public entertainments and the unique role of the middling classes to "thanklessly toil toward national progress." The newspaper *La Clase Media* offers a nonstop espousal of such a view, beginning with its first edition on June 1, 1908.

87. For information on Carreño and his *Manual de urbanidad y buenas maneras*, first published in 1853 and now past the fortieth edition, see Bauer, *Goods, Power, History*, 134–37. See also La Condesa de Tramar, *El trato social: Costumbres de la sociedad moderna en todas las circumstancia de la vida. Nueva guía de la gente elegante, traducido, anotado y adaptado á la sociedad de México con la colaboración de distinguidas damas mexicanas* (Paris: Librería de la Viuda de Ch. Bouret, 1906); and José Rosas Moreno, *Nuevo manual en verso de urbanidad y buenas maneras* (Mexico City: Antigua Librería de Murguía, [1880?]). These are just a few of the many manuals in circulation at this time.

88. *Le Courrier du Mexique*, February 27, 1907, 3.

89. For example, *El Imparcial*, September 16, 1899, 1–2; *El Mundo Ilustrado*, January 13, 1901, 4–5; and September 21, 1902, 5–6.

90. In particular, see *El Tiempo Ilustrado*, May 4, 1903, 210–11. For the Fiesta Floral, or Flower War, the Surtidor store draped flowers and Persian rugs over its second- and fourth-floor railings along with an enormous banner above that announced, "THE BEST SELECTION OF RUGS AND TAPESTRIES IN THE CAPITAL."

91. For American Independence (El Importador, Palacio de Hierro, Puerto de Veracruz, Ciudad de Londres), *Mexican Herald*, July 3, 1910, 6, 7, 11, 16; for Spanish Fiestas de Covadonga, *El Imparcial*, September 9, 1904, 1.

92. *Le Courrier du Mexique*, July 16, 1899, 2; *El Imparcial* July 15, 1899, 1; *Le Courrier du Mexique*, July 15, 1900, 2.

93. For a chronological range of this practice, consult *Le Courrier du Mexique*, July 9, 1888, 3; and *Le Courrier du Mexique*, July 19, 1908, 2.

94. Sam Bass Warner, "Slums and Skyscrapers: Urban Images, Symbols, and Ideology," in *Cities of the Mind: Images and Themes of the City in the Social Sciences*, ed.

L. Rodwin and R. Hollister (New York: Plenum Press, 1984), 183. This, along with the idea of the city as a cultural creation, is cited in Daniel R. Brower, *The Russian City between Tradition and Modernity, 1850–1900* (Berkeley: University of California Press, 1990), 2.

95. Domingo Sarmiento, *Facundo; or, Civilization and Barbarism*, trans. Mary Peabody Mann (1845; reprint, New York: Penguin Books, 1998). For the impact of Sarmiento and his views on the making of Argentina (and for a taste of similar intellectual currents throughout Latin America during the nineteenth century), see Nicolas Shumway, *The Invention of Argentina* (Berkeley: University of California Press, 1993), esp. 130–40. For a fine synopsis of the meaning of the city in colonial Latin America see Bauer, *Goods, Power, History*, 58–63.

96. Sources on this issue are many. Here are two: Alan Knight, *The Mexican Revolution* (Lincoln: University of Nebraska Press, 1990), 1:78–170; and French, *Peaceful and Working People*. For the allure of the city for small-town Porfirians, see González, *San José de Gracia*, 96–102.

97. Although the Hapsburg period was not completely devoid of such efforts, officials sought public support for their rule through policies favorable toward popular culture and society. For an illustration of the sharp distinction in ruling philosophies between Hapsburg and Bourbon officials, see Linda A. Curcio-Nagy, *The Great Festivals of Colonial Mexico City: Performing Power and Identity* (Albuquerque: University of New Mexico Press, 2004); and Curcio-Nagy, "Giants and Gypsies."

98. Juan Pedro Viqueira Albán, *¿Relajados o reprimidos? Diversiones públicas y vida social en la ciudad de México durante el Siglo de las Luces* (Mexico City: Fondo de Cultura Económica, 1987), 229.

99. Viqueira Albán, *¿Relajados o reprimidos?*, stands out as a classic text on this subject. See also Curcio, *Great Festivals*; and Clara García Ayluardo, "A World of Images: Cult, Ritual, and Society in Colonial Mexico City," in Beezley, Martin, and French, *Rituals of Rule*, 77–94.

100. Anne Staples, "Policía y Buen Gobierno: Municipal Efforts to Regulate Public Behavior, 1821–1857," in Beezley, Martin, and French, *Rituals of Rule*, 115–26; Shannon Baker Tuller, "Santa Anna's Legacy: Caudillismo in Early Republican Mexico (Antonio López de Santa Anna)" (PhD diss., Texas Christian University, 1999).

101. For a visual tour of the losses suffered by ecclesiastical properties in the name of urban development, see Guillermo Tovar de Teresa, *La Ciudad de los Palacios: Crónica de un patrimonio perdido*, vol. 2 (Mexico City: Vuelta, 1992). For the scope of the transformation, note the map on page 6.On the comprehensive planning and redevelopment of downtown Newcastle, see Lancaster, *Department Store*, 8.

102. Tenenbaum, "Streetwise History," esp. 128–29.

103. Among the many: Tenenbaum, "Streetwise History"; Beezley, *Judas at the Jockey Club*; Bunker, "Consumers of Good Taste"; and Sandra Kuntz Ficker and Priscilla Connolly, coords., *Ferrocarriles y obras públicas* (Mexico City: Instituto Mora, 1992).

104. On the regulation of morality, a moral geography of vice, and its importance in defining citizenship in modern Mexico, see French, *Peaceful and Working People*; Robert M. Buffington and William E. French, "The Culture of Modernity," in *The Oxford History of Mexico*, ed. Michael C. Meyer and William H. Beezley (New York: Oxford University Press, 2000); Piccato, *City of Suspects*; and Robert Buffington, *Criminal and Citizen in Modern Mexico* (Lincoln: University of Nebraska Press, 1999).

105. Riedel, *Practical Guide*, 178, 185.

106. Today the Portal de las Flores has given way to the offices of the Department of the Federal District (DDF) as well as the widening of the Callejuela, now named Veinte de Noviembre, a project that took place in the 1930s. Tovar de Teresa, *Ciudad de los palacios*, 2:109–12.

107. Tovar de Teresa, *Ciudad de los palacios*, 2:40–41. A petition to the ayuntamiento in 1885 by the merchants of the portal confirms this French dominance. See Gregorio Llacuria and five others (all French) to Juan Bribiesca (Comisión de Hacienda y Mercados), December 21, 1885, exp. 50, Portales 1559–1918, tomo I, AACM.

108. Chabrand, *De Barcelonnette*, 375.

109. Elías, *150 años*, 42.

110. Ibid., 63.

111. Ibid., 68.

112. See the ad in *El Norte*, June 4, 1915, 4, displaying two spiffily dressed soldiers under the heading "Para artículos militares: La ciudad de Londres."

113. *Le Courrier du Mexique*, June 2, 1910, 2, states that the suggestion of the National Chamber patronizing the celebrations on their own day came from Eugène Roux, the president of the French Chamber of Commerce in Mexico.

114. *Le Courrier du Mexique*, June 11, 1910, 2.

115. *Artes y Letras*, September 11, 1910, 2.

116. *Le Courrier du Mexique*, September 5, 1910, 2.

117. For photographs of the event, especially the allegorical cars, see the eight-page edition of *Artes y Letras*, September 11, 1910.

118. *Le Mexique*, September 5, 1910, 267.

119. *Artes y Letras*, September 11, 1910, 4.

120. *La Clase Media*, March 27, 1910, 22.

121. *Le Courrier du Mexique*, September 3, 1910, 3.

122. *Le Courrier du Mexique*, July 11, 1910, 3.

123. For plans, see *Le Courrier du Mexique*, August 19, 1910, 3; and August 25, 1910, 2. For a description of the garden party and for photographs, see *Artes y Letras*, September 11, 1910, 8.

Chapter 5

1. The above account is a composite of several shoplifting cases, descriptions of shoplifters, and accounts of customer-clerk interactions. For photos of Juana and

María, see the "Página negra" feature in *La Gaceta de Policía*, January 7, 1906, 11. Other sources for this shoplifting scene are *La Gaceta de Policía*, February 4, 1906, 15; February 11, 1906, 15; October 16, 1906, 15; *Echo du Mexique*, April 9, 1897, 2; and Zola, *Au bonheur des dames* (Paris: Charpentier, 1883), 176. For one example of customer-clerk dialogue, see *La Semana en el Hogar*, July 22, 1895, 3. For another interaction revealing the sexual tension represented by the counter trade, see *El Imparcial*, December 18, 1897, 2, which reproduces the sexual advances of a male employee on a female customer trying on gloves. The article blames "this commercial epidemic of flirting on pulp-fiction novels [*novelas de bibliotecas económicas*]." For more on these novels, refer to chapter 2 and its account of the story and sales of *Los 41*, one of the most famous of these novels during the Porfiriato. See Irwin, McCaughan, and Rocío Nasser, *Famous 41*.

2. Not all newspapers reported on crime. Of the many that did, I have concentrated on the following: *Le Courrier du Mexique* and *L'Echo du Mexique* as the voice of the French colony and the largest department and clothing store interests and as representatives of extremely influential foreign "civilizing" opinion; *La Semana Mercantil* as the voice of the National Chamber of Commerce and an advocate of national economic and cultural modernization; *El Imparcial* as the largest-circulation daily and a practitioner of sensationalist journalism; and *La Gaceta de Policía* as both pure, sensationalist tabloid on the issue of law and order as well as a rich source of editorializing and mug shots of criminals, featured on its regular "Página negra" (Black page).

3. Abelson, *When Ladies Go A-Thieving*; Patricia O'Brien, "Bourgeois Women and Theft," *Journal of Social History* 17, no.1 (Fall 1983): 65–77; Miller, *Bon Marché*, 197–205.

4. Lancaster, *Department Store*, 184–86.

5. *L'Echo du Mexique*, July 7, 1896, 2; October 24, 1896, 2; April 9, 1897, 2.

6. *La Gaceta de Policía*, October 7, 1906, 15.

7. *El Imparcial*, January 7, 1899, 2.

8. *La Gaceta de Policía*, February 4, 1906, 15.

9. *La Gaceta de Policía*, February 11, 1906, 15.

10. *L'Echo du Mexique*, January 14, 1893, 2.

11. *La Gaceta de Policía*, October 7, 1906, 15.

12. Weeklies such as *El Mundo Ilustrado* usually boasted a column assisting women in proper etiquette and fashion. *El Mundo Ilustrado* offered "consultas de las damas" in which it often recommended requesting samples from stores as well as advised readers on swatches of fabric that they had sent to the newspaper. The best account of á vistas comes from *La Semana Mercantil*, May 20, 1889, 299–300, and its listing of items often requested and the social networks through which goods passed before returning to the store.

13. *El Mundo Ilustrado*, February 18, 1900, 18–20; *La Semana Mercantil*, May 20, 1889, 299–300.

14. See *El Imparcial*, September 2, 1902, 1; and September 3, 1902, 4. The first report describes what appears to be a robbery as two beautiful, well-dressed young

women unknown to the store supposedly entrance the young male clerk, receive jewels worth 600 pesos to take "á vistas," and drive off in a carriage before the owner hears the story and calls the police. This appears to be a classic case of theft by *elegantes*. The next day, however, the women return without knowing of the controversy and ask to purchase the jewels. The jeweler, embarrassed, begs their forgiveness as they begin to cry. He redoubles his efforts, "making comic manifestations of repentance."

15. Abelson, *When Ladies Go A-Thieving*, 82–83.

16. Marie Eileen Francois, *A Culture of Everyday Credit*.

17. *La Semana Mercantil*, December 2, 1895, 568–69.

18. For more on the bicycle mania sweeping the capital, see Beezley, *Judas at the Jockey Club*.

19. *L'Echo du Mexique*, October 2, 1896, 2. In this case, thieves broke into the depot of the Standard Bike Co. on trendy San Francisco Avenue and stole seven bikes worth 1,500 pesos. Police immediately informed local pawnshops.

20. See "Los robos en los Almacenes," *La Semana Mercantil*, May 15, 1905, 233; *Le Courrier du Mexique*, May 6, 1905, 3; May 10, 1905, 3.

21. *El Imparcial*, October 4, 1899, 3.

22. See, for example, Winter, *Mexico and Her People Today*, 340; and Carson, *Mexico: Wonderland of the South*, 95.

23. *Le Courrier du Mexique*, June 9, 1905, 3.

24. Abelson, *When Ladies Go A-Thieving*, 86.

25. The Chamber of Commerce continued to complain through the end of the Porfiriato—and beyond—as seen in *La Semana Mercantil*, May 24, 1909, 283–84.

26. Francisco J. Santamaria, *Diccionario de mejicanismos* (Mexico City: Editorial Porrua, 1959), 314. I confess that in my early research on department stores with a related interest in crime I passed over this term quite a few times before realizing what it meant. The dictionaries of contemporary Spanish that I consulted had left me more confused than enlightened. This experience drove home yet again the value of reference materials such as dictionaries specific to the historical period under consideration. Carlos Roumagnac defines *cruzadoras* (not *cruzadores*) as "women who rob clothing stores" in his list of Mexican street slang. See Roumagnac, *Los criminales en México: Ensayo de psicología criminal* (Mexico City: Tip. "El Fenix," 1904), 378.

27. For a foreigner's view of this urban type, see the full-page article in the monthly newsmagazine *Modern Mexico*, March 1903, 32.

28. C. C. H. Marc, *De la folie considerée dans ses rapports avec les questions medico-judiciaires*, 2 vols. (Paris: J.-B. Baillière, 1840).

29. Miller, *Bon Marché*, 205.

30. Abelson, *When Ladies Go A-Thieving*, 11.

31. Ibid., 161–62.

32. Miller, *Bon Marché*, 197.

33. Abelson, *When Ladies Go A-Thieving*, 10.

34. *L'Echo du Mexique*, October 24, 1896, 2.
35. For France, see Weber, *France*; for Germany, see Breckman, "Disciplining Consumption"; for Mexico through the lens of masculinity, consult Macías-González, "Mexican Aristocracy"; for the United States, Gail Bederman, *Manliness and Civilization: A Cultural History of Gender and Race in the United States, 1880–1917* (Chicago: University of Chicago Press, 1995).
36. William E. French, "Moralizing the Masses," chapter 2 in *Peaceful and Working People*, 35–62; Pablo Piccato, "The Discourse About Alcoholism and Criminality in Mexico City, 1890–1917" (master's thesis, University of Texas at Austin, 1993).
37. A few examples of the mug shot galleries may be found in the following editions of *La Gaceta de Policía*: December 17, 1905, 9; December 24, 1905, 11; January 7, 1906, 11; January 21, 1906, 13; February 11, 1906, 15; February 15, 1906, 15; February 18, 1906, 15; August 12, 1906, 15; October 7, 1906, 15; November 11, 1906, 16; and April 19, 1908, 15.
38. In late 1897 an article in the French newspaper *L'Echo du Mexique* documents how a woman entered a jewelry store and stole a watch left on the counter while the clerks were otherwise occupied. *L'Echo du Mexique*, October 7, 1897, 2. What makes this not-infrequent event remarkable for the reader of dozens of these accounts is that the woman is described as "une femme du peuple," meaning she was a traditionally dressed Indian and probably quite poor. This is not to say that press coverage of criminal acts by the lower classes was a novelty. Nothing could be further from the truth, as newspapers covered popular criminality ad nauseam. The point is that the criminal did not match the crime in terms of habitual coverage in the press. When a singular account such as this shakes the reader from an assumed trajectory in the text, then the idea should be entertained that for consumers of the Porfirian press a narrative of shoplifting had already formed by the 1890s.
39. "La mona vestida en seda, mona se queda."
40. *El Imparcial*, December 30, 1903, 1.
41. *La Gaceta de Policía*, August 2, 1906, 15.
42. Bakhtin, *Rabelais and His World*; Le Roy Ladurie, *Carnival in Romans*. For specific cases of transformed Carnival celebrations in Chihuahua and Monterrey during the Porfiriato, see Steven B. Bunker, "Making the Good Old Days: Invented Tradition and Civic Ritual in Northern Mexico, 1880–1910" (honours essay, University of British Columbia, 1992), 43–51.
43. *El Imparcial*, November 11, 1897, 2.
44. The original Spanish, *interpretado*, is best translated as "performed" in the theatrical sense. Many journalists used such vocabulary as a reflection of the popularity of both theater and light operas (*zarzuelas*) in the capital.
45. French, "Prostitutes and Guardian Angels: Women, Work, and the Family," chapter 4 in *Peaceful and Working People*, 87–108.
46. *La Gaceta de Policía*, December 24, 1905, 11.
47. Buffington and Piccato, "Tales of Two Women," 417. This notion of individual acts influencing the health and welfare of the larger social organism—the nation—is a

central tenet of modernity; thus the influence of nineteenth-century societies in particular to create a virtuous citizenry through public education, morality and manners, surveillance, and patterns of consumption. For more on this idea, see Buffington and French, "Culture of Modernity"; French, *Peaceful and Working People*; Piccato, *City of Suspects*; and Buffington, *Criminal and Citizen*.

48. Beezley, *Judas at the Jockey Club*, initiated this line of analysis. Since then a variety of studies have amplified this seminal work.

49. In the press, see *El Imparcial*, August 17, 1897, 1; and December 6, 1898, 1. For a more private account of such beliefs, see Rafael Reyes Spíndola to José Yves Limantour, Mexico City, September 22, 1893, CDLIV 1883–1899, roll 12, carp. 44, JYL-CEHM. In this correspondence Reyes Spíndola supports a proposal to increase drastically (180 percent) the tariff on "manta"—the cheap cotton cloth associated with Indian consumers—because "it would contribute to federal revenues to which the Indians never contribute."

50. Breckman, "Disciplining Consumption," 490.

51. On meals-included vacations, see *La Semana Mercantil*, September 4, 1893, 426–27. Other articles in the same paper advocating the lash for thievery include October 9, 1893, 486; and April 23, 1894, 198–99. For another source, see *L'Echo du Mexique*, March 30, 1894, 2, which promotes adding the shaving of heads to the call for whipping.

52. *La Semana Mercantil* had championed for years this solution for Mexico's apparent wave of crime. See, for example, the article on November 27, 1899, 662, in which it calls for turning these illegal consumers into producers "at agricultural labors in the National Valley and other locations."

53. *El Imparcial*, February 5, 1904, 1.

54. Breckman, "Disciplining Consumption," 489.

55. González Navarro, *El Porfiriato: La vida social*, 389.

56. One estimate of middle-class demographics numbered them as just under 8 percent nationally and 30 percent in urban areas in 1895. José E. Iturriaga, *La estructura social y cultural de México* (Mexico City: Fondo de Cultura Económica, 1951), quoted in González Navarro, *El Porfiriato: La vida social*, 387.

57. *El Mundo Ilustrado*, August 25, 1901, 16–17.

58. French, *Peaceful and Working People*, 87–108; Carmen Ramos Escandón, "Gender Construction in a Progressive Society: Mexico, 1870–1917," Texas Papers on Mexico no. 90–07, Mexican Center, Institute of Latin American Studies, University of Texas, Austin, 1990. For the United States and the influence of Republicanism on this process, see Linda K. Kerber, *Women of the Republic: Intellect and Ideology in Revolutionary America* (Chapel Hill: University of North Carolina Press, 1980); and Nancy Cott, *The Bonds of Womanhood: "Woman's Sphere" in New England, 1780–1835* (New Haven, CT: Yale University Press, 1977). For France, one study is Bonnie G. Smith, *Ladies of the Leisure Class: The Bourgeoises of Northern France in the Nineteenth Century* (Princeton, NJ: Princeton University Press, 1981).

59. Ramos Escandón, "Señoritas Porfirianas," 143–61.

60. *El Mundo Ilustrado*, January 13, 1900, 18.

61. An example of a Roman Catholic assault on growing materialism and the role of women is Marchal, *La mujer perfecta*, esp. 159–61, 163. Useful etiquette manuals widely used in Mexico include those for women (La Condesa de Tramar, *El trato social*) and for men ([D. J. Cuesta?], *Nuevo manual de urbanidad, cortesanía, decoro y etiqueta; ó, El hombre fino* [Madrid: Lib. de Hijos de D. J. Cuesta, 1889]).

62. *El Mundo Ilustrado*, December 1, 1901, 21. Again, illustrations of furniture and clothing fashions cram the pages surrounding this article as well as the facing page. Another exceptional article rapping women who dress beyond their economic and social station may be found in *El Mundo Ilustrado*, September 9, 1900, 14.

63. *El Mundo Ilustrado*, December 29, 1901, 14.

64. Both of these short stories come from *Novelas cortas de varios autores*, vol. 2 (Mexico City: V. Agueros, 1901).

65. A sampling of newspaper reports on shoplifting in department stores includes: *El Imparcial*, February 1, 1900, 2; September 25, 1901, 2; October 13, 1904, 3; *Le Courrier du Mexique*, February 2, 1900, 2; December 16, 1900, 3; *L'Echo du Mexique*, May 10, 1896, 2; July 7, 1896, 2; May 7, 1897, 2; May 9, 1897, 2; December 21, 1905, 2.

66. *El Imparcial*, March 4, 1899, 2.

67. *El Imparcial*, February 7, 1906, 5; *Le Courrier du Mexique*, February 8, 1906, 3. This common form of swindle can be seen a decade earlier in a similar crime against the Palacio de Hierro documented in *Le Courrier du Mexique*, February 8, 1906, 3.

68. See the case in *El Imparcial*, March 4, 1905, 3, in which a cargador walked off with almost 600 pesos in merchandise from the Importador store.

69. *La Semana Mercantil*, February 11, 1907, 70–71.

70. *El Imparcial*, December 23, 1900, 1; March 7, 1901, 2.

71. *El Imparcial*, August 16, 1898, 1. For another instance of employee and outsider cooperation with an emphasis on the employee, see *El Imparcial*, July 18, 1902, 3. The "Página negra" section of *La Gaceta de Policía* listed numerous thieves who worked the trains not only locally but in most cases throughout the republic: December 17, 1905, 9; December 24, 1905, 11; January 28, 1906, 13; February 4, 1906, 15; February 18, 1906, 15; and October 7, 1906, 15, among others.

72. *L'Echo du Mexique*, May 3, 1896, 2; *Le Courrier du Mexique*, May 18, 1898, 2. For an even earlier account, see *L'Echo du Mexique*, June 8, 1893, 4.

73. *L'Echo du Mexique*, November 16, 1895, 2.

74. *El Imparcial*, January 12, 1900, 2; *L'Echo du Mexique*, May 4, 1895, 2.

75. *L'Echo du Mexique*, May 1, 1894, 2.

76. *El Imparcial*, December 5, 1901, 2.

77. *Le Courrier du Mexique*, June 6, 1910, 2.

78. See Macedo, *La criminalidad en México*. On page 23, for example, he notes that homicides per 100,000 residents in Mexico City were 100 compared to 7.6 for Madrid. See González Navarro, *El Porfiriato: La vida social*, 427, for the confusion and likely error in these numbers. For an excellent account of how public policy and police practices can strongly influence criminal statistics, see Pablo Piccato,

"*Cuidado con los Rateros*: The Making of Criminals in Modern Mexico City," in *Crime and Punishment in Latin America: Law and Society Since Late Colonial Times*, ed. Ricardo D. Salvatore, Carlos Aguirre, and Gilbert M. Joseph (Durham, NC: Duke University Press, 2001).

79. Macedo, *La criminalidad en México*, 40.

80. *La Semana Mercantil*, June 1, 1891, 256–57.

81. Laurence Rohlfes, "Police and Penal Correction in Mexico City, 1876–1911: A Study of Order and Progress in Porfirian Mexico" (PhD diss., Tulane University, 1983); Robert Buffington, "Forging the Fatherland: Criminality and Citizenship in Modern Mexico" (PhD diss., University of Arizona, 1994).

82. *Catálogo de la biblioteca Limantour*. Volumes from experts abroad, such as the Italian César Lombroso and Frenchman Paul Dubuisson, mingled with Mexican criminologists like Miguel Macedo, Julio Guerrero, and Carlos Roumagnac.

83. Macedo, *La criminalidad en México*, 6; Guerrero, *La génesis del crimen*, xi–xii; Roumagnac, *Los criminales en México*.

84. *El Imparcial*, March 10, 1902, 1.

85. Paul Vanderwood, *Disorder and Progress: Bandits, Police, and Mexican Development*, rev. and enlarged ed. (Wilmington, DE: Scholarly Resources, 1992).

86. *El Imparcial*, June 25, 1904, 1.

87. T. J. Jackson Lears, *No Place of Grace: Antimodernism and the Transformation of American Culture, 1880–1920* (New York: Pantheon Books, 1981).

88. Eugen Weber, *Peasants into Frenchmen: The Modernization of Rural France, 1870–1914* (Stanford, CA: Stanford University Press, 1976), esp. 264–77, 289–91.

89. *L'Echo du Mexique*, July 9, 1894, 2; *La Gaceta de Policía*, January 28, 1906, 13; *Le Courrier du Mexique*, April 11, 1900, 2; *L'Echo du Mexique*, May 8, 1894; January 3, 1897, 2.

90. Émile Durkheim, *The Rules of the Sociological Method*, trans. Sarah A. Salovay and Hohn M. Mueller, 8th ed. (Chicago: University of Chicago Press, 1938), 65–73.

91. This perceived transition from violence au vol (violence to theft) with the onset of modernization anticipated the most enduring paradigm found today in the history of criminology. This later twentieth-century approach is more sophisticated than most approaches to nineteenth-century urban environments, which viewed cities as chaotic jungles seething with crime, disorder, and vice. It discounts the notion that urban growth breeds social disorganization and anomie, crime, and popular disorder. Tossed out at the same time is the causal dichotomy of crime as either "greed or need." Instead it looks at increased opportunities for crime in the city, the greater difficulty of crime solutions in a larger community, and the replacement of old "rural" value systems by a newer set of modern "urban" values. Modernizing urban crime characterized by property theft rather than violence is not a product of normlessness caused by the urbanization process but rather the adopting of new norms to fit the new environment. As many observe, the majority of property theft is committed not by recent immigrants to the city but rather by those already comfortable in the environment. "Greed or need" becomes relative; the sense of

deprivation in the city's complex social and economic structure is relative rather than absolute. Crucial to their argument and, I believe, for understanding the changes occurring in Porfirian Mexico City, is the idea that people may steal because they are in need, but the assessment of need depends on what they have been led to expect to desire. This theory of relative deprivation is central to the modernizing crime theory and is commonly called the Merton-Gurr argument, as one of the most widely acclaimed examples of the use of the theory as an explanation for social action is Ted Robert Gurr, *Why Men Rebel* (Princeton, NJ: Princeton University Press, 1971). The clearest and most convincing application of the modernizing crime theory is Howard Zehr, *Crime and the Development of Modern Society: Patterns of Criminality in Nineteenth-Century Germany and France* (Totowa, NJ: Rowman and Littlefield, 1976), esp. 79–81. This theory is generally considered European in origin and has acquired detractors. Most commonly criticism comes from academics in the United States who point out how the violence in American cities during the 1970s and 1980s suggests the weakness of the violence au vol argument. Interestingly, they often use European case studies to make their point. For the best of these arguments, see Eric A. Johnson, *Urbanization and Crime: Germany 1871–1914* (New York: Cambridge University Press, 1995).

92. "El codigo penal y las nuevas sociedades: El robo y la civilización," *El Imparcial*, July 8, 1904, 1.

93. "Criminales modernistas," *El Imparcial*, July 18, 1904, 1.

94. "El peligro del progreso," *El Diablito Rojo*, July 13, 1908, 2.

95. For headlines, see *El Imparcial*, October 24, 1900, 2; and *L'Echo du Mexique*, March 10, 1894, 2. On the use of new technologies and strategies, see *El Imparcial*, July 21, 1904, 1; June 17, 1903, 1; and *Le Courrier du Mexique*, February 15, 1901, 3. Examples of other revelations of new crimes include *L'Echo du Mexique*, November 9, 1897, 2; and *El Imparcial*, August 14, 1904, 3.

96. *Le Courrier du Mexique*, June 14, 1903, 2.

97. Orlove, *Allure of the Foreign*.

98. For example, *El Imparcial*, November 24, 1904, 3.

99. Buffington and Piccato, "Tales of Two Women"; James A. Garza, "Dominance and Submission in Don Porfirio's Belle Époque: The Case of Luis and Piedad," in *Masculinity and Sexuality in Modern Mexico*, ed. Víctor M. Macías-González and Anne Rubenstein, 79–100 (Albuquerque: University of New Mexico Press, 2012); Pablo Piccato, "El chalequero, or 'The Mexican Jack the Ripper': The Meaning of Sexual Violence in Turn-of-the-Century Mexico City," *Hispanic American Historical Review* 81, nos. 3–4 (2001): 623–51.

100. Weber, *France*, 9–26, esp. 13–14. See also Weber, *Peasants into Frenchmen*, 478.

101. González, *San José de Gracia*, esp. chapter 3, "The *Ranchos* and the Town (1900–1910)," 78–112.

Chapter 6

1. James Alex Garza provides a differing description and interpretation of this crime in *Imagined Underworld*, 111–29.

2. Regarding the position of Hernández in the community and the size of his store, see *La Voz de México*, February 24, 1891, 1; on the public attraction of his finest pieces, see *La Voz de México*, April 3, 1891, 2; and for a map of commercial interests in central Mexico City, see Enrique Krauze, *El Poder*, vol. 4 of *Porfirio* (Mexico City: Editorial Clío, 1993), 20–21.

3. On the stock carried by La Esmeralda, see *El Tiempo Ilustrado*, August 9, 1891, 10; on general stock carried by La Profesa, see *La Voz de México*, February 24, 1891, 1; on space and class in the city, see John Lear, "Mexico City: Space and Class in the Porfirian Capital, 1884–1910," *Journal of Urban History* 22, no. 4 (May 1996): 454–92, esp. 459 for elite residence; on Porfirian mentality, see Beezley, *Judas at the Jockey Club*, and French, *Peaceful and Working People*. For the elite mind-set and the importance of conspicuous consumption, see Beezley, "Porfirian Smart Set."

4. For broadsheet drawings of the crime and trial, see Ron Tyler, *Posada's Mexico* (Washington, D.C.: Library of Congress, 1979), 218–20; Roberto Berdecio and Stanley Appelbaum, eds., *Posada's Popular Mexican Prints: 273 Cuts by José Guadalupe Posada* (New York: Dover, 1972), 48–55; and Frank, *Posada's Broadsheets*. Consult *La Voz de México* on the planning of the crime (March 15, 1891, 3); on waiting in the park (April 2, 1891, 2); and on the disguises and route taken (April 25, 1891, 2). For the previously arranged appointment, see *Two Republics*, April 10, 1891, 4.

5. *La Voz de México*, April 25, 1891, 3.

6. *La Voz de México*, April 2, 1891, 2; April 3, 1891, 2; April 23, 1891, 2. On the diamond bracelet, see *La Voz de México*, April 24, 1891, 2; and April 25, 1891, 3. On the stabbing, see *La Voz de México*, April 25, 1891, 3; and *Two Republics*, April 10, 1891, 4. On Martínez's alleged quote, see *La Voz de México*, April 3, 1891, 2.

7. Experts deemed the final value of the crime to be 4,000–8,000 pesos and leaned toward the latter amount, as noted in *La Voz de México*, April 26, 1891, 2. A contradictory sum of 100,000 pesos may be found in Patrick Frank, "Art and Life in Broadsheets by Posada" (unpublished manuscript, University of Colorado, 1996), 176, which is the manuscript published as Frank, *Posada's Broadsheets*. Perhaps his source, a March 2, 1926, article from the newspaper *Universal Gráfico*, adjusted the figure to match the inflationary value of the Mexican peso by 1926. For a description of the appearance, diversity, and value of the individual pieces of jewelry, see *La Voz de México*, March 21, 1891, 3; March 22, 1891, 1; April 23, 1891, 2; and April 26, 1891, 2. On the melting down of gold and pawning of the jewelry, see *La Voz de México*, April 23, 1891, 2; April 25, 1891, 2–3; and April 26, 1891, 2. On the ready street market for stolen goods, see stories in newspapers such as *Two Republics*, January 16, 1891, 4; and July 31, 1891, 4. On the criminal code punishment for theft, see González Navarro, *El Porfiriato: La vida social*, 437.

8. *Two Republics*, February 21, 1891, 4; *La Voz de México*, February 22, 1891, 2–3; February 24, 1891, 1. On the first modern crime claim, see *El Universal Gráfico*, March 2, 1926, 2, cited in Frank, *Posada's Broadsheets*, 107.

9. On rewards, see *La Voz de México*, February 25, 1891, 2; on Díaz's coaxings, see *La Voz de México*, March 3, 1891, 2; and on his usual distance from police affairs, see Rohlfes, "Police and Penal Correction," 50.

10. On Martínez's capture, see *La Voz de México*, March 7, 1891, 2; on Nevraumont's capture, see *La Voz de México*, March 21, 1891, 1.

11. For information on positivism, see Leopoldo Zea, *Positivism in Mexico* (Austin: University of Texas Press, 1974). For a concise account of social Darwinism, consult Mike Hawkins, *Social Darwinism in European and American Thought, 1860–1945: Nature as Model and Nature as Threat* (New York: Cambridge University Press, 1997). For its place in Porfirian criminology, see Buffington and Piccato, "Tales of Two Women." For an elaboration of this paragraph, see chapter 5.

12. On commentator bewilderment, see *La Voz de México*, February 22, 1891, 3; on the stakeout of Hernández, see *La Voz de México*, March 6, 1891, 3. On Chucho el Roto, see Fernando Ferrari, *Chucho el Roto* (Mexico City: Secretaría de Educación Pública, Conasupo, 1989); Carlos Isla, *Chucho el Roto* (Mexico City: Jorge Porrua, 1985); and Jonathan Kandell, *La Capital: The Biography of Mexico City* (New York: Random House, 1988), 365. For an overlapping but alternative analysis of this crime, see Frank, *Posada's Broadsheets*, 107–16.

13. On commodity fetishism, see Needell, *Tropical Belle Epoque*, 158; for a specific instance of Porfirian attention to elite women's pecuniary decency, see the two-day description of the women at the Jockey Club Ball in *Two Republics*, May 19–20, 1891, 4, and Beezley, "Porfirian Smart Set"; on the general theory of a leisure class, see Veblen, *Theory of the Leisure Class*.

14. David Cannadine and David Reeder, eds., *Exploring the Urban Past: Essays in Urban History by J. J. Dyos* (Cambridge: Cambridge University Press, 1982), 73.

15. John Lear, "The Social Geography of the Porfirian Capital," in *Workers, Neighbors, and Citizens*, 15–48. See also Pablo Piccato, "The Modern City," in *City of Suspects*, 17–33, for this "Ideal City," as Piccato calls it, but also for how labor needs in affluent and commercial zones as well as the very symbols of a modern city, such as trams, undermined this social spatial segregation.

16. Macedo, *La criminalidad en México*, 4–5. For information on the geographic stratification project, see Lear, "Mexico City: Space and Class"; on moral regulation during the Porfiriato, see French, *Peaceful and Working People*, 63–85ff; for information on Porfirian leisure activities, see González Navarro, *El Porfiriato: La vida social*, 693–790ff.

17. For examples of *La Voz de México* outrage, see February 22, 1891, 3; February 25, 1891, 1–2; February 26, 1891, 1; April 2, 1891, 2; and April 28, 1891, 3. The sword of Damocles refers to the Greek myth in which an ancient courtier of Syracuse, Damocles, sat at a banquet beneath a sword hung by a single hair. On the newspaper account of the Porfirian equivalent, see *La Voz de México*, February 25, 1891, 1. On rush hour,

see *La Voz de México*, April 2, 1891, 2. The account of curious onlookers may be found in *La Voz de México*, February 25, 1891, 2; and February 26, 1891, 1.

18. On paving, complaints, and street sweeping, see *Two Republics*, January 25, 1891, 4; February 26, 1891, 4; and April 22, 1891, 4; on the daily habits of Hernández, *La Voz de México*, February 24, 1891, 4; on pavement blocks, *Two Republics*, March 3, 1891, 4; and on sliding horses and equestrian-related deaths, *Two Republics*, May 6, 1891, 4; May 24, 1891, 4; and *La Voz de México*, May 6, 1891. For urchin delights, see *Two Republics*, April 29, 1891, 4.

19. For enchilada threats, see *La Voz de México*, June 4, 1891, 4; on the placard, see *La Voz de México*, January 23, 1891, 4; on mixed-housing arrangements, see Lear, "Mexico City: Space and Class," 459.

20. For the socially constructed fear of a "crime wave" in Mexico City beginning in the late 1880s, see Garza, *Imagined Underworld*; and Piccato, *City of Suspects*.

21. On the replacement of the Resguardo Diurno and Nocturno with gendarmes and mounted police, see Rohlfes, "Police and Penal Correction," 38–40. On the distance between policemen and their public visibility, see Thomas Unett Brocklehurst, *Mexico Today: A Country with a Great Future, and a Glance at the Prehistoric Remains and Antiquities of the Montezumas*, 2nd ed. (London: John Murray, 1883); and Curtis, *Capitals of Spanish America*, both cited in Rohlfes, "Police and Penal Correction," 81. The urban crime wave is evident in *Two Republics*, January 15, 1891, 4; February 27, 1891, 4; April 3, 1891, 4; April 30, 1891, 4; and daily in *La Voz de México*.

22. On the previous robbery, see *La Voz de México*, February 24, 1891, 4; on alarm systems from New York, see *Two Republics*, July 5, 1891, 4; and for advertisement, see *El Tiempo Ilustrado*, March 12, 1892, 10. On Chucho el Roto stealing from Hernández, see *La Voz de México*, February 24, 1891, 1; and on Chucho's other conquests, see Ferrari, *Chucho el Roto*, 74.

23. *La Voz de México*, February 22, 1891, 3; February 25, 1891, 2.

24. On Carballeda and inspectors general, see Rohlfes, "Police and Penal Correction," 51, 57; on the secret police, see ibid., 65–69; charges leveled against Cabrera are found in *La Voz de México*, April 26, 1891, 2; and May 6, 1891, 1.

25. *Two Republics*, March 5, 1891, 4; March 22, 1891, 4; March 28, 1891, 4; April 1, 1891, 4. For studies on the existence of a criminal class, see Cynthia Story Bisson, "Crime and the Transition to Modernity in Nineteenth-Century France: The Morbihan, 1825–1925, a Case Study" (PhD diss., Ohio State University, 1989); Jennifer Davis, "The London Garrotting Panic of 1862: A Moral Panic and the Creation of a Criminal Class in Mid-Victorian England," in *Crime and the Law: The Social History of Crime in Western Europe Since 1500*, ed. V. A. C. Gatrell, Bruce Lenman, and Geoffrey Parker (London: Europa Publications, 1980), 190–213; Clive Emsley, *Crime and Society in England, 1750–1900* (London: Longman Group, UK, 1987); George Rudé, *Criminal and Victim: Crime and Society in Early Nineteenth-Century England* (Oxford: Clarendon Press, 1985), esp. 73; and Zehr, *Crime and the Development of Modern Society*. For a fascinating account of the Victorian pickpocket, see Michael

Crichton, *The Great Train Robbery* (New York: Alfred A. Knopf, 1975), 29–32. For the Parisian crime, see *El Universal Gráfico*, March 4, 1926, 13.

26. For information on the preceding two paragraphs, see Friedrich Katz, "Mexico: Restored Republic and Porfiriato, 1867–1910" in *The Cambridge History of Latin America*, vol. 5, ed. Leslie Bethel (Cambridge: Cambridge University Press, 1987), 3–78; and Colin MacLachlan and William H. Beezley, *El Gran Pueblo: A History of Greater Mexico* (Englewood Cliffs, NJ: Prentice-Hall, 1994), 1–130. On railroads and foreign investments, see Coatsworth, *Growth Against Development*; Kuntz Ficker, *Empresa extranjera*; and Schell, *Integral Outsiders*. On railroads and banditry, see Vanderwood, *Disorder and Progress*.

27. Vanderwood, *Disorder and Progress*, 88. On social banditry more generally, consult Eric J. Hobsbawm, *Primitive Rebels: Studies in Archaic Forms of Social Movement in the 19th and 20th Centuries* (New York: W. W. Norton, 1965).

28. On specifically urban crimes, see Rudé, *Criminal and Victim*, 80.

29. On the judges Medina y Ormacchea, see Rohlfes, "Police and Penal Correction," 217; on the trial preparation, see *Two Republics*, April 15, 1891, 4.

30. *La Voz de México*, April 21, 1891, 3; *Two Republics*, April 21, 1891, 4.

31. *Two Republics*, April 21, 1891, 4. On Limantour's presence and that of other important guests, see *La Voz de México*, April 16, 1891, 2; and April 24, 1891, 2. Lear, "Mexico City: Space and Class," 464, provides a short description of Limantour's role among Mexico City's power elite.

32. For a list of the newspapers present, see *La Voz de México*, April 25, 1891, 2, which includes all the major dailies and representatives from the American, Spanish, and French communities. A sampling of Posada's work on this trial exists in Tyler, *Posada's Mexico*, 218–20; and Berdecio and Appelbaum, *Posada's Popular Mexican Prints*, 48–55.

33. *Two Republics*, April 21, 1891, 4; April 22, 1891, 4.

34. *La Voz de México*, April 22, 1891, 2.

35. *La Voz de México*, March 6, 1891, 3; March 15, 1891, 3; April 28, 1891, 3.

36. Rohlfes, "Police and Penal Correction," 204–5.

37. *La Voz de México*, April 28, 1891, 2.

38. *La Voz de México*, April 24, 1891, 2.

39. *La Voz de México*, April 25, 1891, 2; April 26, 1891, 2.

40. *La Voz de México*, March 7, 1891, 2. This use of photography in 1891 contradicts Rohlfes, "Police and Penal Correction," 92, who argues that the police first bought a camera in 1897 and even then barely used the new technology. In *Two Republics*, September 6, 1891, the city council approved 124 pesos to pay for the photos of 1,508 criminals who had stood before the courts.

41. *La Voz de México*, March 19, 1891, 2; April 25, 1891, 3.

42. *La Voz de México*, March 19, 1891, 1; March 21, 1891, 1; March 21, 1891, 3; March 22, 1891, 3; April 25, 1891, 3.

43. *La Voz de México*, April 24, 1891, 1.

44. *La Voz de México*, April 25, 1891, 2.

45. *La Voz de México*, March 6, 1891, 2; April 25, 1891, 2.
46. For Sousa, see *La Voz de México*, April 24, 1891, 2; for Nevraumont, see *La Voz de México*, April 28, 1891, 3.
47. *La Voz de México*, April 24, 1891, 2.
48. *La Voz de México*, April 25, 1891, 3; April 26, 1891, 3.
49. See Stephen Neufeld, "Servants of the Nation: The Military in the Making of the Nation, 1876–1911" (PhD diss., University of Arizona, 2009); Daniel Gutiérrez Santos, *Historia Militar de México, 1876–1914* (Mexico City: Ediciones Ateneo, 1955); and David Coffey, "Brothers of the Sword: Military Tradition in Porfirian Mexico" (paper presented at Texas Christian University, Fall 1996). For the role of the military in forging a modern citizenry and a national identity, see Weber, *Peasants into Frenchmen*, 292–302.
50. *La Voz de México*, April 28, 1891, 3. For information on the Plan de Noria, see Laurens Ballard Perry, *Juárez and Díaz: Machine Politics in Mexico* (DeKalb: Northern Illinois University Press, 1978).
51. *La Voz de México*, March 4, 1891, 2.
52. For further information on the discourse of femininity and gender during the Porfiriato, see Franco, *Plotting Women*; French, "Prostitutes and Guardian Angels"; and Ramos Escandón, "Señoritas Porfirianas."
53. *La Voz de México*, April 24, 1891, 2.
54. *La Voz de México*, April 26, 1891, 2.
55. Ibid.
56. Ibid.
57. *La Voz de México*, April 25, 1891, 3.
58. *La Voz de México*, March 6, 1891, 3.
59. *La Voz de México*, April 25, 1891, 2.
60. *La Voz de México*, March 6, 1891, 3.
61. *La Voz de México*, April 26, 1891, 3.
62. *La Voz de México*, April 28, 1891, 2. For a contemporary perspective on phrenology and its intellectual currency, see Francisco Martínez Baca and Manuel Vergara, *Estudios de antropología criminal* (Puebla: Imprenta Lit. y Encuadernación de Benjamin Lara, 1892).
63. *La Voz de México*, April 28, 1891, 2.
64. *La Voz de México*, April 26, 1891, 2.
65. *La Voz de México*, April 25, 1891, 2.
66. *Two Republics*, April 29, 1891, 4.
67. Rohlfes, "Police and Penal Correction," 312; my emphasis.
68. On Ulúa, see Rohlfes, "Police and Penal Correction," 224–26. Of crucial importance is the issue of when the practice of transportation resumed. Rohlfes says this occurred in 1892 (pp. 225–26), but the La Profesa robbers started their sentence in mid-1891. I believe this is strong evidence to support the claim that the La Profesa robbery resulted in the reinstitution of transport to Ulúa.
69. I am indebted to Patrick Frank for the information on Treffel's later prosperity

and the confirmation that the other four died. The source is *Universal Gráfico*, March 4, 1926. Nevertheless, I question the accuracy of this account due to a flurry of front-page newspaper reports on Treffel after he left prison in 1901. He again became the center of public attention during his trial and conviction for attempting to swindle a firm by claiming to be a successful alchemist, capable of manufacturing gold and diamonds. The judge sent him back to prison to serve the remaining eight years of his original sentence for the La Profesa robbery. Much of the jewelry stolen in the robbery had yet to be found. See *El Imparcial*, April 17, 1901, 1; April 17, 1901, 2; April 18, 1901, 1; April 19, 1901, 2; April 22, 1901, 1; and May 8, 1901, 2.

70. *Two Republics*, April 30, 1891, 4.

71. See Frank, *Posada's Broadsheets*, 115, for the above information on the defiance, escape, resolution, and knife of Martínez.

72. *La Voz de México*, January 8, 1892, 2. In this account of the execution Martínez wounded Cabrera in the arm, but Patrick Frank states that the police detective's neck received the injury. Frank, *Posada's Broadsheets*, 115. On the regular necessity of finishing shots, see Rohlfes, "Police and Penal Correction," 315.

73. On the secret police, see Frank, *Posada's Broadsheets*, 107. On early closings, see *Two Republics*, May 5, 1891, 4.

74. Joy Wiltenburg, "True Crime: The Origins of Modern Sensationalism," *American Historical Review* 109, no. 5 (December 2004): 1377–404.

75. For more on the role of the press and crafting a community narrative, whether national or urban, see Anderson, *Imagined Communities*; and Schwartz, *Spectacular Realities*.

76. Guerrero, *La génesis del crimen*; Roumagnac, *Los criminales en México*. Federico Gamboa became one the most famous late-Porfirian novelists after publishing *Santa* (Mexico City: Editorial Grijalbo, 1979), a work centered on the prostitute Santa that exposed the vices and immorality of the Porfirian metropolis.

77. González, *San José de Gracia*, 64–104ff.

78. For further information on Jesús Negrete, see Frank, *Posada's Broadsheets*, 116–27.

79. *Two Republics*, May 3, 1891, 4, mentioned that several dailies circulated this rumor. In the United States, criminals of the nineteenth century had a long tradition of writing accounts of their exploits; see David Ray Papke, *Framing the Criminal: Crime, Cultural Work, and the Loss of Critical Perspective, 1830–1900* (Hamden, CT: Archon Books, 1987).

80. Rudé, *Criminal and Victim*, 78. Dugdale and Colajanni are cited in Crichton, *Great Train Robbery*, xvi.

81. On the Ocean Bank robbery, see Larry K. Hartsfield, *The American Response to Professional Crime* (Westport, CT: Greenwood Press, 1985); and Crichton, *Great Train Robbery*, 264.

Conclusion

1. Buchenau, *Tools of Progress*; and Francois, *Culture of Everyday Credit*.

2. One of the first revisions in Porfirian historiography is Kuntz Ficker, *Empresa extranjera*. For a discussion of this issue in Latin American historiography, read Orlove and Bauer, "Giving Importance to Imports."

3. See the articles by Joseph Love, John Coatsworth, and Sandra Kuntz Ficker in the Research Forum "From Structuralism to the New Institutional Economics: A Half Century of Latin American Economic Historiography," *Latin American Research Review* 40, no. 3 (October 2005): 97–162.

4. Among historians publishing in English, Robert Buffington and Pablo Piccato are the leading scholars shaping the issues. Buffington, *Criminal and Citizen*; and Piccato, *City of Suspects*.

5. William E. French and Katherine E. Bliss, eds., *Gender, Sexuality, and Power in Latin America Since Independence* (Lanham, MD: Rowman and Littlefield, 2007); French, *Peaceful and Working People*; Ramos Escandón, *Presencia y transparencia*; and Macías-González, "Mexican Aristocracy."

6. The literature on prostitution is vast. Some of the more important texts are Judith Walkowitz, *Prostitution and Victorian Society: Women, Class, and the Stage* (Cambridge: Cambridge University Press, 1980); Alain Corbin, *Women for Hire: Sexuality in France After 1850*, trans. Alan Sheridan (Cambridge, MA: Harvard University Press, 1990); Jill Harsin, *Policing Prostitution in Nineteenth-Century Paris* (Princeton, NJ: Princeton University Press, 1985); Jann Matlock, *Scenes of Seduction: Prostitution, Hysteria, and Reading Difference in Nineteenth-Century France* (New York: Columbia University Press, 1994); and Ruth Rosen, *The Lost Sisterhood: Prostitution in America, 1900–1918* (Baltimore: Johns Hopkins University Press, 1982).

7. Gamboa, *Santa*.

8. Such an approach complements works such as Gil Joseph and Daniel Nugent, eds. *Everyday Forms of State Formation: Revolution and Negotiation of Rule in Modern Mexico* (Durham, NC: Duke University Press, 1994). Of course, other historians have already begun to incorporate the business community in these processes, but commodities and consumption remain absent. For one of the earliest and most forceful of these works, see Haber, *Industry and Underdevelopment*. See also Susan M. Gauss, "Made in Mexico: The Rise of Mexican Industrialism, 1938–1952" (PhD diss., SUNY Stony Brook, 2002).

9. Schell, *Integral Outsiders*; Hart, *Empire and Revolution*.

10. Moreno, *Yankee Don't Go Home!*

11. The phrase comes from an editorial written by Alfonso Luis Velasco in *El Avisador Comercial*, May 12, 1889, 2.

12. Eduardo Maynez to José Yves Limantour, Parras, October 23, 1902, CDLIV 1902, roll 16, carp. 21, JYL-CEHM.

13. González, *San José de Gracia*, 100.

14. Ibid., 88.

15. Ibid., 106.

SELECTED BIBLIOGRAPHY

Archives

Mexico

Archivo General de la Nación, Mexico City
    Fondo Felipe Teixidor
    Fondo Instrucción Pública y Bellas Artes
    Fondo Secretaría de Comercio y Fomento Industrial
    Justicia
    Trabajo
Archivo Palacio de Hierro, Mexico City
Archivos del ex-Ayuntamiento de la Ciudad de México, Mexico City
    Alumbrado
    Diversiones Públicas
    Letreros
    Mercados
    Paseos
    Plaza Mayor
Biblioteca Miguel Lerdo de Tejada, Mexico City
    Hemeroteca
Centro de Estudios de Historia de México Carso, Chimalistac, Mexico City
    Archivo Bernardo Reyes
    Archivo José Yves Limantour
    Biblioteca
Instituto José María Mora, Mexico City
Universidad Nacional Autónoma de México, Mexico City
    Biblioteca Nacional, Centro Cultural Universitario
    Fondo Reservado de la Hemeroteca Nacional de México, Centro Cultural Universitario

United States of America

Library of Congress, Washington, D.C.
    Hispanic Division
    Rare Books
New Mexico State University, Las Cruces, New Mexico
    Amador Trade Catalog Collection
Texas Christian University, Fort Worth, Texas
    Department of Special Collections
        Bell Family Collection
    University Library
University of California at Berkeley, Berkeley, California
    Bancroft Library
University of Texas at Austin, Austin, Texas
    Nettie Lee Benson Latin American Collections
    University Library
University of Texas at El Paso, El Paso, Texas
    Department of Special Collections
        Juan Terrazas Cuilty Papers, 1883–1911
        Mexican Revolution Photograph Collection
    University Library

Periodicals

Actualidades (Mexico City)
Artes y Letras (Mexico City)
El Anunciador Mexicano (Mexico City)
El Avisador Comercial (Mexico City)
La Cagarruta (Mexico City)
El Centro Mercantil (Mexico City)
El Chango (Mexico City)
El Chile Piquín (Mexico City)
La Clase Media (Mexico City)
El Correo de Chihuahua (Chihuahua City)
El Correo de Comercio (Mexico City)
Le Courrier du Mexique (Mexico City)
El Diablito Bromista (Mexico City)
El Diablito Rojo (Mexico City)
Don Cucufate (Mexico City)
El Duende (Mexico City)
L'Echo du Mexique (Mexico City)
El Eco Nacional (Mexico City)

El Economista Mexicano (Mexico City)
El Entreacto (Mexico City)
Frivolidades (Mexico City)
La Gaceta de Policía (Mexico City)
La Guacamaya (Mexico City)
El Imparcial (Mexico City)
El Mensajero (Mexico City)
Mexican Herald (Mexico City)
México Gráfico (Mexico City)
Le Mexique (Mexico City)
Modern Mexico (Mexico City)
El Moquete (Mexico City)
El Mundo Ilustrado (Mexico City)
El Norte (Mexico City)
La Palanca (Mexico City)
El Papagayo (Mexico City)
El Periódico Oficial (Oaxaca City)
El Pinche (Mexico City)
El Popular (Mexico City)
La Risa (Mexico City)
La Semana en el Hogar (Mexico City)
La Semana Ilustrada (Mexico City)
La Semana Mercantil (Mexico City)
El Tiempo Ilustrado (Mexico City)
Le Trait d'Union (Mexico City)
La Tranca (Mexico City)
Two Republics (Mexico City)
La Victoria (Oaxaca City)
La Voz de México (Mexico City)

Primary Sources

Álbum oficial del Comité Nacional del Comercio: Premier centenario de la independencia de México, 1810–1910. Mexico City: Gómez de la Puente, 1910.

Baca, Francisco Martínez, and Manuel Vergara. *Estudios de antropología criminal.* Puebla, Mexico: Imprenta Lit. y Encuadernación de Benjamin Lara, 1892.

Barajas, Hilarión. *Pequeño manual de usos y costumbres de México, y breve colección de algunas frases y modismos figurados, de varios refranes y de muchas otras frases Latinas, impuestas unas por el buen gusto é introducidas las otras por el uso y modo común de hablar.* Mexico City: Tip. Guadalupana, de Reyes Velasco, 1901.

Barros, Eugenio Espino. *Crónica gráfica de la Ciudad de México en el centenario de la independencia.* Mexico City: Departamento del Distrito Federal, Secretaría General de Desarrollo Social, Comité Interno de Ediciones Gubernamentales, 1988.

Bianconi, F. *Le Mexique á la portée des industriels, des capitalistes, des negociants importateurs et des travailleurs*. Paris: Imprimerie Chaix, 1899.

Bigot, Raoul. *Le Mexique moderne*. Paris: Pierre Roger, 1910.

Bishop, William Henry. *Old Mexico and Her Lost Provinces*. New York: Harper and Brothers, 1883.

Böhme, Margarete. *The Department Store: A Novel of To-Day*. Trans. Ethel Colburn Mayne. New York: D. Appleton, 1912.

Brenner, Anita. *The Wind That Swept Mexico*. Austin: University of Texas Press, 1971.

Calderón de la Barca, Fanny. *Life in Mexico During a Residence of Two Years in That Country*. London: E. P. Dutton, 1917.

Campo, Ángel de. *Ocios y apuntes y La rumba*. Mexico City: Editorial Porrua, 1995.

Carson, W. E. *Mexico: The Wonderland of the South*. New York: MacMillan, 1909.

Catálogo de la biblioteca del señor licenciado don José Y. Limantour. Mexico City, 1913.

Chabrand, Émile. *De Barcelonnette au Mexique*. Paris: Plon, Nourrit, 1892.

Cuéllar, José T. *Baile y cochino, ensalada de pollos, los fuereños*. Mexico City: Promexa Editores, 1979.

[Cuesta, D. J.?]. *Nuevo manual de urbanidad, cortesanía, decoro y etiqueta; ó, El hombre fino*. Madrid: Lib. de Hijos de D. J. Cuesta, 1889.

Cumplido, Ignacio, ed. *El album mexicano*. 2 vols. Mexico City: Imprenta de Ignacio Cumplido, 1849.

Curtis, William. *The Capitals of Spanish America*. New York: Harper and Bros., 1888.

Domenech, J. Figueroa. *Guía general descriptiva de la República Mexicana*. 2 vols. Mexico City: Ramón de S. N. Araluce, 1899.

Dubuisson, Paul. *Les voleuses de grands magasins*. Paris: A. Storck, 1902.

Fergusson, Arthur W. *Mexico*. Washington, D.C.: Bureau of the American Republics, 1891.

Gamboa, Federico. *Santa*. Mexico City: Editorial Grijalbo, 1979.

Garrido, Felipe. *Luz y sombra: Los inicios del cine en la prensa de la ciudad de México*. Mexico City: Consejo Nacional Para la Cultura y las Artes, 1997.

Génin, Auguste. *Notes sur le Mexique*. Mexico City: Imprenta Lacaud, 1908–1910.

Grandes almacenes de "El Palacio de Hierro." Obsequio a nuestros favorecedores. Agenda para el año 1900. Mexico City: Tip. El Lápiz de Aguila, 1900.

Guerrero, Julio. *La génesis del crimen en México: Ensayo de psiquiatría social*. Mexico City: Imprenta de la Vda. de Ch. Bouret, 1901.

Honoré, M. F. *Les employés de commerce á Paris au point de vue social*. Paris, 1895.

Inclán, Luis G. *Astucia: El jefe de los hermanos de la hoja; ó, Los charros contrabandistas de la rama*. Mexico City: Librería de la vda. de Ch. Bouret, 1908.

Kahlo, Guillermo. *Mexiko 1904*. Mexico City: Universidad Iberoamericana, 2002.

Leacock, Stephen. *Arcadian Adventures with the Idle Rich*. Toronto: Cromwell, 1914.

Leroy, Lucien. *Mexico: Ses colonies française, suisse et belge et l'etat économique, politique et financier du Mexique en 1898*. Mexico City: Imprimerie Bouligny y Schmidt Sucs., 1898.

Macedo, Miguel. *La criminalidad en México: Medios de combatirla*. Mexico City: Oficina tip. de la Secretaría de Fomento, 1897.

Maillefert, Eugenio. *Directorio del comercio del Imperio Mexicano para el año de 1867.* 1867. Reprint, Mexico City: Instituto Mora, 1992.

Marchal, R. P. V. *La mujer perfecta.* Trans. S. P. Vicens y Marco. Barcelona: Gustavo Gili, 1908.

Martin, Percy F. *Mexico of the Twentieth Century.* Vol. 1. London: Edward Arnold, 1907.

The Massey-Gilbert Blue Book of Mexico: A Directory in English of the City of Mexico. Mexico City: Massey-Gilbert, 1901.

Mexicanos: Los pintados por si mismos. Mexico City: Casa de M. Murguia, portal del Aguila de oro, 1853.

Molina Enriquez, Andrés. *Los grandes problemas nacionales.* Mexico City: Impr. de A. Carranza e Hijos, 1909.

Mora, José María Luis. *Obras completas.* Mexico City: Secretaría de Educación Pública—Instituto de Investigaciones Dr. José María Luis Mora, 1987.

Novelas cortas de varios autores. Vol. 2. Mexico City: V. Agueros, 1901.

Phillip, George, ed. *British Documents on Foreign Affairs: Reports and Papers from the Foreign Office Confidential Print.* Part 1, *From the Mid-Nineteenth Century to the First World War.* Series D, *Latin America, 1845–1914.* Vol. 4, *Mexico, 1861–1910.* Bethesda, MD: University Publications of America, 1998.

Riedel, Emil. *Practical Guide of the City and Valley of Mexico with Excursions to Toluca, Tula, Pachuca, Puebla, Cuernavaca, etc.* Mexico City: I. Epstein, 1892.

Rosas Moreno, José. *Nuevo manual en verso de urbanidad y buenas maneras.* Mexico City: Antigua Librería de Murguía, [1880?].

Roumagnac, Carlos. *Los criminales en México: Ensayo de psicología criminal.* Mexico City: Tip. "El Fenix," 1904.

Routier, Gaston. *Le Mexique.* Paris: Lille Imp. L. Danel, 1891.

Santamaria, Francisco J. *Diccionario de mejicanismos.* Mexico City: Editorial Porrua, 1959.

Sarmiento, Domingo. *Facundo; or, Civilization and Barbarism.* Trans. Mary Peabody Mann. New York: Penguin Books, 1998.

Tablada, José Juan. *Las sombras largas.* Mexico City: Consejo Nacional para la Cultura y las Artes, 1993.

Thompson, Wallace. *The Mexican Mind: A Study of National Psychology.* Boston: Little, Brown, 1922.

Tramar, La Condesa de. *El trato social: Costumbres de la sociedad moderna en todas las circumstancia de la vida. Nueva guía de la gente elegante, traducido, anotado y adaptado á la sociedad de México con la colaboración de distinguidas damas mexicanas.* Paris: Librería de la Viuda de Ch. Bouret, 1906.

Tweedie, Mrs. Alec. *Maker of Modern Mexico: Porfirio Díaz.* New York: J. Lane, 1906.

Veblen, Thorstein. *The Theory of the Leisure Class.* 1899. Reprint, New York: Penguin Books, 1994.

Verdugo, Agustin, Jorge Vera Estañol, and Manuel Calero y Sierra. *El Buen Tono y la 'Bonsack Machine Company.' Sentencia de la suprema corte de justicia de la nación y ptras pieza relativas al juicio seguido entre 'El Buen Tono' y el Sr. W. H. Butler.* Mexico City: Imprenta de Ignacio Escalante, 1900.

Winter, Nevin O. *Mexico and Her People of Today: An Account of the Customs, Characteristics, Amusements, History and Advancement of the Mexicans, and the Development and Resources of Their Country*. Rev. ed. Boston: L. C. Page, 1923. Originally published 1907.

Zola, Emile. *Au bonheur des dames*. Paris: Charpentier, 1883.

Secondary Sources

Abel, Richard. *The Ciné Goes to Town: French Cinema, 1896–1914*. Rev. and expanded ed. Berkeley: University of California Press, 1998.

———. *The Red Rooster Scare: Making Cinema American, 1900–1910*. Berkeley: University of California Press, 1999.

Abelson, Elaine. *When Ladies Go A-Thieving: Middle-Class Shoplifters and the Victorian Department Store*. New York: Oxford University Press, 1989.

Amerlinck, María Concepción. *Historia y cultura del tabaco en México*. Mexico City: Tabacos Mexicanos, 1988.

Anderson, Benedict. *Imagined Communities: Reflections on the Origin and Spread of Nationalism*. 2nd ed. London: Verso, 1991.

Antiq-Auvaro, Raymonde. *L'emigration des Barcelonnettes au Mexique*. Nice: Editions Serre, 1992.

Arnaud, François, Anselme Charpenel, Léon Martin, André Signoret, and Elie Borel, eds. *Les Barcelonnettes au Mexique: Récits et témoignages*. Barcelonnette, France: Sabença de la Valeia, 1994.

Asociación Mexicana de Agencias de Publicidad. *Crónica de la publicidad en México: 1901–2001*. Mexico City: Editorial Clío, 2002.

Aurrecocchea, Juan Manuel, and Armanda Batra. *Puros cuentos: La historia de la historieta en México*. Vol. 1. Mexico City: Editorial Grijalbo, 1988.

Auslander, Leora. *Taste and Power: Furnishing Modern France*. Berkeley: University of California Press, 1996.

Bakhtin, Mikhail. *Rabelais and His World*. Trans. Helen Iswolsky. Cambridge, MA: MIT Press, 1968.

Baldwin, Deborah J. *Protestants and the Mexican Revolution: Missionaries, Ministers, and Social Change*. Urbana: University of Illinois Press, 1990.

Bastian, Jean-Pierre. *Los disidentes: Sociedades protestantes y revolución en México, 1872–1911*. Mexico City: Fondo de Cultura Económica, 1989.

Bauer, Arnold J. *Goods, Power, History: Latin America's Material Culture*. New York: Cambridge University Press, 2001.

Beatty, Edward. *Institutions and Investment: The Political Basis of Industrialization in Mexico Before 1911*. Stanford, CA: Stanford University Press, 2001.

Bederman, Gail. *Manliness and Civilization: A Cultural History of Gender and Race in the United States, 1880–1917*. Chicago: University of Chicago Press, 1995.

Beezley, William H., ed. *A Companion to Mexican History and Culture*. Malden, MA: Blackwell, 2011

———. *Judas at the Jockey Club and Other Episodes of Porfirian Mexico*. Lincoln: University of Nebraska Press, 1987.

———. *Mexican National Identity: Memory, Innuendo, and Popular Culture*. Tucson: University of Arizona Press, 2008.

———. "The Porfirian Smart Set Anticipates Thorstein Veblen in Guadalajara." In Beezley, Martin, and French, *Rituals of Rule*, 173–90.

Beezley, William H., Cheryl English Martin, and William E. French, eds. *Rituals of Rule, Rituals of Resistance: Public Celebrations and Popular Culture in Mexico*. Wilmington, DE: Scholarly Resources, 1994.

Benson, John, and Gareth Shaw, eds. *The Evolution of Retail Systems, c. 1800–1914*. Leicester, UK: Leicester University Press, 1992.

Benson, Susan Porter. *Counter Cultures: Saleswomen, Managers, and Customers in American Department Stores, 1890–1940*. Urbana: University of Illinois Press, 1986.

Berdecio, Roberto, and Stanley Appelbaum, eds. *Posada's Popular Mexican Prints: 273 Cuts by José Guadalupe Posada*. New York: Dover, 1972.

Bowler, Peter J. *Evolution: The History of an Idea*. Berkeley: University of California Press, 2009.

Breckman, Warren G. "Disciplining Consumption: The Debate About Luxury in Wilhelmine Germany, 1890–1914." *Journal of Social History* 24, no. 3 (Spring 1991): 485–505.

Breen, T. H. *The Marketplace of Revolution: How Consumer Politics Shaped American Independence*. New York: Oxford University Press, 2004.

Brewer, John, and Roy Porter, eds. *Consumption and the World of Goods*. London: Routledge, 1993.

Briseño Senosiain, Lillian. *Candil de la calle, oscuridad de su casa. La iluminación de la ciudad de México durante el porfiriato*. Mexico City: Tecnológico de Monterrey, Instituto Mora, 2008.

Brower, Daniel R. *The Russian City between Tradition and Modernity, 1850–1900*. Berkeley: University of California Press, 1990.

Buchenau, Jürgen. *Tools of Progress: A German Merchant Family in Mexico City, 1865–Present*. Albuquerque: University of New Mexico Press, 2004.

Buffington, Robert. *Criminal and Citizen in Modern Mexico*. Lincoln: University of Nebraska Press, 2000.

Buffington, Robert, and Carlos A. Aguirre, eds. *Reconstructing Criminality in Latin America*. Wilmington, DE: Scholarly Resources, 2000.

Buffington, Robert, and William E. French. "The Culture of Modernity." In *The Oxford History of Mexico*, edited by Michael C. Meyer and William H. Beezley, 397–432. New York: Oxford University Press, 2000.

Buffington, Robert, and Pablo Piccato. "Tales of Two Women: The Narrative Construal of Porfirian Reality." *The Americas* 55, no. 3 (January 1999): 391–424.

Bunker, Steven B. "'Consumers of Good Taste': Marketing Modernity in Northern Mexico, 1890–1910." *Mexican Studies/Estudios Mexicanos* 13, no. 2 (Summer 1997): 227–69.

Bunker, Steven B., and Víctor M. Macías-González. "Consumption and Material Culture from Pre-contact through the Porfiriato." In Beezley, *Companion to Mexican History*, 54–82.

Bunker, Steven B., and Víctor M. Macías-González. "Consumption and Material Culture in the Twentieth Century." In Beezley, *Companion to Mexican History and Culture*, 83–118.

Camacho Morfín, Thelma. *Imágenes de México: Las historietas de El Buen Tono de Juan B. Urrutia, 1909–1912*. Mexico City: Instituto Mora, 2002.

Cannadine, David, and David Reeder, eds. *Exploring the Urban Past: Essays in Urban History by J. J. Dyos*. Cambridge: Cambridge University Press, 1982.

Casanova, Manuel González. *Los escritores mexicanos y los inicios del cine*. Mexico City: UNAM, 1995.

Casasola, Gustavo. *Seis siglos de historia gráfica de México, 1325–1925*. Mexico City: Editorial Gustavo Casasola, 1968.

Cerda González, Luis C. *Historia financiera del Banco Nacional de México: Porfiriato, 1884–1910*. Vol. 2. Mexico City: Fomento Cultural Banamex, 1994.

Certeau, Michel de. *The Practice of Everyday Life*. Trans. Steven Randall. Berkeley: University of California Press, 2002.

Cerutti, Mario. *Burguesía, capitales e industria en el norte de México: Monterrey y su ámbito regional*. Monterrey, Mexico: Alianza Editorial, 1992.

Chenut, Helen Harden. *The Fabric of Gender: Working-Class Culture in Third Republic France*. University Park: Pennsylvania State University Press, 2005.

Coatsworth, John H. *Growth Against Development: The Economic Impact of Railroads in Porfirian Mexico*. Dekalb: University of Northern Illinois Press, 1981.

Coerver, Don M. *The Porfirian Interregnum: The Presidency of Manuel González of Mexico, 1880–1884*. Fort Worth: Texas Christian University Press, 1979.

Cohen, Lizbeth. "The Class Experience of Mass Consumption: Workers as Consumers in Interwar America." In *The Power of Culture: Critical Essays in American History*, edited by Richard Wightman Fox and T. J. Jackson Lears, 135–62. Chicago: University of Chicago Press, 1993.

Crichton, Michael. *The Great Train Robbery*. New York: Alfred A. Knopf, 1975.

Crossick, Geoffrey, and Serge Jaumain, eds. *Cathedrals of Consumption: The European Department Store: 1850–1939*. Aldershot, UK: Ashgate Publishing, 1999.

Curcio-Nagy, Linda A. "Giants and Gypsies: Corpus Christi in Colonial Mexico City." In Beezley, Martin, and French, *Rituals of Rule*, 1–26.

———. *The Great Festivals of Colonial Mexico City: Performing Power and Identity*. Albuquerque: University of New Mexico Press, 2004.

Davis, Jennifer. "The London Garrotting Panic of 1862: A Moral Panic and the Creation of a Criminal Class in Mid-Victorian England." In *Crime and Law: The Social History of Crime in Western Europe Since 1500*, edited by V. A. C. Gatrell, Bruce Lenman, and Geoffrey Parker, 190–213. London: Europa Publications, 1980.

Deans-Smith, Susan. *Bureaucrats, Planters, and Workers: The Making of the Tobacco Monopoly in Bourbon Mexico*. Austin: University of Texas Press, 1992.

de Grazia, Victoria, and Ellen Furlough, eds. *The Sex of Things: Gender and Consumption in Historical Perspective*. Berkeley: University of California Press, 1996.

Delamare, François, and Bernard Guineau. *Colors: The Story of Dyes and Pigments*. Trans. Sophie Hawkes. New York: Harry N. Abrams, 2000.

Díaz, María Elena. "The Satiric Penny Press for Workers in Mexico, 1900–1910: A Case Study in the Politicisation of Popular Culture." *Journal of Latin American Studies* 22, no. 3 (October 1990): 497–526.

d'Olwer, Luis Nicolau, et al. *El Porfiriato: La vida económica*. Vol. 7 of *Historia moderna de México*, edited by Daniel Cosío Villegas. Mexico City: Editorial Hermes, 1955–1972.

Douglas, Mary, and Baron Isherwood. *The World of Goods: Towards an Anthropology of Consumption*. New York: W. W. Norton, 1978.

Dreiser, Theodore. *Sister Carrie*. New York: Penguin, 1981.

Durkheim, Émile. *The Rules of the Sociological Method*. Trans. Sarah A. Salovay and Hohn M. Mueller. Chicago: University of Chicago Press, 1938.

Elías, Anilú. *150 años de costumbres, modas y Liverpool*. Mexico City: El Puerto de Liverpool, 1997.

Emsley, Clive. *Crime and Society in England, 1750–1900*. London: Longman Group, UK, 1987.

Eskilson, Stephen J. *Graphic Design: A New History*. New Haven, CT: Yale University Press, 2007.

Esquivel, Gerardo, and Graciela Márquez Colín. "Some Economic Effects of Closing the Economy: The Mexican Experience in the Mid-twentieth Century." In *The Decline of Latin American Economies: Growth, Institutions, and Crises*, edited by Sebastian Edwards, Gerardo Esquivel, and Graciela Márquez Colín, 333–62. Chicago: University of Chicago Press, 2007.

Estadísticas históricas de México. Mexico City: INEGI, 1984.

Fairchilds, Cissie. "The Production and Marketing of Populuxe Goods in Eighteenth-Century Paris." In *Consumption and the World of Goods*, edited by John Brewer and Roy Porter, 228–48. London: Routledge, 1993.

Ferrari, Fernando. *Chucho el Roto*. Mexico City: Secretaría de Educación Pública, Conasupo, 1989.

Franco, Jean. *Plotting Women: Gender and Representation in Mexico*. New York: Columbia University Press, 1989.

Francois, Marie Eileen. *A Culture of Everyday Credit: Housekeeping, Pawnbroking, and Governance in Mexico City, 1750–1920*. Lincoln: University of Nebraska Press, 2006.

Frank, Patrick. *Posada's Broadsheets: Mexican Popular Imagery, 1890–1910*. Albuquerque: University of New Mexico Press, 1998.

Fraser, W. Hamish. *The Coming of the Mass Market, 1850–1914*. Hamden, CT: Archon Books, 1981.

French, William E. "Living the Vida Local: Contours of Everyday Life." In Beezley, *Companion to Mexican History*, 13–33.

———. *A Peaceful and Working People: Manners, Morals, and Class Formation in Northern Mexico*. Albuquerque: University of New Mexico Press, 1996.

———. "Prostitutes and Guardian Angels: Women, Work, and the Family in Porfirian Mexico." *Hispanic American Historical Review* 72, no. 4 (November 1992): 529–52.

Gamboa Ojeda, Leticia. "Los Barcelonnettes en la ciudad de Puebla: Panorama de sus actividades económicas en el porfiriato." In *México Francia: Memoria de una sensibilidad común, siglos XIX–XX*, coordinated by Javier Pérez Siller, 171–94. Mexico City: Editorial Ducere, 1998.

García Márquez, Gabriel. *One Hundred Years of Solitude.* Trans. Gregory Rabassa. New York: Alfred A. Knopf, 1998.

Garner, Paul. *British Lions and Mexican Eagles: Business, Politics, and Empire in the Career of Weetman Pearson in Mexico, 1889–1919.* Stanford, CA: Stanford University Press, 2011.

———. *Porfirio Díaz.* Harlow: Pearson Education, 2001.

Garza, James A. *The Imagined Underworld: Sex, Crime, and Vice in Porfirian Mexico City.* Lincoln: University of Nebraska Press, 2007.

———. "Dominance and Submission in Don Porfirio's Belle Époque: The Case of Luis and Piedad." In *Masculinity and Sexuality in Modern Mexico*, edited by Víctor M. Macías-González and Anne Rubenstein, 79–100. Albuquerque: University of New Mexico Press, 2012.

Glickman, Lawrence B. *American Workers and the Making of Consumer Society.* Ithaca, NY: Cornell University Press, 1997.

Gómez Galvarriato Freer, Aurora. "Industrialización, empresas y trabajadores industriales del Porfiriato á la Revolución: La nueva historiografía." *Historia Mexicana* 52, no. 3 (January–March 2003): 773–804.

Gómez Galvarriato Freer, Aurora, and Aldo Musacchio. "Organizational Choice in a French Civil Law Underdeveloped Economy: Paternships, Corporations, and the Chartering of Business in Mexico, 1886–1910." Harvard Business School Working Paper No. 05–024, Harvard University, 2004.

González, Luis. *San José de Gracia: Mexican Village in Transition.* Trans. John Upton. Austin: University of Texas Press, 1974.

González Navarro, Moisés. *Estadísticas sociales del Porfiriato, 1877–1910.* Mexico City: Talleres Gráficos de la Nación, 1956.

———. *El Porfiriato: La vida social.* Vol. 4 of *Historia moderna de México*, edited by Daniel Cosío Villegas. Mexico City: Editorial Hermes, 1955–1972.

Gouy, Patrice. *Pérégrinations des "Barcelonnettes" au Mexique.* Grenoble, France: Presses Universitaires de Grenoble, 1980.

Gray, Tim. *The Political Philosophy of Herbert Spencer: Individualism and Organicism.* Brookfield, VT: Avebury, 1996.

Gurr, Ted Robert. *Why Men Rebel.* Princeton, NJ: Princeton University Press, 1971.

Haber, Stephen H. *Industry and Underdevelopment: The Industrialization of Mexico, 1890–1940.* Stanford, CA: Stanford University Press, 1989.

Hahn, H. Hazel. *Scenes of Parisian Modernity: Culture and Consumption in the Nineteenth Century.* New York: Palgrave-MacMillan, 2009.

Hall, Stuart, David Held, Don Hubert, and Kenneth Thompson, eds. *Modernity: An Introduction to Modern Societies.* Malden, MA: Blackwell Publishers, 1996.

Hartsfield, Larry K. *The Great American Response to Professional Crime*. Westport, CT: Greenwood Press, 1985.

Hawkins, Mike. *Social Darwinism in European and American Thought, 1860–1945: Nature as Model and Nature as Threat*. New York: Cambridge University Press, 1997.

Hellion, Denise. *Exposición permanente: Anuncios y anunciantes en* El Mundo Ilustrado. Mexico City: INAH/UAM-Azcapotzalco, 2008.

Hibino, Barbara. "Cervecería Cuauhtémoc: A Case Study of Technological and Industrial Development in Mexico." *Mexican Studies/Estudios Mexicanos* 8, no. 1 (Winter 1992): 23–43.

Hobsbawm, Eric. *Bandits*. Rev. ed. New York: New Press, 2000.

———. *Primitive Rebels: Studies in Archaic Forms of Social Movement in the 19th and 20th Centuries*. New York: W. W. Norton, 1965.

Hower, Ralph M. *The History of an Advertising Agency: N. W. Ayer & Son at Work, 1869–1949*. Cambridge, MA: Harvard University Press, 1949.

Irwin, Robert McKee, Edward J. McCaughan, and Michelle Rocío Nasser, eds. *The Famous 41: Sexuality and Social Control in Mexico, 1901*. New York: Palgrave MacMillan, 2003.

Isla, Carlos. *Chucho el roto*. Mexico City: Jorge Porrua, 1985.

Jardine, Lisa. *Worldly Goods: A New History of the Renaissance*. New York: W. W. Norton, 1996.

Jay, Robert. *The Trade Card in Nineteenth-Century America*. Columbia: University of Missouri Press, 1987.

Johns, Michael. *The City of Mexico and the Age of Díaz*. Austin: University of Texas Press, 1997.

Johnson, Eric A. *Urbanization and Crime: Germany, 1871–1914*. New York: Cambridge University Press, 1995.

Kandell, Jonathan. *La Capital: The Biography of Mexico City*. New York: Random House, 1988.

Keremetsis, Dawn. *La industria textil Mexicana en el siglo XIX*. Mexico City: SepSetentas, 1973.

Knight, Alan. *The Mexican Revolution*. 2 vols. Lincoln: University of Nebraska Press, 1990.

———. "Patterns and Prescriptions in Mexican Historiography." *Bulletin of Latin American Research* 25, no. 3 (2006): 340–66.

Kourí, Emilio. *A Pueblo Divided: Business, Property, and Community in Papantla, Mexico*. Stanford, CA: Stanford University Press, 2004.

Kuchta, David. "The Making of the Self-Made Man: Class, Clothing, and English Masculinity, 1688–1832." In *The Sex of Things: Gender and Consumption in Historical Perspective*, edited by Victoria de Grazia, 54–78. Berkeley: University of California Press, 1996.

Kuhn, Gary. "Fiestas and Fiascoes—Balloon Flights in Nineteenth-Century Mexico." *Journal of Sports History* 13, no. 2 (Summer 1986): 111–18.

Kuntz Ficker, Sandra. *Empresa extranjera y mercado interno: El Ferrocarril Central Mexicano, 1880–1907*. Mexico City: El Colegio de México, 1995.

Kuntz Ficker, Sandra, and Priscilla Connolly, coords. *Ferrocarriles y obras públicas.* Mexico City: Instituto Mora, 1999.

Kuri, Ariel Rodríguez. *La experiencia olvidada. El Ayuntamiento de México: Política y gobierno, 1876–1912.* Mexico City: El Colegio de México, 1996.

Lancaster, Bill. *The Department Store: A Social History.* London: Leicester University Press, 1995.

Leach, William R. *Land of Desire: Merchants, Power, and the Rise of a New American Culture.* New York: Pantheon Books, 1993.

———. "Transformations in a Culture of Consumption: Women and Department Stores, 1890–1925." *Journal of American History* 71, no. 2 (September 1984): 319–42.

Leal, Juan Felipe, Eduardo Barraza, and Carlos Flores. *El arcón de las vistas: Cartelera del cine en México, 1896–1910.* Mexico City: UNAM, 1994.

Lear, John. "Mexico City: Popular Classes and Revolutionary Politics." In *Cities of Hope: People, Protests, and Progress in Urbanizing Latin America, 1870–1930,* edited by Ronn Pineo and James A. Baer, 53–87. Boulder, CO: Westview Press, 1988.

———. "Mexico City: Space and Class in the Porfirian Capital, 1884–1910." *Journal of Urban History* 22, no. 4 (May 1996): 454–92.

———. *Workers, Neighbors, and Citizens: The Revolution in Mexico City.* Lincoln: University of Nebraska Press, 2001.

Lears, T. J. Jackson. *Fables of Abundance: A Cultural History of Advertising in America.* New York: Basic Books, 1994.

———. *No Place of Grace: Antimodernism and the Transformation of American Culture, 1880–1920.* New York: Pantheon Books, 1981.

Le Roy Ladurie, Emmanuel. *Carnival in Romans.* Trans. Mary Feeney. New York: George Braziller, 1980.

Lüdtke, Alf. "Introduction: What Is the History of Everyday Life and Who Are Its Practitioners?" In *The History of Everyday Life: Reconstructing Historical Experiences and Ways of Life,* edited by Alf Lüdtke, translated by William Templer, 3–40. Princeton, NJ: Princeton University Press, 1995.

Lysack, Krista. *Come Buy, Come Buy: Shopping and the Culture of Consumption in Victorian Women's Writing.* Athens: Ohio University Press, 2008.

MacFarlane, Alan, and Gerry Martin. *Glass: A World History.* Chicago: University of Chicago Press, 2002.

Macías-González, Víctor M. "The *Lagartijo* at *The High Life*: Masculine Consumption and Homosexuality in Porfirian Mexico." In Irwin, McCaughan, and Rocío Nasser, eds., *Famous 41,* 227–50.

Maldonado, Victor Alfonso. *México: A principios de siglo.* Mexico City: Agualarga Editores, 1996.

Martínez Gutiérrez, Patricia. *El Palacio de Hierro: Arranque de la modernidad arquitectónica en la Ciudad de México.* Mexico City: Instituto de Investigaciones Estéticas, UNAM, 2005.

Marzio, Peter. *The Democratic Art: Chromolithography, 1840–1900: Pictures for a Nineteenth-Century America.* Boston: David R. Godine, 1979.

Mason, Roger. *The Economics of Conspicuous Consumption: Theory and Thought Since 1700*. Cheltenham: Edward Elgar, 1998.

Mauss, Marcel. *The Gift: The Form and Reason for Exchange in Archaic Societies*. London: Routledge, 1990.

McCracken, Grant. *Culture and Consumption: New Approaches to the Symbolic Character of Consumer Goods and Activities*. Bloomington: Indiana University Press, 1988.

McCrossen, Alexis, ed. *Land of Necessity: Consumer Culture in the United States–Mexico Borderlands*. Durham, NC: Duke University Press, 2009.

McKendrick, Neil, John Brewer, and J. H. Plumb. *The Birth of a Consumer Society: The Commercialization of Eighteenth-Century England*. Bloomington: Indiana University Press, 1982.

México, ¿quieres tomarte una foto conmigo? Cien años de consumo. Mexico City: PROFECO/Editorial Gustavo Casasola, 1996.

Meyer, Jean. "Les français au Mexique au XIXème siècle." *Cahiers des Amériques Latines* 9–10 (1974): 62–64.

Miller, Michael B. *The Bon Marché: Bourgeois Culture and the Department Store, 1869–1920*. Princeton, NJ: Princeton University Press, 1981.

Moreno, Julio. *Yankee Don't Go Home! Mexican Nationalism, American Business Culture, and the Shaping of Modern Mexico, 1920–1950*. Chapel Hill: University of North Carolina Press, 2003.

Morgan, Tony. "Proletarians, Politicos, and Patriarchs: The Use and Abuse of Cultural Customs in the Early Industrialization of Mexico City, 1880–1910." In Beezley, Martin, and French, *Rituals of Rule*, 151–71.

Mukerji, Chandra. *From Graven Images: Patterns of Modern Materialism*. New York: Columbia University Press, 1983.

Needell, Jeffrey D. *A Tropical Belle Epoque: Elite Culture and Turn-of-the-Century Rio de Janeiro*. Cambridge: Cambridge University Press, 1987.

Nolan, Mary. *Visions of Modernity: American Business and the Modernization of Germany*. New York: Oxford University Press, 1994.

Novo, Salvador. *Apuntes para una historia de la publicidad en la Ciudad de México*. Mexico City: Organización Editorial Novaro, 1967.

O'Brien, Patricia. "Bourgeois Women and Theft." *Journal of Social History* 17 (Fall 1983): 65–77.

Orlove, Benjamin, ed. *The Allure of the Foreign: Imported Goods in Postcolonial Latin America*. Ann Arbor: University of Michigan Press, 1997.

Ortiz Gaitán, Julieta. *Imágenes del deseo: Arte y publicidad en la prensa ilustrada mexicana (1894–1939)*. Mexico City: UNAM, 2003.

Papke, David Ray. *Framing the Criminal: Crime, Cultural Work, and the Loss of Critical Perspective, 1830–1900*. Hamden, CT: Archon Books, 1987.

Pérez-Rayón, Nora. "La publicidad en México a fines del siglo XIX: Expresión del progreso económico y la modernidad porfirista, transmisora de nuevos valores y modelos culturales." *Sociológica* 9, no.1 (September–December 1994): 195–226.

Pérez-Rayón Elizundia, Nora. *México 1900: Percepciones y valores en la gran prensa capitalina*. Mexico City: UAM-Azcapotzalco, 2001.

Pérez-Siller, Javier, coord. *México-Francia: Memoria de una sensibilidad común, siglos XIX–XX.* Vol. 1. Mexico City: Editorial Ducere, 1998.

Pérez-Siller, Javier, and Chantal Cramaussal, coords. *México-Francia: Memoria de una sensibilidad común, siglos XIX–XX.* Vol. 2. Puebla, Mexico: BUAP/El Colegio de Michoacán/CEMCA, 2004.

Piccato, Pablo. *City of Suspects: Crime in Mexico City, 1900–1931.* Durham, NC: Duke University Press, 2001.

———. "*Cuidado con los Rateros*: The Making of Criminals in Modern Mexico City." In *Crime and Punishment in Latin America: Law and Society Since Late Colonial Times,* edited by Ricardo D. Salvatore, Carlos Aguirre, and Gilbert M. Joseph, 233–72. Durham, NC: University of North Carolina Press, 2001.

———. "'El Paso de Venus por el disco del Sol': Criminality and Alcoholism in the Late Porfiriato." *Mexican Studies/Estudios Mexicanos* 11, no. 2 (Summer 1995): 203–41.

Pilcher, Jeffrey. "Fajitas and the Failure of Refrigerated Meatpacking in Mexico: Consumer Culture and Porfirian Capitalism." *The Americas* 60, no. 3 (January 2004): 411–29.

Polanyi, Karl. *The Great Transformation: The Political and Economic Origins of Our Time.* Boston: Beacon Hill Press, 1957.

Porter, Susie S. *Working Women in Mexico City: Public Discourses and Material Conditions, 1879–1931.* Tucson: University of Arizona Press, 2003.

Poster, Mark. *Cultural History and Postmodernity.* New York: Columbia University Press, 1997.

Prestholdt, Jeremy. "On the Global Repercussions of East African Consumerism." *American Historical Review* 109, no. 3 (June 2004): 755–81.

Proal, Maurice, and Pierre Martin Charpenel. *Los Barcelonnettes en México.* Mexico City: Editorial Clio, 1998.

Ramos-Escandón, Carmen, ed. *Presencia y transparencia: La mujer en la historia de México.* Mexico City: El Colegio de México, 1992.

———. "Señoritas Porfirianistas: Mujeres e ideología en el México progresista, 1880–1910." In *Presencia y transparencia: La mujer en la historia de México,* edited by Carmen Ramos Escandón, 143–62. Mexico City: El Colegio de México, 1992.

Reyes, Aurelio de los. *Los origenes del cine en México (1896–1900).* Mexico City: Fondo de Cultura Económica, 1983.

Roach, Joseph. *Cities of the Dead: Circum-Atlantic Performance.* New York: Columbia University Press, 1996.

Roberts, Mary Louise. "Gender, Consumption, and Commodity Culture." *American Historical Review* 103, no. 3 (June 1998): 817–44.

Robina, Lucía de. *Reconciliación de México y Francia (1870–1880).* Mexico City: Secretaría de Relaciones Exteriores, 1963.

Rocchi, Fernando. *Chimneys in the Desert: Industrialization in Argentina During the Export Boom Years, 1870–1930.* Stanford, CA: Stanford University Press, 2006.

Ruane, Christine. "Clothes Shopping in Imperial Russia: The Development of a Consumer Culture." *Journal of Social History* 28 (Summer 1995): 765–82.

Rubenstein, Anne. *Bad Language, Naked Ladies, and Other Threats to the Nation: A Political History of Comic Books in Mexico.* Durham, NC: Duke University Press, 1998.

Rudé, George. *Criminal and Victim: Crime and Society in Early Nineteenth-Century England*. Oxford: Clarendon Press, 1985.

Saragoza, Alexander. *The Monterrey Elite and the Mexican State, 1880–1940*. Austin: University of Texas Press, 1988.

Scanlon, Jennifer, ed. *The Gender and Consumer Culture Reader*. New York: New York University Press, 2000.

Schell, William. *Integral Outsiders: The American Colony in Mexico City, 1876–1911*. Wilmington, DE: Scholarly Resources, 2001.

Schudson, Michael. *Advertising, the Uneasy Persuasion*. New York: Basic Books, 1984.

Schwartz, Vanessa R. *Spectacular Realities: Early Mass Culture in Fin-de-Siècle Paris*. Berkeley: University of California Press, 1998.

Schivelbusch, Wolfgang. *Disenchanted Night: The Industrialization of Light in the Nineteenth Century*. Trans. Angela Davies. Berkeley: University of California Press, 1988.

Scott, James. *Domination and the Arts of Resistance: Hidden Transcripts*. New Haven, CT: Yale University Press, 1990.

Shammas, Carole. *The Pre-industrial Consumer in England and America*. Oxford: Clarendon Press, 1990.

Shaya, Gregory. "The *Flâneur*, the *Badaud*, and the Making of a Mass Public in France, circa 1860–1910." *American Historical Review* 109, no. 1 (February 2004): 41–77.

Smith, Adam. *The Wealth of Nations*. Amherst, NY: Prometheus Books, 1991.

Smith, Bonnie G. *Ladies of the Leisure Class: The Bourgeoises of Northern France in the Nineteenth Century*. Princeton, NJ: Princeton University Press, 1981.

Stearns, Peter N. *Consumerism in World History: The Global Transformation of Desire*. London: Routledge, 2006.

———. "Stages of Consumerism: Recent Work on the Issues of Periodization." *Journal of Modern History* 69 (March 1997): 102–17.

Tello Peón, Berta. "Intención decorativo en los objetos de uso cotidiano de los interiores domésticos del Porfiriato." In *El arte y la vida cotidiana*, edited by Elena Estrada de Gerleso, 139–54. Mexico City: UNAM Instituto de Investigaciones Estéticas, 1995.

Tenenbaum, Barbara. "Streetwise History: The Paseo de la Reforma and the Porfirian State, 1876–1910." In Beezley, Martin, and French, *Rituals of Rule*, 127–51.

Tenorio-Trillo, Mauricio. *Mexico at the World's Fairs: Crafting a Modern Nation*. Berkeley: University of California Press, 1996.

———. "1910 Mexico City: Space and Nation in the City of the *Centenario*." *Journal of Latin American Studies* 28, no. 1 (1996): 75–104.

Thompson, E. P. "Time, Work-Discipline, and Industrial Capitalism." *Past and Present* 38 (1967): 56–97.

Tinker Salas, Miguel. *In the Shadow of the Eagles: Sonora and the Transformation of the Border During the Porfiriato*. Berkeley: University of California Press, 1997.

Toussaint, Florence. *Escenario de la prensa en el Porfiriato*. Mexico City: Fundación Manuel Buendía, 1989.

Tovar de Teresa, Guillermo. *La Ciudad de los palacios: Crónica de un patrimonio perdido*. Vol. 2. Mexico City: Vuelta, 1992.

Trentmann, Frank. "Beyond Consumerism: New Historical Perspectives on Consumption." *Journal of Contemporary History* 39, no. 3 (July 2004): 373–401.

Tyler, Ron. *Posada's Mexico.* Washington, D.C.: Library of Congress, 1979.

Vanderwood, Paul. *Disorder and Progress: Bandits, Police, and Mexican Development.* Rev. and enlarged ed. Wilmington, DE: Scholarly Resources, 1992.

Van Young, Eric . "The New Cultural History Comes to Old Mexico." *Hispanic American Historical Review* 79, no. 2 (May 1999): 211–47.

———. "La pareja dispareja: Breves comentarios acerca de la relación entre historia económica y cultural." *Historia Mexicana* 52, no. 3 (January–March 2003): 831–72.

Vaughan, Mary Kay. "Primary Education and Literacy in Nineteenth-Century Mexico: Research Trends, 1968–1988." *Latin American Research Review* 25, no. 1 (1990): 31–66.

Villamil Duarte, José Alberto. *Publicidad mexicana: Su historia, sus instituciones, sus hombres.* Mexico City: Demoscopia, 1971.

Viqueira Albán, Juan Pedro. *¿Relajados o reprimidos? Diversiones públicas y vida social en la Ciudad de México durante el Siglo de las Luces.* Mexico City: Fondo de Cultura Económica, 1987.

Voekel, Pamela. "Peeing on the Palace: Bodily Resistance to Bourbon Reforms in Mexico City." *Journal of Historical Sociology* 5, no. 2 (June 1992): 183–208.

Walton, Whitney. *France at the Crystal Palace: Bourgeois Taste and Artisan Manufacture in the Nineteenth Century.* Berkeley: University of California Press, 1992.

Warner, Sam Bass. "Slums and Skyscrapers: Urban Images, Symbols, and Ideology." In *Cities of the Mind: Images and Themes of the City in the Social Sciences,* edited by L. Rodwin and R. Hollister, 181–96. New York: Plenum Press, 1984.

Weber, Eugen. *France: Fin de Siécle.* Cambridge, MA: Belknap Press of Harvard University Press, 1986.

———. *Peasants into Frenchmen: The Modernization of Rural France, 1870–1914.* Stanford, CA: Stanford University Press, 1976.

Wells, Allen, and Gilbert M. Joseph. "Modernizing Visions, *Chilango* Blueprints, and Provincial Growing Pains: Mérida at the Turn of the Century." *Mexican Studies/ Estudios Mexicanos* 8, no. 2 (Summer 1992): 167–215.

West, Sally. *I Shop in Moscow: Advertising and the Creation of Consumer Culture in Late Tsarist Russia.* DeKalb: Northern Illinois University Press, 2011.

Widdifield, Stacie G. *The Embodiment of the National in Late Nineteenth-Century Mexican Painting.* Tucson: University of Arizona Press, 1996.

Wiesen, S. Jonathan. *Creating the Nazi Marketplace: Commerce and Consumption in the Third Reich.* New York: Cambridge University Press, 2011.

Williams, Rosalind. *Dream Worlds: Mass Consumption in Late Nineteenth-Century France.* Berkeley: University of California Press, 1982.

Wiltenburg, Joy. "True Crime: The Origins of Modern Sensationalism." *American Historical Review* 109, no. 5 (December 2004): 1377–404.

Wood, Andrew Grant. *Revolution in the Street: Women, Workers, and Urban Protest in Veracruz, 1870–1927.* Wilmington, DE: Scholarly Resources, 2001.

Wright, Cynthia. "'Feminine Trifles of Vast Importance': Writing Gender into the History of Consumption." In *Gender Conflicts: New Essays in Women's History*, edited by Franca Iacovetta and Mariana Valverde, 229–60. Toronto: University of Toronto Press, 1992.

Zamora Casillas, Yolanda. "Alacena publicitaria." *Revista Mexicana de Ciencias Políticas y Sociales* 109 (1982): 47–54.

Zea, Leopoldo. *Positivism in Mexico*. Austin: University of Texas Press, 1974.

Zehr, Howard. *Crime and the Development of Modern Society: Patterns of Criminality in Nineteenth-Century Germany and France*. Totowa, NJ: Rowman and Littlefield, 1976.

Zolov, Eric. *Refried Elvis: The Rise of the Mexican Counterculture*. Berkeley: University of California Press, 1999.

Theses, Dissertations, and Other Unpublished Works

Avent, Glenn. "A Popular and Wholesome Resort: Gender, Class, and the YMCA in Porfirian Mexico." Master's thesis, University of British Columbia, 1993.

Bisson, Cynthia Story. "Crime and Transition to Modernity in Nineteenth-Century France: The Morbihan, 1825–1925, a Case Study." PhD diss., Ohio State University, 1989.

Buffington, Robert. "Forging the Fatherland: Criminality and Citizenship in Modern Mexico." PhD diss., University of Arizona, 1994.

Bunker, Steven B. "Making the Good Old Days: Invented Tradition and Civic Ritual in Northern Mexico, 1880–1910." Honours essay, University of British Columbia, 1992.

Gómez-Galvarriato, Aurora. "The Impact of Revolution: Business and Labor in the Mexican Textile Industry, Orizaba, Veracruz, 1900–1930." PhD diss., Harvard University, 1999.

———. "Apuntes geneológicas de la elite porfiriana." Unpublished manuscript, ca. 1994–1999.

Macías-González, Víctor Manuel. "The Mexican Aristocracy and Porfirio Díaz, 1876–1911." PhD diss., Texas Christian University, 1999.

Montano, Diana Jeaneth. "Electrifying Mexico: Cultural Response to a New Technology, 1880s–1960s." PhD diss., University of Arizona, forthcoming.

Pérez-Siller, Javier. "Fiscalité, economie et pouvoir au Mexique (1867–1911): Instauration, consolidation et chute d'un regime." Vol. 1. PhD diss., Université de Paris I, Panthéon-Sorbonne, 1994.

Piccato, Pablo. "The Discourse about Alcoholism and Criminality in Mexico City, 1890–1917." Master's thesis, University of Texas at Austin, 1993.

Rohlfes, Laurence. "Police and Penal Correction in Mexico City, 1876–1911: A Study of Order and Progress in Porfirian Mexico." PhD diss., Tulane University, 1983.

Schell, Patience. "Teaching the Children of the Revolution: Church and State Education in Mexico City, 1917–1926." PhD diss., St. Anthony's College, Oxford University, 1998.

Singleton, Lisa. "Economic Origins of the Mexican Welfare State, 1840–1890." PhD diss., Tulane University, 2011.

Smith, Phyllis. "Contentious Voices amid the Order: The Porfirian Press in Mexico City, 1876–1911." PhD diss., University of Arizona, 1996.

INDEX

Page numbers in italic text indicate illustrations.

CPSIA information can be obtained
at www.ICGtesting.com
Printed in the USA
LVHW102313150722
723616LV00005B/129

9 780826 344557